SPECIAL EDUCATION
IN THE
CRIMINAL JUSTICE SYSTEM

Edited by

C. MICHAEL NELSON
University of Kentucky

ROBERT B. RUTHERFORD, JR.
Arizona State University

BRUCE I. WOLFORD
Eastern Kentucky University

Merrill Publishing Company
A Bell & Howell Information Company
Columbus   Toronto   London   Melbourne

Published by Merrill Publishing Company
A Bell & Howell Information Company
Columbus, Ohio 43216

This book was set in Aster

Administrative Editor: Vicki Knight
Production Coordinator: JoEllen Gohr
Cover Designer: Cathy Watterson

Library of Congress Catalog Card Number: 86-63914
International Standard Book Number: 0-675-20477-1
Printed in the United States of America
1 2 3 4 5 6 7 8 9—91 90 89 88 87

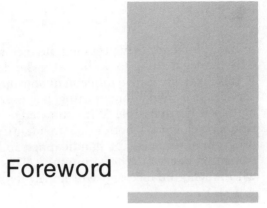

Foreword

Special Education in the Criminal Justice System is the first book of its kind, filling not only a tremendous need but also a void. Every year thousands of handicapped criminal offenders move through the labyrinth of the U.S. criminal justice system. At every step along the way—from arrest to pretrial detention in a local jail, appearance in court, incarceration, and eventual release—the handicapped offender poses a special challenge and frequently a special problem. Often, for lack of information and training in this area, criminal justice personnel neither recognize nor understand the special needs and characteristics of the mentally retarded, the learning disabled, or the behaviorally disordered. The result is often inappropriate, even unjust, treatment of the handicapped offender as well as costly, frustrating problems for criminal justice agencies and society in general.

When PL 94–142—*The Education of All Handicapped Children Act*—was enacted, it held out promise for younger incarcerated, handicapped offenders by including them in its mandate. The act was written with public school children in mind, however, and many of its provisions are difficult to implement in a correctional setting. As a result, the promise soon turned into frustration, which in turn frequently led to inaction. Many criminal justice agencies are currently out of compliance with the law and provide few or inadequate services for handicapped offenders.

This text provides criminal justice practitioners and policy makers with a wealth of background knowledge and practical advice in terms of the implementation of special education services for handicapped offenders. It is based on both research and tested practice. Without being prescriptive or dogmatic, it provides numerous recommendations concerning what can be done to satisfy the mandate of the law with eligible but incarcerated persons. The authors reflect professionalism and know-how as well as real concern and commitment. Their emphasis is not on compliance with PL 94–142 as an end in itself. Instead, they provide guidance to sound practice because it is not only the legal thing to do but also the decent thing to do.

It is far from easy to implement appropriate special education and related services in a correctional setting; however, as the authors of this text testify, neither is it impossible. With knowledge and concern criminal justice practitioners can do a better job in identifying, assessing, and meeting the programmatic needs of handicapped individuals and preparing them for transition back into the community. This text provides these professionals with much guidance and will hopefully serve as a catalyst to action.

Osa D. Coffey
Institute for Economic and Policy Studies, Inc.

Preface

Producing the first book of its kind is exciting, yet also risky. Until a few years ago there was no field that could be called correctional special education. Editing a text entitled *Special Education in the Criminal Justice System* thus may seem presumptuous or premature. Although correctional educators have known for some time that a large proportion of incarcerated youth have significant educational handicaps, until recently relatively few systematic special education services had been implemented to meet the needs of handicapped youthful offenders.

Two factors have contributed to the infancy of special education in the criminal justice system. First, correctional education programs are just beginning to respond to the mandate of the Education for All Handicapped Children Act of 1975 (PL 94–142) to serve handicapped offenders under the age of 22. Second, the professional knowledge base underlying the educational services provided for this population has been sparse and scattered.

The mandate of PL 94–142 to serve all handicapped youth specifically includes those in state correctional facilities. However, since the law was implemented in 1978, state and federal monitoring of compliance with PL 94–142 has focused primarily on public school programs. Only within the past several years has emphasis been placed on compliance in correctional settings. Despite this new focus correctional educators have often found it difficult to meet inmates' special needs in accordance with the regulations of PL 94–142 and corresponding state legislation. Programs and states have often been reluctant to make public the large numbers of handicapped youth in correctional education programs, because litigation and loss of state and federal funds are potential consequences of noncompliance.

Problems of noncompliance notwithstanding, a few researchers have studied the characteristics and educational needs of handicapped offenders. For example, Dr. Miles Santamour has exposed and analyzed the special problems of mentally retarded offenders. And since the mid-1970s Dr. Ingo Keilitz and his colleagues have been investigating the relationship between juvenile delinquency and learning disabilities. In addition, several facets of the relationship between behavior disorders and criminal behavior were explored in the early volumes of the journal *Behavioral Disorders*. These and other pioneer efforts provided the foundation for the field that has come to be known as correctional special education. Still, in the more than 10 years since PL 94–142 became law, relatively few attempts have been made to develop comprehensive and effective special education programs for incarcerated handicapped youth and young adults.

The origins of this text date back to the first conference on Programming for the Needs of Behaviorally Disordered Adolescents, held in Minneapolis in 1982; there a group of correctional and special educators met informally and established a special interest group on correctional special education. Correctional educators, who provide educational programs to youthful offenders (many with significant educational handicaps) in correctional facilities, began an exchange of information and contacts with special educators, who provided special education services to many of these same adolescents and young adults prior to incarceration. Together, these two groups formed a network of professionals concerned with the needs of handicapped offenders in the criminal justice system.

In 1983 the Correctional Special Education Training Project (C/SET) was funded by the Office of Special Education and Rehabilitative Services (OSERS) to develop special education training materials for correctional education programs and to develop linkages between correctional and special educators within states and across the country, including both juvenile and adult corrections. Concurrent with C/SET's activities has been an infusion of correctional special education content into the correctional and special education literature. Such journals as the *Journal of Correctional Education, Journal of Special Education, Corrections Today, Remedial and Special Education,* and *Behavioral Disorders* have recently published articles on correctional special education. In addition, OSERS has designated as a priority the needs of young handicapped adults, *including those who are incarcerated.* The National Institute of Corrections has designated learning handicapped adult offenders as a funding priority in 1986 and 1987. Higher education training programs to prepare correctional special educators have been established in Maryland, North Carolina, Illinois, Washington, D.C., Oregon, and Wisconsin. In 1986 ten proposals were submitted to the Division of Personnel Preparation of OSERS to train correctional special educators to work with adjudicated handicapped adolescents and young adults (D. Sutherland, personal communication, January 1986). States and correctional education programs have increased their efforts to define compliance with the federal mandate and to comply with the regulations of PL 94–142.

Despite these advances the field of correctional special education is still in its formative stages. The information presented in this text does not represent typical correctional special education practices. Neither does it represent an idealized futuristic state. *Special Education in the Criminal Justice System* represents what we believe to be current best practices in light of present needs and resources. In sailing these uncharted waters, we acknowledge the risk that our representations of both what is real and what is possible may not match the perceptions of learned colleagues. But we are attempting to provide a beginning: some initial data for others to assemble, add to, and discard as this field evolves. We hope that time will prove this a useful beginning.

The text is organized into three sections: "Background Information," "Characteristics and Needs of Handicapped Offenders," and "Components of Effective Correctional Special Education Programming." The first section provides information regarding the foundations of correctional special education: an overview of handicapped persons in the criminal justice system, an introduction to that system, educational interventions within the system, and legal issues in correctional special education. The second section provides information about the three major special education populations that are overrepresented in correctional programs: the mentally retarded offender, the learning disabled offender, and the behaviorally disordered offender. The third section provides an overview of the components of correctional special education that we feel are essential to effective service delivery: functional evaluation in correctional settings, a functional curriculum, instruction in social skills for antisocial adolescents, issues in transition from correctional facilities to public schools, and teaching handicapped learners in correctional education programs.

Readers will observe that some of the curriculum and program models described in these later chapters (especially chapters 9 and 10) were developed and implemented in public school or other community settings rather than in correctional institutions. However, we believe that these curricula and programs are relevant to correctional education for several reasons. First, correctional special education, in its current stage of evolution, lacks the resources to develop its own innovative programs for handicapped offenders incarcerated in secure facilities. Second, the learner skills that are emphasized in these community programs are needed but have not been taught in traditional correctional education programs. Third, both handicapped and nonhandicapped incarcerated youth have been shown to lack many functional living skills, and evidence is accumulating to suggest that deficits in these skill domains contribute to recidivism. Program models that emphasize these skills should be carefully considered. These chapters present resources and strategies that will prove valuable to correctional educators, especially those working with handicapped students.

The importance of generalizing to natural community environments the skills learned in restrictive settings presents a challenge to all criminal justice professionals. That challenge is to design alternative correctional programs that provide opportunities for offenders to practice and master critical skills in the environments where they will be most needed. The information contained in Part III should be viewed as building blocks. The task for creative and daring criminal justice professionals is to design strategies for implementing effective correctional special education programs from these building blocks, whether in diversion programs, in institutions, or during aftercare and follow-up.

Interspersed among all these chapters are a variety of vignettes that provide case study information, personal perspectives, and program descriptions. The purpose of these vignettes is to add practical information and interest, to make the content of the text more vivid.

This text would not have been published without the efforts of a number of people. The most obvious contributors are the authors of the chapters that follow; these experts have provided the essential core of the text. Their knowledge in their particular areas of expertise and their ability to communicate that knowledge have contributed greatly to the field of correctional special education. The vignette authors have also contributed valuable insight into the many facets of special education in the criminal justice system.

In addition, we acknowledge Merrill Publishing Company and particularly Vicki Knight for their courage in taking on a venture with such an unpredictable outcome. And we thank the following individuals, who reviewed this text and made suggestions to improve it: Dr. Raymond Bell, Lehigh University; Dr. Gail Schwartz, George Washington University; Dr. John F. Littlefield, The Ohio State University; Dr. John Mesinger, University of Virginia; and Dr. Ronnie Wilkins, Memphis State University. Several others, including Jo'lene Ralston, Susan Bigelow, and Kathy Fejes, provided invaluable assistance in developing this text.

C. Michael Nelson began his special education career as a teacher of adolescents with learning and behavior disorders. After earning a master's degree in school psychology, he worked as a child psychologist at the University of Kansas Medical Center, while simultaneously pursuing a doctorate in special education with an emphasis on behavioral disorders. He received his Ed.D. in 1969 and took a position with the special education faculty at the University of Kentucky. With Robert Rutherford and Bruce Wolford, he co-authored the Correctional/Special Education Training Project and served as the coordinator of in-service curriculum development. He currently is a professor of special education at the University of Kentucky and is a past president of the Council for Children with Behavioral Disorders.

Robert B. Rutherford, Jr., is a professor of special education at Arizona State University. He received his doctorate in special education from George Peabody College in 1971. He has taught emotionally disturbed children and adolescents and directed a 4-year alternative school program for adjudicated youth. Dr. Rutherford is past president of Teacher Educators of Children with Behavioral Disorders and was the director of the Correctional Special Education Training (C/SET) Project. He is currently editor of *Behavioral Disorders* and the monograph series of the Council for Children with Behavior Disorders, *Severe Behavior Disorders of Children and Youth*. He has written a number of journal articles and book chapters in the areas of behavior disorders and special education in the criminal justice system.

Bruce I. Wolford is an associate professor of correctional services at Eastern Kentucky University in Richmond, Kentucky. He worked for 5 years as a correctional educator in Ohio adult institutions. Dr. Wolford is a past editor of the *Journal of Correctional Education* and has served as the president of the Correctional Education Association. He earned a doctorate degree from Ohio State University in adult education and public administration of corrections.

Contents

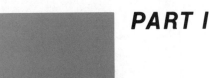

PART I

Background

INTRODUCTION   *Robert B. Rutherford, Jr.*

In order to understand the role of special education in the criminal justice system, we must be able to identify and describe those individuals we refer to as handicapped offenders, the characteristics and scope of the criminal justice system, the educational interventions employed in the criminal justice system, and the legal issues—both legislative and judicial—related to serving handicapped youthful offenders within that system.

The first part of the text contains four chapters that provide background information on the role of special education for handicapped youth and young adults in the criminal justice system. In chapter 1 Nelson presents prevalence data on the number of incarcerated handicapped offenders in juvenile and adult corrections who are in need of and eligible for special education services. He then describes the essential components of effective correctional special education and provides an orientation for the remaining chapters of the book in relating to these components.

In chapter 2 Snarr describes the United States criminal justice system in terms of what constitutes crime in our society and how we, as a society, respond to crime. He describes the three major components of the system—police, courts, and corrections—as they relate to juveniles and adults who commit crimes.

In chapter 3 Wolford presents a comprehensive overview of the role of educational interventions in the treatment and rehabilitation of offenders within the criminal justice system. Correctional education has a long history in the U.S. criminal justice system. Wolford describes the major contributions of correctional educators and presents a perspective on what constitutes quality correctional education.

In chapter 4 Wood reviews special education law and its relation to correctional education. He differentiates among litigation, legislation, and regulation and explains how each relates to the legal mandate of providing special education services to handicapped youthful offenders.

Handicapped Offenders in the Criminal Justice System

CHAPTER 1   *C. Michael Nelson*

One of the first revelations to a newcomer in the field of correctional education is the alarming statistics regarding crime and punishment in the United States. The crime rate in this country, particularly for violent offenses (homicide, rape, assault), is among the highest in the world. Over 41 million crimes were reported in 1981. Ten percent of all households were struck by burglary or violent crime during that year. Yet even these statistics fail to reflect the enormity of the problem because it is estimated that only a third of all crimes are reported to the police (U. S. Bureau of Justice Statistics, 1983).

Many of the perpetrators of these crimes are young people; half of the persons arrested for serious crimes are under the age of 20 (U. S. Bureau of Justice Statistics, 1983). Snarr and Wolford (1985) indicate that of every 1,000 arrests, 300 are juvenile cases. They also point out that youthful offenders account for over 40% of all violent crimes in the United States and that nearly 50% of those arrested for property offenses are juveniles. The overrepresentation of young persons in these statistics is apparent, given that juveniles comprise 20% of the total population (Ryan, 1983).

Although only about 10% of all juveniles and adults who are arrested for crimes are sentenced to corrections (Snarr & Wolford, 1985), it is estimated that nearly $2\frac{1}{2}$ million persons are under some form of correctional care, custody, or supervision (U. S. Bureau of Justice Statistics, 1983). Adults comprise almost 2 million of this population, whereas juveniles account for the remaining $\frac{1}{2}$ million. The latter figure represents 1.5% of all juveniles aged 10 to 17. Three out of every four persons under the sanction of the correctional system are being supervised in the community; nevertheless, almost 500,000 persons are incarcerated in adult correctional institutions, and an estimated 74,000 juveniles are in detention. This rate of incarceration also is among the highest in the world (U. S. Bureau of Justice Statistics, 1983). It should be noted that 117,000 offenders in adult institutions are under the age of 22 (Gerry, 1983), and that as many as 500,000 juveniles are annually in secure detention (i.e., confined to jails and detention centers without being sentenced to corrections) (Snarr & Wolford, 1983).

HANDICAPPED YOUTH IN CORRECTIONS

Because relatively scarce financial and human resources must be allocated according to fluctuating national priorities, estimates of the prevalence of handicapped persons in any human services program tend to be affected by sociopolitical variables. As Mesinger (1986) notes, such fluctuation has been characteristic of prevalence estimates within the population of juvenile offenders.

> Since the 1950s the literature has ranged from "nearly all delinquents are normal," a sociologist's perspective; to "nearly all delinquents are deviant," a psychologist/psychiatrist's perspective; to "nearly all delinquents have learning disabilities," a special educator's view. (p. 99)

Recent surveys of correctional populations reveal that handicapped persons are significantly overrepresented, and if anything, these estimates are conservative. Morgan (1979) found that 42% of those incarcerated in the juvenile detention facilities he sampled were handicapped according to PL 94–142 definitions. Santamour and West (1979) reported that the prevalence of mental retardation in corrections is three times that found in the general population. Coffey (1983) observed that learning disabled persons are similarly represented. In a national survey of state departments of correctional and special education, Rutherford, Nelson, and Wolford (1985) found 28% to be the average of handicapped offenders in state juvenile correctional programs, and 10% the average in state adult correctional institutions. The authors acknowledge that these figures are likely to be conservative because they were based on administrators' estimates. Bell (1985) assessed more than 1,000 adult inmates and reported that 42% manifested significant educational deficiencies, and 34% were potentially learning disabled. By comparison the Office of Special Education and Rehabilitation Services estimates that 10.76% of the school population (ages 3 through 21) are handicapped (Murphy, 1986).

Even though the federal mandate to provide a free and appropriate education to all handicapped persons under the age of 22 specifically extends to correctional education programs, incarcerated individuals have been neglected at all levels of the criminal justice system. Keilitz and Miller (1980) suggest that criminal justice personnel do not understand or recognize handicapped persons and thus tend to respond prejudicially. Murray (1976) indicates that the probability of adjudication is 220% greater if a youthful offender appearing in court is learning handicapped. It also has been observed that incarcerated handicapped offenders are more frequent targets of physical, sexual, and economic abuse by other inmates (Santamour & West,

1979; Snarr & Wolford, 1985). With regard to mentally retarded offenders, Santamour & West (1979) explain that, because these persons more often fail to understand prison rules or to advocate for their rights in prison, they tend to serve out their entire sentences; therefore, their periods of incarceration average 2 to 3 years longer than those of nonretarded inmates.

The preceding comments suggest that the treatment of handicapped persons by the criminal justice system has been negligent; however, it should be noted that when a program attempts to identify *all* handicapped offenders, it is often revealed that many learning handicapped delinquents were not identified by their local public schools. For example, Mesinger (1986) reports that a survey of youths in Virginia correctional programs in 1983 found that 38% ($n = 454$) had some disability, but that only 179 of these young offenders had been previously identified in their own communities. Findings such as these indicate that the public schools may be overlooking a significant number of exceptional youth.

SPECIAL EDUCATION SERVICES IN CORRECTIONS

Special education programs generally are not as readily available in correctional institutions as they are in the public schools, even though education is mandatory in most juvenile correctional programs. Nor are many correctional education programs able to offer the same quality of services to handicapped students as that available in the public schools (Rutherford et al., 1985). The reasons are numerous. First, there is an attitude among some criminal justice professionals and the public that criminals do not deserve the same educational and other benefits that law-abiding citizens merit. However, the demographics regarding incarcerated offenders strongly suggest a relationship between crime and educational deficiencies. For example, only 40% of the inmate population has a high school diploma, compared with 85% of the general population. Six percent of offenders have never been to school or attended only kindergarten. Many offenders perform below the sixth grade level in basic academic skill areas. Their social backgrounds often include a turbulent home life, a lack of family ties, more frequent histories of child abuse, and neurological abnormalities (U. S. Bureau of Justice Statistics, 1983). Although these correctional data do not establish causation, it is reasonable to assume that the lack of an appropriate education and marketable skills increases the probability that youths will engage in criminal behaviors.

Another reason for the unavailability of good special educational programs in corrections is the shortage of qualified personnel. Rutherford et al. (1985) reported that 28% of juvenile correctional education teachers are certified in special education. This figure may suggest that the gap between availability of and need for trained special educators in corrections is closing, given the prevalence rates for handicapped populations. However, this figure is only an average; the percent reported for individual states ranged from 4% to 100%. Furthermore, some states (i.e., Alabama, Delaware, Kansas, Massachusetts, and New Jersey) have designated 80% or more of their juvenile correctional population as handicapped. The national average for certified special education teachers in adult correctional education programs is 9%, but this figure must be interpreted in light of the reported incidence of handicaps in adult inmate populations (a conservative 10%) and the observation that far fewer adult offenders are in education programs. In a later survey of a sample of state departments of juvenile correctional education, Rutherford, Nelson, and Wolford (1986) noted little improvement. The ratio of handicapped juvenile offenders to certified special education teachers in this more recent survey was 17 to 1. Although this ratio may seem adequate to persons familiar with public school resource room programs, it should be kept in mind that special education teachers are not evenly distributed across correctional institutions. A few years ago the ratio of special educators to correctional programs averaged less than one per institution (Wolford, 1983).

The specific qualifications of certified special education teachers working in correctional settings have not been addressed on a national level. Whereas public school special education teachers generally are required to be certified in the disability areas in which they are teaching (e.g., educable mentally handicapped, learning disabled, behaviorally disordered), any type of special education certification may be accepted by correctional education agencies. For example, the majority of endorsed special education teachers working in corrections in the state of Virginia are certified in mental retardation—even though this population has the lowest incidence in correctional education programs (J. F. Mesinger, personal communication, April 1986).

A third reason for the unavailability of special education services in correctional programs is the difficulty of implementing PL 94–142 in correctional settings. The law obviously was designed for public schools, not for corrections (Coffey, 1983). In chapter 3 Wolford describes correctional education programs available to youths under correctional supervision. Clearly, the conditions of confinement often require substantial departures from the delivery of educational services seen in public schools, for handicapped and nonhandicapped students alike. In the case of incarcerated handicapped youth, the regulations concerning the least restrictive environment and parental involvement are particularly difficult to implement (Rutherford et al., 1985). Fewer than 10% of correctional education programs are estimated to be in full compliance with the law (Coffey, 1983; Rutherford et al., 1985).

Other factors that interfere with the provision of appropriate special education services in corrections include inadequate funding, the lack of interagency agreements and cooperation, rapid population turnover (a 6 months' average in juvenile programs), failure to obtain previous school records, inadequate screening and assessment procedures, and administrative policies that place institutional security above education (Kerr, Nelson, & Lambert, 1987; Leone, 1986; Rutherford et al., 1986; Warboys & Shauffer, 1986)

THE NEED

The larger numbers of handicapped offenders and the lack of appropriate special education programs in the criminal justice system provide dramatic evidence of the need for special education services. But exactly what types of handicapped persons are found in the system? What are their educational rights, and what constitutes appropriate special educational programming in correctional settings? Is special education for these persons effective; that is, can it reduce the tendency of offenders to return to criminal activities when they are released? These and other important questions are addressed in subsequent chapters of this text. This section provides an overview of these issues.

Handicapped Populations in Corrections

The entire range of handicapping conditions is not found in correctional programs. Persons with severe and profound developmental disabilities, for example, are not likely to have the opportunity to commit criminal offenses, nor are they likely to be incarcerated. For the most part they require lifelong supervision in sheltered living and working environments. Furthermore, their handicaps are so apparent that if they ever broke the law, law enforcement or court officers would refer them to state or community mental health or mental retardation programs for treatment. This is not to suggest that all severely handicapped persons are excluded from correctional programs. Many states provide segregated correctional programs for seriously disturbed offenders. However, in the criminal justice system persons with special education needs are predominantly those with mild to moderate handicaps: the mentally retarded, the learning disabled, and the behaviorally disordered.

Murphy (1986) conducted an extensive review of prevalence studies of handicapped juvenile delinquents by categorical labels, in comparison to their reported prevalence in the general population. These data are summarized in Tables 1.1, 1.2, and 1.3. The overall prevalence estimates range from 30% to 60%, with extreme discrepancies even between estimates provided by administrators in the same state. Murphy suggests that the reasons for such differences include inconsistencies in defining handicaps and juvenile status among states and correctional agencies, as well as the heterogeneity of the offenders' learning and behavioral characteristics themselves.

Prevalence data regarding mental retardation among juvenile delinquents is reported in Table 1.1. Murphy (1986) indicates that the IQs of delinquents average 8 points lower than those of nondelinquents. Morgan (1979) reports

Prevalence Reports of Mental Retardation Among Juvenile Delinquents and Students in the General Population

Table 1.1

Study	Population	Source of Data	Criteria	% Handicapped (Range)
General Population				
Comptroller General, 1981	All school-age children	Estimates from Stanford Research Institute, 1977	NA	(1.3–2.3)
OSE, in press[a]	All students in grades K–12	SEAs	Counts of MR children receiving special education	1.86
Delinquent Population				
Bullock & Reilly, 1979	188 JDs referred to psychologist (age = 13–17)	Case files	NA	25.0
Day & Joyce, 1982	202 adjudicated JDs in OH (age = 14–19)	Court records	IQ<70	7.4
Kardash & Rutherford, 1983	Approx. 350 JDs in AZ Dept. Corrections	Administrators of education, juvenile services, corrections	EMR	3.4
Mesinger, 1976	1360 JDs in state care in VA (age = 12–17)	RDC evaluation[b]	IQ 74–60 IQ<60	12.5 1.6
Morgan, 1979	All JDs in state juvenile correctional facilities	Survey responses of 204 correctional administrators	EMR TMR (Based on P.L. 94–142 definition of MR)	7.69 1.84
Pasternack & Lyon, 1982	40 JDs from detention home in NM ($\overline{X}$ age = 15.4)	Psychometric assessment	State regulations	30.0
Prescott & Van Houten, 1982	950 JDs in NJ correctional facilities (age = 11–21)	Corrections data	IQ<70	6.0
Prout, 1981	166 JDs in 2 juvenile facilities in WI (age = 13–17)	RDC evaluation, community agency records	IQ<75	15.0
Sylvester, 1982	Approx. 2,000 JDs processed annually through SC Dept. Youth Services	RDC evaluation	EMR	10.0
Young et al., 1983	All JDs in public & private facilities for juvenile offenders	Survey responses of directors of facilities	NA	10.3

Notes: NA = Not Available; SEA = State Education Agency; JD = Juvenile Delinquent; RDC = Reception & Diagnostic Center; EMR is generally considered to mean IQ between 50 and 76; TMR is generally considered to mean IQ between 50 and 25.

[a]Office of Special Education Programs, U.S. Department of Education (L. Danielson, personal communication, 1985).
[b]IQ based on Otis Beta nonverbal test.

Source: From "The Prevalence of Handicapping Conditions Among Juvenile Delinquents" by D. M. Murphy, 1986, *Remedial and Special Education, 7,* p. 11. Copyright 1986 by Pro-Ed. Reprinted by permission.

Table 1.2   Prevalence Reports of Learning Disabilities Among Juvenile Delinquents and Students in the General Population

Study	Population	Source of Data	Criteria	% Handicapped (range)
General Population				
Comptroller General, 1981	All school-age children	Estimates from Stanford Research Institute, 1977	NA	(1.0–3.0)
OSE, in press[a]	All students in grades K–12	SEAs	Counts of LD children receiving special education	4.49
Delinquent Population				
Broder et al., 1981	633 adjudicated JD & status-offender boys in 3 cities (age = 12–15)	Psychometric assessment following screening of records	Generally, 2 or more yrs. discrepancy between IQ & achievement	36.5
Bullock & Reilly, 1979	188 JDs referred to psychologist (age = 13–17)	Case files	NA	9.0
Kardash & Rutherford, 1983	Approx. 350 JDs in AZ Dept. Corrections	Administrators of education, juvenile services, corrections	NA	20.0
Lenz et al., 1980	117 misdemeanor offenders in KS diversion program (grade = 7–12)	Psychometric assessment following screening by teacher	NA	(5.98–11.1)
Morgan, 1979	All JDs in state juvenile correctional facilities	Survey responses of 204 correctional administrators	P.L. 94–142 definition of LD	10.59
Pasternack & Lyon, 1982	40 JDs from detention home in NM ($\bar{X}$ age = 15.4)	Psychometric assessment	Below 10th percentile in achievement, processing problems	12.5
Prout, 1981	166 JDs in 2 juvenile facilities in WI (age = 13–17)	RDC evaluation, community agency records	Significant deficit between IQ & at least 1 achievement area	(13.0–42.0)
Zimmermann et al., 1979	687 adjudicated JDs & status offenders (age = 12–17)	Psychometric assessment following screening of records	Generally, 2 or more yrs. discrepancy between IQ & achievement	33.0

Notes: NA = Not Available; SEA = State Education Agency; JD = Juvenile Delinquent; RDC = Reception & Diagnostic Center; all subjects within normal range of IQ.

[a]Office of Special Education Programs, U.S. Department of Education (L. Danielson, personal communication, 1985).

Source: From "The Prevalence of Handicapping Conditions Among Juvenile Delinquents" by D. M. Murphy, 1986, *Remedial and Special Education, 7,* p. 12. Copyright 1986 by Pro-Ed. Reprinted by permission.

Prevalence Reports of Emotional Disturbance Among Juvenile Delinquents and Students in the General Population Table 1.3

Study	Population	Source of Data	Criteria	% Handicapped (range)
General Population				
Comptroller General, 1981	All school-age children	Estimates from Stanford Research Institute, 1977	NA	(1.2–2.0)
OSE, in press[a]	All students in grades K–12	SEAs	Counts of ED children receiving special education	.9
Delinquent Population				
Kardash & Rutherford, 1983	Approx. 350 JDs in AZ Dept. Corrections	Administrators of education, juvenile services, corrections	NA	36.0
Morgan, 1979	All JDs in state juvenile correctional facilities	Survey responses of 204 correctional administrators	P.L. 94–142 definition of ED	16.23
Pasternack & Lyon, 1982	40 JDs from detention home in NM ($\bar{X}$ age = 15.4)	Psychometric assessment	State regulations	20.0[b]
Prout, 1981	166 JDs in 2 juvenile facilities in WI (age = 13–17)	Records from RDC, community agencies	Significant behavioral or emotional problems in at least 2 settings	50.0[b]
Young et al., 1983	All JDs in public & private facilities for juvenile offenders	Survey responses of directors of facilities	Severe ED Moderate ED	17.4 36.0

Notes: NA = Not Available; SEA = State Education Agency; JD = Juvenile Delinquent; RDC = Reception & Diagnostic Center.
[a]Office of Special Education Programs, U.S. Department of Education (L. Danielson, personal communication, 1985).
[b]Authors use term "Behaviorally Disordered."

Source: From "The Prevalence of Handicapping Conditions Among Juvenile Delinquents" by D. M. Murphy, 1986, *Remedial and Special Education, 7,* p. 1. Copyright 1986 by Pro-Ed. Reprinted by permission.

an average prevalence estimate of 9.5%, using PL 94–142 criteria, as compared with 1% in the general population. Most retarded persons in correctional programs function in the educable mentally retarded range. For example, Brown and Courtless (1971) report that only 1.6% of their sample had IQs of less than 55, and Morgan (1979) reports an average of 1.84% with IQs in the moderately retarded range. Murphy (1986) indicates that persons manifesting such degrees of retardation lack the skills to plan and carry out felony crimes. In chapter 5 Santamour discusses mentally retarded offenders from the perspective of his extensive research in this area.

No exceptional population has received more attention concerning its involvement with the criminal justice system than the learning disabled. Prevalence data related to juvenile offenders with learning disabilities are reported in Table 1.2. Murphy (1986) indicates that estimates from studies of this population including some not summarized in Table 1.1 range from 12% to 70%, compared with 1% to 3% in the general population according to General Accounting Office (GAO) estimates. (However, as Murphy points out, the GAO data are very conservative; other surveys have reported rates of learning disabilities from 16% to 19% in the general population.) Keilitz and Dunivant have conducted extensive research in the relationship between learning disabilities and juvenile delinquency. In chapter 6 they discuss their research, as well as other issues related to learning disabilities among criminal offenders.

Table 1.3 summarizes prevalence reports of behavioral disorders. Prevalence estimates concerning this population are particularly variable; behavioral disorders are difficult to identify reliably in any setting. Also, whereas federal law specifically excludes from the definition of seriously emotionally disturbed those socially maladjusted persons who have not been otherwise diagnosed as emotionally disturbed, characteristics that clearly distinguish behavioral disorders from social maladjustment have not been established. The multitude of ambiguous definitions of behavioral disorders or serious emotional disturbances is another complication (Murphy, 1986). The average prevalence estimate in Morgan's (1979) survey was 16.23%; the range was 0% to 80%. In chapter 7 Gilliam and Scott discuss the population of behaviorally disordered offenders and provide data indicating that youths labeled socially maladjusted or seriously emotionally disturbed do not come from completely separate populations.

Data from prevalence studies of other handicapping conditions among correctional populations are reported in Table 1.4. As Murphy (1986) observes, very few studies have been conducted of conditions other than learning disabilities, behavioral disorders, and mental retardation. Morgan (1979) found lower estimates of speech impairments among juvenile delinquents than within the general population but higher estimates of hearing and visual impairments. His data regarding orthopedic and other health impairments are close to the estimates for the general population. However, other studies summarized by Murphy suggest that all of these disabilities are far more prevalent in correctional populations than is suggested in Morgan's survey. More research is needed.

Murphy (1986) expresses the concern of many researchers:

> The transient nature of the population of adjudicated juveniles and the absence of communication between a delinquent's school and the correctional system (or among any of the numerous correctional and social service agencies with which a delinquent might come in contact) significantly reduce the chances that handicapped offenders will be identified and provided with special education services. (p. 17)

Prevalence Reports of Other Handicapping Conditions Among Juvenile Delinquents and Students in the General Population   **Table 1**

Study	Population	Source of Data	Criteria	% Handicapped Conditions (Range)				
				Speech Impaired	Hearing Impaired	Visually Impaired	Ortho-pedically Impaired	Other Health Impaired
			General Population					
Comptroller General, 1981	All school-age children	Estimates from Stanford Research Institute, 1977	NA	(2.4–4.0)	(.3–.5) hard of hearing; (0.8–.19) deaf	(.05–.16)	(.1–.75)	(.1–.75)
OSE, in press[a]	All students in grades K–12	SEAs	Counts of handicapped children receiving special education	2.8	.18	.08	.14	.14
			Delinquent Population					
Kardash & Rutherford, 1983	Approx. 350 JDs in AZ Dept. Corrections	Administrators of edution, juvenile services, corrections	NA	2.8				
Mesinger, 1976	1360 JDs in state care in VA (age = 12–17)	RDC evaluation	NA	1.4 moderate; .1 severe	.1 moderate			
Morgan, 1979	All JDs in state juvenile tional facilities	Survey responses of 204 correctional administrators	P.L. 94–142 definitions	1.66	1.36 hard of hearing; .03 deaf	1.59	.27	.78
Snavely, 1985[b]	Approx. 700 JDs in CA Youth Authority (age = 12–24)	Adolescent & adult speech/language screening	NA	65.0				
Young et al., 1983	All JDs in public & private facilities for juvenile offenders	Survey responses of directors of facilities	NA				8.2[c]	9.4[d]

Notes: NA = Not Available; SEA = State Education Agency; JD = Juvenile Delinquent; RDC = Reception & Diagnostic Center.

[a]Office of Special Education Programs, U.S. Department of Education (L. Danielson, personal communication, 1985).
[b]Speech/Language/Cognitive Rehabilitation Program (personal communication).
[c]"Physically Handicapped."
[d]"Chronically Physically Ill."

Source: From "The Prevalence of Handicapping Conditions Among Juvenile Delinquents" by D. M. Murphy, 1986, *Remedial and Special Education, 7,* p. 14. Copyright 1986 by Pro-Ed. Reprinted by permission.

Educational Needs of Handicapped Offenders

As indicated earlier, educators are concerned that handicapped youthful offenders are not receiving adequate special education services. The implementing regulations for PL 94–142 clearly specify the components of an appropriate special education program, as well as the procedural safeguards
for handicapped students and their parents. The intent of the law is to (1)
ensure that a free and appropriate education be made available to all handicapped students; (2) help local and state education agencies provide this
education; (3) assess the effects of these efforts; and (4) provide due process
assurances to handicapped students and their parents (Blackhurst, 1985). According to Blackhurst (1985) the major provisions of PL 94–142 include the
following:

1. Procedural safeguards concerning the identification, evaluation, and
   placement of handicapped pupils. Parents must be notified when their
   children are to be tested and must give their permission for testing and
   for placement in special education.
2. Whenever appropriate, handicapped students must be educated with
   pupils who are not handicapped. This is known as "mainstreaming." The
   principle upon which mainstreaming is based is that handicapped pupils
   should be educated in the "least restrictive environment"—that is, the
   educational setting that imposes the fewest restrictions on their functioning as normal students.
3. Tests and testing procedures used to determined whether students are
   eligible for special education must not be racially or culturally biased.
   Testing must be conducted in the pupil's native language, and educational
   decisions cannot be made on the basis of a single test score.
4. In consultation with a student's parents and based on the data obtained
   from the assessment, an individualized educational plan (IEP) must be
   developed for each student placed in special education. This IEP must
   be reviewed at least annually and revised as necessary.
5. Parents have the right to review their child's school records at any time,
   and no one else except authorized school personnel may have access to
   information contained in those records without written parental
   permission.
6. If a student's parents or legal guardians are not available, a surrogate
   parent must be appointed to serve as an advocate for the pupil in the
   parents' role.
7. Schools are required to make their first priority the provision of special
   education services to handicapped students who currently are unserved.
   Their second priority is to provide appropriate programs for those who
   are inadequately served. All handicapped pupils, both those who are
   served in special education and those who are not, must be identified.
8. Handicapped students who have not received a high school diploma must
   be served through the age of 21.

9. Even handicapped students placed in privately operated educational programs are entitled to the same educational benefits and safeguards as are those educated in publicly supported programs.
10. State and local education agencies receive additional funds from the federal government to defray the extra costs of educating handicapped students. However, the program must spend as much of its own money to educate handicapped pupils as it spends to educate those who are not handicapped.
11. Both the state and local education agencies must submit plans (the former to the U. S. Department of Education, the latter to the appropriate state Department of Education) detailing how they will provide a free and appropriate education to all handicapped students in their jurisdictions. These plans must be reviewed annually. The state education agency is specifically responsible for monitoring the special education programs operated at the local level.

Correctional education programs have found a number of these provisions extremely difficult to implement. For example, it is frequently impossible to locate an offender's parents to obtain their permission to test or place a student or to obtain their cooperation in developing an IEP. Although the provisions clearly indicate that surrogate parents may be used, locating and training such persons imposes an additional burden on correctional education staff; therefore, they tend to use other correctional staff members (e.g., educational counselors, prerelease workers) as parent surrogates, even though such practices are expressly forbidden (Gerry, 1983). Another difficulty is posed by the variability among states in responsibility for the administration and supervision of correctional education programs. Some states permit local public school districts to operate correctional education programs, some establish the state education agency as a special school district for operating institutional education programs, and some states allow the correctional education program in each penal institution to operate as an independent school district (Warboys & Shauffer, 1986). Nevertheless, PL 94–142 assigns formal responsibility for supervision of special education programs to the state education agency. Efforts to provide quality supervision are hampered by a lack of communication and collaboration between state departments of education and corrections (Rutherford et al., 1985).

Section 504 of the Vocational Rehabilitation Act of 1973 even more dramatically emphasizes the rights of handicapped persons. Section 504 mandates that handicapped individuals not be excluded solely on the basis of their handicaps from any program receiving federal assistance (Blackhurst, 1985). This law contains no funding authorization; however, evidence of discrimination against handicapped persons can jeopardize a state's receipt of any federal funds (Warboys & Shauffer, 1986). Legal issues pertaining to handicapped incarcerated youth are discussed in greater detail by Wood in chapter 4.

These legal mandates provide the basis for correctional special education programs and attempt to assure that services meet minimum standards of quality, but they do not prescribe the content of an effective program for handicapped young persons who are incarcerated. Rutherford et al. (1985) describe what they feel to be the essential components of an effective correctional special education program.

1. *Functional assessments of the deficits and learning needs of handicapped offenders.* Such assessments require more than standardized, one-time paper-and-pencil testing of groups in a central reception center. (These procedures often fail to identify handicapped persons.) Furthermore, functional assessment requires the identification of skill deficits that impede students' ability to function successfully as independent citizens. Even though the remediation of basic academic skill deficiencies is a reasonable goal, it cannot be the *only* goal if the lack of appropriate community living and job-related skills is what prevents the offender from adjusting to the demands of independent living. In chapter 8 Howell delineates the process of functional assessment and evaluation.

2. *A functional curriculum; that is, one that meets a student's individual needs.* The curricula of many correctional education programs focus on basic adult education (i.e., adult literacy) and the attainment of Carnegie units or preparation for the general education diploma (GED). Rutherford and his colleagues (1985) question the validity of such a focus if the offender lacks the skills to find a job or take care of daily living needs. Chapter 9 by Fredericks and Evans and chapter 10 by Goldstein address the components and development of a functional curriculum for handicapped youth.

3. *Vocational training opportunities that are specifically tailored to the needs of handicapped persons.* In the majority of correctional programs, vocational education programs are dictated by the needs and characteristics of the institution and/or are restricted to students having minimum levels of academic competence. Such training programs tend to discriminate against the handicapped. Vocational special education is still new to corrections; consequently, little information about this area is currently available. However, correctional educators should make every effort to learn about federal and state regulations concerning vocational special education, as well as to apprise themselves of new developments in this field. Vocational special education also is touched on in chapter 9.

4. *Transition services that effectively link the correctional education program to a student's previous educational program, as well as to the educational and human services needed to support the handicapped offender following incarceration.* This component appears to be a major weakness of many correctional education programs and is especially critical to the community adjustment of handicapped persons. Edgar, Webb, and Maddox describe a model for the provision of transition services in chapter 11.

5. *A comprehensive system for providing a full range of education and related services to handicapped offenders.* This involves cooperation and collaboration within and among the many human service agencies that represent the criminal justice system, as well as other agencies that deal with handicapped youth and adults. Such coordination is plainly absent in the agencies serving offenders. A major goal of this text is to provide a common knowledge base upon which to build such a system. The chapters by Snarr and Wolford contribute important information about correctional education programs and the criminal justice system within which they operate.

6. *Effective training in correctional special education to improve the skills of educators currently serving handicapped offenders, as well as to develop skills in preservice special educators and to attract neophyte special educators to the developing field of correctional special education.* In chapter 12 Leone discusses the challenges and realities of teaching handicapped persons in correctional settings.

CONCLUSION

This chapter has attempted to provide a context for the emerging discipline of correctional special education, as well as some preliminary demographics regarding incarcerated handicapped offenders and the special education services presently available to them. In addition, the basic parameters of effective correctional special education services have been given. The following chapters draw upon the expertise of numerous colleagues to fill in the details.

The majority of persons incarcerated in this country are young and poorly educated, both in the amount of schooling received and the levels of functional academic and social competence attained. A significant portion of these offenders meet state and federal definitional criteria for the handicapped. Depending on the type of correctional program, it costs $12,000 to $30,000 a year to incarcerate one person (Snarr & Wolford, 1985). Providing adequate special education services in correctional programs will undoubtedly increase these costs. The question we must answer is, will correctional special education justify increased costs by reducing recidivism? There are several related questions: Is education an effective treatment? Are we willing to commit sufficient professional and financial resources to test this hypothesis, or would we rather keep recycling handicapped youth through the criminal justice system? The difficulty of evaluating an intervention as varied and multifaceted as education must be acknowledged, but the general failure of the lock-them-up-and-leave-them policy must also be recognized. The position shared by the editors and authors of this volume is that the acquisition of appropriate adult living skills will help incarcerated young persons, once released, to stay out of prison. Some readers will react to this thesis with skepticism, and some degree of skepticism is healthy. However, we hope it will be tempered with a willingness to consider the possibility that appropriate correctional special education can deter mildly handicapped young persons from repeating criminal offenses.

REFERENCES

Bell, R. (1985). *National Institute of Justice Research: Learning deficiencies of adult inmates.* Paper presented at the National Conference on Corrections, Washington, DC.

Blackhurst, A. E. (1985). Issues in special education. In W. H. Berdine & A. E. Blackhurst (Eds.), *An introduction to special education* (2nd ed., pp. 45–85). Boston: Little, Brown.

Broder, P. K., Dunivant, N., Smith, E. C., & Sutton, L. P. (1981). Further observations on the link between learning disabilities and juvenile delinquency. *Journal of Educational Psychology, 73,* 838–850.

Brown, B. S., & Courtless, T. F. (1971). *The mentally retarded offender* (DHEW Publication No. HSM 72–90–39). Washington, DC: U. S. Government Printing Office.

Bullock, L. M., & Reilly, T. F. (1979). A descriptive profile of the adjudicated adolescent: A status report. In R. B. Rutherford, Jr., & A. G. Prieto (Eds.), *Monograph in severe behavioral disorders of children and youth* (Vol. 2, pp. 153–161). Reston, VA: Council for Children with Behavioral Disorders.

Coffey, O. D. (1983). Meeting the needs of youth from a corrections viewpoint. In S. Braaten, R. B. Rutherford, Jr., & C. A. Kardash (Eds.), *Programming for adolescents with behavioral disorders* (Vol. 1, pp. 79–84). Reston, VA: Council for Children with Behavioral Disorders.

Comptroller General of the U. S. (1981). *Disparities still exist in who gets special education.* Report to the chairman, Subcommittee on Select Education, Committee on Education and Labor, House of Representatives of the United States, September 30, 1981. Gaithersburg, MD: General Accounting Office.

Day, E., & Joyce, K. (1982). Mentally retarded youth in Cuyahoga County Juvenile Court: Juvenile court work research group. In M. B. Santamour & P. S. Watson (Eds.), *The retarded offender* (pp. 141–165). New York: Praeger.

Gerry, M. H. (1983). *Monitoring the special education programs of correctional institutions.* Washington, DC: U. S. Department of Education.

Kardash, C. A., & Rutherford, R. B., Jr. (1983). Meeting the special education needs of adolescents in the Arizona Department of Corrections. *Journal of Correctional Education, 34*(3), 97–98.

Keilitz, I., & Miller, S. L. (1980). Handicapped adolescents and young adults in the criminal justice system. *Exceptional Education Quarterly, 2,* 117–126.

Kerr, M. M., Nelson, C. M., & Lambert, D. 1987. *Helping adolescents with learning and behavior problems.* Columbus, OH: Merrill.

Lenz, B. K., Warner, M. M., Alley, G. R., & Deshler, D. D. (1980). *A comparison of youths who have committed delinquent acts with learning disabled, low-achieving, and normally achieving adolescents* (Research Report No. 29). Lawrence: University of Kansas, Institute for Research in Learning Disabilities.

Leone, P. E. (1986). Teacher training in corrections and special education. *Remedial and Special Education, 7,* 41–47.

Mesinger, J. F. (1976). Juvenile delinquents: A relatively untapped population for special education professionals. *Behavioral Disorders, 2,* 22–28.

Mesinger, J. F. (1986). Alternative education for behaviorally disordered youths: A promise yet unfulfilled. *Behavioral Disorders, 11,* 98–108.

Morgan, D. J. (1979). Prevalence and types of handicapping conditions found in juvenile correctional institutions: A national survey. *Journal of Special Education, 13,* 283–295.

Murphy, D. M. (1986). The prevalence of handicapping conditions among juvenile delinquents. *Remedial and Special Education, 7,* 7–17.

Murray, C. A. (1976). *The link between learning disabilities and juvenile delinquency: Current theory and knowledge.* Washington, DC: National Criminal Justice Reference Service.

Pasternack, R., & Lyon, R. (1982). Clinical and empirical identification of learning disabled juvenile delinquents. *Journal of Correctional Education, 33*(2), 7–13.

Prescott, M., & Van Houten, E. (1982). The retarded juvenile offender in New Jersey: A report on research in correctional facilities and mental retardation facilities. In M. B. Santamour & P. S. Watson (Eds.), *The retarded offender* (pp. 166–175). New York: Praeger.

Prout, H. T. (1981). The incidence of suspected exceptional educational needs among youth in juvenile facilities. *Journal of Correctional Education, 32*(4), 22–24.

Rutherford, R. B., Jr., Nelson, C. M., & Wolford, B. I. (1985). Special education in the most restrictive environment: Correctional special education. *Journal of Special Education, 19*, 59–71.

Rutherford, R. B., Jr., Nelson, C. M., & Wolford, B. I. (1986). Special education programming in juvenile corrections. *Remedial and Special Education, 7*, 27–33.

Ryan, T. A. (1983). Prevention and control of juvenile delinquency. *Journal for Vocational Special Needs Education, 5*, 5–12.

Santamour, M. B., & West, B. (1979). *Retardation and criminal justice: A training manual for criminal justice personnel.* Washington, D.C.: President's Committee on Mental Retardation.

Snarr, R. W., & Wolford, B. I. (1985). *Introduction to corrections.* Dubuque, IA: William C. Brown.

Sylvester, B. T. (1982). Opportunities and barriers in interagency collaboration: Perspectives of a juvenile justice board member. In M. B. Santamour & P. S. Watson (Eds.), *The retarded offender* (pp. 491–495). New York: Praeger.

U. S. Bureau of Justice Statistics. (1983). *Report to the nation on crime and justice: The data.* Washington DC: U. S. Department of Justice.

Warboys, L. M., & Shauffer, C. B. (1986). Legal issues in providing special educational services to handicapped inmates. *Remedial and Special Education, 7*, 34–40.

Young, T. M., Pappenfort, D. M., & Marlow, C. R. (1983). *Residential group care, 1966 and 1981: Facilities for children and youth with special problems and needs.* Preliminary report of selected findings from the National Survey of Residential Group Care Facilities, School of Social Service Administration, University of Chicago.

Zimmerman, J., Rich, W. D., Keilitz, I., & Broder, P. K. (1979). *Some observations on the link between learning disabilities and juvenile delinquency* (LDJD–003). Williamsburg, VA: National Center for State Courts.

VIGNETTE   Report Finds D.C. Delinquents Are Denied Special Education

WASHINGTON—Despite the fact that almost half of the District of Columbia's juvenile delinquents have been identified as handicapped, most are not receiving special-education services, according to testimony given before a House panel this month.

Gene L. Dodaro, associate director of the general-government division in the General Accounting Office, told the House Subcommittee on Fiscal Affairs and Health for the District of Columbia that according to a G.A.O. study, approximaely 46 percent, or about 595, of the 1,287 juvenile delinquents studied were identified as handicapped in 1983. Almost all the delinquents identified as handicapped were learning disabled or emotionally disturbed, he said.

The juveniles were typically between the ages of 10 and 18, and most had been arrested for more than one crime, including burglary, robbery, and assault, Mr. Dodaro said. He also noted that handicapped delinquents tended to be younger and arrested more often than nonhandicapped delinquents.

The subcommittee requested the G.A.O. audit, a staff aide said, because of complaints by lawyers and parents about the treatment of such juvenile offenders.

Federal Response

Madeleine C. Will, assistant secretary for the Education Department's office of special education and rehabilitative services, told the panel that her office was aware of some of the problems addressed in the G.A.O. report. She said it was the responsibility of each state agency—or in the case of the District of Columbia, the local board of education—to monitor the facilities that are responsible for providing special-education services.

Ms. Will said her office has found that, in addition to the District of Columbia, a number of states are failing to ensure that their agencies provide adequate services for all handicapped children in compliance with P. L. 94–142, the Education for All Handicapped Children Act.

"Although significant progress has been made in implementing the requirements of [P. L. 94–142], the area of general supervision—which is closely tied to the broader problems of interagency cooperation—has been a persistent problem of national scope," she said.

Services Not Provided

In the District of Columbia, juvenile-delinquent cases are handled in several ways, according to Anthony N. Salvemini, senior evaluator with the Washington regional office of the G.A.O.

If a juvenile is found guilty of a criminal offense, he or she could be allowed to continue in school under the supervision of a probation officer or placed in a public or private residential facility.

Mr. Salvemini told the subcommittee that about 63 percent of the 595 handicapped delinquents identified did not receive the kind of individualized education program (I.E.P.) required for all special-education students under P. L. 94–142. Of those who did receive an I.E.P., about 73 percent were placed in programs that did not meet all the requirements of P. L. 94–142.

He also noted that the Education Department found in 1983 that teachers in the facilities serving juvenile delinquents did not meet certification standards required under federal law.

"The reason for these problems is fundamental," Mr. Dodaro said. "The District has not implemented an effective system to ensure compliance with P. L. 94–142, as it relates to handicapped delinquents. The current system of coordination, information exchange, and program monitoring needs improvement."

—A.T.

Editors' note: On July 24, 1986, a consent decree was entered with the Superior Court of the District of Columbia, Civil Division, in the case of *Jerry M. et al. v. District of Columbia et al.* The defendants agreed to fully comply with the requirements of PL 94–142 and its implementing regulations by September 1, 1987.

Carolyn Eggleston

Correctional Special Education: Our Rich History   VIGNETTE

The passage in 1975 of Public Law 94–142, the Education for All Handicapped Children Act, has had a profound effect on public education. The act's inclusion of confined populations placed correctional special education on a dramatic new trajectory. It was not, however, the first appearance of special education in corrections. Programs for the handicapped pioneered in corrections, although services flourished and receded over time. We will look at just a few of the most significant examples.

Concern for the "defective delinquent," "idiot," or "morally insane" individual has been expressed throughout our country's history, most often in protecting society from such persons, as reflected in the swiftness with which we built our first hospital for the insane. The hospital was opened in 1773, in Williamsburg, Virginia, while the country was still composed of colonies (National Conference of Charities & Correction, 1901). It was in the very same year that the Walnut Street Jail was opened in Philadelphia; it became a prison in 1790 (Wallack, 1939). The need to keep undesirables out of mainstream society was identified as an early priority.

The first training school in the country, the New York City House of Refuge, was established in 1824; it provided some educational training for delinquent and dependent youth (Dell'Apa, 1973). Efforts were hindered in the 1830s by a trend toward characterizing some prisoners as subhuman. Charles Caldwell wrote that in "youthful offenders. . .the brain. . .resembles too much that of the Carib, who is perfectly animal, and never feels a virtuous emotion" (p. 34). This attitude slowed the growth of educational programs for the special-needs offender, because it was felt such an offender could not improve. The 1873 Report of the Prison Association of New York notes a high percentage of inmates with special problems in reading and/or writing.

One of the first major programs for the handicapped offender began at Elmira Reformatory in Elmira, New York. This "pioneer reformatory" was opened in 1876; it is considered the first adult reformatory for males in the United States (Chenault, 1951). Elmira was established to accommodate the rising problem of urban offenders. Students were dropping out of school in record numbers, and, without jobs or direction, they committed crimes. Programs were developed at Elmira to manage these students. The Elmira education program covered a broad range of subjects, including academic subjects, marching, drill, and vocational training.

In addition to a school program for the "regular" inmates, Elmira started a series of programs for handicapped inmates. In 1883, classes were developed for "dullards" who were not interested in school. *Dullard* was a commonly used term to describe slow learners, although the criteria for this category were not clear. The courses focused on industrial arts; Waden Zebulon Brockway brought in a professor from Syracuse University to teach them (Brockway, 1912). The primary class, as it was called, lasted only 3 months but was considered a success. Brockway brought in a visiting physician, Dr. Hamilton Wey, in 1886 to teach another class. Wey organized a special class for "low grade intractable convicts." The program was comprehensive in scope and included special diets, exercise, and massage, as well as early morning academic training (McKelvey, 1977).

In 1889 Brockway opened a gymnasium equipped with hot baths and massage rooms as one more effort to improve the overall functioning of the inmate. It was used by Dr. Wey for "specific physical renovation, to improve defectives and dullards in their moral habitudes" (Brockway, 1912, p. 302). Brockway estimated that about 10% of Elmira's inmates took part in the experiment. He felt that, without the benefits of this total program, the inmates would have remained "incorrigible."

In 1892 a "scientific dietary experiment" was implemented at Elmira (Brockway, 1912). It represented an early attempt to link poor diet with educational and emotional problems—a topic of major interest in recent years.

An interesting special education program was initiated at Elmira in 1896. This program was designed for inmates who were unable to behave properly or who had an academic deficiency in one specific area. Individualized attention was of major concern in the program. It included the physical therapy procedures proven successful in previous Elmira programs, and it emphasized manual and technical instruction (Brockway, 1912). This may have been one of the earliest programs for the learning disabled in this country. It was designed for people who were "exceptionally stupid or deficient in a single facility such as the arithmetical" (p. 360).

Elmira quickly became the model of exemplary correctional education programs. It set the standard for other systems to emulate. In a paper presented before the Social Science Association in 1894, Charles Warner discussed the mission and efforts of the Elmira system. He said, "To rectify the bodies, to develop and train abnormal minds—this is glorious work. . .if we were having no effect, we should not be opposed. . .but daily we get a little more light, and the area of darkness withdraws" (Brockway, 1912, p. 338).

Correctional special education experienced a rebirth in the 1930s. This was due in large part to the efforts of Austin MacCormack, the "father of modern correctional education." He conducted a national correctional education study in the late 1920s and published *The Education of Adult Prisoners* in 1931, which remains a standard for correctional education today. MacCormack(1931) found that inmates exhibited a higher frequency of emotional disturbances and psychological problems than the population at large. He included in his book information on special education, highlighting individualized instruction, incremental gain, and the holistic approach.

In 1939 *Correctional Education Today* was published by the American Prison Association's Committee on Education (Wallack, 1939). This book, edited by Walter Wallack, included a chapter on "Special Types of Education," which focused on the special-needs offender. It provided a series of educational strategies for deficit remediation. A "Considerations for Teaching" section included a list of suggestions, some of which remain relevant today.

> (1) everything which is taught must be within the comprehension of the individual, (2) short units are essential so that they will come well within the limits of attention, (3) realization of attainment must come within short periods of time and not be projected into the future, (4) tasks should be of a repetitive nature but graded in learning sequence, . . . (7) the program as a whole should be directed towards improvement of physical condition so that coordination of motor activities may be naturally stimulated, and, (8) . . .the whole program should be representative of a satisfactory way of living within attainable limits so that social competence within such limits can be vividly illustrated." (Wallack, 1939, p. 245)

The chapter included characteristics of incarcerated students. Some special cautions were given for considering program development: "(1) low mental level, (2) low adaptability, (3) low type motor abilities, (4) personal factors, such as being and having been easily discouraged, (5) possible emotional instability, (6) suggestability, (7) slowness in recognizing hazards, and, (8) lack of appreciation of goals, little perseverance and lack of ability for self-criticism" (Wallack, 1939, p. 245).

The innovations proposed by MacCormack began to be seen in a number of institutions. Some specialized projects continued at Elmira (Wallack, Kendall, & Briggs, 1939). At the Napanoch, New York, Institution for Defective Delinquents, a study was conducted to find out if "low grade defectives could and should be taught to read" (Wallack, 1939, p. 247). The Institution at Woodbourne, New York, started programs for deaf inmates, to teach them to read lips; and stuttering inmates at Attica Prison were provided with remedial speech programs (Wallack, 1939).

After this period little activity in correctional special education was noted until the 1960s. Right-to-treatment considerations for inmates were initiated during this decade. These considerations were to have a dramatic impact on services to the handicapped offender. Right-to-treatment concerns for inmates focused on several rights guaranteed in the U.S. Constitution.

In 1968 a national survey was initiated to study programs for the mentally retarded in correctional facilities. Brown and Courtless (cited in Woody, 1974) found that 56% of the facilities studied had no special programs for the retarded and that only 4.5% had comprehensive programs. This was one of the earliest attempts to investigate programming for the handicapped using modern classification and evaluation techniques.

The increase in right-to-treatment cases has been directed toward both adult and juvenile programming. In 1972 a class action suit was brought on behalf of boys incarcerated in a training school in Indiana, for violation of 1st, 8th, and 14th Amendment rights (Keenan & Hammond, 1979). In *Nelson v. Heyne* an "affirmative right to treatment" was specified. It was determined that the individual needs of the student had to be considered in providing treatment.

Education as a treatment right began to be seen during this period, including education for the handicapped. Pope (1983) makes a compelling argument for educating the incarcerated: "A state is not obligated under the Constitution of the United States to provide any educational opportunities. However, if a state chooses to provide educational opportunities for some children, then the Equal Protection Clause of the 14th Amendment mandates that the state provide that opportunity 'equally' to all" (p. 1).

The passage of PL 93–112 in 1973 and PL 94–142 in 1975 is fully applicable to the incarcerated. These mandates have provided direction to recent efforts aimed at establishing services for the handicapped offender. However, the precedent for these efforts comes from the handful of pioneering programs started well over a century ago.

REFERENCES

Brockway, Z. (1969). *Fifty years of prison service: An autobiography* Montclair, NJ: Patterson Smith. (Reprint of a 1912 edition)

Caldwell, C. (1829). *New views of penitentiary discipline and moral education reform*. Philadelphia: Wm. Brown. (1951, October).

Chenault, P. (1951, October). *Inmate education in the Department of Correction of New York State, 1847–1949*. (*Corrections Magazine* reprints, 1949–1951)

Dell'Apa, F. (1973). *Education for the youthful offender in correctional institutions: Issues*. Boulder, CO: Western Interstate Commission for Higher Education.

Keenan, P., & Hammond, C. (1979). The institutionalized child's claim to special education: A federal codification of the right to treatment. *University of Detroit Journal of Urban Law, 56* (2), 337–404.

MacCormack, A. H. (1931). *The education of adult prisoners*. New York: National Society of Penal Information.

McKelvey, B. (1977). *American prisons: A history of good intentions*. Montclair, NJ: Patterson Smith.

Proceedings of the National Conference of Charities and Correction. (1901, September). New York: National Conference of Charities and Correction.

Nelson v. Heyne, 491 F.2d 352 (7th Cir. 1974).

Pope, L. (1983). Does delinquency mean second class: Providing equal educational opportunity to adolescents adjudicated delinquent. Unpublished manuscript.

Prison Association of New York. (1873). *Twenty-Eighth Annual Report of the Executive Committee of the Prison Association of New York and accompanying documents for the year 1872*. Albany: Argus.

Wallack, W. (Ed.). (1939). *Correctional education today*. New York: American Prison Association.

Wallack, W., Kendall, G., & Briggs, H. (1939). *Education within prison walls*. New York: Columbia University, Teachers College, Bureau of Publication.

Woody, R. (1974). *Legal aspects of mental retardation*. Springfield, IL: Charles C. Thomas.

The Criminal Justice System

CHAPTER 2   *Richard W. Snarr*

All societies place limits on human behavior and establish both formal and informal means to deal with those who exceed the limits. Formal means find expression in written laws and institutional structures that identify, charge, convict, and sentence violators; this crime control apparatus is referred to as the criminal justice system. Several basic features of this system in the United States will be elaborated upon here.

First, the system is composed of three major components—police, courts, and corrections. The role of police includes enforcing laws through investigation and arrest; the courts interpret law, consider charges, determine whether a person is guilty, and issue sentences; the responsibilities of corrections include carrying out sentences, protecting the public, and attempting to change offender behavior. Critics maintain that throughout the system victim needs and rights are not satisfactorily met.

Second, the criminal justice system operates according to certain democratic fundamentals specified by the United States Constitution, the Bill of Rights, and our system of laws. Governmental power is subdivided at both federal and state levels; separate enforcement, court, and correctional functions exist at both levels. In addition, numerous due process features have been established throughout the system to protect all persons' civil rights.

Third, the justice system is fragmented into an adult system and a separate juvenile system, which has jurisdiction (i.e., authority to decide cases) for children through age 17, with certain exceptions in certain states. For example, in a few states the maximum jurisdictional age is 16, and some state laws provide that a youth committing a serious offense, such as murder, be tried in the adult system. In philosophic terms the juvenile system is to be less harsh and oriented more toward rehabilitation than the adult system.

Fourth, both adult and juvenile systems are marked by a high degree of discretionary decision making. In many instances officials are permitted wide latitude regarding a person's entry into, movement through, and exit from the system. For example, police exercise discretion in deciding whether to arrest; prosecutors decide which charges to file; judges decide whether to incarcerate offenders; parole board members decide whether to release prisoners before they have served full terms. A comparison of decisions often indicates significant disparity between cases, which generates considerable criticism and ongoing controversy.

Fifth, the justice system is one part of a larger society and therefore must function according to existing relationships and decisions made by other entities. Legislators play key roles in this respect; they reflect public sentiment, enact legislation, and authorize funding from limited resources. The role of the judicial branch includes interpreting law, which impacts on the procedures by which criminal justice personnel perform their jobs and are held accountable. For example, beginning in the 1960s, courts dropped their hands-off doctrine toward intervening in correctional operations; their intervention has brought considerable change in such areas as prison discipline, revocation of parole, and visitation rights. More recently, the rise of privately funded and managed correctional facilities contracting with the public sector indicates an emerging and strengthening of this linkage between corrections and the rest of society.

LEGAL STRUCTURE AND PROCESS

From among the different types of law, our discussion will focus on that segment known as criminal law. Criminal law exists to promote a more peaceful, predictable, and orderly society. It is generally agreed that persons living in civilized society should not be subjected to bodily harm or to destruction or theft of their private property (Pound, 1959). Criminal law is a formal, written means of describing such illegal behaviors and denoting punishments. Criminal behaviors are considered public threats and are therefore treated as crimes against the state; thus, the government rather than an individual citizen acts as prosecutor. By contrast, civil law is designed to control private matters; the government provides a court forum to settle disputed matters in suits brought by individual citizens.

Jurisdictions throughout the United States designate crimes as felonies or misdemeanors, based on several factors. Felonies are considered to be more serious offenses than misdemeanors. Felonies include murder, rape, burglary and arson; misdemeanors include petty larceny, traffic offenses, and disorderly conduct. Important distinctions are also made in the maximum level of designated punishment. Felony offenses may warrant capital punishment (the death sentence) or confinement in state prisons for terms in excess of 1 year. Maximum penalties specified for misdemeanors are less than 1 year's incarceration in a local jail and/or a fine (Kerper & Israel, 1979). These distinctions are somewhat arbitrary and vary slightly from jurisdiction to jurisdiction. The same behavior may be designated a felony in one jurisdiction and a misdemeanor in another; but the most serious behaviors are never misdemeanors, and the most minor are never felonies. Consequences of a felony conviction are usually more severe; a convicted felon will likely experience greater social stigma and may be barred from certain types of employment as well as from holding public office.

A designation of felony or misdemeanor also affects the processing of cases in the justice system. In some jurisdictions all felony cases must secure a grand jury indictment. In addition, jurisdiction in some lower level or magistrate courts is limited to misdemeanor cases only; and when tried by a jury, misdemeanor cases are often heard by a 6-person rather than a 12-person jury.

Substantive and Procedural Law

One division of criminal law is the distinction between substantive and procedural law. Substantive law describes those activities designated as crimes and specifies penalties for violations. Statutes prohibiting burglary, kidnapping, driving under the influence of alcohol, and disorderly conduct are examples of substantive law. On the other hand, procedural law describes legal processes that are permitted in order to enforce and implement substantive law, thereby affecting the entire justice process. Procedural laws are numerous and include such matters as investigation, arrest, search and seizure, court hearing, sentencing, parole, and appeal. Rights of accused and convicted citizens are within the purview of procedural law.

At this point, it should be repeated that juvenile laws are applied only to persons within a specific age range. Juvenile, as well as adult, statutes contain designations both substantive and procedural in nature and are discussed later in this chapter.

ACTIVITIES CONSTITUTING CRIME

We have just noted that the substantive portion of criminal law defines various behaviors constituting crime. A listing and definition of serious crimes, accompanied by summary data, are presented in Table 2.1. Behaviors resulting in personal injury, such as rape, homicide, and assault, are referred to as crimes against persons. Crimes such as burglary and motor vehicle theft, which do not involve use or threat of force against a person, are commonly designated as property offenses.

Measuring Criminal Activity

Two widely used measures of the extent of crime in the United States are the Uniform Crime Reports (UCR) and the National Crime Survey (NCS). Each approaches measurement differently and therefore yields different data. Each serves different purposes and enhances our understanding of crime.

Characteristics of the Most Common Serious Crimes

Table 2.1

Homicide: causing the death of another person without legal justification or excuse.

- Homicide is the least frequent violent crime.
- 93% of the victims are slain in single-victim situations.
- At least 55% of murders are carried out by relatives or acquaintances of the victims.
- 24% of all murders occur or are suspected to occur as the result of some felonious activity.

Rape: unlawful heterosexual intercourse by force or without legal or factual consent.

- Most rapes involve a lone offender and a lone victim.
- About 36% of rapes are committed in victims' homes.
- 58% of rapes occur at night between 6:00 P.M. and 6:00 A.M.

Robbery: unlawful taking or attempted taking of property that is in the immediate possession of another, by force or threat of force.

- Robbery is a violent crime that typically involves more than one offender (in about half of all cases).
- Slightly fewer than half of all robberies involve the use of a weapon.
- Fewer than 2% of the robberies reported to the police are bank robberies.

Assault: unlawful, intentional inflicting or attempted inflicting of injury upon another person. Aggravated assault is the unlawful, intentional inflicting of serious bodily injury or unlawful threat or attempt to inflict bodily injury or death by means of a deadly or dangerous weapon, with or without actual infliction of injury. Simple assault is the unlawful, intentional inflicting of less than serious bodily injury without a deadly or dangerous weapon or an attempt or threat to inflict bodily injury without a deadly or dangerous weapon.

- Simple assault occurs more frequently than aggravated assault.
- Assault is the most common type of violent crime.

Burglary: unlawful entry of any fixed structure, vehicle, or vessel used for regular residence, industry, or business, with or without force, with the intent to commit a felony or larceny.

- 42% of all household burglaries occur without forced entry.
- In the burglary of several million U.S. households, the offenders enter through an unlocked window or door or use a key (for example, a key "hidden" under a doormat).
- About 34% of no-force household burglaries occur between 6:00 A.M. and 6:00 P.M.

**Table 2.1
(continued)**

- Residential property is targeted in 67% of reported burlgaries; nonresidential property accounts for the remaining 33%.
- Three-quarters of nonresidential burglaries for which the time of occurrence is known take place at night.

Larceny: unlawful taking or attempted taking of property other than a motor vehicle from the possession of another, by stealth, without force and without deceit, with intent to permanently deprive the owner of the property.

- Pocket picking and purse snatching most frequently occur inside nonresidential buildings or in street locations.
- Unlike most other crimes, pocket picking and purse snatching affect the elderly as much as other age groups.
- Most personal larcenies with contact occur during the daytime, but most household larcenies occur at night.

Motor vehicle theft: unlawful taking or attempted taking of a self-propelled road vehicle owned by another with the intent of permanently or temporarily depriving the owner of it.

- Motor vehicle theft is relatively well reported to the police because reporting is required for insurance claims, and vehicles are more likely than other stolen property to be recovered.
- About three-fifths of all motor vehicle thefts occur at night.

Arson: intentional damaging or destruction or attempted damaging or destruction by means of fire or explosion of the property without the consent of the owner, or of one's own property or that of another by fire or explosives with or without the intent to defraud.

- Single-family residences are the most frequent targets of arson.
- More than 17% of all structures where arson occurs are not in use.

The UCR measures crime that is reported to police. Police departments report this information on a voluntary basis to the Federal Bureau of Investigation for processing. Offenses are classified in two categories. Serious crimes are designated as Part I or index crimes; their volume is measured according to the following criminal offenses:

- □ homicide
- □ rape
- □ robbery (personal and commercial)
- □ assault (aggravated)
- □ burglary (household and commercial)

□ larceny (household and commercial)
□ motor vehicle theft
□ arson

Part II offenses (e.g., gambling, fraud, liquor law violations) are considered less serious in nature and are not included in the crime volume index. A significant limitation of the UCR is that most crimes are not reported to the police. Current evidence suggests that only about one-third of all crimes are reported to the police (Bureau of Justice Statistics, 1983b, p. 24).

The NCS was begun in 1973 to learn more about those crimes not reported to police and to gain information from victims of crime. To measure the total number of crimes committed, this survey periodically asks a national sample of 60,000 households about their experiences as victims of crime during a specified period of time. Offenses measured are

□ rape
□ robbery (personal)
□ assault (aggravated and simple)
□ household burglary
□ larceny
□ motor vehicle theft

The results of the NCS survey indicate that more than 41 million victimizations occurred during 1981 (Bureau of Justice Statistics, 1981). Data are summarized in Table 2.2. Contrary to popular belief, the NCS has shown that the percentage of households victimized by crime decreased 6% from 1975 to 1984 (Bureau of Justice Statistics, 1985). Comparisons of the UCR and NCS are presented in Table 2.3.

National Crime Survey Victimization Results   **Table 2.2**

Crimes	Number of Victims
Personal crimes of violence:	
Rape	178,000
Robbery	1,381,000
Aggravated assault	1,796,000
Simple assault	3,228,000
Personal crimes of theft:	
Larceny with contact	605,000
Larceny without contact	15,258,000
Household crimes:	
Burglary	7,394,000
Larceny	10,176,000
Motor vehicle theft	1,439,000
Total	41,455,000

Source: From the Bureau of Justice Statistics National Crime Survey, 1981.

Table 2.3 **Comparison of Uniform Crime Reports and National Crime Survey**

	Uniform Crime Reports	National Crime Survey
Offenses measured	Homicide Rape Robbery (personal and commercial) Assault (aggravated) Burglary (commercial and household) Larceny (commercial and household) Motor vehicle theft Arson	Rape Robbery (personal) Assault (aggravated and simple) Burglary (household) Larceny (personal and household) Motor vehicle theft
Scope	Crimes reported to the police in most jurisdictions; considerable flexibility in developing small-area data	Crimes both reported to police and unreported; all data for the nation as a whole; some data available for a few large geographic areas
Collection method	Police department reports to FBI	Survey interviews; periodic national sample of 60,000 households representing 135,000 persons over the age of 12, asking about their experiences as victims of crime during a specified period
Kinds of information	Provides counts of offenses and information on persons arrested, persons charged, law enforcement officers killed or assaulted, and characteristics of homicide victims	Provides details about victims (e.g., age, race, sex, education, income, and relationship of victim to offender) and about crimes (e.g., time and place of occurrence, any report to police, use of weapons, resulting injury, and economic consequences)
Sponsor	Department of Justice Federal Bureau of Investigation	Department of Justice Bureau of Justice Statistics

SYSTEMS THAT RESPOND TO CRIME

The response to crime in the United States is fragmented, largely because of the division of governmental powers. Each branch and level of government is involved in the various decision-making processes aimed at identifying and sentencing law violators. Since the response to crime in many instances occurs at the state and local level, there are really many criminal justice systems rather than a single system, although all are required to be administered according to due-process guarantees provided by the United States Constitution. Although the processing of cases may vary by jurisdiction, the flow chart in Figure 2.1 illustrates the route of cases in the adult and juvenile systems.

Entry into the System

The justice system does not respond to most crime because crime is often not discovered or reported. Law enforcement agencies usually learn about crime from the reports of citizens, discovery by a police officer in the field, or investigative and intelligence work.

Once a law enforcement agency has established that a crime has been committed, a suspect must be identified and apprehended for the case to proceed through the system. Sometimes a suspect is apprehended at the scene; however, identification of a suspect usually requires extensive investigation. Very often no one is identified or apprehended for a crime.

Prosecution and Pretrial Services

After an arrest law enforcement agencies present information about the case and the accused to the prosecutor, who decides whether formal charges will be filed with the court. If no charges are filed, the accused must be released.

A suspect who is charged with a crime must be taken before a judge or magistrate without unnecessary delay. At the initial appearance the judge or magistrate informs the accused of the charges and decides whether there is probable cause to detain the accused person. In some jurisdictions a pretrial-release decision is made, and defense counsel is assigned at the initial appearance. If the offense is minor, the determination of guilt and assessment of a penalty may also occur at this stage. In many jurisdictions the initial appearance may be followed by a preliminary hearing. The main function of this hearing is to discover whether there is probable cause to believe that the accused committed a known crime within the jurisdiction of the court. If the judge does not find probable cause, the case is dismissed; however, if the judge or magistrate finds probable cause for such a belief, or the accused waives the right to a preliminary hearing, the case may be bound over to a grand jury.

A grand jury hears evidence against the accused presented by the prosecutor and decides whether there is sufficient evidence to cause the accused to be brought to trial. If the grand jury finds sufficient evidence, it submits to the court an indictment (a written statement of the essential facts of the offense charged against the accused). The grand jury can also investigate criminal activity generally and issue indictments called grand jury originals that initiate criminal cases.

Some felony cases and misdemeanor cases proceed from the issuance of an information (a formal, written accusation submitted to the court by a prosecutor rather than a grand jury). Indictments are usually required in felony cases. However, the accused may choose to waive a grand jury indictment and instead accept service of an information for the crime.

Figure 2.1   Sequence of Events in the Criminal Justice System

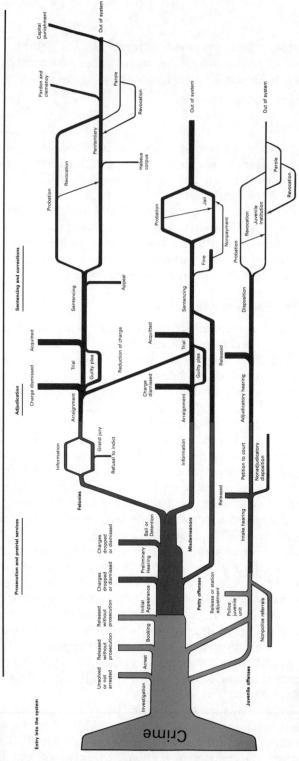

Note: This chart gives a simplified view of caseflow through the criminal justice system. Procedures vary among jurisdictions. The weights of the lines are not intended to show the actual size of caseloads.

Source: From "The Response to Crime" by M.W. Zawitz, T.R. Mina, C.M. Kuykendall, L.A. Greenfeld, and J.L. White in *Report to the Nation on Crime and Justice: The Data* (pp. 42–43) by the Bureau of Justice Statistics, 1983. Washington, DC: U.S. Department of Justice.

Adjudication

Once an indictment or information has been filed with the trial court, the accused is scheduled for arraignment. At the arraignment the accused is informed of the charges, advised of the rights of criminal defendants, and asked to enter a plea to the charges. If the accused pleads guilty or nolo contendere (accepting penalty without admitting guilt), the judge may accept or reject the plea. If the plea is accepted, no trial is held, and the offender is sentenced at this proceeding or at a later date. The plea may be rejected if, for example, the judge believes that the accused may have been coerced. In that situation the case may proceed to trial.

If the accused pleads not guilty or not guilty by reason of insanity, a date is set for a trial. A person accused of a serious crime is guaranteed a trial by jury. However, the accused has the right to ask for a bench trial, in which a judge, rather than a jury, serves as the finder of fact. In both instances the prosecutor and the defense present evidence by questioning witnesses whereas the judge decides on issues of law. A trial results in acquittal or conviction on the original charges or on lesser included offenses.

After a trial a defendant may request appellate review of the conviction or sentence. In many criminal cases appeals are a matter of right; all states with the death penalty provide for automatic appeal of a death sentence. However, under some circumstances, and in some jurisdictions, appeals may be subject to the discretion of the appellate court and may be granted only upon acceptance of a defendant's petition for a writ of certiorari.

Sentencing and Corrections

After a guilty plea or verdict, sentence is imposed. In most cases the judge decides on the sentence, but in some states the sentence for capital offenses, such as murder, is decided by the jury.

In an attempt to arrive at an appropriate sentence, a sentencing hearing may be held at which evidence of aggravating or mitigating circumstances will be considered. In assessing the circumstances surrounding a convicted person's criminal behavior, courts often rely on presentence investigations performed by probation agencies or other designated authorities. The sentencing choices available to judges and juries vary widely among jurisdictions.

- □ Death penalty
- □ Incarceration in a prison, jail, or other detention facility
- □ Probation, allowing the convicted person to remain at liberty but subject to certain conditions and restrictions
- □ Fines, primarily applied as penalties for minor offenses
- □ Restitution, which requires the offender to provide financial compensation to the victim

If sentenced to prison, the convicted person may be eligible for parole after serving a specific portion of the sentence. Parole is the conditional release of a prisoner before the prisoner's full sentence has been served. The decision to grant parole is made by a paroling authority such as a parole board, which has power to grant or revoke parole or to discharge a parolee altogether. The manner in which parole decisions are made varies widely among jurisdictions.

The Juvenile Justice System

The processing of juvenile offenders is not entirely dissimilar to adult criminal processing, but there are crucial differences in procedures. Many juveniles are referred to juvenile courts by law enforcement officers, but many others are referred by school officials, social service agencies, neighbors, and even parents for behavior or conditions that are determined to require intervention by the formal systems for social control.

When a juvenile is referred to juvenile court, an intake unit or prosecuting attorney determines whether sufficient grounds exist to warrant the filing of a petition requesting an adjudicatory hearing or a request to transfer jurisdiction to criminal court. In a few states, and at the federal level, a prosecutor under certain circumstances may file criminal charges against a youth directly in adult court.

The court with jurisdiction over juvenile matters may reject the petition, or the juvenile may be diverted to another agency or program in lieu of further court intervention. Examples of diversion programs include alcohol or drug counseling and psychiatric therapy.

If a petition for an adjudicatory hearing is accepted, the juvenile may be brought before a court quite unlike the court with jurisdiction over adult offenders. In disposing of cases, juvenile courts usually have far more discretion than adult courts. In addition to such options as probation, commitment to correctional institutions, restitution, or fines, state laws grant juvenile courts the power to order removal of children from their homes for placement in foster homes or treatment facilities. Juvenile courts may also order participation in special programs aimed at shoplifting prevention, drug counseling, or driver education. They may also order referral to criminal court for trial as an adult.

Despite the considerable discretion associated with juvenile court proceedings, juveniles are afforded most of the due-process safeguards associated with adult criminal trials. Sixteen states permit the use of juries in juvenile courts; however, in light of the U.S. Supreme Court's holding that juries are not essential to juvenile hearings, most states do not make provisions for juries in juvenile courts.

POLICE

Police functions in the United States are performed by a variety of agencies at the state, local, and federal levels, reflecting in large measure the unwillingness of society to centralize police authority in a way often found under less democratic forms of government. Most policing agencies—such as municipal, county, township, and sheriff's departments—are under local governmental control. Each of the 50 states has state police/highway patrol agencies as well as some specialized enforcement agencies. More than 50 law enforcement agencies such as the Federal Bureau of Investigation, the Postal Inspection Service, and the Drug Enforcement Administration exist at the federal level.

Police officers perform three basic roles: law enforcement, maintenance of order, and service activities. The focus of this discussion is the enforcement of criminal law because it relates to entry of cases into the criminal justice system.

Police must determine through investigation whether a crime has been committed, identify who committed the crime, apprehend a suspect, and collect and present evidence for prosecution. It should be remembered that investigative procedures are subject to various constitutional requirements. Notable in this regard is the Fifth Amendment protection against self-incrimination and Sixth Amendment specification of an accused person's right to legal counsel.

The nature and type of investigation undertaken by police vary considerably and are determined mainly by the specifics of each case. In some instances police themselves may witness a crime and arrest a suspect at the scene with little or no additional investigation necessary. Crimes may also come to the attention of police through victim and witness reports when the perpetrator has fled and no one was arrested at the scene. Such cases often necessitate a time-consuming and complex investigation accomplished in many jurisdictions, especially larger ones, by a detective division. Such investigations may include (1) searches, (2) interrogation, (3) identification of suspects, and (4) arrest, with each procedure subject to constitutional requirements aimed at protecting the innocent and reducing mistakes. For example, the Fourth Amendment provides protection against unreasonable searches and seizures and generally specifies that searches without probable cause and a court search warrant are unlawful. Some exceptions are permitted, such as searches incidental to a lawful arrest, provided that a suspect is searched in the immediate area at the time of arrest.

The Fifth Amendment provides protection from self-incrimination during interrogation. Any statement issued by a defendant must be shown to have been made voluntarily. The U.S. Supreme Court ruled in *Miranda v. Arizona* (1966) that persons in custody must be told that

1. they have the right to remain silent
2. if they decide to make a statement, the statement can and will be used against them
3. they have the right to have an attorney present at the time of the interrogation, or they will have an opportunity to consult with an attorney
4. if they cannot afford an attorney, one will be appointed by the state

Special consideration of the ability of the learning handicapped to understand this warning may be required.

The Sixth Amendment provides that accused persons have a right to counsel in all criminal prosecutions. This right has generally been interpreted to begin when an arrested person is presented before a court magistrate at the first appearance and to continue through the criminal proceedings. The right to counsel provided at state expense is also guaranteed if an accused person is indigent.

Arrest

Although some cases enter the justice system by a grand jury indictment or a citation requiring court appearance, most cases enter through the arrest procedure. An arrest is the legally authorized taking of a person into custody to answer a charge. It is usually accomplished by a police officer, based on probable cause, and deprives a person of liberty. More than 10.8 million arrests were reported in 1981 (U.S. Department of Justice, 1982, p. 162). For every five offenses reported to police, there is approximately one arrest (FBI, 1981).

The police role is often difficult and complex. Officers are permitted wide discretion in deciding whether to arrest, but their judgments are not often open to review. In general, the arrest process is characterized by the application of a somewhat indefinite probable cause standard and an absence or minimum of specific departmental policy. As a result considerable disparity and lack of fairness can sometimes be observed.

THE COURTS

Beginning Court Processes: The Prosecutor

Once a suspect is arrested, that case is referred to the public prosecutor, who represents the government in criminal cases. Prosecutors play a central role and are permitted considerable discretionary decision making. For example, they can decide whether to drop a case, what charges to file, whether to reduce charges, and what sentences to recommend, thereby greatly influencing the path of cases. In one instance a prosecutor may refuse to charge, and the case exits the system. In another instance a prosecutor may file a charge that provides mandatory incarceration if guilt is established. Prosecutors are also active in plea bargaining with the defense.

The Defense Attorney

The Sixth Amendment to the United States Constitution provides for the right to counsel for the defendant. This right has been held by the Supreme Court to apply during such processes as police questioning and lineups, preliminary court hearings, appeals, and probation and parole revocation hearings. The counsel for the defendant is identified as the defense attorney and is the counterpart of the prosecuting attorney. Indigent defendants facing possible incarceration as a penalty must be provided legal counsel by the state. The defense attorney represents the accused throughout the criminal process, which is adversarial in nature, and functions to protect the legal rights of the defendant.

Once charges are entered, it is decided whether a defendant should remain in custody (usually jail) or be released prior to possible trial. Increasingly, during this pretrial phase defendants are being released on recognizance (ROR), on conditional release, and/or on payment of only a percentage of bail (usually 10%) or on unsecured bail (no payment of money but liability for full amount for failure to appear). Various pretrial release programs have been developed throughout the United States and have been successful in the sense that most defendants (85% and up) qualify for release (usually with minimal or no bail money required), and only a small percent (less than 5%) willfully fail to appear in court when scheduled. These programs are an attempt to provide a fairer system whereby qualified defendants may be released regardless of whether financial resources permit payment of full bail.

Court Structure

The court system in the United States is divided into two major differentiations: one establishes a separation between juvenile and adult jurisdictions, and another distinguishes among courts at the federal, state, and local levels of government.

Juvenile Court. Juvenile courts were first established in 1899 in Illinois and were developed essentially to be treatment-oriented rather than punishment-oriented. In this sense the court was not seen as a court per se because it was to provide for the protection and rehabilitation of juveniles. Two primary considerations were that children were not totally responsible for their behavior and that the state had some duty to help "socialize" its children. Table 2.4 provides a quick reference to differentiate between the characteristic features of juvenile courts and adult criminal courts.

Criminal Court. Consistent with the governmental structure of federalism, a dual system of courts exists in the United States, with federal courts at one level and state and local courts at another level. The typical organization of state judicial systems is shown in Figure 2.2.

Nearly all cases originate at the level of "minor" or "major" courts. Jurisdiction in minor courts is usually limited to misdemeanors and other cases of specific nature, such as traffic, divorce, and probate cases. Most serious criminal cases are initiated at the major court level. Cases may be appealed on points of law to a higher level court. A majority of states (32 of 50) have intermediate appeals courts, but all states have a court of last resort. State courts are characterized by a diversity of administrative organization and a considerable lack of uniformity. Judges in state level courts are selected by a variety of means, including appointment, popular election, and merit selection.

The Federal Judiciary Act of 1789 created separate state and federal judicial systems. The resulting federal level court structure is depicted in Figure 2.3. The federal court system includes 94 district courts and various

Table 2.4   **Comparison of Juvenile Court and Adult Criminal Court**

Characteristic Feature	Juvenile Court	Adult Court
Purpose	Protect/treat	Punish
Jurisdiction	Based mainly on age	Based on offense
Responsible for noncriminal acts	Yes (status offenses)	No
Court proceedings	More informal/private	Formal/public
Proceedings considered to be criminal	No	Yes
Release of identifying information to press	No	Yes
Parental involvement	Usually possible	No
Release to parental custody	Frequently	Occasionally
Plea bargaining	Rare; open admission of guilt common	Frequently
Right to jury trial	No (*McKeiver* case)	Yes
Right to treatment under 14th Amendment	Yes	No
Sealing/expungement of records	Usually possible	No

Figure 2.2   **Organization of State Courts**

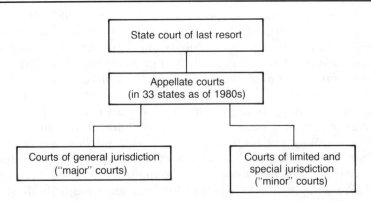

special courts that have general jurisdiction. Twelve courts of appeal exist throughout the country, and the Supreme Court of the United States operates mainly as the court of last resort. Federal judges are selected by presidential appointment, normally after consultation with members of Congress from the jurisdictional area involved.

Organization of Federal Courts

Figure 2.3

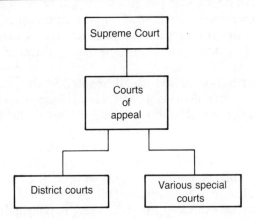

Court Process

Once a case has been brought before the court for adjudication, the criminal defendant enters a plea of guilty, not guilty, or nolo contendere. Most cases result in guilty pleas, which sometimes exceed 90% of obtained convictions.

As many as 90% of guilty pleas result from a process known as plea bargaining, in which a defendant pleads guilty in exchange for some consideration, such as a reduction of the charge and/or a lighter sentence. Involved in this exchange are the defendant and the defense attorney, the prosecuting attorney, and in some jurisdictions the judge (Newman, 1956). Plea bargaining is a controversial but permitted practice in most jurisdictions, although it is prohibited in some. Certain observers believe that this practice individualizes justice and is an administrative necessity to prevent hopeless backlogs of cases. Others discourage plea bargaining because it encourages defendants to waive the right to a trial, increases sentencing disparity, and increases the possibility of an innocent person pleading guilty in order to receive a lighter sentence rather than risking a possibly greater sentence resulting from a trial.

For defendants pleading not guilty, the Sixth Amendment includes a right to a jury trial, which may be, and many times is, waived by defendants, more often in misdemeanor than in felony cases. Fewer than 10% of cases actually proceed to a jury trial; most cases are tried in court before a judge without a jury.

Sentencing

Sentencing is an authorized judicial process for penalizing a guilty person and reflects the complex processes by which society meets its objectives for dealing with those guilty of crimes. These objectives are often categorized as (1) incapacitation, (2) retribution, (3) rehabilitation, and (4) reintegration.

Each objective reflects various attitudes and sometimes conflicting opinions and places varying degrees of penalty upon guilty persons.

Incapacitation separates offenders from the community, thereby denying them the opportunity for further criminal activity. Current policy in the United States relies heavily on this approach, through incarceration in prisons and jails.

The idea of retribution is historically rooted in the concept of revenge. This notion carries a strong message of societal disapproval and implies payment of a debt to society. Retribution emphasizes punishment per se with little specific emphasis on crime prevention.

By contrast, the objective of rehabilitation is to treat offenders to bring about behavior changes, thereby restoring or bringing about a socially acceptable and law abiding condition. This approach is based on a medical model and looks closely at the individual to determine and remediate cases. This model is based on examining an individual, making a diagnosis, prescribing and carrying out treatment, and then conducting a reexamination.

The concept of reintegration emphasizes finding ways to fit offenders into the community as productive citizens. Central to this idea is that the community shares some responsibility for deviance among its members and has an important role to play in changing such behavior.

Attitudes and practices reflect considerable diversity regarding sentencing objectives and illustrate a lack of consensus among those in the criminal justice system. This is often evident in the great differences in sentences imposed by judges. Judges are generally permitted a wide range of sentencing discretion, which often manifests itself in inequitable sentences that cannot be justified (i.e., sentencing disparity). Furthermore, legislators, criminal justice practitioners, and the public often display divergent opinions regarding the purposes to be served by sentencing. A major difference in opinion relates to whether sentences may be served in the community or whether incarceration in jail or prison is required.

Sentencing Alternatives: Noninstitutional. Legislative bodies have authorized a variety of sentences that the courts may give to offenders. Some sentences result in an institutional commitment (incarceration) whereas others do not. The types of sentences not requiring incarceration include

□ *Fines:* an economic penalty that requires the offender to pay a specific sum of money within the limit set by law. Fines are often imposed in addition to probation or as an alternative to incarceration.

□ *Community service:* the requirement that the offender provide a specific number of hours of public service work, such as collecting trash in parks or other public facilities.

□ *Restitution:* the requirement that the offender provide financial remuneration for the losses incurred by the victim.

□ *Probation:* the sentencing of an offender to community supervision by a probation agency, often the result of suspending a sentence of confinement. Such supervision normally requires adherence to specific rules of conduct while the offender is in the community. If violated, a sentencing judge may impose a sentence of confinement. Probation is the most widely used correctional disposition in the United States.

□ *Other community-based programs:* many programs were developed and enhanced, mainly during the 1970s, to involve the community and provide services without incarceration.

Sentencing Alternatives: Institutional.   Sentences imposing a period of institutional commitment display marked variation in who controls the sentence selection and who controls the length of incarceration (Snarr & Wolford, 1985). This results in diverse sentencing structures and a lack of standard definitions and terms. The types of sentences requiring incarceration include

□ *Split sentences and shock probation:* a penalty that explicitly requires the convicted person to serve a period of confinement in a local, state, or federal facility (the shock), followed by a period of probation. This penalty attempts to combine the use of community supervision with a short incarceration experience.

□ *Incarceration:* the confinement of a convicted criminal in a federal or state prison or a local jail to serve a court-imposed sentence. Custody is usually within a jail, administered locally, or a prison, operated by the state or the federal government. In many states offenders sentenced to less than 1 year are held in a jail; those sentenced to longer terms are committed to the state prison.

Sentences imposing incarceration may be broadly classified as (1) nondiscretionary, (2) limited discretionary, and (3) discretionary. A nondiscretionary sentence makes a prison term mandatory; the incarceration is specified by statutory law and must be given upon conviction. Judges have no discretionary power to grant probation or suspend sentence, and in some jurisdictions parole is not possible. This manner of sentencing is currently increasing.

Limited discretionary sentences usually allow for a suspended sentence, probation, or, if a judge chooses incarceration, a fixed amount of time that usually may be reduced by parole and/or good behavior time. This classification includes determinate sentences.

Discretionary sentences provide the most latitude. Judges may suspend sentence, grant probation, or, if incarceration is chosen, fix the period of time to be served within a range from a low minimum to a high maximum. Commonly called indeterminate sentences, these sentences often give parole authorities substantial control over the length of time served.

CORRECTIONS

That segment of the criminal justice system in which society seeks to protect the public, punish offenders, change offender behavior, and compensate victims is commonly known as corrections (Snarr & Wolford, 1985). Since a wide range of social objectives are expressed in the criminal justice process and a wide range of offender behavior exists, multiple philosophies and various forms of correctional supervision are in operation. Supervision ranges from a minimal amount within the community to maximum security incarceration.

Data from the Bureau of Justice Statistics (1983a) indicate that just over 1% of the U.S. population is under some form of correctional supervision (over 2.4 million persons), and even though three out of four persons under correctional sanction are being supervised in the community, prison populations are increasing. Although the data are constantly changing, latest available estimates of the number of persons under each form of correctional supervision are shown in Table 2.5.

Table 2.5   **Numbers of Persons Under Correctional Supervision**

	Adults			Juveniles	
	Number	Percent		Number	Percent
Probation	1,335,359	61	Probation	328,000	72
Jail	208,000	9	Detention[a]	74,000	16
Prison	412,303	19	Aftercare	53,000	12
Parole/other	243,880	11	Total	455,000	100
Total	2,199,542	100			

[a]In public and private facilities.

Source: From Bureau of Justice Statistics (p. 2), 1983a, and Office of Juvenile Justice and Delinquency Prevention (p. 4), 1983.

Probation

Offenders granted probation avoid incarceration and remain in the community under supervision of a probation officer. At both adult and juvenile levels this is the most frequently imposed sentence with over 60% of sentenced adults and over 70% of adjudicated juveniles being placed on probation.

Probation is considered a viable alternative when an offender is considered not to be a danger to public safety. Negative aspects of incarceration can be avoided, reduced costs to taxpayers are probable, and more effective treatment may be possible through placement in community settings.

The granting of probation is left to the discretion of the trial court and may be revoked if the probationer violates the law during the period of probation. The decision to grant probation is often based on a presentence investigation (PSI) report prepared by a probation officer for the court. Such a report contains a variety of information, including the offender's educa-

tional level, employment history, prior record, and evaluation of the feasibili-
ty of granting probation.

Probationers are supervised in the community by probation officers. The
quality and amount of time officers are able to spend in actual supervision
varies considerably, fluctuating with the size of an officer's caseload and the
number of other assignments, such as preparing PSI reports.

Jails

Jails are among the oldest and most widely used forms of confinement. Current estimates place the number of jails in the United States at about 3,500,
with over 200,000 persons being held in local jails on any given day. Jails
are administered by local governments in most instances; in a majority of
jurisdictions this responsibility is placed with the sheriff's department.

Jails house a diverse group of people, including men, women, and even
some children; younger and older persons; many unemployed and poor; some
in poor health; and many with a chemical dependence on alcohol or other
drugs. A majority (57%) of these are unconvicted as they are awaiting arraignment or trial whereas 43% have been convicted and are serving a jail
term or are awaiting transfer to a prison (Bureau of Justice Statistics, 1983a).

Prisons

Policy Matters.   As a result of policy, the United States currently confines
offenders in prisons and jails at the rate of about 244 per 100,000 population, an all-time high (National Moratorium on Prison Construction, 1981).
This is among the higher per capita rates worldwide, exceeded only by South
Africa (400 per 100,000) and the Soviet Union (391 per 100,000). By contrast,
the rate in the Netherlands is 21 per 100,000; in Japan, 44 per 100,000; and
in Great Britain, 80 per 100,000 (Doleschol & Newton, 1981).

The current number of persons in prisons and jails in the United States
has also reached an all-time high. The total currently exceeds 600,000, with
more than 412,000 in prisons and more than 208,000 in jails (U.S. Department of Justice, 1983; Bureau of Justice Statistics, 1983a). Included in the
factors contributing to this growth are changes in sentencing laws and
practices, a larger number of persons in a higher risk age group, and changing political and public opinion. The wisdom of policies resulting in an ever-
expanding number of prisoners is controversial and is frequently debated,
especially because incarceration represents the most expensive form of correctional supervision and because the deterrence value of imprisonment is
minimal.

Facilities.   Prisons are operated at both state and federal levels of government to hold those convicted under state or federal law. Prisons are usually
categorized according to the amount of security they provide—maximum,
medium, or minimum. Maximum security facilities often have high walls,
armed guards in observation towers, and large interior cell blocks. Medium

security prisons typically have armed posts, high fences, and outside cell block units. Minimum security facilities are characterized by no armed posts or fences and dormitory-type housing. A summary of selected features characterizing prisons in the United States is presented in Table 2.6.

Classification of Prisoners.   Classification is an ongoing decision-making process in which both juvenile and adult inmates are assigned to various levels of security, programs, and work activities. Initial classification for adults is usually part of a statewide system of classification. In such a system all inmates are evaluated at a central reception/classification center and are then assigned residence at an appropriate institution. Most juvenile systems do not have statewide, centralized classification; this process is accomplished in the field or within each facility.

Once an institutional assignment has been determined, a classification committee at that facility continues the process by reviewing inmate needs and problems and making specific assignments, such as housing units, and

Table 2.6

Prison Facility Characteristics

Characteristics	Federal	State
Number of prisons	38	521
Security level:		
Maximum	13	140
Medium	17	207
Minimum	8	174
Inmate population:		
Less than 500	10	366
500–999	18	80
1,000 or more	10	75
Year built:		
Before 1875	0	25
1875–1924	3	76
1925–1949	16	125
1950–1969	8	156
1970–1978	11	139
Prisoners housed:		
Males only	31	460
Females only	2	40
Males and females	5	21
Prison employees:		
Number	8,626	83,535
Percent administrative	2.2	2.2
Percent custodial	42.4	62.9
Percent service	23.0	15.9
Percent other	32.4	19.0

Source: From "Prison Facility Characteristics, March 1978," 1980, *American Prisons and Jails*, 3.

health and educational programs. The continuing review, monitoring, and adjustment of assignments constitute the phase known as reclassification. Such review can result in a recommendation for parole in one instance or denial in another.

Numerous factors may be evaluated in making classification decisions: test results, criminal history, any prior institutional record, employment history, education, and personality traits. However, in most instances the overwhelming concern is determination of the level of custody and control of the prisoner. At the state level this means, in operational terms, placing the inmate in a minimum, medium, or maximum security institution. Security designations at the federal level range from a Type 1 institution, which provides the least restrictive security, to a Type 6, which provides the most security.

For several reasons the promise and potential of classification is yet to be realized. Classification decisions are weighted so much toward custody considerations that an inmate often is restricted in accessing programs and activities designed to meet needs and solve problems. Scarce resources are allocated first for security, many times severely limiting resources for treatment. Overcrowding and lack of bed space create conditions in which program capacities are reached and waiting lists develop. In many instances a necessary range of programs simply does not exist, especially when one considers the special education needs of handicapped inmates. An awareness of such needs is just beginning, as a result of efforts by some educators, legislators, and correctional officials. These efforts are essential if the potential inherent in the classification process is to be achieved and more complete individualized treatment is to become a reality.

Living in Prison. Numerous features characterize life in prison. First of all, inmates are there against their will; it has been mandated that they spend time confined. Prisons are a form of total institutionalization marked by isolation from the outside world, regimentation of schedule, close supervision, and sharing of limited space by numerous inmates, many of whom seek to exploit others. Such a situation is, in a word, stressful and requires adjustments that most inmates are able to make. In the process individuals become enmeshed in the informal social structure of the inmates and become identified with various prison roles. Prolonged exposure can lead to what has been identified as prisonization, wherein an individual becomes so adapted to prison life that it becomes increasingly difficult to live on the "outside," in society at large.

Unfortunately, prisons historically contain scenes of brutality, sometimes even resulting in the death of inmates. Such treatment first existed, in part, because the courts refused to hear grievances brought on behalf of prisoners, following a "hands-off doctrine." However, during the 1960s courts began to drop this doctrine and consider prisoners' civil rights. As a result, nearly every aspect of prison life—medical care, prison crowding, use of isolation, visitations, physical abuse, censorship of mail—has undergone judicial scrutiny.

Release from Prison.   Two important points to remember are that near-ly all prisoners are released at some point and most are released prior to serving the maximum possible sentence. More than three-fourths of all prisoners are released on parole. The remainder receive either mandatory releases, in which earned "good time" reduces sentence length, or "serve outs," in which the maximum term imposed has been served and the offender is released with no further conditions or supervision.

Granting parole is a discretionary decision vested in an authorized parole board. Often this process is long, complex, and controversial. Examples of wide disparity in the granting of paroles have resulted in some efforts to improve the process and others to reduce or, in a few instances, eliminate the power of parole boards.

Although a considerable range exists, prisoners typically become eligible for initial parole reviews after serving about one-third of their sentences. For many a prison sentence results in a nearly equal length of incarceration time and community supervision time, which together account for about two-thirds of the maximum sentence.

Courts have ruled that there is no constitutional guarantee of parole, but an inmate is entitled to a written reason if parole is denied. A parolee is sub-ject to certain conditions, usually including employment specifications and is placed in the community under the supervision of a parole officer. The court may revoke parole for technical or legal infractions but in so doing must conduct a hearing according to certain due process standards, which include written notice of violation, opportunity to be heard in person, and written reasons if parole is revoked.

Prison Costs.   Currently, more people are being sentenced to prisons than there is space to accommodate. At the same time the issue of prison crowding is receiving considerable court attention. Approximately 70% of the states are under court order or face litigation because of crowding. This situation is forcing states to consider alternatives: more programs that do not require incarceration, more prisons, and in some instances contracts for services with private vendors. Because of the high costs involved, prisons are being increasingly treated as a scarce resource. Average per prisoner bed construc-tion costs in current dollar amounts are estimated to be $58,000 for max-imum security, $46,000 for medium security, and $26,000 for minimum security (Camp & Camp, 1982). Thus, a 500-bed minimum security prison might cost $13 million. In addition, the average annual cost to house an adult offender ranges from $5,000 to $23,000 (Bureau of Justice Statistics, 1983a, p. 92). Using a mid-figure of $12,000, a 500-bed institution would cost $6 million per year to operate.

JUVENILE DISPOSITIONS

Juvenile offenders receive dispositions that are generally indeterminate. That is, a juvenile remains under supervision until authorities deem that youth to be rehabilitated or legally an adult. In most states the juvenile correctional agency is granted this release authorization. In a few instances this authority resides with the committing judge or a juvenile parole agency.

Although unable to issue death penalties or life sentences, juvenile courts nationwide have a variety of dispositional alternatives available. In many jurisdictions the range of alternatives is limited. Dispositions are commonly viewed as moving from a least restrictive alternative to a most restrictive alternative. Under the former, youthful offenders continue living at home while participating in a particular program—customarily classified as a nonresidential program. This arrangement is often accomplished as a part of probation, which has been noted as the most frequently used form of supervision for juveniles.

Other youth may require closer supervision away from home—in residential programs. Group homes and facilities for youthful offenders, both public and private, provide varying degrees of security for the approximately 74,000 young persons in detention in the United States.

Upon release from a particular program, a small proportion of youth are provided with aftercare services analogous to adult parole. This is the least-developed and least-used form of supervision, and it is the type of care most in need of improvement for juvenile corrections.

CONCLUSION

The criminal justice system is designed to control crime and contribute toward the goal of a safe and orderly society. There are really many criminal justice systems, and the response to crime usually involves local officials. The total system seeks to properly identify law violators, establish guilt, issue an appropriate sanction, and change offender behavior. These responsibilities are carried out by police, courts, and corrections components within a framework of democratic principles designed to protect all individuals' civil rights. Officials are legally permitted to exercise wide discretion in determining a person's entry into, movement through, and exit from the system.

Criminal law describes behaviors that constitute crime. Enforcement of such law is a major responsibility of policing agencies. Entry into the criminal justice system usually results from a police arrest. A suspect's case is then referred to the prosecutor for possible court action.

The court system is fragmented between juvenile and adult jurisdictions and among courts at the federal, state, and local levels. In most cases a plea of guilty is entered. Once guilt is established, the court issues a sentence. Some sentences require incarceration whereas others, such as probation, do not.

Supervision in the carrying out of sentences is provided by the corrections segment of the criminal justice system and is directed toward protecting the public, punishing offenders, attempting to change offender behavior, and compensating victims. Current policy decisions have resulted in a large number of incarcerations and prison overcrowding. Providing a wider range of treatment programs is essential if the special individual needs of persons under correctional supervision are to be met.

REFERENCES

Bureau of Justice Statistics. (1981). *National crime survey*. Washington, DC: United States Department of Justice.

Bureau of Justice Statistics. (1983a). *Probation and parole, 1982*. Washington, DC: United States Department of Justice.

Bureau of Justice Statistics. (1983b). *Report to the nation on crime and justice: The data*. Washington, DC: United States Department of Justice.

Bureau of Justice Statistics. (1985, June). *Households touched by crime, 1984*. Washington, DC: United States Department of Justice.

Camp, G., & Camp, C. (1982). *The corrections yearbook: Instant answers to key questions in corrections*. Pound Ridge, NY: Criminal Justice Institute.

Doleschal, E., & Newton, A. (1981). *International rates of imprisonment*. San Francisco, CA: National Council on Crime and Delinquency.

Federal Bureau of Investigation. (1981). *Uniform crime reports*. Washington, DC: Government Printing Office.

Kerper, H. B., & Israel, H. (1979). *Introduction to criminal justice* (2nd ed.). St. Paul, MN: West.

Miranda v. Arizona, 383 U.S. 436 (1966).

National Moratorium on Prison Construction. (Winter, 1981). United States incarceration and prison construction. *Jericho, 24*, 6–7.

Newman, D. J. (1956). Pleading guilty for consideration: A study of bargain justice. *Journal of Criminal Law, Criminology and Police Science, 46*, 780–90.

Office of Juvenile Justice and Delinquency Prevention. (1980). *Children in custody: Advance reports on the census of private and public juvenile facilities*. Washington, DC: United States Department of Justice.

Pound, R. (1959). *Jurisprudence*. St. Paul, MN: West.

Snarr, R. W., & Wolford, B. I. (1985). *Introduction to corrections*. Dubuque, IA: Wm. C. Brown.

U.S. Department of Justice. (1982). *Crime in the United States*. Washington, DC: Government Printing Office.

Victor Clark

The Handicaps in Teaching the Handicapped in the Criminal Justice System

VIGNETTE

The most difficult part of teaching the handicapped in the criminal justice system is not necessarily the disabilities of the imprisoned, but often the inabilities and limitations of those who are responsible for educating them.

The disabilities of the students themselves can be assessed, diagnosed, and then matched with goals to surmount them; but the handicaps imposed by the attitudes of those who are hired to teach the handicapped are the real deterrents to progress. The inabilities and prejudices of correctional staff impose additional restrictions on student achievement. Prejudice toward disabilities, race, ethnicity, and incarceration and insensitivity to human needs as well as a lack of initiative on the part of educators are the greatest disabilities to be overcome before inroads can be made in this area.

The result of these combined inabilities is a lack of effective communication between educators and pupils and between the administrative heirarchy and the educational staff. Effective communication is fundamental to enhancing the learning processes of students. All effective teaching techniques are predicated on the establishment of a basic exchange of communication between educators and pupils.

For many reasons I believe the lack of effective communication to be an acute problem in the penal system. In other public education programs effective communication is facilitated by educators who have had previous experience living in the environment and/or who demonstrate an affinity toward their target populations. This creates an initial empathy. Unfortunately, persons hired as educators in prisons generally have never been exposed to the life-style and realities of the penal experience. They have, however, been exposed to negative labeling and attitudes about prisons and prisoners (e.g., all inmates lie; all inmates steal; all inmates spend their days plotting ways to "con" you; all inmates are verbally/physically abusive, illiterate, and without desire to change/educate themselves). To compound the problem, the penal institutions that hire correctional educators indoctrinate new staff in these preconceived notions and prejudices. Educators of the imprisoned are taught to view students as inmates, residents, incarcerates, prisoners, criminals, and convicts as opposed to persons.

On one occasion a visitor to the deaf and/or blind unit where I work asked me, "What sex is an inmate?" I didn't understand the question, so I asked her what she meant. She replied, "Well, I noticed while walking past the toilets that the signs read 'Men,' 'Women,' and 'Inmates.' Are inmates a different sex)" At first I saw her question as cute and charming, but later I perceived the implications of it.

Imprisoned handicapped persons are treated much like children, regardless of their age. This treatment often extends to their interactions with resources outside the penal institution and can result in significant problems. For example, the visually impaired need to receive textbooks on tape and/or in braille, yet they are not allowed to receive them directly; they must go through intermediaries, whereas their nonhandicapped peers may obtain resources directly from outside agencies without such restrictions. After completion of his general education diploma, Billy, a student of mine, enrolled in a college curriculum. All of his textbooks were to be taped by Recorders for the Blind. However, because he was not able to arrange for the taping of materials himself, Billy was forced to work through prison library personnel, package room personnel, supervisory staff, and security personnel. The process was delayed so much through these channels that not one single textbook arrived on tape until the semester was over. Billy's inmate classification caused additional problems with the Reader's Aid Program, which is sponsored by the Office of Vocational Rehabilitation (OVR) and is responsible for the fee for readers. Besides reading one-to-one, readers are also responsible for tutoring as necessary and for notetaking in class. Monies are sent by OVR to the local higher education institution, which dispenses these funds equitably to the readers. However, in the case of inmates, the prison intervenes. Although a specific sum is sent, the prison does not allow that sum to be distributed directly to the readers but instead gives the amount they deem suitable. Thus, not only is the imprisoned handicapped person prevented from further education because of a lack of materials, but the motivation for readers to assist with classroom assignments is drastically curtailed.

This sort of occurrence happens with Library of Congress materials as well. The imprisoned handicapped have no control over whether and when materials (disks, tapes, tape players, record players, headphones, braille equipment) arrive or leave the facility.

Another illustration of neglectful treatment is the poor and often nonexistent services provided by the Office of Vocational Rehabilitation. Imprisoned handicapped persons must receive medical verification of their handicap(s) before being eligible for OVR services. Most institutions do not have the personnel or monies needed to send handicapped inmates to appropriate medical services to qualify them for OVR services. Handicapped persons end up either paroled, having received no services while incarcerated, or denied parole because they did not take advantage of rehabilitation services—in which they could not take part because they could not get the medical examinations to do so.

I have myself been the victim of two learning disabilities: being labeled a slow learner in public school and being born a member of a minority group. I became involved in special education because I viewed it as a viable alternative to past and present educational and social experiences for this exceptional population. My life experiences, coupled with traditional educational experiences, have helped foster alternatives—from an insider's approach, so to speak.

I am a high school dropout, a Vietnam vet with 16 months of combat duty. I was arrested less than a year after discharge from the Marine Corps and sentenced to 20 years to life for felony homicide. During imprisonment I had to take my GED exam twice before successfully completing it. Subsequently, I have gone on to obtain an A.A. in liberal arts, a B.A. in psychology (magna cum laude and valedictorian), and an M.S. in education with special education concentration, graduating with a 4.0 cumulative average. I am presently enrolled in another graduate program, working toward an M.A. in sociology. While still an undergraduate, I took my internship in a psychiatric unit of a maximum security prison. There I witnessed a multitude of psychological dysfunctions, all of which were treated in the same manner: every patient was heavily medicated and left in a stupor. There I developed educational programs instituting mainstreaming within the educational component of the facility. Prior to this program, the men in this psychiatric unit demonstrated a lack of initiative in cleaning themselves, communicating rationally, or changing their plight. With the program in place, they began to participate actively in their own development. I worked with approximately 36 patients representing a multitude of nationalities and personalities. I worked with two assistants and a corrections officer, who had over 30 years on the job and also wanted to help people. Together we worked toward helping these inmates. This was the first time I found correctional personnel accepting advice from someone who was incarcerated (I had been imprisoned 9 years at that time).

During the 3 years that I worked in that setting, every patient was actively involved in an educational endeavor or a therapeutic program, and there were no disciplinary problems resulting in confinement to cells. The technique that seemed most effective was getting correctional personnel involved in the patients' activities, whether school, work, or recreation. The patients began to trust the correctional staff, and that led to patient acceptance of other programs that we implemented to assist them. This acceptance can be attributed to the sincerity of the staff's involvement. We established a nurturing family atmosphere in that unit.

After receiving my M.S. in education, I was transferred to another facility under construction for use by visually and hearing impaired inmates. This unit was called the sensorial disabled unit (SDU). When I arrived, there were no civilian staff members who had ever worked with or had knowledge about the development of such a unit. I designed and coordinated a complete educational and recreational program for this select imprisoned group. The unit has turned out to be one of a kind in the nation for educating the imprisoned sensorially handicapped. With the use of signing and braille, the unit is capable of handling the educational needs of the hearing and visually impaired in a manner equal to the way in which the needs of the nonsensorially impaired are met.

I work now with seven educational assistants whom I have trained. I stress that the students' needs must come first and that all students must be afforded proper respect. I try to instill in the assistants that academics is not the only learning process going on in the classroom; there is also the use of social skills. The assistants must strive to be positive role models in dress, manner, and communication.

A unique approach to discipline and classroom management is incorporated within the academic arena. All educational assistants not only demonstrate consistency in modeling positive attitudes and behaviors, but also illustrate integrity. They show the students sincerity and fairness and nurture trust in addition to building rapport. One would have to experience this class to witness the contradictions with traditional classroom behavior. For example, students must be chased out of the room and their work folders taken away to prevent them from continuing their assignments when the officers are closing the rooms for the day. Students have filed complaints with the administration for closing the academic area when civilians were not available to open up (only nonimprisoned persons may possess keys) and will request that assignments be given to them when extended holiday vacations are impending (Christmas, Easter, summer break).

I cannot say exactly what it is that causes such a remarkable learning atmosphere, but we keep doing what seemingly works and remain flexible to future changes. The results show a healthy attitude, higher academic grades, and achievement of goals, not to mention higher self-esteem.

No attitude/behavior is too small to confront, and no educator is too powerful to admit a wrong decision and/or action to a student. I ask the educators to use an abundance of positive strokes, but with sincerity. If students are in error, the educators should tell them so but should also show them how to correct the problem; and if students are correct, the educator should praise them. I stress that the educators should demonstrate patience and kindness yet maintain strictness and integrity. Often when a behavior/attitude is considered dangerous, I speak loudly enough to the responsible student so that everyone in the classroom receives the benefit of the lesson. We call this a *camera shot*. It exposes significant others to the lesson intended for one student. Most important is that each student is different, and each technique is employed differently. I cannot stress enough that each student's individuality is important. None of our techniques are written in stone; we must be flexible at all times and leave room for errors in judgment, as well as growth and change.

Though I maintain supervision of the classroom area, including development and maintenance of daily individualized lesson plans, and I facilitate communication between the hearing impaired and the hearing staff of this facility, many staff members still perceive incarcerated persons as being capable of performing only menial tasks. It is a constant battle to encourage the imprisoned handicapped to view themselves as viable entities in society when the educational system does not positively acknowledge the imprisoned for their accomplishments.

Correctional Education: Training and Education Opportunities for Delinquent and Criminal Offenders

CHAPTER 3   *Bruce I. Wolford*

Correctional education programs for the 2.4 million persons under correctional supervision in the United States are operated at the local, state, and federal levels. The largest and most comprehensive educational programs are found in the nation's state and federal adult correctional institutions, which house over 400,000 criminal offenders (Bureau of Justice Statistics, 1983a). Other programs exist in juvenile correctional facilities, jails, and various community settings such as court and alternative schools. For many offenders enrollment in correctional education is their last extended participation in a formal education experience.

A number of factors brought correctional education to the nation's attention in the 1980s. First, the total number of individuals under correctional supervision has grown dramatically in recent years; there has been a 100% increase in the adult prison population in the last 15 years (Bureau of Justice Statistics, 1983a). Second, the relatively recent movement away from rehabilitation toward a punitive response to crime has left education as the only formal opportunity for positive change available to many individuals under correctional supervision in many jurisdictions. Third, federal and state court intervention into the administration and operation of correctional facilities has repeatedly resulted in calls for improved education programs. Finally, much attention already has been focused on correctional education because of the staggering levels of illiteracy and related educational problems among offenders (Bureau of Justice Statistics, 1983a).

With regard to this last factor, the results of a recent National Institute of Justice examination of learning deficiencies among incarcerated adult offenders provide a bleak profile of the correctional client (Bell, Conard, & Suppa, 1984). Nearly half of the offenders studied did not appear to have the literacy skills necessary to function effectively in society. Forty-two percent of the sample were found to be functioning below the fifth grade level. The average IQ score was one standard deviation below the national norm, and 15% of the sample had IQ scores below 75. The vast majority of offender records reviewed in this study indicated culturally and educationally deprived backgrounds. Offenders had received little or no relevant vocational training and had no consistent work history. Over 50% of the sample were members of ethnic minorities. These offenders also had extensive criminal records, with over 60% previously adjudicated as delinquent. And these incarcerated adults had grown up in unstable families. In many cases (over 80%) the offender not only had dropped out of public school, but also had dropped out of or had been rejected by society (Porter & Porter, 1984).

Although the population eligible for correctional education programs has grown in recent years, the weaknesses and limitations of correctional education have remained fundamentally unchanged for 50 years (Conrad, 1981; Horvath, 1982). Because of limited resources, staff, and expertise, correctional education programs traditionally have directed their efforts toward those few offenders who seek out education as a means of self-improvement or who have hopes of favorably impressing correctional releasing authorities. The majority of offenders, who shy away from correctional education, have all too often been forgotten (Arbuthnot & Gordon, 1983). And all too often those individuals who are unserved or underserved by correctional programs have been the low-functioning adults and juveniles. These offenders have been unable or unmotivated to enter the traditional adult programs of basic education and GED preparation, which have been the mainstay of most correctional education systems. Many of these individuals, if properly screened and identified, would certainly qualify for special education services. Probably almost all of the offenders in need of educational services but not participating have experienced previous failures in and rejection by public education institutions.

Only limited vocational education opportunities exist for adult offenders, and very few training programs in marketable skills are available for delinquents. Despite offenders' lower-than-normal scores or measures of social and moral reasoning development (Arbuthnot & Gordon, 1983), many correctional education programs still do not provide opportunities for life skills or values training. Limited available resources and pressing needs for literacy training have led correctional educators to concentrate only on offenders' basic educational needs (Bell, Conard, & Suppa, 1984).

The goals and directions of correctional education are shaped not so much by educational needs as by political and practical realities. Correctional education operates as an institiution within the larger institution of corrections (Horvath, 1982). Correctional considerations such as security, protection of society, and institutional operations, rather than the needs of offenders or the considered opinions of educators, often dictate educational programming decisions. However, despite rather formidable challenges and in the face of great demands for limited resources, correctional educators have been able to develop and maintain an impressive array of education programs for adult and juvenile offenders.

PROGRAM MODELS

Correctional education programs differ in terms of their approach, administration, setting, and students served. The three examples included in this section may provide a brief view of some typical service delivery models.

The Kalamazoo Way

The Kalamazoo, Michigan, Juvenile Home Youth Center School (JHYCS) is an example of a local community response to the educational needs of adjudicated delinquents. Operated by the county government in conjunction with a juvenile detention facility, the school serves a maximum of 58 male and female youths between the ages of 12 and 18. Funding for the educational programs comes from the local school districts and federal programs such as Chapter 1. The staff consists of six special education teachers, four aides, one counselor, one tutor, one administrator, and a secretary. The youths may be in the center from 1 day to 1 year or longer, but most stays are very short with under 30 days a typical period of confinement.

The school provides a full-day program that includes English/reading, math, social sciences, prevocational training, health and family planning, as well as art, industrial arts, home economics, and physical education. The stated goals of the program are to assess behavioral and academic strengths and needs, provide an opportunity for youths to acquire skills, and provide on-the-job and career exploration experiences. The program must achieve these goals in a small, secure detention facility, within a very limited period of time, and with a transient population that is being, or has recently been, adjudicated by the juvenile court (Miller, 1982).

Jail Education in Cook County

More than 7 million people pass through U.S. jails each year. Although the typical stay is short (less than 11 days), some individuals spend up to 1 year or longer in such facilities. Jails clearly have the highest volume of the correctional system components. On any given day the 3,500 jails in the United States may have well over 200,000 residents. Based on recent reports, it is estimated that 3% of the U.S. population goes to jail in a calendar year. Jails, like the crimes that feed them, are urban dominated. More than 40% of all jail inmates are in the nation's 100 largest cities (Bureau of Justice Statistics, 1983a). Education programs are available in only one of every five U.S. jails. Those jails providing education programs tend to be in more densely populated areas where a higher daily population of inmates is found.

Jail programs vary greatly, ranging from part-time or volunteer adult basic education or literacy programs to full-service education systems. One of the most unique jail education programs operates in the Cook County Jail in Chicago. The PACE Institute is a private corporation that provides the educational programs for the jail's residents; it relies on support from private donations as well as federal and state education programs. PACE provides adult basic education, GED, prerelease, vocational, on-the-job training, and transitional programs for both male and female jail residents. Materials and techniques used at the Cook County Jail have been duplicated throughout the nation.

Wisconsin Correctional Education

The Division of Corrections in Wisconsin is responsible for both juvenile and adult correctional services. The division operates statewide adult and juvenile correctional institutions with maximum, medium, and minimum security levels and a total incarcerated population of over 5,000 men and women. The educational programs are supervised by the director of education and employment services and an advisory staff. Educational programs in Wisconsin correctional institutions include adult basic education, literacy, special education, GED preparatory classes, high school diploma courses, English-as-a-second-language classes, independent life skills courses, vocational training, and associate level postsecondary classes.

The Wisconsin correctional education system employs 250 teachers, counselors, and administrators. Wisconsin has a comprehensive curriculum configuration for all of the correctional education programs, which facilitates planning, transfer of residents, and staff in-service training. The curriculum was developed around a set of basic assumptions:

1. All educational programs and/or program components will address the development or enhancement of literacy and job skills.
2. All educational services will focus on the development of entry level skills and individual employability.
3. All educational programs will be competency-based, defined and organized around clusters of modules designed to meet specific employment needs.
4. The selection, development, and evaluation of occupations training programs will be in line with labor market forecasts.
5. Each inmate will be assigned to educational programs on the basis of a comprehensive assessment and evaluation of employment and education skills and deficits and an individualized plan for achievement.
6. Inmates can progress through their individual education program plans as they move through security levels and/or from one institution to another.
7. All inmates will receive comprehensive pre-release training, including job placement and pre-parole services.
8. Work and study release programs appropriately selected to meet individual employment needs are an integral part of a system-wide educational configuration.
9. All educational program plans, course outlines, student transactions, definition of admission requirements, and program completion are policy matters and, therefore, fall under the jurisdiction of the Division Administrator. (Wisconsin Division of Corrections, 1986)

Offenders entering the correctional system are first received at assessment and evaluation centers, where all inmates are evaluated as to academic and vocational needs and referred to appropriate programs. The Wisconsin system uses a mobile resource team for special education assessment, placement, and supervision. Special education services are provided at juvenile facilities and at each security level in adult correctional institutions.

These three examples reflect the diversity of settings and the size of correctional education programs. These and other correctional education programs remain in a developmental stage. Only in 1984 did the U.S. Department of Education issue a policy statement on correctional education, indicating that "education is a necessity for every American including the more than 2.2 million adults and juveniles who are under the jurisdiction of the criminal justice system." Correctional educators have already faced many challenges in their efforts to provide viable services to the adults and juveniles under correctional supervision. The future of correctional education remains uncertain but appears to include growth and improvement.

ISSUES IN CORRECTIONAL EDUCATION

The Correctional Education Association[1], the international organization that represents the interests of professional educators working in correctional settings, has defined correctional education (CE) as

> an organized and individualized self-help strategy to interrupt nonsocial or antisocial behavior through vocational and academic learning activities that foster social attitudes and equip students in contact with the criminal justice system for lives as responsible community members. (Gehring, 1984, p. 4)

Although this definition appears clear and concise, the practice of correctional education varies greatly within and among jurisdictions.

Correctional education is a professional area attempting to define its goals and purposes in a complex and often hostile environment. In its report to Congress on correctional education in adult institutions, the General Accounting Office found that offenders were not adequately prepared by institutional programs to live and work in free society. The report found that inmates need basic education, social skills, and marketable job skills if they are to enter the work force and lead a crime-free life (GAO, 1979). The GAO is not alone in its identification of the shortcomings of corrections in providing adequate educational opportunities for offenders (Bell, 1979; Conrad, 1981; Horvath, 1982; MacCormack, 1931). Correctional educators face numerous dilemmas in their attempts to improve service delivery to offenders.

---

[1]For additional information on the Correctional Education Association, write the organization's national office at 4321 Hartwick Road, Suite L–208, College Park, MD 20740.

Purposes of Correctional Education

Much of the confusion and conflict existing in correctional education is associated with the varying purposes of corrections. There are four generally accepted rationales for correctional services: retribution, incapacitation, resocialization, and reintegration (Snarr & Wolford, 1985). The application of any or all of these rationales varies by jurisdiction, agency, institution, and practitioner. With such divergent rationales it is not surprising that educators who work in correctional settings have difficulty defining their roles and responsibilities.

The goals of correctional education within custodial settings can be grouped into six categories:

1. to provide institutional work assignments
2. to provide passive control of inmate behavior
3. to provide inmates with basic academic and vocational skills
4. to reduce recidivism
5. to provide inmates with an opportunity to change their personal behavior and values
6. to support the operational needs of the correctional institution

There exist significant differences among correctional educators and between correctional educators and administrators as to the priority of these goals in correctional education (Wolford, 1985).

Nearly all groups agree that the desired product of corrections is more than just an educated criminal (Duguid, 1981). The causes of crime and the problems faced by offenders are complex and clearly include more than limited education and a lack of vocational skills. How much can and should the correctional educator be expected to do to aid in the reformation of offenders? Some would argue that correctional educators should concentrate their efforts on meeting the basic educational needs of the vast majority of inmates. Providing opportunities, literacy, and vocational skills should be the primary scope of correctional education (Bell, Conard, & Suppa, 1984). These are measurable goals that educators can help to reach, given adequate resources and time.

However, a recent movement in correctional education and in other areas of education has been toward life skills or competency-based education (Shelton, 1985). This orientation maintains that basic literacy and vocational skills taught in isolation from real world application are of questionable worth. Competency-based programs such as the Adult Performance Level (APL) Project have received increasing interest and use in correctional settings.

The most comprehensive approach to correctional education includes elements of both basic and life skills education, along with the concept of habilitation.

> The educational approach does not assume irrationality, sickness or the necessity to convert or replace, but rather assumes that most prisoners

are simply deficient in certain analytic problem-solving skills, interpersonal and social skills and in ethical/moral development. Each of these deficits can be addressed most effectively through education, through a process of habilitation rather than rehabilitation. (Duguid, 1981, p. 86)

This approach to correctional education is built on the works of Kohlberg and others and has received its widest application in European and Canadian correctional systems. Correctional education in this approach must have two essential elements: it must have a "central concern for ethics and morality and provide facilitation of critical thinking skills through an issues-oriented curriculum" (Duguid, 1981). This approach supports Kohlberg's findings that offenders, both adult and juvenile, are generally characterized by lower-than-normal moral reasoning development. Kohlberg's stages of moral development and the perspective on law represented by each stage (as suggested by Arbuthnot & Gordon, 1983) are presented in Table 3.1.

Public Support of Correctional Education

It has long been assumed that correctional education programs do not have strong support from the general public. The attitude of some vocal individuals within corrections and the general public has been that free education for criminals is a reward and these men and women should be punished for their criminal acts. Education programs for juvenile delinquents have existed for many years, and state mandatory education laws have supported such programs; but support of educational programs for adult offenders has not been widespread.

Few public opinion polls have addressed this issue, but one survey conducted in Kentucky indicates broad general support for most correctional education efforts (Faine & Bohlander, 1979). This study, commissioned by the Kentucky Corrections Cabinet, found well over 80% of the sample population in support of adult basic, vocational, and life skills programs for inmates incarcerated in the Commonwealth's correctional institutions. However, only 20% of the sample was supportive of higher education programs for the same population. This survey indicates that the public does recognize the need for correctional education programs.

Standards of Correctional Education

The standards and accreditation process developed for adult and juvenile correctional institutions by the American Correctional Association through the Commission on Accreditation for Corrections include many provisions for education programs. However, it is distressing that no mandatory standards exist for correctional education programs in adult institutions, where the largest number of individuals are incarcerated. In addition, few, if any, states have educational laws or administrative regulations governing correctional education. Without accepted measures of quality programming, it is not possible to effectively measure or monitor correctional education efforts.

Table 3.1   Kohlberg's Stages of Moral Development with Perspectives on Law

Level	Stage (Characteristics of Reasoning)	Law Issue
I. *Preconventional* Social perspective is centered around self. Events are perceived in terms of physical dimensions or consequences. General lack of awareness of purpose of rules and conventions.	1. *Heteronomous morality.* Equates right behavior with concrete rules backed by power and punishment. Concern with size and importance of damage and participants.	Laws are seen as simple labels. (Breaking laws would result in punishment.)
II. *Conventional* Social perspective is centered on larger group or society. Concern for opinions of others and need for rules to regulate desired behavior. Member-of-society perspective.	2. *Individualism, instrumental purpose, and exchange.* Right behavior is that which serves one's own interests. Aware of other's needs, but not of rights. Fairness is strict, right. Reciprocal agreements are very pragmatic.	Laws are seen as intentions of lawmakers. (Breaking laws would result in loss to self.)
III. *Post-Conventional, or Principled* Social perspective is prior-to-society. Laws should be based on principles of justice. Human rights and respect for individual dignity are universal.	3. *Mutual interpersonal expectations, relationships, and interpersonal conformity.* Right behavior is the "good" time that is approved by significant others. Concern for expectations of others, proper role of behavior.	Laws relate to prosocial motives and conduct; diffuse normative expectations. (Breaking laws is selfish, deceitful, will make people think badly of you.)
	4. *Social system and conscience.* Right behavior is meeting agreed upon obligations, following rules of society to preserve order, contributing to the good of society and its institutions.	Laws protect specific rights, practices, and institutions necessary for the social system. (Breaking laws undermines various rights; engenders disrespect for the law and can lead to social instability.) Laws protect fundamental human rights against infringement by others. (Breaking laws is generally unacceptable since they are made with common agreement; may be broken if they violate fundamental human rights.)
	5. *Social contract or utility; individual rights; universal ethical principles.* Right behavior is determined by universal ethics, principles of justice.	

Source: From "Moral Reasoning Development in Correctional Intervention" by J. Arbuthnot and D. A. Gordon, 1983, *Journal of Correctional Education, 34,* pp. 133–138. Copyright 1983 by the *Journal of Correctional Education.* Reprinted by permission.

Motivation for Participation in Correctional Education Programs

One remaining issue is the motivation underlying offender participation in correctional education programs. It already has been noted that for many individuals in the criminal justice system, correctional education programs will be their last formal learning experience. In juvenile institutions and community settings, education is mandated by compulsory education laws. The organization of most juvenile correctional systems is on a purely indeterminate sentence basis, which encourages participation in self-improvement programs. In addition, youths in these programs have limited work assignments, which promote their participation in educational programs.

In adult correctional institutions education has been viewed by inmates as a voluntary option and in some systems as a privilege that must be earned through hard work and good behavior. The "gaming" theory maintains that inmates enroll in education and other programs only to favorably influence the releasing authority. However, in an examination of parole release criteria in Florida, Lombardi (1984) found that participation in education and other treatment programs was an insignificant variable in the parole release process. In states where paroling authorities still operate, offense severity and length of sentence remain the primary release determinants. If, however, inmates perceive educational participation as an aid to early release, they will continue to play the nongame, regardless of the reality.

In many jurisdictions parole/indeterminate release systems have been eliminated and replaced with some form of determinate sentencing or flat time. In some of these systems elaborate "good time" provisions have been established. Good time provisions provide a formula for sentence reduction for good behavior and other specified activities. The Texas Department of Corrections has a significant educational good time release formula that can grant an inmate up to 15 days per month in sentence reduction for full participation in educational programs.

Other jurisdictions, such as Maryland and the Federal Bureau of Prisons, have established mandatory education participation programs. The programs require any resident testing below prescribed levels on standardized achievement tests to enroll in educational programs for minimum periods of time. The effects of mandatory and good time education provisions on inmate participation and motivation have yet to be measured and reported. It remains a challenge for correctional educators to attract and keep offenders motivated to participate in educational programs.

THE ADMINISTRATION OF CORRECTIONAL EDUCATION

The multilevel governmental system operating in the United States ensures that most public service systems have complex networks of administration, funding, and service delivery (see Table 3.2). The responsibility for correctional education programs is unequally divided among local, state, and

Table 3.2   **Governmental Responsibility for Correctional Education**

	Government Level		
	Federal	State	Local
Direct services	Federal Bureau of Prisons and military correctional centers	Adult and juvenile correctional facilities and some community-based programs in certain jurisdictions	Alternative schools, court schools, jail and detention education programs, group homes and other community-based services
Financial support	Full responsibility for federally operated institutions; indirect support for correctional programs through federal education programs (e.g., adult education, PL 94–142, Pell grants)	Through corrections and education departments, full responsibility for state facilities and partial responsibility for community programs in some jurisdictions	Shared responsibility with state government, courts, and local school districts
Supervision and monitoring	Supervision and monitoring of federally operated programs; indirect monitoring of state education agencies regarding correctional education	Supervision and monitoring of state programs; monitoring through state education agencies and corrections departments of some local programs	Supervision of local programs; self-monitoring of community programs

federal government agencies. Direct educational services to offenders remain primarily a state responsibility; the largest correctional education programs can be found in state-operated adult and juvenile correctional institutions. Local governments are commonly responsible for the delivery of education services in jails, group homes, juvenile detention centers, and alternative/court schools. The federal government provides direct educational services only in the 42 facilities of the Federal Bureau of Prisons and in military correctional centers.

The funding for correctional education programs is more difficult to track. State governments provide the largest portion of correctional education funding; they devote an average of 3% of their total budgets to correctional services, but less than 1% of the total correctional budget is targeted for correctional education (National Institute of Corrections, 1984). Most states use additional funds from education department budgets for correctional programs.

The federal government provides funding for programs operated in federal facilities. In addition, federal education programs such as vocational, adult, and bilingual education, ESEA/Chapter I, and Pell grants provide support for state and local programs. There has been no comprehensive report to date on total federal funding for correctional education. It is estimated that federal support, although significant, does not exceed state expenditures for correctional education.

Local government support for correctional education comes primarily from public school districts, which provide staff and materials for community-based programs. There has been no calculation of how many dollars are contributed to correctional education by local governments.

State governments assume responsibility for supervision and monitoring of state institutional programs, as well as monitoring of local programs. In addition, the U.S. Department of Education assumes some state monitoring relative to federal statutes such as PL 94-142. The federal government monitors and supervises federal institutional programs. The only responsibility of most local governments is to operate and supervise community-based programs.

A variety of agencies within state and local government share responsibility for the delivery of correctional education services. State correctional or human service agencies share responsibility for correctional education in juvenile institutions. Partial or full funding frequently is provided through state education sources. Departments of corrections are generally responsible for funding education programs in adult institutions, with supplemental funding coming from federal and, in some cases, state educational agencies.

State departments of education or local school districts in some jurisdictions provide educational services for incarcerated juveniles. State education agencies provide only limited funding for adult correctional education programs, except in a few states where primary responsibility has been shifted from corrections. A majority of state education funding for adult correctional education programs is directed toward those under age 22.

Other agencies providing juvenile correctional education include the courts and some private firms. Because the majority of U.S. jails are operated by sheriffs, the responsibility for correctional education in local detention often rests with a law enforcement agency.

ADMINISTRATIVE STRUCTURES

It is difficult to identify any clear administrative structures for locally operated correctional education programs. The most common arrangements are under a special division of the local school system or with a director of programs/services in a correctional or law enforcement agency.

State correctional education programs have been organized under various typologies (Pecht, 1983). There are a total of 85 distinct state correctional education systems in the United States (35 adult systems, 35 juvenile systems, and 15 combined adult/juvenile correctional education programs (Rutherford, Nelson, & Wolford, 1985). Four basic administrative structures operate in those 85 systems: decentralization, centralization, separate educational agency, and contract/autonomy. Traditionally, education programs have been the responsibility of the local prison/institution administrator. In most systems today the local correctional administrator, regardless of the correctional education administrative structure, is highly influential in the operation of education programs within that institution.

Decentralization

The decentralized system places primary responsibility for curriculum, staffing, and funding with the local institutional staff. This arrangement is most common in sparsely populated states where no central administrative position has been established for correctional education. The correctional agency assumes nearly all responsibility for education in these systems.

Centralization

Under a centralized system the correctional agency still retains responsibility for educational programming, but supervisory authority is divided between a central office and the local institution. There generally is at least a state director of correctional education and, in some cases, a support staff of professional educators at the state level.

Two significant variations of this arrangement should be mentioned, relating to budgetary authority and a separate school district. In many systems the central office administrator does not control a line-item budget for education. The administrator may or may not control the flow of state and federal funds for education into the corrections agency. When budgetary authority remains with the local institution administrator, the power and influence of the central office education staff is significantly reduced. When the central office education administrator does control the entire education budget, a pure centralized system is created.

The other variation is seen in eight systems, where a correctional school district has been established (Carlson, 1983). These school districts are chartered by the state education agency and in many ways enjoy equal status with other public school districts in the state. The school district may or may not control a line-item budget. An analysis of federal support for correctional education indicates that over 40% of the funds were directed to those eight school district systems.

Separate Educational Agency

In some states partial or full responsibility for education services has been delegated to state or local education agencies. In Maryland and Pennsylvania the state department of education operates the correctional education programs in adult and juvenile institutions (Galley & Steurer, 1985). These are centralized systems maintaining full responsibility for educational services, including budgetary control. The organizational chart for Maryland's system is represented in Figure 3.1. The corrections departments in these jurisdic-

Organizational Chart of Maryland's Adult Correctional Education

Figure 3.1

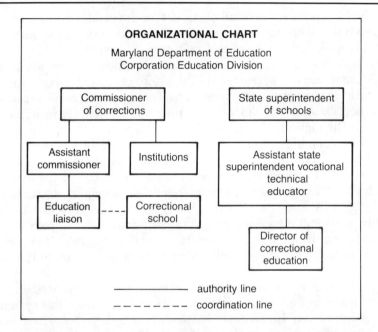

Source: From "Correctional Education Administered by the State Education Agency—Six Years Experience" by J. P. Galley and S. J. Steurer, 1986, *Journal of Correctional Education, 36*(1), p. 32. Copyright 1986 by the *Journal of Correctional Education.* Reprinted by permission.

tions designate a liaison to work with the state education agency to monitor services and programs.

In some juvenile systems local public school districts provide education services for incarcerated youth within their jurisdictions. This arrangement is accomplished through a contractual or interagency agreement. This may represent the most decentralized system. For example, in Kentucky, correctional education services for incarcerated youth are provided by 19 independent school districts throughout the state. Typically the correctional agency designates an education liaison in these systems.

The operation of correctional education programs by education agencies has both positive and negative aspects. Galley and Steurer (1985) identified the following strengths and limitations, based on the Maryland experience.

Strengths
Substantial growth in state and federal support
Increased training for educational staff
Growth in program and support services

Limitations
Created coordination and scheduling problems
Correctional education budget in competition with public schools for funds (p. 32)

Contract/Autonomy

In other jurisdictions some or all of the correctional education programs are contracted out to community colleges or other education units. Both Alabama and Illinois make extensive use of contracted services.

In Virginia the state legislature created and funded a separate state agency (the Department of Correctional Education) to provide programs in adult and juvenile institutions. The contractual and autonomous arrangements seem to meet local needs but do not appear to be gaining in popularity or application throughout the nation.

Two other variables affecting the administration of correctional education are institutional security levels and classification. In general the higher the security level, the greater the control and authority of the local correctional administrator (warden, superintendent, or manager). Regardless of the correctional education administrative structure, significant differences among institutional education programs typically exist in part because of the security requirements of the institutions. For example, it is common to find very limited vocational education offerings in maximum security institutions.

A related factor is the assignment and movement of inmates into and between institutions and programs. Correctional classification systems control the assignment of incarcerated offenders. These systems base decisions primarily on institutional and security needs; seldom do educational considerations figure into the process. Although educational personnel may participate on classification committees, decisions made by these groups seldom take into account offenders' educational needs. Functional assessment and placement to maximize educational experience will not occur on a system-wide basis until educational needs become a basis for decision making in the classification process.

The effective administration of correctional education is one of the key factors influencing the quality and range of services available to offenders. A thorough analysis of the relative merits of the various administrative arrangements is needed. States should determine the most appropriate options available in their jurisdictions.

CORRECTIONAL EDUCATION IN THE JUVENILE JUSTICE SYSTEM[2]

The years of adolescence are a time to experiment, to test one's own limits, and to challenge the control and authority of the adult world that rules over young lives. It should not be surprising to discover that the peak years for criminal behavior (seen in both property and violent crimes) are during and

---

[2]Significant portions of this section are reprinted by permission of author and publisher from "Educational Interventions in the Juvenile Justice System," by B.I. Wolford, 1985. In S. Braaten, R.B. Rutherford, and W. Evans (Eds.), *Programming for Adolescents with Behavioral Disorders*, 2, pp. 78–79. Copyright © 1985 by the Council for Children with Behavior Disorders, Reprinted by permission.

immediately following adolescence (Bureau of Justice Statistics, 1983b). Nearly one in every three juveniles will have some contact with the police (Wolfgang, Figlio, & Sellin, 1979). One young person in nine will appear in juvenile court before the age of 18 (Bronfenbrenner, 1974).

The learning handicapped adolescent appears with disproportionate frequency in correctional settings. Throughout the juvenile justice system the learning-related problems of youths work against them. Their level of suggestibility and capacity to be manipulated by peers and others often lead handicapped youths into delinquent acts. Similarly, their lack of sophistication and limited knowledge of the justice system make them likely arrestees and unlikely divertees from the system. Many judges and lawyers tend to focus on IQ scores and are not typically well-informed about handicapping conditions (Schilit, 1983). When handicapped offenders reach a juvenile correctional facility, they are unlikely to find personnel or programs designed to meet their needs (Rutherford, Nelson, & Wolford, 1985). However, educational alternatives and programs are possible within the juvenile justice system.

Figure 3.2 illustrates movement through the juvenile justice system and indicates the points at which educational interventions can be applied. Those intervention points can be organized into four stages, described as predelinquent, diversionary and adjudicatory, dispositional, and reentry. Predelinquent interventions are aimed at preventing delinquent behavior. Diversionary and adjudicatory interventions can occur at any time after a youth's initial encounter with the police, up to and through the adjudication process. Dispositional interventions, on the other hand, occur only after adjudication, and reentry interventions take place during transition from the correctional system.

Predelinquent Interventions

Prevention, so goes the old adage, is superior to cure. Educational interventions that can forestall delinquency are the most desirable and often the most economical. When one considers that in 1980 the cost of incarcerating one juvenile for a year ranged from $20,000 to $30,000 (Abt Associates, 1980), it seems economically prudent to investigate preventive measures.

Alternative education programs directed at reducing the 20% dropout rate in U.S. schools have been demonstrated to be effective in many communities (U.S. Department of Justice, 1980). Alternative programs commonly incorporate individualized instruction, rewards for positive behavior, goal-oriented work, and small student populations. These programs can be operated by a school system and/or juvenile court. Parent education programs directed at both providing parenting skills and identifying families in need of additional assistance and support constitute another preventive intervention. On a different level, individual teachers can include law-related educational components within their curricula.

Figure 3.2   **Educational Intervention in the Juvenile Justice System**

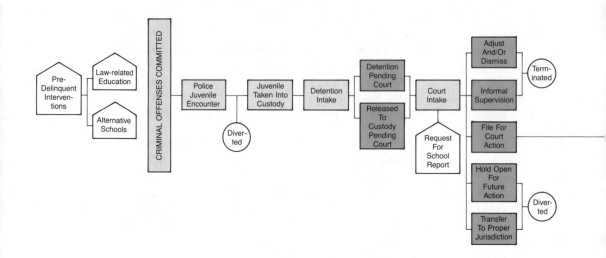

Diversion and Intervention During Adjudication

At least two forms of educational intervention are available during the adjudication process. Educational programs such as court and alternative
schools and job programs or a cooperative occupational experience can be
used to divert young people from the justice system (Meers, 1983). Youths
can agree to enter community programs and remain outside the juvenile
justice system, based upon their continued participation and noncriminal
behavior. Increasingly these community programs are being operated by non-

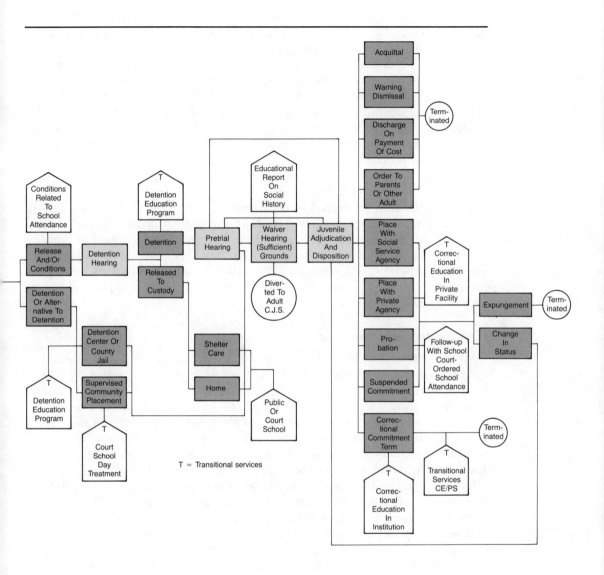

profit agencies under performance contracts with government agencies (Nelson, 1982).

One of the most extensive court school programs is found in California. The Los Angeles County Juvenile Court schools serve over 4,000 youngsters daily and approximately 45,000 students annually at 39 different facilities, including day schools, juvenile halls, shelters, and camps (Leone, Price, & Vitolo, 1985). The program is operated by the county office of education and receives funding from the California Department of Education on a per pupil revenue formula. A full range of educational programs, with an emphasis on individualized instruction and functional skills, is made available to delinquent youth in the Los Angeles court schools.

Detention education programs are a different intervention available to most individuals who do not qualify for diversion or who reside in an area where diversion programs are not available. Detention education programs primarily serve youth involved in the adjudicatory process but can also be made available in some short-term dispositional cases. In communities that have separate juvenile detention facilities or units, educational programs are generally available. In many smaller communities juveniles are held in special sections of local jails, where appropriate educational programs are generally unavailable (Cottle, 1979).

Despite the limited period of confinement in most detention facilities (6 months or less), educational programming remains important both to aid in transition and to enhance academic skills. Short-term remedial reading programs based on behavior modification have been successful with delinquents (Gagne, 1977). Delinquents entering detention facilities anticipate punishment; it may be only through reward conditions that improved performance can be achieved.

Dispositional Interventions

Dispositional alternatives can occur during probation and in community, residential, and institutional settings. Education plays an important role in each of these areas. Conditions of probation for juveniles (the most frequently used dispositional alternative) commonly include regular school attendance. Teachers and educational counselors, with the active support of the courts and probation staff, can sometimes reach youth who have previously avoided school. In addition, according to Burchard and Lane (1982), service providers such as probation officers can be trained to use behavior modification effectively. In the best of circumstances the typically adversarial relationship that often exists between probationer and probation officer can be turned into one of positive reinforcement.

Community-based residential facilities have long been noted for their use of behavioral and other educational approaches. The Teaching Family Model, which originated in Lawrence, Kansas, is a home-style treatment program for delinquents. The program employs the family teaching approach through a token economy. Behavioral approaches have found their greatest acceptance in the national array of group homes patterned after the Teaching Family Model.

Despite a significant reduction in the number of youth held in long-term facilities, an extensive system of state-operated juvenile correctional facilities still exists in the United States. These long-term facilities represent the most punitive and highly controlled intervention in the juvenile justice system. The length of stay in these facilities varies greatly among jurisdictions, with averages ranging from 6 months to over 1 year.

Educational programs in these facilities often are the largest and most extensive available to delinquent youth. Juvenile correctional education programs in institutions commonly provide high school credit programs, remedial and special education programs, as well as prevocational and life skills programs. Some institutions have developed modified comprehensive schools operating within the confines of the correctional facility.

Reentry Interventions

It is not sufficient to bring about rehabilitation without a transition program and modification of the natural environment to which a juvenile offender returns (Burchard & Lane, 1982). Transitional services are needed throughout the juvenile justice system to facilitate the transfer of educational records and the continuation of educational programs, from community to institution and back to community.

Youths leaving correctional facilities need transitional support services to assure their participation in community educational programs. Frequently youths fail to reenroll in school and, lacking adequate education, job, and life skills, find themselves reentering the criminal justice system rather than society. Significant issues have been raised about the generalization of skills from institutional programs to the community. Transitional programs have been the most neglected components of educational programming for delinquents. Only recently have demonstration programs been funded in this vital area.

Many opportunities exist for teachers to intervene in the juvenile justice system as resource persons, advocates, trainers, and correctional educators. The task remains to find the most appropriate approaches and locations for such interventions.

Observations on Educational Interventions in the Juvenile Justice System

The role of education in our society is second only to that of the family. For youths whose families have abdicated or ignored their responsibilities, the task of education often falls entirely on the school and other social agencies. It is generally agreed that delinquent/criminal behavior is learned and that adolescents can learn not to engage in such behavior. Juvenile delinquents and other adolescents need more than basic education. Educational programs must recognize that delinquency is a complex problem that defies simple solutions. In addition to enhancing both academic and life skills, schools should provide an opportunity for all youth to experience success. The learning handicapped youth also needs to be exposed to information about the criminal justice system, its operation, and the realities of crime and punishment in this nation.

Correctional education should provide programs supporting the reestablishment of ties in a normalized setting. Transitional services between the community and the correctional setting must be given the highest priority. The continuum of educational services should not be broken either by entering or by leaving the correctional environment.

CORRECTIONAL EDUCATION IN THE ADULT JUSTICE SYSTEM

Correctional education opportunities for adults are concentrated in correctional facilities (jails and prisons). Community-based and transitional programs for adult offenders are very limited and, where available, are generally provided by local adult basic education/literacy programs or employment service offices.

Jail Education Programs

Jail education programs are available in only 30% of the nation's short-term detention facilities (Kerle & Ford, 1982). Because of the relatively short period of incarceration (in most jails the average is less than 72 hours), small populations, and limited funding for programming, most jail education programs are found in larger urban facilities. The types of programs are summarized in Table 3.3. Jail education has only recently been given much attention by the criminal justice system and the judiciary. The coming years should see a considerable growth in adult detention education programs.

Education Programs in Long-Term Institutions

Although many of the issues discussed in the remainder of this section apply equally to jails and prisons, the focus will be on long-term correctional institutions, where the bulk of education programs for offenders presently operate. Adult illiterates, unable to function productively, are estimated to include 60% to 80% of the nation's prison population (Bell, Conard, & Suppa, 1984; Omang, 1982). Based on recent adult corrections population figures, these percentages translate to between 214,000 and 285,000 illiterate adults

Table 3.3   **Jail Education Programs in the United States**

Type of Program	Number of Jails	Percent of Jails
GED preparatory	774	29.1
Adult basic education	383	14.4
Life skills	114	4.3
Vocational training	214	8.0
Job placement	417	15.7

Note: Based on a survey of 2,664 U.S. jails in 1982 (Kerle & Ford, 1982).

currently in prison. Bush (1982) estimates that $6.6 billion a year are spent to keep illiterate offenders in the nation's prisons and jails.

Nearly all long-term correctional institutions (those authorized to house offenders for longer than 1 year) have some form of educational programming. The scope of education services available generally shows a positive correlation with the size of the institution. Factors such as security level, location of the facility, and special nature of the incarcerated population can significantly affect the educational program. More than 7,000 correctional educators provide programs for 120,000 offenders in the nation's prisons.

Education programs for adult offenders are generally voluntary and in many systems are largely part-time, evening, or weekend activities in which inmates participate after completing their work assignments. The number of inmates enrolled in educational programs varies widely among jurisdictions, ranging from 3% to 58% with a national average of 30% participation (Rutherford, Nelson, & Wolford, 1985). The largest programs are adult basic education and literacy training. Other programs include GED preparatory classes, vocational training, high school completion, prerelease, and life skills. On the average, only 1% of the adult prison population is enrolled in a special education program, despite the high numbers identified as learning handicapped.

GED Programs. The traditional orientation of adult correctional education programs has been toward earning the GED. This test-driven system has raised concern that correctional education has been certifying and not educating offenders (Smith, 1983). The GED completion program does provide a tangible goal for inmates to pursue while incarcerated, and the GED is commonly recognized and accepted in the "free world." It also lends itself to the quantification and documentation required by most correctional record-keeping systems. For those higher functioning inmates serving relatively short sentences, the GED serves a useful purpose. However, for many prison residents the GED is at best a long-term goal, often beyond their reach.

Some jurisdictions have begun to question the merits of a GED-driven educational program and have modified their curriculum, based on a more functional orientation. The Illinois Department of Corrections has adopted a policy that inmates pursuing a GED must pass sequentially ordered competency-based tests covering 80% of the overall objectives in the system's English, math, and reading curricula before becoming eligible to take the GED. The purpose of this policy is to foster acquisition of the fundamental knowledge and basic skills necessary for social and economic survival (Smith, 1983).

Adult Basic Education Programs. Adult Basic Education (ABE) programs for inmates also have been a mainstay of correctional education. Supported in part by federal funding through the Adult Education Act, ABE programs have been developed in nearly all correctional facilities. These programs are typically self-paced/learner-oriented and often use programmed material in a learning laboratory arrangement. Advancement through an ABE program is based on periodic testing using a standardized instrument, such as the California Test of Adult Basic Education (TABE). The ABE program is generally viewed as a feeder system for a GED preparatory class.

Adult Literacy Programs.   Although literacy programs are not always distinguishable from ABE efforts, they recently have gained increased acceptance. For many years the primary person responsible for correctional education was an inmate teacher. The institutional classification system would identify more highly educated offenders and would send them to the prison school, where a small, trained educational staff would use these recruits as teachers. Beginning in the 1930s in the Federal Bureau of Prisons and in some state systems, a movement developed to professionalize correctional education. A result of this effort was an increase in the number of certified noninmate teachers. Inmates became teacher aides and in some systems performed only clerical roles.

The national literacy effort begun in the 1980s has resulted in a reexamination of the use of inmates as well as community and institutional volunteers in the educational process. Based on one of the main literacy programs (e.g., Laubach Literacy or Literacy Volunteers of America), correctional education programs have greatly increased their use of inmate and nonprison tutors to assist illiterate offenders and to enhance existing educational programs.

The most significant contribution of literacy efforts in correctional education has been the development of systematic and effective training programs for volunteer tutors, and this training of volunteers has been a key to the growth of literacy programs in corrections. Although most correctional literacy volunteers are inmates, many systems do solicit the services of nonresidents. In Pennsylvania the State Department of Education operates correctional education programs and trains and uses correctional officers as volunteer literacy tutors. This approach not only provides the system with a supplement to the supply of inmate tutors, but also has proven to be an excellent educational advocacy effort within the correctional institution.

Life Skills Programs.   Most, if not all, inmates have been sentenced to prison for reasons that directly or indirectly relate to their inability to function effectively in society (Shelton, 1985). In response to the need for a life-skills-oriented adult education curriculum, a number of programs have been developed. The Adult Performance Level (APL) Project is the most widely used life skills program in the correctional setting. APL was initially pilot-tested in a number of adult education settings, including correctional agencies, and has been used ever since its initial pilot test in the Windham School System operated by the Texas Department of Corrections.

The APL is a competency-based high school diploma program that allows students to advance at their own pace through seven steps: counseling, diagnosis, instruction, mastery, life skills, individualized competency assessment, and certification. The program is used both as a supplement to traditional ABE/GED programs and as an alternative learning approach.

Vocational Education Programs. Vocational programs in adult institutions provide both preapprenticeship and certificate programs as well as on-the-job training. Correctional vocational education can be defined as instruction offered to enable offenders to be more readily employed upon their return to free society. It involves the development of basic skills, specific occupational training, and job retention training, focusing on such things as motivation for work and positive work habits (Day & McCane, 1982).

Vocational programs have been supported by federal and state vocational education funding, departments of corrections, and employment services programs funded under the Job Training Partnership Act (JTPA) and earlier manpower programs. With the return to the production of prison industry products marketable in the private sector, an increasing interest has developed in the relationship between vocational education and prison industries.

Correctional vocational programs face a number of challenges in the delivery of training.

1. overcoming limitations in training based on security needs
2. developing marketable and practical training programs within institutions
3. meeting the training needs of incarcerated females
4. balancing the responsibilities of training while meeting institutional maintenance and production demands
5. working with academic programs and penal industries to assure that vocational students gain both basic literacy skills and relevant work experience

The need for employable job skills far exceeds the capacity of correctional vocational programs. Additional programs and delivery mechanisms are needed.

Special Education Programs. Special education programs have been the latest addition to adult correctional education. Fewer than 10% of the identified learning handicapped inmates are receiving special education services (Rutherford, Nelson, & Wolford, 1985). These limited services can be explained by the relatively recent attention paid to adult facilities by special educators. Because most educational programs are voluntary and special funding is generally provided only for inmates under the age of 22, many residents do not receive appropriate services.

Transitional Programs. Transitional services are provided in only a limited number of jurisdictions. Most existing programs are tied to employment and do not address the needs of the learning handicapped. A prerelease program funded by the Job Training Partnership Act and operated by the Ohio Department of Rehabilitation and Corrections is a prototype for employment transition. All Ohio inmates complete a vocational and educational evaluation and assessment upon commitment to the corrections department. The residents' aptitudes, abilities, and interests are matched to prison education programs and work assignments. As space becomes available, inmates are placed in appropriate education and work assignments. The Ohio Plan is described here to illustrate comprehensive correctional education programming for adult offenders.

The Ohio Plan

The Ohio Department of Rehabilitation and Correction has developed a comprehensive plan for the education, training and employment of offenders assigned to adult correctional institutions.

Inmate Work and Education Assignments. Upon reception in prison, inmates are tested to determine their aptitude, skills and interests for certain types of jobs. If the inmate is below a certain educational level, he/she will be enrolled in the mandatory adult basic education program. There are two categories of jobs, those linked to "specialized tracks" which combine requirements for education and training to the work assignment, and those which are a part of a service track. The service track jobs are generally institutional-need placements. They are used for inmates who do not wish to enter a specialized track, for short-term inmates who have too little time to complete enough of a track and for inmates waiting to enter a specialized track or phase of a track.

For inmates who wish to enter a specialized track and apply for a specific type of work assignment, the approach is similar to what any Ohio citizen would encounter if seeking employment through the Ohio Bureau of Employment Services (OBES) or other job placement alternatives. Following aptitude and interest testing, there is job counseling and the development of an educational and training career phase to complete prior to assignment to the job. There can be jobs which allow the completion of education and training requirements while on the job.

The tracks available to inmates include

1. *Academic track.* This track is designed for inmates whose primary interest/need is academic education and who wish to proceed through ABE/GED completion to post-secondary training. Inmates completing post-secondary course work are assigned to appropriate institutional jobs where such academic preparation is required. Additionally, this track includes tutorial programs and English-as-a-second-language programs. Mandatory ABE inmates who are not yet enrolled in another track are placed in this track.
2. *Vocational/Apprenticeship track.* This often begins with ABE/GED programming. Inmates would then be placed into a vocational or apprenticeship program in areas of their interests and aptitudes. While a variety of vocational or apprenticeship programs are offered, there also are a variety of skills and aptitudes required for admission into these programs. Vocational areas are further divided into "hi-tech" programs such as computer programming, drafting or electronics, with placement in similar types of institutional jobs. Other vocational areas include "trades" programs including building maintenance or carpentry. Every institution has building maintenance or other training programs which should be completed before assignment to an institutional maintenance job. There is a third group of vocational programs in the "service" area. Examples are food or health services, with training followed by an appropriate job assignment.
3. *Industrial track.* The industrial track also begins with ABE/GED educational programming which then leads to pre-industrial training or specific vocational

training. Following education and training, inmates are placed into an Ohio Penal Industry (OPI) job. The many ongoing improvements in OPI to make these assignments similar to private sector operations are important to the success of the industrial track.

4. *Service Track.* This track is the initial work assignment for many offenders entering the system as well as for those not wishing to enter a specialized track, those on a waiting list, or those with insufficient time to complete a specialized track. Included in this track are the laundry worker, food server, custodian, grounds keeper, sanitation worker, and farm laborer. Farm laborer is included in this track based upon custody/supervision restrictions. The importance of this track should not be minimized because the workers assigned will be responsible for the cleanliness, safety and sanitation of the institution.

5. *Special Needs Track.* This track is specialized to the individual's needs. It is designed for those inmates whose individual needs preclude them from participation in the conventional tracks. However, inmates will be mainstreamed whenever feasible. Those identified as special needs inmates are the educably mentally impaired, the physically handicapped, the geriatric, and those being treated for psychological problems.

The department's pre-release program emphasizes the transition from institutional to community living. While basic living skills such as consumer economics should continue, the primary emphasis is on extending the inmates' institutional work activities to the community. Links to OBES, resumé and interview skills development, and counseling or job searching are critical. (Ohio Department of Rehabilitation and Correction, 1986)

Aftercare Programs

Upon notification of parole eligibility, residents may be transferred to a prerelease institution, where they complete an intensive prerelease and employment preparation program.

Residents may then be sent to community-based minimum security prerelease centers located in major metropolitan areas. Once in the community centers offenders are linked to local employment service personnel. The soon-to-be-released men and women are assisted in obtaining employment and additional education and training. This approach provides a comprehensive transition from institutions to community.

Postsecondary Programs

Postsecondary correctional education programs have operated in prisons since the early 1960s. Presently over 350 colleges and universities provide educational programs for over 27,000 institutional residents. Most programs are operated by 2-year publicly funded community/junior or technical colleges. Although advanced degrees are available through correspondence and some on-site programs, most inmates pursue associate degrees or certificates.

Postsecondary programs are funded by federal and state education voucher systems, contracts, and special arrangements. The variety of educational offerings are as diverse as the higher education institutions involved in correctional education. Although the primary emphasis is on the completion of general education, some colleges provide comprehensive programs. Project Talent, a correctional education program developed by Wilmington College, provides a wide range of educational programs in Ohio's Lebanon Correctional Institution. Project Talent provides both associate and bachelor degree programming in technical fields, liberal arts, and social sciences. Project Talent is also involved in educational and employment transition, family counseling services, and cultural enrichment for incarcerated students.

Correctional education programs in adult institutions face the challenges associated with operating in an often-hostile environment. Many inmates are initially resistant to education as a result of earlier experiences and learning handicaps. In addition, the prison is oriented toward custodial needs that often do not conform to educational goals. And many programs operate with limited budgets and suffer from isolation and neglect. Despite some rather significant obstacles, many fine educational programs presently operate in the more than 1,000 long-term correctional institutions in the United States.

SPECIAL EDUCATION IN CORRECTIONS

Correctional settings have been the last major area to respond to the mandate to provide free and appropriate education to all handicapped youth. The delay in responding can be attributed in part to the very nature of corrections. Society has chosen to isolate correctional programs from the general community. Juvenile and adult institutions often are impenetrable facilities located in remote and sparsely populated areas. This removal of convicted offenders from public contact and scrutiny has denied handicapped offenders the benefits of public advocacy and attention. Historically, correctional agencies have chosen one of three alternatives in dealing with the handicapped offender:

1. ignore special education needs
2. significantly change the educational process to meet correctional needs
3. group the learning handicapped with the psychopath, sociopath, and sexual deviant incarcerated populations (Schilit, 1983)

Along with the isolation of correctional programs, a number of other problems have limited the development of special education programs. Correctional education programs frequently are viewed as being outside the governance and standards of state and local education authorities. Many state education statutes and regulations fail to specifically address the needs of adjudicated youth. Only recently have such states as California developed education statutes and policies specifically directed toward correctional populations (Leone, Price, & Vitolo, 1985).

Further limiting is the fact that the handicapped correctional population is highly mobile both prior to and after incarceration. On the streets, prior to adjudication, a handicapped youth is frequently truant from school and often resides in numerous jurisdictions. Upon incarceration that youth becomes correctionally mobile, going from local detention to state facility, then moving within the correctional system according to security, program, and institutional needs. After what is often a short stay in corrections, this individual may be returned to a community corrections program or, more typically, dumped back onto the streets with few or no educational transition services. A recent study of youth leaving the Wisconsin Division of Corrections determined that the vast majority did not return to public schools and therefore did not complete high school (Haberman & Lerman, 1982).

In additon, most adult correctional systems are faced with burgeoning populations and are forced to make institutional assignments based almost exclusively on security and space determinations. Typically, the correctional classification process neither considers educational needs nor effectively screens new arrivals for educational needs. Institutional educational programs are typically voluntary and have no effective process for identifying handicapped offenders; the potential special education student slips into a correctional crack, avoiding the school program in which he or she has already failed on the streets.

As a result of public pressure through such legislation as the Juvenile Justice Delinquency and Prevention Act (JJPDA), juvenile correctional programs have been largely deinstitutionalized. Following the principle of the least restrictive alternative, fewer juveniles have been held in long-term facilities, and those incarcerated have often had brief periods of confinement (less than 6 months). The deinstitutionalization movement has resulted in the development of less punitive community-oriented programs, but it has also inadvertently worked to reduce specialized programs, which are viewed as more cost-effective in larger long-term facilities.

Given the public school orientation of existing handicapped education statutes, the numerous limitations faced by correctional educators and administrators attempting to meet the mandates of special education laws, and the tremendous need for services that exists within correctional populations, some have suggested that a realistic goal for correctional special education may be to meet the spirit, if not the letter, of the law (Leone, Price, & Vitolo, 1985).

To reach the goal of having meaningful special education programs in all correctional settings, both effective monitoring of services and strong public advocacy are needed. Each state education agency (SEA) is required to periodically monitor educational programs within its jurisdiction. This monitoring requirement includes programs operated in correctional settings (Gerry, 1985). However, for largely the same reasons that special education programs have been slow to develop in correctional settings, SEA monitoring of correctional settings has been limited. The pressure of outside scrutiny and the assistance available from SEA staffs can play a significant role in the development and refinement of special education services for offenders.

Public and professional advocacy for the learning handicapped has been a crucial factor in the development of special education programs and legislation in the United States. Correctional education has suffered from a lack of public attention and advocacy. Meaningful special education programs in correctional settings need advocates within the general public and the education profession. With a basic knowledge of special education and its operations, what is needed for highly effective advocacy is a core of knowledge regarding the criminal justice system. Schilit (1983) has suggested that students entering the field of special education and interested citizens/advocates need to understand the following:

1. the types of violations of the law
2. the ways in which violators are arrested
3. the procedures that are followed when a person is arrested
4. the ways in which criminals are punished
5. the release-from-confinement process

Effective correctional special education programs will not be developed and maintained without public and professional assistance and attention.

CONCLUSION

> A nation's treatment of criminals is one of the unfailing tests of its civilization.
>
> —Winston Churchill

Much public attention, as well as political and policy orientation in recent years, has been directed toward simple retribution in the treatment of criminal offenders. However, it must be remembered that most incarcerated offenders will one day return to the community; the majority of convicted offenders never even leave the local setting but remain in free society under the terms of a probated sentence. The public cannot escape the realities of crime; given present resources and alternatives, society is unable to isolate permanently or incapacitate all identified criminals. One clearly identified and addressable need shared by most criminals is greater educational and vocational skills.

Although recidivism remains the ultimate success measure of all correctional programs, an adequate education and marketable job skills cannot be expected to assure a law-abiding life-style. Education alone cannot erase the effects of social, economic, and cultural deprivation, in which most offenders have been raised. Correctional education can, however, provide those individuals who are capable, willing, and interested with the opportunity to seek a new direction. The future of correctional education lies in making quality programs available to all offenders, including those with learning handicaps.

REFERENCES

Abt Associates. (1980). *American prisons and jails.* Washington, DC: National Institute of Justice.

Arbuthnot, J., & Gordon, D. A. (1983). Moral reasoning development in correctional intervention. *Journal of Correctional Education, 34,* 133–138.

Bell, R. (1979). *Correctional education programs for inmates.* Washington, DC: Government Printing Office.

Bell, R., Conard, E. H., & Suppa, R. J. (1984). The findings and recommendations of the national study on learning deficiencies in adult inmates. *Journal of Correctional Education, 35,* 129–137.

Bronfenbrenner, U. (1974). The origins of alienation. *Scientific American, 231,* 53–61.

Burchard, J. D., & Lane, T. W. (1982). Crime and delinquency. In A. S. Bellak, M. Hersen, & A. E. Kazdin (Eds.), *International handbook of behavior modification and therapy* (pp. 613–652). New York: Plenum.

Bureau of Justice Statistics. (1983a). *Jail inmates, 1982.* Washington, DC: U.S. Department of Justice.

Bureau of Justice Statistics. (1983b). *Report to the nation on crime and justice: The data.* Washington, DC: U.S. Department of Justice.

Bush, B. (1982, May 17). *U.S. News and World Report,* p. 4.

Carlson, R. (1983). *Vocational education in the prison system.* Washington, DC: U.S. Department of Education.

Conrad, J. P. (1981). *Adult offender education programs.* Washington, DC: U.S. Department of Education.

Cottle, T. J. (1979). Children in jail. *Crime and Delinquency, 25,* 318–334.

Day, S. R., & McCane, M. R. (1982). *Vocational education in corrections.* Columbus, OH: National Center for Research in Vocational Education.

Duguid, S. (1981). Prison education and criminal choice: The context of decision-making. In L. Morin (Ed.), *On prison education* (pp. 83–98). Ottawa: Canadian Government Publishing Centre.

Faine, J., & Bohlander, E. (1979). Public response to correctional programs in Kentucky. *Kentucky Criminal Justice Research Series #6.* Bowling Green: Western Kentucky University.

Gagne, E. E. (1977). Educating delinquents: A review of research. *Journal of Special Education, 11,* 13–28.

Galley, J. P., & Steurer, S. J. (1985). Correctional education administered by the state education agency—six years' experience. *Journal of Correctional Education, 36,* 31–34.

Gehring, T. (1984). CEA executive board approves resolutions, begins implementation. *Journal of Correctional Education, 35,* 137–141.

General Accounting Office. (1979). *Report to Congress: Correctional institutions can do more to improve the employability of offenders.* Washington, DC: Author.

Gerry, M. H. (1985). *Monitoring the special education programs of correctional institutions.* Washington, DC: National Association of State Directors in Special Education and the Correctional/Special Education Training Project.

Haberman, D. M., & Lerman, P. E. (1982). *Educational follow-up study of juveniles released from Ethan Allen and Lincoln Hills Schools.* Madison, WI: Employment and Training Institute.

Horvath, G. J. (1982). Issues in correctional education: A conundrum of conflict. *Journal of Correctional Education, 33,* 8–15.

Kerle, K. E., & Ford, F. R. (1982). *The state of our nation's jails.* Washington, DC: National Sheriffs Association.

Lombardi, J. (1984). The impact of correctional education on length of incarceration: Nonsupport for new paroling policy motivation. *Journal of Correctional Education, 35,* 64–67.

MacCormack, A. H. (1931). *The education of adult prisoners.* New York: National Society for Penal Information.

Meers, G. D. (1983). Vocational teachers' role in serving juvenile offenders. *Journal for Vocational Special Needs Education, 5,* 30–34.

Miller, L. (1982). *Detention education, the Kalamazoo way.* Kalamazoo, MI: Kalamazoo County Juvenile Home Youth Center School.

National Institute of Corrections. (1984). *State expenditures for corrections 1970–1983.* Boulder, CO: NIC Information Center.

Nelson, E. K. (1982). New patterns for public programs: The youth services example. In *Employment, crime and policy issues.* Washington, DC: American University.

Ohio Department of Rehabilitation and Correction. (1986). *The Ohio plan.* Columbus, OH: Author.

Omang, J. (1982, November 25–27). *The Washington Post.*

Pecht, H. E. (1983). The emergent CE profession: Special problems require tested criteria for the selection of effective teachers. *Journal of Correctional Education, 34,* 85–88.

Porter, R. F., & Porter, J. G. (1984). Survey of attitudes of incarcerated felons on dropping out of public schools. *Journal of Correctional Education, 35,* 80–82.

Rutherford, R. B., Nelson, C. M., & Wolford, B. I. (1985). Special education in the most restrictive environment: Correctional/special education. *Journal of Special Education, 19,* 1, 59–71.

Schilit, J. (1983). Learning behavior problem adolescent offenders. In B. J. D'Alonzo (Ed.), *Educating adolescents with learning and behavior problems* (pp. 67–90). Rockville, MD: Aspen Systems.

Shelton, E. (1985). The implementation of a life coping skills program within a correctional setting. *Journal of Correctional Education, 36,* 41–45.

Smith, D. (1983). Certification versus education in correctional schools: A major problem and its solution. *Journal of Correctional Education, 34,* 99–100.

Snarr, R. W., & Wolford, B. I. (1985). *Introduction to corrections.* Dubuque, IA: Wm. C. Brown.

U.S. Department of Education. (1984). Correctional education policy statement. *Federal Register, 49,* 85, 18607–8.

U.S. Department of Justice. (1980). *Prevention of delinquency through alternative education.* Washington, DC: Government Printing Office.

Wisconsin Division of Corrections. (1986). *Basic assumptions for curriculum development.* Madison, WI: Author.

Wolfgang, M. E., Figlio, R. M., & Sellin, T. (1979). *Delinquency in a birth cohort.* Chicago: University of Chicago Press.

Wolford, B. I. (1985). Balancing the educational and custodial functions of the correctional educator. In T. Appoloni (Ed.), *Education training handbook* (pp. 129–163). Sacramento: California Department of Corrections.

Terry L. Baumgardner

Summer Therapy   **VIGNETTE**

I don't believe a summer has passed since I've been here that they haven't come. Usually it's 15 to 20 smiling but suspicious-acting people looking up at me as I enter the administration receiving area. They have come, my fellow teachers and administrators from the public schools, to tour the correctional facility where I labor and to gain a day off from the summer school professor who sent them in lieu of a regular class meeting.

As I began to perform the 118th production of my canned welcome and introduction speech, that little flame of caution begins to spark inside, warning me to be extra cautious about how much I really tell these people. After all, these are professionals from a different world of education, who do things quite differently from the way we do them "inside the fence." I always find my anxiety rising when I think they may judge me inferior if I'm not clear or thorough enough in explaining why our system is so different from theirs. Will they judge me and my "school" based on their superficial view from this rather cursory tour, or will they try to dig beneath the surface, ask the important questions, and really understand why we do business the way we do? Lord knows, I want to impress them!

As I talk on, I am able to monitor what I say and reflect on how these people and I really do differ. I realize that these fellow professionals work within a system with a mission to educate and they are principal players in that system. How wonderful, I muse, to work in an environment that is organized to educate students rather than to confine them. To be part of a process in which one's work is primary rather than ancillary would be refreshing. It would be exhilarating to labor in a place where learning to read, write, and do math was equal in priority to a student's doing his living quarter chores on time or raking enough rocks on work detail. Anyone who attempts to be an educator in a correctional setting has to come to grips with the fact the organization is not designed primarily to educate, but rather to correct antisocial behavior.

My train of thought is quickly broken when someone asks a question about how many "semesters" a student must be enrolled. I quickly respond that students who are wards enter and leave according to the dictates of the criminal justice system and not according to semesters. I explain that 10 or more students will quit classes this week, will leave the institution, and that a number of new faces will be ushered in to fill their vacant desks as soon as the gate slams behind those who are released. I tell them how the correctional system of open entry and exit forces a teacher to abandon the image of an eloquent lecturer in front of knowledge-thirsty students in favor of an image of a learning manager looking over the shoulder of each student working on the individualized work prepared for him or her. The vision of stimulating class discussions and of students in hot, intellectual debate probing the meaning behind a difficult concept also must be abandoned. It must be replaced with one of every student working on something different; and because of learning disabilities (sometimes half the class will be learning handicapped), these students will need assistance with the most elementary materials. What a different situation from a system where most students begin, learn, and complete academic pursuits together. I wonder how many of these visitors could adapt their teaching style for every class, every day, for 12 months of each year.

My talk becomes almost therapeutic for me. My feelings of inferiority begin to subside as I share in some detail the aspects of my work that the group appears to be genuinely excited about. I tell them that all our instruction, because it is individualized, is diagnostic/prescriptive and is targeted to students' weaknesses. I describe the great amount of freedom instructors have here in determining curriculum scope, sequence, and materials. I tell them that most classes are no larger than 12 to 15 students, with special education classes being much smaller. Mentioning that teachers and administrators carry the authority to administer a wide range of sanctions (some quite severe) for inappropriate behavior brings the group to a full buzz of conversation.

A few "amens" are heard when I share that educators are encouraged to fully participate in treatment teams, which allows them freedom to don the roles of counselor, advocate, and therapist. And when I tell them that all of these positive aspects are a part of my freedom—freedom to provide the educational experiences I feel strongly about in a way I think most effective, freedom to discipline, freedom to get involved in students' lives, and freedom to be different—they look excited enough to line up for applications. What a paradox—that one can be freer behind walls!

Special Education Law and Correctional Education

CHAPTER 4   *Frank H. Wood*

Citizens of the United States have demonstrated a continuing concern with defining their civil rights. Through the courts they have extended those rights to persons accused or convicted of committing crimes and delinquent acts and to individuals with special needs. Recent court decisions and legislation have defined more specifically the right of those with educational handicaps to a free and appropriate public education. The issue of whether this right applies to law violators of school age is receiving attention. Because there is evidence that the percentage of youth with educational handicaps is three to four times greater in the adjudicated population than in the general population (Mesinger, 1977; Morgan, 1979; Murphy, 1986; Wolford, 1983), clarification of a state's responsibilities for providing special education has been given a high priority by correctional educators (Smith, Ramirez, & Rutherford, 1983; Wolford, 1983). A recent survey by Rutherford, Nelson, and Wolford (1986) indicates that there has been some improvement in the quality and quantity of special education provided in the 15 states surveyed, but the authors conclude that "the goal of providing a free and appropriate education for all handicapped juvenile offenders has not yet been realized" (p. 32). This chapter reviews the legal mandate that directs efforts to reach that goal.

LITIGATION, LEGISLATION, AND REGULATION

Definition of the right of all U.S. citizens to a free and appropriate public education comes from interpretation of the Constitution and existing legislation, litigation in various state and federal courts, and passage of new legislation that details the patterns of educational services to be provided and allocates necessary funds for implementation. The scope of new legislation is further detailed in the rules and regulations developed by local, state, and national agencies. Interpretation of the law and its implementing regulations then becomes the subject of further argument and litigation. Deciding how new developments in any related area affect our responsibilities as educators is not an easy task. Review of some basic principles may be helpful.[1]

The right of students with handicapping conditions to a free and appropriate education has been mandated by the U.S. Congress in a series of acts, beginning with the Education of the Handicapped Act passed in 1970 (PL 91–230) and subsequently amended by PL 93–380 and PL 94–142 (LaVor, 1976). The legislative intent of PL 91–230 and of the PL 94–142 amendments (20 U.S.C. §1401–1468) has been further detailed in federal regulations, most notably those published in the *Federal Register* in 1977 following the passage of PL 94–142 and subsequently in the *Code of Federal Regulations* (30 C.F.R. Part 300).

The programs specified by this legislation and its amendments are "discretionary": those states that do not accept the funding provided under PL 94–142 are not explicitly bound by its requirements. However, because the most critical features of this legislation are built on the mandatory provisions of Section 504 of Title V of the Rehabilitation Act of 1973 (PL 93–112), those states receiving any federal monies are bound by those provisions, whether or not they agree to the provisions of PL 94–142 (*New Mexico Association for Retarded Citizens v. The State of New Mexico*, 1979). The mandatory provisions include the requirement that due process procedures be followed in planning access to a free and appropriate public education in the least restrictive environment. Where PL 94–142 applies, the Supreme Court has ruled that it provides the "exclusive remedy" to correct any violations of these provisions (*Smith v. Robinson*, 1984).

Section 1412 (6) of PL 94–142, the Education for All Handicapped Children Act of 1975, specifically applies its provisions to students placed in institutional settings by stating that they apply to "all education programs within the state, including all such programs administered by any other state or local agency," and the implementing regulations make specific reference to "state correctional facilities" (§300.2 [b][4]). (Unless otherwise noted, citations are to the implementing regulations as published in the *Code of Federal Regulations*, 54 C.R.F. 300).

Most laws are reasonably clear in intent when originally drafted. However, during the complicated legislative process, the original language can be amended many times. Sections can be added so that specific concerns will be clearly covered. Other additions can seek to weaken or diffuse the impact of the legislation. Litigation over precise meaning is the inevitable result. Issues of constitutionality are also frequently raised in lawsuits. The most important of the resulting decisions become accepted interpretations of the original law with an impact far wider than the court's actual jurisdiction. Examples important in clarifying the right to an education of students with special needs include *Brown v. Board of Education of Topeka* (1954) and

---

[1]In developing this section, the author has drawn heavily from the work of Grosenick, Huntze, Kochan, Peterson, Robertshaw, and Wood, 1981.

Mills v. Board of Education of the District of Columbia (1972), as well as the *Pennsylvania Association for Retarded Citizens* (1971) consent decree.

Implementing regulations promulgated by administrative agencies attempt to clarify the intent of Congress, but the meaning and appropriateness of such regulations may also be challenged in administrative hearings or lawsuits. The regulations, which are adopted following publication in the *Federal Register* and public comment, can be recalled and modified at any time by action of the agency that issued them. As a case in point, the Office of Special Education and Rehabilitation proposed a major revision of the regulations implementing PL 94–142 during 1981 and 1982. However, following widespread criticism, the revised regulations were withdrawn prior to promulgation.

Disagreement about the appropriateness of regulations leads to discussion about the intent of the original legislative mandate. As a result, there is a substantial body of case law ruling on specific issues that have been raised in the courts. Technically, those court decisions apply only to the specific issues addressed in the cases, and the actual authority of most court decisions is further limited by the jurisdiction of the court issuing the opinion. The Supreme Court of the United States has final jurisdiction in all cases involving federal law and in any cases involving constitutionally protected rights, such as the right to an education. Ranking below the Supreme Court in jurisdiction are the 11 federal circuit courts and below them, more than 90 federal district courts. Again, technically, a decision handed down in one of these lower courts applies only to the specific case under consideration and is binding as a precedent only within that court's jurisdiction. Although the Supreme Court is the final court of appeal, on many issues of importance the opinions of judges of lower federal courts are never reviewed by that court. In fact, thoughtful, well-written decisions issued at any level of the court system have widespread influence. State law and its implementing regulations are interpreted independently by the appropriate state courts unless federal and state law appear to be in conflict, in which case a separate ruling may be sought to establish jurisdiction.[2]

Major decisions about the education of handicapped students are also made through court-approved agreements between the litigants in particular cases and through the administrative hearing process. For example, one of the major court cases involving the educational rights of handicapped citizens was decided without a formal legal judgment. The court approved a consent agreement in the form of a consent decree under which the defendants voluntarily bound themselves to carry out specific reforms under the supervision of the court, with the understanding that the case might be reopened if the results were not satisfactory to the plaintiffs (*Pennsylvania Association for Retarded Citizens v. The Commonwealth of Pennsylvania*, 1971). The administrative hearing process provided for in the "procedural safeguards" section of PL 94–142 (§1415) is also widely used in efforts to settle serious

---

[2]For a more thorough discussion of these complex matters, see Turnbull, 1986, pp. 5–7.

disputes about what is a free and appropriate public education for an individual student. The courts have generally ruled that the administrative remedies provided by the act must be exhausted before a case is filed in the courts (*Sessions v. Livingston Parish*, 1980).

Educators who wish to keep up to date on the most important of the decisions handed down in courts and administrative hearings each year will find useful the *Education for the Handicapped Law Report* (1977–present), a specialized legal reference. Valuable reviews and additional discussion can be found in Turnbull (1986) and Warboys and Shauffer (1986).

The remainder of this chapter presents the major requirements of laws relating to the provision of special education programs for youthful offenders in correctional institutions and reviews various court decisions regarding questions of interpretation.

MAJOR PROVISIONS OF PL 94–142

The Education for All Handicapped Children Act of 1975 (PL 94–142) established the right of children and youth of school age (through age 21 in most states) to a free and appropriate public education adjusted to meet their individual educational needs, regardless of any handicapping conditions. Major provisions of the law and the implementing regulations related to youthful offenders with handicaps are listed here and discussed in more detail in the sections that follow.

1. The state education agency (SEA) is designated as the "sole state agency" responsible for ensuring a free and appropriate public education for every student with special educational needs because of handicapping conditions (§300.134).
2. The SEA is required to oversee development of written, interagency cooperative agreements that assure a free and appropriate public education to any student in agencies other than the public schools, regardless of the type of agency (§300.134).
3. An individualized education program (IEP) must be developed by the school with the participation of the parents for each student with special needs (§300.340–349).
4. Procedural safeguards must be followed so that (a) parent and student rights are protected in decisions regarding evaluation and placement (§300.500–514); (b) evaluation and placement are without bias (§300.530–534); (c) the student's special education placement is in the least restrictive environment (LRE) in which an appropriate education can be provided (§300.550–556); and (d) confidentiality is observed in the use and storage of all documents related to the student's evaluation and placement (§300.560–576).
5. Procedures must be established for (a) child identification (§300.128, 220); (b) the setting of priorities for service (§300.320–324); and (c) a comprehensive system of personnel development (§300.380–387).

SOLE STATE AGENCY STATUS OF THE SEA AND INTERAGENCY AGREEMENTS

Because of the special status of correctional institutions as agencies of the state with rights and responsibilities that may conflict with those assigned the SEA under PL 94–142, additional discussion is needed to clarify the law's application to such settings. The state education agency (SEA) has responsibility for assuring that institutions serving school-aged youth but administered by other state agencies provide an educational program meeting the requirements of PL 94–142. State correctional agencies have the responsibility to provide housing and rehabilitation programs for youth whom the courts have ordered detained. The correctional agency's responsibility for the education of juvenile offenders is usually made clear in state legislation, but in practice it may be given lower priority than their detention (Smith, Ramirez, & Rutherford, 1983). This is especially the case in adult institutions, where education often has lower priority than "work" in the eyes of both inmates and staff, and disciplinary suspension from education and similar "privileged" activities may occur more frequently and for longer periods than in juvenile institutions (Gerry, 1982, p. 18). The courts have ruled that compelling administrative considerations associated with the responsibility for security and detention may take precedence over rehabilitative programming (*Hayes v. Cuyler*, 1979). However, depriving adult prisoners of meaningful education programs is a violation of their constitutional rights (*Holt v. Sarver*, 1970). Other courts have affirmed that juvenile prisoners also have a constitutional as well as a statutory right to rehabilitative treatment (*Martarella v. Kelly*, 1972; *Nelson v. Heyne*, 1974) and that administrators of juvenile correctional facilities are responsible for seeing that such programs are available without discrimination to all imprisoned youth (*Santiago v. City of Philadelphia*, 1977). The specific application of the provisions of PL 94–142 to correctional institutions has already been noted.

The SEA, as the state agency with the primary responsibility for monitoring compliance with the requirements of PL 94–142, is charged with discovering any deficiencies in the educational programs being provided incarcerated youthful offenders with handicapping conditions, but correction of violations is often made difficult by the absence of mechanisms for interagency cooperation.

This problem is often exacerbated by the variety of administrative arrangements under which educational services are provided to students in correctional institutions. Educational services may be provided by the state correctional agency acting as a local education agency (LEA) for all institutions under its administration, by individual correctional institutions acting as LEAs, or by the public school in whose district the correctional institution is located. Grosenick and Huntze (1980) cite a report to Congress on implementation of PL 94–42 that states that "in some cases responsibility for educational services to handicapped children may be shared by as many as six different agencies" (p. 111). Among these may be public agencies concerned with welfare, mental health, and vocational education/rehabilitation, in addition to education and corrections, at the local as well as the state level. Occasionally contracts with private agencies must also be considered.

Grosenick and Huntze (1980) examined 1979 and 1980 state annual program plans, required under PL 94–142, for all 50 states and five territories. They estimated that 40% of the states had some interagency agreements in place, generally between education and corrections. However, they reported, "The amount of detail incorporated into the documents (interagency agreements) varies considerably. In some instances the agreements consist of assurance that the above (PL 94–142) obligations will be met. In other cases, the agreement included information relative to actual implementation" (p. 114).

SEAs monitoring the compliance of educational programs in correctional institutions with the provisions of PL 94–142 must take into consideration the problems associated with the conflict between correctional and educational priorities and those related to system characteristics, such as the short period of incarceration for many youth and shortages of funds and trained personnel. Such problems do not, of course, excuse correctional agencies from compliance. In *Green v. Johnson* (1981) a U.S. District Court (Massachusetts) ruled that youthful offenders under the age of 22 who had not received a diploma did not lose their right to an education appropriate to their needs because of incarceration. The defendants in this case were several Massachusetts county houses of corrections where staff either were not trained to provide special education services, such as nonbiased assessment and individualized instruction, or had failed to provide such services. The SEA and the correctional institutions were charged with correcting the deficiencies noted in the decision. Further, in *Willie M. v. Hunt* (1980), a class action on behalf of North Carolina children under the age of 18 with histories of violent or assaulting behavior who were placed in residential programs, the consent decree charged the state with providing appropriate treatment and education. Although based only in part on PL 94–142, this decree appears to support the right to appropriate education of juveniles convicted of the most serious offenses, even when the conditions required for effective detention make implementing that right quite costly to the state. In 1982 the North Carolina legislature established a reserve fund of $10 million to provide the necessary additional services.

Faced with the heavy burden of supervising the implementation of PL 94–142 in their states' local education districts, some SEAs have been slow to turn their attention to the needs of youthful offenders. *Green v. Johnson* is an indication that failure to comply may lead to intervention by the courts.

A FREE AND APPROPRIATE PUBLIC EDUCATION

A free and appropriate public education "means special education and related services which: (a) Are provided at public expense, under public supervision and direction, and without charge, (b) Meet the standards of the State

educational agency. . . , (c) Include preschool, elementary school, or secondary school education in the State involved, and (d) are provided in accordance
with an individualized education program. . ." (§300.4). Other sections of the
regulations make it clear that this education must be provided to "all handicapped children aged three through twenty-one" (§300.122 [a]), including those
in "state correctional facilities" (§300.2 [b][4]). The only common exception
to this requirement is that educational programming need not be continued
in most states after a student receives a high school diploma.

The schools have a responsibility to provide related services as needed
to assist students to benefit from the educational program. "Related services" are defined as "transportation and such developmental, corrective, and
other *supportive services as are required to assist a handicapped child to benefit from special education* [italics added], and include speech pathology and
audiology, psychological services, physical and occupational therapy, recreation, early identification and assessment of disabilities in children, counseling services, and medical services for diagnostic or evaluation purposes
(§300.13 [a]).

The exact meaning of the related services requirement has been the subject of much discussion and litigation. The U.S. Supreme Court, in *Board of
Education of the Hendrik Hudson Central School District v. Rowley* (1982),
supported the free and appropriate public education provisions of PL 94–142
and noted the intent of Congress that all handicapped children receive special
education as needed in each individual case. But the court's judgment was
that related services were necessary only to the extent that, without them,
the child would not benefit from the education program provided. In the opinion of the justices of the majority view, the intent of Congress was only "to
bring previously excluded handicapped children into the public education
systems of the States and to require the States to adopt procedures which
would result in individualized consideration of and instruction of each child"
(458 U.S. 189). Access to and benefit from special education are the key concepts. The " 'basic floor of opportunity' provided by the Act consists of access
to specialized instruction and related services which are individually designed
to provide educational benefit to the handicapped child" (458 U.S. 201). In
the case at issue, Amy Rowley, a deaf child placed in a regular classroom,
was making progress in ("benefiting from") the educational program provided, without the services of an interpreter for the deaf, which her parents
requested. The possibility that Amy might make greater progress if an interpreter were provided was not considered sufficient reason to require the LEA
to provide one.

The extent to which a school district may be required to provide psychotherapy as a related service has been the subject of conflicting rulings by
various courts and hearing officers (Grosenick, Huntze, Kochan, Peterson,
Robertshaw, & Wood, 1982). The U.S. Supreme Court has not yet accepted
for review a case dealing with this issue. Some districts have provided psychotherapy at LEA expense; most have not. The *Rowley* decision suggests that
the key may be whether or not the related service is necessary for the stu-

dent to benefit from the special education program provided. In *Irving Independent School District v. Tatro* (1984) the Supreme Court ruled that schools must provide nonmedical related services, in this case catheterization, if such services are necessary to permit a student to benefit from special education. However, this finding does not necessarily apply to a service such as psychotherapy or counseling. This issue may be moot for correctional institutions that provide extensive counseling as part of their rehabilitative services, as long as that counseling meets individual student needs as reflected in the IEP. States that do not do so at present may feel prompted to develop adequate counseling programs voluntarily, as a result of class action suits such as *Willie M.* .

DEVELOPMENT OF AN INDIVIDUALIZED EDUCATION PROGRAM (IEP)

The requirement that an individualized education program be developed for each student in a process involving the student's parents is one of the key provisions of PL 94–142. Not only is the IEP the basis for an appropriate educational placement, but as Smith and Hockenberry (1980) point out, the transmission of the IEP can serve as a basis for interagency cooperation.

As judges develop greater understanding of the importance of the IEP provision, their decisions in cases where interagency cooperation is necessary may place greater stress on it. In *Green v. Johnson* (1981) the court ruled that the lack of an IEP prepared prior to a student's admission to a correctional facility did not excuse the correctional education program from the responsibility of developing an appropriate plan and providing special education, even when the anticipated period of incarceration was brief. In the *Maynard* case (1982) the court order directed the school district to provide an education program appropriately adjusted to a student's handicapping condition, which had been discovered after the juvenile court's involvement.

Even though there are great potential benefits from using the IEP as a focus of interagency communication and cooperation, we should not close our eyes to the difficulties involved (Wood, 1982). Transmission of information between schools, even those within the same LEA, often is not well accomplished, and there is every reason to expect transmission of information between agencies to be even more difficult. Attention must be given to due process considerations, which can further slow the process. Smith and Hockenberry (1980) mention that Massachusetts "has implemented a program, the Special Education Coodinator Project, which assigns a special education coordinator to a handicapped student who is leaving the correctional facility and needs community services" (p. 14). This idea sounds promising.

An educational program may be appropriate and yet not lead to a diploma if the state sets additional standards that the student is unable to meet, according to the New York Appeals Court (*Board of Education of Northport-East Northport Union Free School District v. Ambach*, 1983). In this case the school district wished to present diplomas to students with handicaps who had not passed the minimum competency examination set by the state board of regents. The court gave precedence to the state's additional requirements. If followed by other courts, this ruling may affect the recognition given students who complete an appropriate special education program.

SAFEGUARDS

Due Process

Gerry (1982) lists the following important procedural rights that must be protected for students and parents, basing his list on the Office of Special Education Monitoring Guide, which follows the actual regulations (§§300.500–300.514).

(a) Opportunity to examine records.
(b) Right to an independent evaluation.
(c) Right to an impartial due process hearing.
(d) Prior notice and parent consent for initial evaluation and all placement changes.
(e) An impartial hearing officer.
(f) Hearing rights.
(g) Right to a hearing decision appeal.
(h) Right to an administrative appeal, impartial review.
(i) Right to pursue civil action.
(j) Adherence to timelines/convenient hearings and review.
(k) Agreement between parents and public agency about the child's status during due process proceedings.
(l) The availability of surrogate parents, if needed.
(m) The knowledge and right to file a formal complaint. (p. 55)

Gerry suggests that all of these issues except (d) and (k), which he feels are superseded by the student's adjudicated status, must be considered in designing a special program in a correctional facility. He believes that "many correctional education programs have not developed separate procedural safeguard procedures. . .but instead have used existing institutionwide offender grievance procedures" (p. 53), thus failing to meet the requirements of PL 94–142. Noting the complex jurisdictional questions that are involved, he recommends careful legal review of the procedures appropriate for application in a correctional institution. Several important due process issues are discussed separately.

Parental Participation

Section 1414 of PL 94–142 provides for the "participation and consultation of the parents or guardian of such [handicapped] children" as part of the procedure for providing these children with full educational opportunities. Because of the nature of the correctional system, in which youthful offenders are gathered into institutions at several locations around the state, often considerably removed from their homes, their parents may not be available for consultation, may even be unknown, and may have had their rights terminated by the courts. In other instances the interests of the parents are clearly not aligned with the best interests of their child. Since representation of the child's interests through a parent or guardian is assigned much importance in the negotiation of an appropriate educational program, any of these situations should be sufficient for the appointment of a surrogate for the parents (Luckasson, 1982; §300.514). The literature contains little information about the use of surrogates for adjudicated youth, although Smith and Hockenberry (1980) state that several states have developed surrogate training programs. The important point at issue is the availability of someone who will advocate for the student during the required due process procedures.

The implementing rules provide further guidance regarding the selection of surrogates. A surrogate should have "no interest that conflicts with the interests of the child he or she represents, and (have) knowledge and skills that insure adequate representation of the child" (§300.514 [c]). Gerry (1982) feels that "in practice, to the extent that surrogate parents are appointed for handicapped students, most correctional education programs use officials of the correctional facility" (p. 56). Such practice would be in direct violation of the requirement in the regulations that employees of an agency involved in the care or education of a child not be permitted to serve as surrogate parents. Conflicting role expectations can make it difficult for these individuals to be free of conflicts of interest. Many would find it difficult to suspend entirely their customary attitudes as corrections officers to advocate vigorously on behalf of a student, should this be in the student's best interests.

The criterion of absence of conflicts of interest would seem to require a surrogate who is independent of both the SEA and the corrections system. Smith and Hockenberry (1980) suggest that the procedure specified in the court order resolving the case of *Mattie T. v. Holladay* (1980) may have relevance, although the case involves the rights of mentally retarded children in a state institution. They describe the recommended procedures as follows:

> For all children placed by a court in the legal custody of a public agency and who are living with foster parents, the foster parents shall serve as surrogate parents.
>
> For all other children placed by a court in the legal custody of a public agency, the agency shall appoint surrogate parents.
>
> For children residing in a residential facility but who have not been placed by a court in the legal custody of a public agency, the agency responsible for their care shall: (1) make and document at least three attempts to contact each child's parents to inform them of special education placement procedures and to explain their role as advocates for their child; but if these efforts fail to involve the parents or if the parents fail twice to attend IEP meetings, (2) the agency shall appoint a sur-

rogate parent for the child unless the child's parents object to the appointment in writing, in which case the agency shall inform the parents that the surrogate is appointed solely for the purpose of representing the child's interests in educational decisions. (pp. 16–17)

The main difficulty with applying these guidelines in correctional settings may be the length of time required for implementation. Whereas retarded youth may need relatively long periods of commitment or foster home placement, many youthful offenders are held in correctional institutions for only short periods of time.

Protection in Evaluation Procedures (PEP)

"Testing and evaluation materials and procedures used for the purposes of evaluation and placement of handicapped children must be selected and administered so as not to be racially or culturally discriminatory" (§300.530 [b]). Given the substantial numbers of culturally different and racial minority students placed in correctional institutions, correctional educators need to give special attention to how this requirement of the law is met. The issue of nonbiased assessment has been much discussed in the professional literature.[3] The importance of following nondiscriminatory procedures in the administration of correctional programs for delinquent youth was affirmed in *Santiago v. City of Philadelphia* (1977), and specific guidelines for nonbiased assessment and placement procedures were part of the consent agreement in *Lora v. New York City Board of Education* (1984; Wood, Johnson, & Jenkins, 1985). Besag and Greene (1981) argue that "the use of standardized tests in nonstandard situations [i.e., correctional settings] is both a violation of common sense and good testing techniques" (p. 17), but the staff of the Louisiana Pupil Appraisal Program (Klingler, Marshall, Price, & Ward, 1983) are more positive about the value of a well-thought-out approach to assessment using both standardized and nonstandardized approaches to measurement. Meeting the PEP requirement will continue to be a challenge to educators.

Education in the Least Restrictive Environment (LRE)

The requirement that education take place in the least restrictive environment in which an appropriate educational program can be delivered is another key provision of PL 94–142. The language of the act is quite specific: "The state [should establish]. . .procedures to assure that, to the maximum extent appropriate, handicapped children, including children in public or private institutions or other care facilities, are educated with children who are not handicapped, and that special classes, separate schooling, or other removal of handicapped children from the regular educational environment occurs only when the nature or severity of the handicap is such that educa-

[3]A thorough discussion of problems and possibilities for nonbiased assessment can be found in a collection of papers available through Research for Better Schools, Inc. (*Exploring Issues*, 1978).

tion in the regular class with the use of supplementary aids and services cannot be achieved satisfactorily" (§1412 [5]). Meeting this requirement is generally considered to require the availability of a full range of educational placements, from highly restrictive special classes or special school placements to maintenance in regular classrooms with only supportive services given the classroom teacher. How is this requirement to be interpreted in the special setting of the correctional institution?

First, it is obvious that most correctional settings are to some extent restrictive environments because of society's mandate to detain offenders. It seems reasonable, then, that meeting the LRE provision in such a setting be interpreted to mean that the educational program should not restrict the social interaction of students with handicapping conditions and their nonhandicapped peers to any greater extent than is required by the nature of the correctional setting itself unless the severity of the handicapping conditions requires additional restrictions. This interpretation would also be consistent with the requirement for nondiscriminatory treatment affirmed in *Santiago v. City of Philadelphia* (1977). An example of inappropriate restrictions is the exclusion of students with handicapping conditions from programs providing vocational training or special tutoring under the provisions of Chapter 1 of PL 97–35 because they are believed to be "too handicapped" to benefit fully from these programs. An example of a desirable approach is the Louisiana Pupil Appraisal Program described by Klingler et al. (1983), in which educational needs are one variable considered when making institutional placement decisions for inmates in the state correctional system.

To date, no major court decisions have focused specifically on the meaning of LRE in institutional environments. Perhaps further interpretation will take place when the IEP and appropriate education provisions of PL 94–142 are more widely and effectively implemented.

Confidentiality

The confidentiality provision of PL 94–142 (§300.560–576) includes such procedural rights as adequate notice to parents, specified rights of access to information, the right to challenge information in student records, and prior consent to disclosure and destruction of information. As with the due process issues discussed earlier, addressing these issues in the context of a correctional institution will require the attention of lawyers sensitive to the needs of youthful offenders with handicapping conditions and knowledgeable of the requirements of PL 94–142 as well as state law on procedures to be followed with adjudicated youth.

OTHER ISSUES

A number of other issues are given attention in PL 94–142 and the implementing regulations. The relevance of the requirement that child identification procedures be established (§300.128) in the special context of the correctional institution is illustrated by *Green v. Johnson* (1981). Also clearly relevant are the requirements that priority for service be given first to students who meet the age requirement for a free and appropriate public education and who "are not receiving any education" (§300.320 [al]) and second to students "who are receiving an inadequate education" (§300.320 [b]), although meeting these requirements in a correctional institution may necessitate a change in current procedures.

Another requirement of the law concerns the "development and implementation of a comprehensive system of personnel development" (§300.380). Various federal funds are earmarked for this purpose, but there is no guarantee that the training available through readily accessible training agencies will meet the special needs of correctional educators. Joint leadership from SEA and corrections personnel may be necessary before this requirement can be met effectively.

INSTITUTIONAL SELF-EVALUATION

As the state agency responsible for the detention and rehabilitation of youth who have violated state laws, the state department of corrections is naturally concerned about its compliance with the requirements of PL 94–142. But because the provisions of the law are complex and self-evaluation is difficult, corrections staff have a tendency to wait until the SEA draws attention to compliance issues while it discharges its monitoring responsibilities. Progressive correctional educators who wish to take a more proactive role in compliance may find the document prepared by Gerry (1982) useful as a guide to self-assessment. Entitled "Illustration of Possible Compliance Issues, Monitoring Questions, Significance Measures, and Information Sources for Initial Screening of Correctional Education Programs," this document presents questions that should be readily answerable without additional data collection. Eight major issues are addressed.

   I. Barriers, pre-conditions, or disincentives to the access of students to overall education program or policies related to their removal.

   II. The existence of program curricular options for handicapped students such as individualized specially designed instruction and access to regular and/or special vocational education, regular and/or adapted physical education, or bilingual education.

   III. The components of any individualized evaluation conducted by central diagnostic or intake centers.

   IV. The existence of procedures for the transfer of student records from and to local education agencies and correctional institutions.

   V. Under-identification of mentally retarded, learning disabled, and seriously emotionally disturbed offenders.

   IV. Limitations on the time available for instruction.

   VII. Isolation of handicapped students in self-contained programs.

VIII. The existence of surrogate parent procedures utilizing persons not in the employ of the correctional agency. (Appendix B)

Compliance can be furthered by the development of comprehensive interagency agreements that attend to funding as well as procedural and service issues and the assignment of supervision for their implementation to personnel with sufficient authority to carry out their charge.

CONCLUSION

"The law is not an end in itself, nor does it provide ends. It is preeminently a means to serve what we think is right." These words of Supreme Court Justice William C. Brennan, Jr. (1957) are a fitting commentary on the law as discussed here. Students with handicapping conditions that interfere with their education are a minority in our schools. Serving what we—their friends, parents, and fellow citizens—believe to be right, our elected representatives have passed legislation to assure that they will receive the free and appropriate public education they require. By explicitly extending the provisions of that law to include students who are in correctional institutions, we have underlined our intention that it be truly an Education for All Handicapped Children Act.

REFERENCES

Besag, F. P., & Greene, J. B. (1981). Once is too much, II: Exceptional education definitions. *Journal of Correctional Education, 32* (3), 17–20.

Board of Education of the Hendrick Hudson Central School District v. Rowley, 458 U.S. 176 (1982).

Board of Education of Northport-East Northport Union Free School District v. Ambach, 458 N.Y.2d 680, 469 N.Y.2d 669 (N.Y. Ct. App. 1983).

Brennan, W. C., Jr. Opinion on Roth v. United States 354 U.S. 476 (1957).

Brown v. Board of Education of Topeka, 374 U.S. 483 (1954).

Education for All Handicapped Children Act of 1975, 20 U.S.C.§ 1400–1461. Implementing regulations codified in 34 C.F.R. § 300.

Education for the Handicapped Law Report. (1977–present). Washington, DC: CRR Publishing.

Exploring issues in the implementation of PL 94–142: PEP: Developing criteria for the evaluation of protection in evaluation procedures provisions. (1978). Philadelphia: Research for Better Schools, Inc. (444 North 3rd Street, Philadelphia, PA 19123).

Gerry, M.H., & Company. (1982). *Monitoring the special education programs of correctional institutions.* Washington, DC: Author.

Green v. Johnson, 513 F. Supp. 965 (D. Mass. 1981).

Grosenick, J.K., & Huntze, S.L. (1980). *National needs analysis in behavior disorders: Adolescent behavior disorders:* Columbia, MO: University of Missouri—Columbia, Department of Special Education.

Grosenick, J. K., Huntze, S. L., Kochan, B., Peterson, R. L., Robertshaw, C. S., & Wood, F. H. (1981). *National needs analysis in behavior disorders working paper: Legislation, litigation, and the handicapped.* Columbia, MO: University of Missouri—Columbia, Department of Special Education.

Grosenick, J. K., Huntze, S. L., Kochan, B., Peterson, R. L., Robertshaw, C. S., & Wood, F. H. (1982). *National needs analysis in behavior disorders working paper: Psychotherapy as a related service.* Columbia, MO: University of Missouri—Columbia, Department of Special Education.

Hayes v. Cuyler, 475 F. Supp. 350 (E.D. Pa. 1979).

Hockenberry, C. M. (1980) *Education of adjudicated handicapped youth: Policy issues and implications.* Reston, VA: Council for Exceptional Children, ERIC Clearinghouse on Handicapped and Gifted Children.

Holt v. Sarver, 309 F. Supp. 362 (E.D. Ark. 1970).

In re Shelly Maynard. Order of the Family Court, Monroe County, N.Y. (Cited in *Education for the Handicapped Law Report,* December 1982, *554,* 195–196)

Irving Independent School District v. Tatro, 104 S. Ct. 3371, 82 Ed. 2d 664 (1984).

Klingler, J. H., Marshall, G. M., Price, A. W., & Ward, K. D. (1983). A pupil appraisal for adults in the Louisiana Department of Corrections. *Journal of Correctional Education, 34,* 46–48.

Kroth, R. (1970). The mirror model of parent involvement. *Pointer, 25,* 18–22.

LaVor, M.L. (1976). Federal legislation for exceptional persons: A history. In F. J. Weintraub, A. Abeson, J. Ballard, & M. L. LaVor (Eds.), *Public policy and the education of exceptional children* (pp. 96–111). Reston, VA: Council for Exceptional Children.

Lora v. Board of Education of the City of New York, 587 F. Supp. 1572 (E.D. N.Y. 1984).

Luckasson, R.A. (1982). Consensus and conflict of parent and child interests: Surrogate parent appointment and other interventions. *Exceptional Education Quarterly, 3,* 9–16.

Matarella v. Kelly, 394 F. Supp. 575 (S.D.N.Y. 1972).

Mattie T. v. Holladay, C.A. No. D.C. 75–31–5 (N.D. Miss. 1980).

Mesinger, J.F. (1977). Juvenile delinquents: A relatively untapped population for special education professionals. *Behavioral Disorders, 2,* 95–101.

Mills v. Board of Education of the District of Columbia, 384 F. Supp. 866 (D.D.C. 1972).

Morgan, D.I. (1979). Prevalence and types of handicapping conditions found in juvenile correctional institutions: A national survey. *Journal of Special Education, 13,* 283–295.

Murphy, D. M. (1986). The prevalence of handicapping conditions among juvenile delinquents. *Remedial and Special Education, 7,* 7–17.

New Mexico Association for Retarded Citizens v. the State of New Mexico, 495 F. Supp. 391 (D.N.M. 1981), rev. 678 F. 2d 847 (10th Cir. 1982).

Nelson v. Heyne, 491F. 2d 353 (7th Cir. 1974).

Pennsylvania Association for Retarded Children v. Commonwealth of Pennsylvania, 334 F. Supp. 1257 (E.D. Pa. 1971), also, 343 F. Supp. 279 (E.D. Pa. 1972).

Rutherford, R. B., Jr., Nelson, C. M., & Wolford, B. I. (1986). Special education programming in juvenile corrections. *Remedial and Special Education, 7,* 27–33.

Santiago v. City of Philadelphia, 435 F. Supp. 136 (E.D. Pa. 1977).

Sessions v. Livingston Parish School Board, 501 F. Supp. 251 (M.D. La. 1980).

Smith v. Robinson, 104 S. Ct. 3457, 82 L. Ed. 2d 746 (1984).

Smith, B. J., & Hockenberry, C. M. (1980). *Implementing the Education for All Handicapped Children Act, P. L. 94–142, in youth correction facilities: Selected issues.* Unpublished Manuscript, Council for Exceptional Children, Reston, VA.

Smith, B. J., Ramirez, B. A., & Rutherford, R. B., Jr. (1983). Special education in youth correctional facilities. *Journal of Correctional Education, 34,* 108–112.

Turnbull, H. R., III. (1986). *Free appropriate public education: The law and children with disabilities.* Denver: Love.

Warboys, L. M. & Shauffer, C.B. (1986). Legal issues in providing special education services to handicapped inmates. *Remedial and Special Education, 7,* 34–40.

Willie M. v. Hunt, C.A. No. CC/79–0249 (W.D.N.C. 1979).

Wolford, B. I. (1983). Correctional education and special education—An emerging partnership; or "born to lose." In R.B. Rutherford & C.M. Nelson (Eds.), *Severe behavior disorders of children and youth* (Vol. 6, pp. 13–19). Reston, VA: The Council for Children with Behavior Disorders.

Wood, F. H. (1982). Cooperative full service delivery to emotionally disturbed students. In M. M. Noel & N. G. Haring (Eds.), *Progress or change: Issues in educating the emotionally disturbed: Vol. 1 Identification and program planning* (pp. 115–134). Seattle: University of Washington, Program Development Assistant System.

Wood, F. H., Johnson, J. L., & Jenkins, J. R., (1986). The Lora Case: Nonbiased referral, assessment, and placement procedures. *Exceptional Children, 52,* 323–331.

Carole B. Shauffer

VIGNETTE The Youth Law Center

Incarcerated children are perhaps the most powerless people in our society. Many adult prisoners have the skills and sophistication to take cases to court by themselves or to contact lawyers. Most children living in the community have parents who can represent them and work to defend their rights. Children in jails, detention centers, and training schools, however, all too often have no one to speak for them. The Youth Law Center was founded to fill this need.

The Youth Law Center is a nonprofit public interest law firm representing incarcerated children throughout the United States. One of the Youth Law Center's goals is to ensure that children held in correctional settings are provided with the rehabilitative treatment and education necessary to remedy the problems that led to their incarceration.

Although a high percentage of children involved with the juvenile or criminal justice systems suffer from handicaps affecting their ability to benefit from education (estimates range as high as 40% to 60%), many institutions fail to provide any form of special education. For example, the Youth Law Center was involved in litigation in a small, pretrial detention center in Washington that offered no educational programming. Although juvenile court judges, detention center staff, and the local school district all recognized the importance of education for these children, each group put the blame on the other and denied any responsiblility for providing such services. Youth Law Center staff sued the county that ran the facility for failing to provide education, and the court ordered the county to provide educational services to all children and diagnostic services to children who appear to have special needs.

In other settings administrators claim to be providing special education but, in fact, are making only token efforts to meet children's needs. In one large training school only 10 children out of a population of 450 were identified as having any special needs. The evaluation process in that school consisted of an interview with an untrained staff member and a cursory review of the student's record. Officials did recognize the fact that many children had speech and hearing problems or needed counseling, but the school had not employed professionals to address these problems. In fact, the only special education services available were two "special needs" classrooms, one of which was designed to serve children with emotional disabilities and the other of which served children with all other forms of educational handicap. Youth Law Center staff litigated to enforce the rights of these children to individualized education programs and a free and appropriate public education.

The problems of incarcerated youth who need special education do not end with their release. In most cases there is no communication between the child's school district and the incarcerating institution. Training schools and detention centers are unable to obtain school records and so cannot appropriately place children. And when the child leaves the institution, no records are transmitted to the receiving school. As a result, the incarceration, which can last from several months to several years, is dead time, and children must repeat much of that education.

In litigation over conditions at training schools, Center staff have also discovered other problems affecting handicapped youth. For example, handicapped youth are often the target of physical and psychological abuse by other children and by staff. Because training school staff members are typically not trained in the special needs of children with emotional disturbances, learning disabilities, and other impairments, they may perceive a child's behavior as being insubordinate or recalcitrant and may punish that child. Many of these children spend their time in isolation units, where they receive no education. Attorneys at the Youth Law Center are focusing on the question of whether this is discrimination against the handicapped that is in violation of the Rehabilitation Act.

Another major problem for handicapped children results from their detention in adult jails. Although the Youth Law Center takes the position that all children should be removed from adult jails, center staff remain concerned about the treatment children receive while they are in adult facilities. In one instance a parent contacted the Youth Law Center to say that her child, who had been receiving special education before he was arrested, was now being detained in a jail and had been denied the right to see a psychiatrist or to obtain any school materials. This policy is typical of jails, which are concerned with security and are not oriented to providing any form of rehabilitation.

The Youth Law Center has also been involved in litigation challenging the ability of the state to incarcerate handicapped children. In a landmark case, *Willie M. v. Hunt*, Youth Law Center attorneys obtained a court order prohibiting the incarceration of persons with serious emotional and cognitive disabilities and requiring that they be provided with services and treatment.

These examples illustrate some of the ways in which the juvenile justice system is ill equipped to meet the needs of handicapped offenders. Through a combination of litigation and legislative advocacy, the Youth Law Center is attempting to ensure that handicapped children in correctional institutions have the same opportunities to receive special education and treatment that children have on the outside.

PART II

Characteristics and Problems of Handicapped Offenders

INTRODUCTION *Robert B. Rutherford, Jr.*

As pointed out in the first part of the text, handicapped offenders constitute a significant percentage of the incarcerated population in juvenile and adult corrections. Although the full range of handicapping conditions is typically found in most correctional facilities, the most common conditions are mental retardation, learning disabilities, and behavioral disorders.

In chapter 5 Santamour describes the mentally retarded offender. Based on his research over the past decade, Santamour presents a description of the characteristics and problems of the mentally retarded in corrections. He also discusses general programming options and specific programs designed for mentally retarded and developmentally disabled offenders.

In chapter 6 Keilitz and Dunivant describe the link between learning disabilities and delinquency. These authors, who have conducted extensive research that describes the learning disabled offender, explain the various theories and hypotheses concerning the relationship between learning disabilities and crime, examine the research strategies designed to investigate this relationship, and suggest ways to weaken the relationship.

In chapter 7 Gilliam and Scott present a description of the behaviorally disordered offender in the criminal justice system. Included are the characteristics of behaviorally disordered, seriously emotionally disturbed, and socially maladjusted individuals in correctional settings.

Variability in content and writing style is perhaps more apparent in these chapters than in any other portion of the text. These differences are due to a number of factors, including individual research interests, perspectives on political issues, and professional experience with the target populations. Chapter 5 is influenced by Santamour's broad experience with, and concern for, the problems encountered by mentally retarded offenders in the criminal justice system. Chapter 6 reflects Keilitz and Dunivant's extensive research into the link between juvenile delinquency and learning disabilities. Readers may be surprised that the population of behaviorally disordered offenders has not been studied so systematically, nor has there been as much professional advocacy for this group. One reason for this neglect surely is the clause in PL 94–142 excluding the socially maladjusted from the seriously emotionally disturbed. Gilliam and Scott address this issue in Chapter 7 and present some original research indicating that individuals considered socially maladjusted may also be classified for special education purposes as seriously emotionally disturbed.

The Mentally Retarded Offender

CHAPTER 5   *Miles B. Santamour*

A new ripple of concern is bringing to consciousness the injustices endured by the offender who is mentally retarded, and the attention of correctional educators is once again beginning to focus on this area of need. In part, this renewed concern has been caused by the recognition given to these offenders by the President's Committee on Mental Retardation, the National Institute of Corrections, the American Correctional Association, and the Association for Retarded Citizens (U.S.A.). Litigation (e.g., *Ruiz v. Estelle*) and legislation such as that in California and Tennessee, which protects offenders with mental retardation, have also focused attention on this long-neglected area.

Recently, the American Bar Association (1983) cited specific standards for assisting defendants and convicted offenders who are mentally retarded. More recently, Madeleine Will, assistant secretary of the U.S. Department of Education, Special Education and Rehabilitation Services, took steps to safeguard the educational rights of inmates who are handicapped. In the fall of 1985, she held a conference of advisors to assist her in determining what steps to take in implementing PL 94–142 regulations in criminal and juvenile justice institutions. In 1986 California became the first state in the nation to implement standards requiring local and county detention facilities to identify mentally retarded inmates and provide them with special handling. In that same year, the National Institute of Corrections provided more than a half million dollars for projects to improve conditions nationwide for mentally retarded inmates.

Numerous local and state forums and three national meetings, together with countless presentations at gatherings attended by both criminal justice and mental retardation professionals, have added additional support in bringing this area of concern to the attention of both fields. Several exemplary programs that serve offenders with mental retardation have been promoted

This chapter was previously published in *The Prison Journal* (1986), Vol. LXVI, by the Pennsylvania Prison Society, Philadelphia. Reprinted by permission.

by a variety of groups, publications, and other news media, thus also furthering the cause.

Despite all this activity, however, the majority of the people with mental retardation who encounter the justice system still suffer gross injustice, which far exceeds that suffered by any other group of offenders. People with mental retardation are more likely than those without retardation to be arrested, to be convicted, to be sentenced to prison, and to be victimized in prison. They receive probation and parole far less readily and far less often than their nonretarded counterparts.

Who are these offenders, what injustices do they suffer, and what can be done about it? These are questions that professionals are just now beginning to ask. Although there is some confusion about certain related issues, most professionals agree that injustices do occur, and they agree that something should be done about it.

A HISTORY OF THE PROBLEM

The relationship between mental retardation and criminal behavior has been a subject of great debate, beginning with efforts by early researchers to demonstrate that retardation predisposes a person to commit criminal acts. Between 1890 and 1920 theorists tried to link retardation with criminality, poverty, insanity, and general moral and physical degeneration. Their explanations of these various phenomena held the individual to be the source of the problem; they often blamed the victim rather than larger societal factors. During this period Goddard (1916) went so far as to assert that the number of criminals falling into the mentally retarded range was close to 100%.

From 1921 to 1960 the debate shifted to include consideration of social factors operating within the environment. Theorists then questioned whether retardation predisposed anyone to commit criminal acts. The focus of blame shifted from the individual to the family unit and stressed such factors as the impact of poverty, poor education, and questionable or nonexistent health care (Jenkins, 1935).

Since 1960, concern for the problem has greatly increased. Many have recognized that the disproportionate numbers of persons with retardation among offenders are, in part, the result of administrative and legal procedures rather than an indication of any direct causal relationship between mental retardation and criminality (President's Panel on Mental Retardation, 1967). Some writers have gone even further, suggesting that unequal opportunity within the societal structure in general, and within the criminal justice system in particular, raises the incidence of mental retardation and alters unfavorably the situation of the person with mental retardation within the criminal justice system.

IDENTIFICATION AND NUMERICAL REPRESENTATION

Estimates of mental retardation in the general population range from 1% to 3% (President's Committee on Mental Retardation, 1977). Recent studies have shown that a disproportionately high percentage of prison inmates are retarded. A comprehensive effort to identify the number of incarcerated offenders with retardation was conducted by Brown and Courtless (1982); they reported that 9.5% of the inmate population was mentally retarded (with an IQ below 70). Zeleny (1983) studied the findings of intelligence tests of over 60,000 inmates and reported that, in fact, the number of offenders with mental retardation was close to 30% of the inmate population.

Other studies have also shown varying percentages. Levy (1967) found that the rate of mental retardation for juvenile offenders (under 21) was less than 10% and closer to 4%. Texas found a rate of 10% for adult offenders and 12% to 16% for juvenile offenders. South Carolina reported a figure of 8% in its department of corrections (1973). In 1975 the Atlanta (Georgia) Association for Retarded Citizens attempted to identify that state's offender population with retardation and placed the percentage at 27%. But Rockowitz (1985) identified only 3.6% of the Monroe County (New York) jail population as being mentally retarded.

The discrepancy between earlier studies and more recent studies may be partially explained by the vastly greater number of community programs now serving citizens with retardation, thus providing courts with alternatives to incarceration. Other reasons for the discrepancy may be the increase in the number of public education classes, the extended length of time education is now offered to students with mental retardation (through age 21), and the increased job opportunities and community residential facilities available to citizens with mental retardation.

The major factor, however, is the change in definition. At the time of the Brown and Courtless (1982) study, adaptive behavior was not a factor in determining mental retardation. In Texas, for instance, more than one-third of the inmates who met the IQ level for mental retardation were excluded from service because of adaptive behavior scores. Currently, a study is being conducted by Douglas Price-Williams and others at the University of California, Los Angeles that may add conclusive data to the prevalence rate.

Determining the number of offenders with retardation is difficult for many reasons. There are no clear guidelines that specify the IQ levels indicative of retardation, even though most studies designate an IQ score of 70 or below. In addition, some studies rigidly adhere to consideration of adaptive behavior in determining mental retardation; others do not. Further problems are variations in tests used for evaluation and the variability of conditions under which the tests are administered.

Use of IQ tests to indicate mental retardation is being seriously questioned, as is the meaning of the IQ score itself. According to the American Association on Mental Deficiency (AAMD), tests applied across cultures, unless properly standardized, are likely to lead to serious errors in individual diagnoses and in reported rates of mental retardation (Grossman, 1983). For example, Brown and Courtless (1982) found the national average of offenders with retardation to be 9.5%, with geographical differences ranging from 2.6% in the mountain states to 24.3% in the east south central states. Assuming the reliability of the study, such geographical variation suggests the operation of sociocultural variables in determining the percentage of offenders with mental retardation.

Consideration of the inadequacy of the IQ test has suggested a necessary broadening of the means used to assess mental retardation. "A Manual on Classification and Terminology in Mental Retardation" (Heber, 1959) stressed the importance of measuring levels of adaptive behavior and provided for four levels of measurement. The present definition of mental retardation includes reference to subaverage general intellectual functioning and deficits in adaptive behavior. Adaptive behavior is defined as the degree to which an individual meets the standards of personal independence and social responsibility expected of his or her age and cultural group (Grossman, 1983); it includes maturation, learning, and social adjustment. However, such wide variations exist in the environmental demands to which individuals are subjected that there may be no consensus on what constitutes socially acceptable adaptive behavior.

Recognizing the problems of both IQ tests and scales of adaptive behavior, the AAMD urges caution in their use rather than denial of their utility. Indices of neither IQ nor adaptive behavior are sufficient independently for individual diagnosis or classification. As dual measures, however, and supplemented by clinical judgment and biomedical data, they can enable a classification system to fulfill its basic purpose (Grossman, 1983).

Certain facets of the literature dealing with the retarded offender are concerned with the quantity and quality of testing being done in the correctional setting. Brown and Courtless (1982) found that close to 70% of the institutions responding to their surveys reported doing routine testing for all admissions. A rather large assortment of tests was being used to measure intelligence, the most common of which was the Wechsler Intelligence Scale for Children and the Wechsler Adult Intelligence Scale. Haskins and Friel (1973), in their national survey of correctional institutions, also found a greater incidence of intelligence testing than had been expected. Approximately 84% of responding institutions reported testing under conditions deemed necessary for reliability.

As to the reliability of institutional testing, however, Brown and Courtless (1982) found that only 75% of a sample of those identified by their institutions as retarded retested below an IQ of 70, using standard measures. These researchers felt that the other 25% verified the lack of standardization in testing procedures. Of those institutions surveyed by Brown and Courtless (1982), 75% reported that IQ tests were given to inmates by psychologists, whereas other institutions reported using social workers, classification officers, and inmates under the supervision of a psychologist. Several institutions did not routinely test and were therefore unable to provide IQ scores. A shortage of mental health staff persons was noted in the responses of the institutions. Standards set by the American Correctional Association with regard to the numbers of psychiatrists, psychologists, social workers, and counselors were not being met.

As noted earlier, attempts to assess the number of incarcerated offenders with retardation have resulted in a wide range of estimates. However, most of these studies have agreed on the heterogeneity of this group in terms of levels of retardation. Although people with mental retardation are often referred to as a group, there are individuals with mild, moderate, severe, or profound retardation; and it is important to consider them separately. For example, individuals who are severely and profoundly retarded (with an IQ under 50) are easily identifiable as retarded at the time of arrest, and most are diverted, shortly after arrest, from the criminal justice system to residential facilities for persons with retardation. This practice was substantiated by Project CAMIO (Haskins & Friel, 1973). And Brown and Courtless (1982) found only 1.6% of those incarcerated in penal and correctional facilities with IQ levels below 55.

It should be noted that no statistics are available on the numbers of offenders with retardation who are residing in facilities for the mentally ill; very few are available for local jails or houses of detention. In addition, there is no estimate of the number of retarded persons who are diverted from the criminal justice system. However, evidence suggests that persons with retardation are diverted less frequently than persons without retardation.

Reasons for the Disproportionate Numbers of Offenders with Retardation

If retardation and criminality are not synonymous and if there is no clear cause-and-effect relationship between the two, then why is there a disproportionate number of offenders with retardation in prison today? An explanation begins with an examination of the disadvantages experienced by the person with mental retardation within society in general and within the criminal justice system in particular.

Social Factors. Theorists today acknowledge that social deviance is far more complex than individual pathology. Social deviance, such as retardation and delinquency, is a phenomenon that takes shape within and is inseparable from the wider social context in which it occurs. That context may include a lack of access to productive work and de facto barriers that support discrimination within the labor market, housing, education, and health care (Kolko, 1962). The criminal justice system also takes shape within this wider social context and bears the impact of a society with unequal opportunities (Wright, 1973).

Among socially disadvantaged people in the United States, studies show a disproportionate number of persons with mental retardation. In addition, the relationship of social class variables to mental retardation appears to be more direct for persons with mild to moderate retardation than for persons with severe retardation. This situation implies that factors responsible for severe retardation are less influenced by social class than are those responsible for mild retardation (Lapouse & Weitzer, 1967). Thus, persons with mild to moderate retardation are more likely to occupy lower social class positions and to bear a number of its concomitant demographic characteristics, including low occupational status, inferior living conditions, poor schools, limited educational opportunities, inadequate health facilities, and high unemployment. Retarded persons are also disproportionately members of minority groups.

Research on the population of offenders with mental retardation has demonstrated that the vast majority of these offenders have obtained only a limited amount of education. They are likely to have completed the sixth to the eighth grade with academic achievement equivalent only to that of the second or third grade (Atlanta Association for Retarded Citizens, 1975). More often than not, offenders with retardation are either unemployed or underemployed in low-skilled jobs prior to their arrest. One study noted that the vast majority (77%) of offenders with retardation were living on standard minimum incomes, with another 12% on welfare (Atlanta Association for Retarded Citizens, 1975). In most studies offenders with retardation have been overwhelmingly members of minority groups (Brown & Courtless, 1982; Haskins & Friel, 1973).

The Disadvantaged Position of Offenders with Retardation.   Within the criminal justice system mentally retarded offenders are at a distinct disadvantage. Consider the following:

1. A person with retardation may not understand the implications of the rights being read to him (Moschella, 1986).
2. People with retardation who have been arrested often confess quickly and react to friendly suggestions and/or intimidation. Many times they try to say what they think another person wants to hear.
3. A person with retardation may have difficulty communicating with a lawyer and with court personnel, thus hampering the preparation of the case.
4. In some cases the condition of mental retardation is not even recognized by the lawyers, judges, and others involved (Allen, 1968; Haggarty, Kane, & Nodall, 1972).
5. A person with retardation often pleads guilty more readily than a person without retardation and is more often convicted of the arresting offense. Plea bargaining to reduce charges, and thereby sentences, is used less frequently today with the retarded person (Brown & Courtless, 1982).
6. Appeals are sought less frequently for persons with retardation, and post-

conviction relief is requested in only a small percentage of cases (Brown & Courtless, 1982).

7. Pretrial psychological exams are seldom requested. One study found this request in only 25% of the cases examined. Presentence testing was requested in only 20% of the cases studied (Brown & Courtless, 1982).

8. Use of probation and other diversionary noninstitutional programs is less frequent with retarded offenders. They are often considered not to be good prospects for such programs, despite a lack of evidence to support this assumption (Haskins & Friel, 1973).

9. In prison the offender with retardation is slower to adjust to routine, has more difficulty in learning regulations, and thus accumulates more rule infractions, lessening his or her chance for admittance into choice programs, living quarters, and so on. This situation also acts to limit parole opportunities (Illinois Correctional Services for the Developmentally Disabled, 1975; Kentucky Legislative Research Commission, 1975; South Carolina Department of Mental Retardation, 1969).

10. Offenders with retardation rarely take part in rehabilitation programs in prison because of their desire to mask their limitations. As a result, they spend much of their time in meaningless inactivity (Kentucky Legislative Research Commission, 1975).

11. Offenders with mental retardation are often the butt of practical jokes and sexual harassment in prison (Kentucky Legislative Research Commission, 1975).

12. Because of their lack of participation in rehabilitation programs in prison, their numerous rule infractions, and their inability to formulate release plans, offenders with retardation are denied parole more frequently, serving sentences 2 to 3 years longer on the average than those of other prisoners incarcerated for the same offenses (Kentucky Legislative Research Commission, 1975).

Characteristics Associated with Retardation.   Additional factors associated with the condition of mental retardation should be considered in an explanation of the relationship between mental retardation and criminal behavior.

1. People with retardation often display poor judgment. They do not understand fully the significance of their actions and the consequences that ensue.

2. Often in an effort to be accepted and/or recognized, retarded persons may unknowingly involve themselves in criminal activity.

3. People with retardation may be more easily led into criminal activity by others because of their heightened suggestibility. A person with retardation may then become the perfect scapegoat in an illegal activity.

These individual characteristics of mental retardation often provide the framework for involvement in criminal activity. They do not, however, explain the problem completely.

THE STATE OF THE ART

In an attempt to draw attention to the need, to correct injustices in the system, and to provide corrective programming for adjudicated offenders with mental retardation, several programs and projects have sprung up. Most were developed by concerned individuals or agency administrators; some came into being as a result of court action.

Conferences and Programs

South Carolina, Florida, and Rhode Island held the first conferences of national significance on the subject of mentally retarded offenders (Santamour & Watson, 1982). All three meetings addressed issues and provided direction to concerned professionals. Their most significant contribution, however, was the publications they produced. Most notable was "The Naïve Offender," which was widely distributed by the President's Committee on Mental Retardation. Although these early meetings did not provide concrete solutions, they focused attention on the needs of offenders with mental retardation and stimulated a number of local and state meetings on the subject.

Two national conferences funded and sponsored by a consortium of national voluntary and public agencies were held in South Carolina in 1975 and 1980. They provided the first forum for professionals actively engaged in working with mentally retarded offenders to come together to evaluate the state of the art and to exchange ideas and practices. Publications from each conference stimulated further interest and had an impact on the development of programs.

Initially, the President's Committee on Mental Retardation, the U.S. Department of Justice (Law Enforcement Assistance Administration), the Juvenile Justice and Delinquency Prevention Agency, and the National Institute on Corrections were the only federal agencies concerned with the problem. Later, the Department of Health and Human Services (Administration on Developmental Disabilities) and the U.S. Department of Education (Special Education and Rehabilitation Services) displayed interest by funding specific programs or promoting research. National voluntary organizations—such as the Association for Retarded Citizens (ARC), the American Association on Mental Deficiency (AAMD), and the American Correctional Association (ACA)—have long supported addressing the problems and have produced publications dealing with the subject matter.

Recently, several projects have been funded by the Administration on Developmental Disabilities and/or state level developmental disabilities planning councils—notably the University of Rochester Medical Center's training grant (1983–1985) and the Nebraska Department of Health's Individual Justice Plan (1985). On the state level South Carolina in 1975, Arizona in 1983, New Mexico and New York in 1984, and Texas in 1985 have held state conferences with money provided by state developmental disabilities planning councils. Similar meetings have been funded by state level groups in more than a dozen other states from 1977 to 1985. All have attempted to bring together officials from the fields of criminal justice and mental retardation to address the problems and to stimulate programming.

An unresolved case in Louisiana (*Hand et. al v. Phelps*) and three other lawsuits (*Ruiz v. Estelle*, 1980; *Guthrie v. Evans*, n.d.; and *Duran v. Anaya*, n.d.) have also had a significant impact on how the offender with mental retardation is treated in prison. In consent agreements in all three resolved cases the states agreed to establish programming specifically designed for offenders with retardation. Most significant was the Texas case (*Ruiz v. Estelle*), in which for the first time in history a state department of corrections developed a screening process to identify inmates with mental retardation and a program to provide individual treatment. The process separates the offender with mental retardation from the regular prison population, thereby safeguarding the retarded offender's vulnerability. In addition, it provides developmental programming based on the individual's adaptive abilities and emotional stability. Each inmate, regardless of age, receives vocational and educational programming based on an individual vocational and/or educational plan. Security staff are individually picked and specially trained to supervise inmates with retardation. The plan also includes tying correctional services into the parole program, thereby facilitating the postincarceration adjustment. Programs in North Carolina, Alabama, Georgia, South Carolina, Virginia, and New Mexico, although less comprehensive, are also trailblazers in this area of criminal justice.

Institutional Services

State mental retardation facilities that have outstanding programs for offenders include Camarillo and Stockton State Hospitals in California. The Utah State School at American Fork also has a special program for offenders. The Oak Ridge Training School in Virginia is the only program within a state-operated juvenile justice facility that is designed to treat juvenile offenders with mental retardation. Camarillo and Stockton also have programs for juveniles, but they are within the administration of the Department of Developmental Disabilities.

Community Services

Community correctional and/or community-based programs are available to offenders in a number of states and localities. Included are programs in Maine, Tennessee, Kentucky, Florida, California, Utah, Washington, Ohio, New York, Texas, and Mississippi. These services include program alternatives to incarceration and parole programs. Typical of these programs are two residences funded by the South Central Los Angeles Regional Center: the Crisp Home is privately operated by a married couple, and the DRRO House by the King/Drew Medical Center. The former serves offenders referred through the Center's jail project, and the latter serves clients who have received treatment in the Camarillo State Hospital Offender Program. Both are highly structured and include job training and placement components. Only two states, New York and Texas, are attempting to network the entire criminal justice system. In New York the effort is being coordinated by the Developmental Disabilities Council, and in Texas by the department of corrections.

Preventive Measures

Dr. Ruth Luckerson, the University of New Mexico, and Stanfield Associates of Santa Monica, California, have developed curricula to teach individuals with mental retardation about the nature of criminal behavior and the consequences of crime. The Northern Virginia Regional Center and the Camarillo State Hospital (California) both have curricula designed to teach defendants with mental retardation what their rights are as well as how to become competent to stand trial. Florida and other states have similar programs.

Training curricula for police and criminal justice personnel have also been developed by a number of state and national groups, including the Association for Retarded Citizens, the President's Committee on Mental Retardation, Georgetown University, and the Universities of Florida, Minnesota, South Carolina, and Wisconsin. The New Jersey Association for Retarded Citizens also has a good curriculum. In Canada the John Howard Society (Calgary, Alberta) has addressed the problem; in England Stanley Hewitt and in Australia the Department of Youth and Community Services have done likewise.

Advocacy

Legal and personal advocacy projects have come and gone, along with the interest and individuals and the availability of funds. Among those still existing are the Baltimore Association's Mentally Retarded Offender Project, South Carolina's Protection and Advocacy Offender Liaison Services, the South Central Los Angeles Regional Center's Law Enforcement Liaison Program, and the Lancaster County (Pennsylvania) Mentally Retarded Offender Program. Similar programs exist in Washington, Oregon, and Nebraska.

THE USE OF PRISON

The National Coalition on Jail Reform and some professionals in the field of mental retardation take a firm stand on where offenders with mental retardation should be housed for treatment. The coalition holds to the policy that no offender with mental retardation or mental illness should be placed in either a jail or a prison. California State Assemblyman Lloyd Connelly has introduced legislation that would prohibit incarcerating people with mental retardation with other nonretarded offenders. Currently, California has a law (SB 579) that automatically diverts offenders with mental retardation from jail for a first conviction or a misdemeanor charge. In determining placement of offenders, two aspects should be taken into account: the principle of normalization and the nature of the prison culture.

The Principle of Normalization

The principle of normalization has received much attention in recent years. In attempting to apply it to the situation of offenders with retardation, professionals argue that such people should not be given different treatment just because they are retarded. According to this position a person with retardation who commits an offense should be treated just as the nonretarded are, once guilt and culpability have been established. According to Haywood (1976) it is not the retardation that requires treatment, but the criminal or delinquent behavior. Treatment should be provided by the justice system, the educational system, the social welfare system, and/or the vocational rehabilitative system. Thus, if the responsibility lies with the criminal justice system, transferring the individual to a facility for people with mental retardation is not the solution. Very often such a transfer results in the lifetime sentencing of the individual to such a facility (Haywood, 1976).

Proponents of normalization feel that the citizen with mental retardation has the right to be treated as nearly as possible like other citizens, which includes bearing responsibility for one's own behavior. This concern for normalization has often led to advocacy for nonsegregated placement of offenders with retardation within a correctional facility (Haywood, 1976). To this author normalization means that planning should be carried out for a retarded offender as it would be for any other offender—and only that. It does not mean treating the individual as though he or she were "normal." It does mean that the offender with retardation should have normal opportunities.

For the most part, persons with mental retardation in correctional settings are quite different from persons currently receiving treatment in institutions for the mentally retarded. Those in prison are more intelligent, more sophisticated or streetwise, better able to mask their limitations, and less physically handicapped. When placed in institutions for people with retardation, they often victimize other residents and disrupt routines. They present security risks and prompt training needs that these institutions are ill equipped to handle; facility design and staffing patterns are geared toward the needs of docile, multiply handicapped individuals. Consequently, it is generally accepted in the field of retardation that the desired setting for rehabilitating and training the retarded offender is some place other than an existing state institution for persons who are mentally retarded.

However, research also indicates problems within correctional facilities in meeting the needs of offenders with retardation. Here they are also out of step with the dominant characteristics of the inmate population. Their training needs are more habilitative than rehabilitative. They are victimized by more sophisticated inmates; and because of their desire to be accepted, the consequences of their maladaptive behavior become intensified as they assume the values of the prison culture. Although their security needs are met in prison, their need for protection from abuse and exploitation is increased. The staff of correctional facilities are also ill equipped to meet the needs of this population.

The Prison Culture

The problem of the prison culture needs elaboration at this point. Much of the sociological literature deals with the question of subcultures, in which it is assumed that a distinct set of values and patterns of behavior exists, different from the dominant culture. Sykes (1972) notes that imprisonment means that many individuals are bound together for long time periods; and such aggregates inevitably give rise to social systems—not just those decreed by the custodians but also those that develop more informally as individuals interact in meeting the problems posed by their particular environment. Therefore, in attempting to understand the meaning of imprisonment, we must see prison life as something more than an arrangement of walls and bars, cells and keys. A prison is a society within a society.

The loss of liberty that prisoners experience marks their "civil death" and severs their association with the dominant culture. At this point the only value system immediately available is that of the criminal surroundings—the prison culture—which other prisoners assume in order to be part of something. For offenders with retardation, who have a greater tendency to be persuaded and manipulated, the negative impact of the prison culture on their development is much greater than it is for nonretarded inmates. And because of their impaired development, the behavior learned in prison by retarded inmates is less apt to be reversed.

Offenders with retardation have often never been accepted by society at large. Becoming a part of the "society of captives" is often their first experience with acceptance—hence its pervasive impact. At Bridgewater State Hospital and Prison in Massachusetts, personnel commenting on the strengths of the association between the inmate wtih retardation and the prison culture noted that it was only the inmates with retardation who returned to the prison for social visits.

PROGRAMMING FOR THE OFFENDER

There is little disagreement among professionals as to what the treatment process for offenders should include and which goals it should set. However, there is disagreement with the term *rehabilitation* as it is used in corrections. In the criminal justice system today rehabilitation refers to the process of restoring the individual to behaviors and values that are socially acceptable. Such behaviors and values are, by definition, not illegal. It is assumed in the rehabilitative process that the individual formerly displayed appropriate behavior and held socially acceptable values and temporarily laid them aside.

The problem is very different for the child or adult with retardation caught up in the justice system. People with retardation cannot be assumed to have learned socially acceptable behaviors and values. For these persons the lag in their developmental processes often results in the absence of certain basic social and cognitive skills. Their learning process has often been hit or miss. Therefore, their need is not so much to relearn acceptable behaviors and values but to become acquainted with them. The term *habilitation*, therefore, is more appropriate than *rehabilitation*.

Habilitation is defined as the process of locating the individual's levels of knowledge and skill and developing a plan that proceeds from those levels toward higher levels of independence. The process involves the pooling of resources and personnel in an effort to enhance the individual's physical, mental, social, vocational, and economic condition to the fullest and most useful extent.

Goals of Treatment

The major treatment goal of correctional education programs serving retarded offenders is to develop and implement a system of services specifically designed to meet the needs of those offenders. The system should include diagnosis; evaluation and classification; development of personal, physical, educational, and vocational skills; courses in human sexuality; and development of social values and independent life skills. The ultimate goal is the reentry of offenders with retardation into the community as independent, law-abiding, and better-adjusted individuals. In setting objectives for offenders with retardation, it is important to keep in mind their right to equal opportunities to develop their full potential. The objectives should include

1. providing the courts with alternatives to the present system of incarceration by making available special programs for people with retardation, at the same time reducing administrative problems caused by the incarceration of offenders with retardation
2. setting up a scheme for diagnosis and classification that approximately defines the intellectual and developmental levels of individuals and places them in the settings appropriate for their personal and security needs
3. creating a developmentally oriented, emotionally supportive, and physically safe environment for offenders with retardation
4. developing an individualized treatment program for each offender, based on an understanding of individual developmental needs and criminal behavior
   a. raising the inmate's level of understanding of personal and social behavior
   b. helping the inmate acquire the skills, resources, and opportunities necessary to survive comfortably in society
   c. obtaining a significant reduction in the incidence of institutional rule infractions by the offender with retardation

5. providing a system of supportive services that will make reentry into the open community easier and will reduce recidivism
6. establishing guidelines for correctional and parole officers working with offenders with retardation

CONCLUSION

The criminal justice system does not operate in a vacuum. It is a social system, reflecting the wider social context. The system bears the impact of a society that affords limited opportunities to some and greater opportunities to others. The statistics speak for themselves; we cannot assume that most attorneys, judges, and probation officers desire and actively seek greater knowledge in handling offenders with mental disorders. Perhaps, considering the present state of affairs in community services for people with mental retardation (specifically the lack of interagency cooperation and our overloaded courts and probation systems), we should not be surprised. The offender with retardation has always been a low priority in both the corrections and the mental retardation systems and likely will continue to be so. Offenders, mentally retarded or not, lack a committed, well-organized, and financially sound advocacy group.

However, the past 6 or 7 years have been a period of optimism. Earlier indications of how offenders with mental retardation could be helped by a coherent philosophy of service have grown into new approaches. But in very practical and concrete ways, people are finding out exactly how complicated it is to build patterns of support for offenders with mental retardation who are incarcerated or are living in the community. These people do not fit tidily into overall schemes. Yet those of us observing today's treatment of offenders with retardation must acknowledge and appreciate the powerful accomplishments that have been realized within a short time period. We must also continue to believe that offenders with mental retardation, regardless of where they live or what crime they committed, have the right to be treated as vital human beings.

REFERENCES

Allen, R. (1968). Legal norms and practices affecting the mentally deficient. *American Journal of Orthopsychiatry, 38*, 635–642.

American Bar Association. (1983). *Criminal justice mental health standards.* Washington, DC: Author.

Atlanta Association for Retarded Citizens. (1975). *A study of Georgia's criminal justice system as it relates to the mentally retarded.* Atlanta: Author.

Bontrager, R. (1985). *Report on study conducted at Lincoln Correctional Center.* Presentation at the IJP Symposium, Omaha, NE.

Brown, B. S., & Courtless, T. F. (1982). *The mentally retarded offender.* Washington, DC: National Institute of Mental Health.

Cohen, J., & Kane, L. A. (1986). *Citizens with mental retardation and the law in process.* Washington, DC: President's Committee on Mental Retardation.

Denkowski, G. C., Denkowski, K. M., & Mabli, J. (1983). A 50-state survey of the current status of residential treatment programs for mentally retarded offenders. *Mental Retardation, 21,* 197–203.

The developmentally disabled offender. (1986). *Prison Journal, 66,* 1–92.

Duran v. Anaya, No. 77–721–JB (Dist. Ct. N. Mex.).

Goddard, H. H. (1916). *Feeblemindedness.* New York: Macmillan.

Grossman, H. J. (Ed.). (1983). *Classification in mental retardation* (Special Publication #9). Washington, DC: American Association of Mental Deficiency.

Guthrie v. Evans, No. 3068 (U.S. Dist. Ct. Ga).

Haggarty, D. E., Kane, L., & Udall, D. K. (1972). As essay on the legal rights of the mentally retarded. *Family Law Quarterly, 6,* 59–71.

Haskins, J., & Friel, C. (1973a). *Project CAMIO: Vol. 3. The mentally retarded and the law project.* Huntsville, TX: Sam Houston State University.

Haskins, J., & Friel, C. (1973b). *Project CAMIO: Vol. 6. The delinquent in a state residential facility for the mentally retarded.* Huntsville, TX: Sam Houston State University.

Haywood, H. C. (1976). Reaction comments. In H. Kindred, J. Cohen, D. Penrod, & T. Shaffer (Eds.), *The mentally retarded citizen and the law* (pp. 677–680). New York: Free Press.

Heber, R. (1959). A manual on terminology and classification in mental retardation. Monograph supplement to *American Journal of Mental Deficiency.*

Illinois Correctional Services for the Developmentally Disabled. (1975, June). *The developmentally disabled offender in the Illinois justice system.* Chicago: Author.

Jenkins, R. L. (1935). The geographical distribution of mental deficiency in the Chicago area. *Journal of Psychoasthenics, 40,* 291–307.

Kapp, M. (1973, Spring). *Legal disposition of the mildly retarded offender: A vote for segregation and special treatment.* Unpublished paper.

Kentucky Legislative Research Commission. (1975, October). *Mentally retarded offenders in adult and juvenile correctional institutions* (Research Report No. 125). Frankfort, KY: Author.

Kolko, G. (1962). *Wealth and power in America.* New York: Praeger.

Lapouse, R., & Weitzer, N. (1967). Epidemiology. *American Journal of Mental Deficiency, 48,* 408–461.

Levy, R. S. (1967). Dimensions of mental retardation among wards of Illinois Youth Commission. *Journal of Correctional Education, 19,* 12–16.

Massachusetts Bar Association. (1977). *The retarded citizens and the law: Focusing on the criminal offender specialized training and advocacy program.* Boston: Author.

The mentally disordered offender. (1985). *Source book.* Washington, DC: U.S. Department of Justice, National Institute of Corrections.

Moschella, A. L. (1986). In search of the mentally retarded offender. *Prison Journal, 66,* 67–76.

President's Committee on Mental Retardation. (1977). *MR76, mental retardation: Past and present* (pp. 143–153). Washington, DC: U.S. Government Printing Office.

President's Panel on Mental Retardation. (1967). *Report of the task force on law.* Washington, DC: Department of Health, Education, and Welfare.

Rockowitz, R. (1985). *Monroe County, New York, Comprehensive Demonstration Project.* Presentation of the IJP Symposium, Omaha, NE.

Ruiz v. Estelle, 503 F. Supp. 1265 (S.D. Tex. 1980), *cert. denied,* 103 S.Ct. 1438.

Rutherford, R. B., Nelson, C. M., & Wolford, B. I. (1985). Special education in the most restrictive environment: Correctional/Special education. *Journal of Special Education, 19,* 59–71.

Santamour, M. B. (1986). Dehogging a state's correctional system. Unpublished manuscript.

Santamour, M. B., & Watson, P. (1982). *The retarded offender.* New York: Praeger.

Santamour, M. B., & West, B. (1977). *The mentally retarded offender and corrections.* Washington, DC: U.S. Department of Justice.

Soule v. Coughlin, N.Y. State Supreme Court, County of Onondaga Index No. 85 6422, November, 1985.

South Carolina Department of Corrections. (1983). *The mentally retarded adult offender: A study of the problem of mental retardation in the South Carolina Department of Corrections.* Columbia, SC: Author.

South Carolina Department of Mental Retardation. (1969). *A plan for the youthful mentally retarded offender* (File Y: 35–83). Columbia, SC: Author.

Sykes, G. (1972). *The society of captives.* Princeton, NJ: Princeton University Press.

Wright, E. O. (1973). *The politics of punishment.* New York: Harper & Row.

Zeleny, L. D. (1933). Feeblemindedness in criminal conduct. *American Journal of Sociology, 139,* 564–576.

The Learning Disabled Offender

CHAPTER 6   *Ingo Keilitz and Noel Dunivant*

Although estimates vary, it is widely acknowledged that learning disabled youth are disproportionately represented among criminal defendants and adjudicated delinquents (Keilitz & Van Duizend, 1984; Morgan, 1979; Rutherford, Nelson, & Wolford, 1985). Indeed, parents, educators, criminal justice professionals, and the courts seem all but convinced that a strong relationship exists between learning disabilities and juvenile delinquency (Elliot & Voss, 1974; Keilitz & Miller, 1985; "The Link," 1985; Murray, 1976; *School Board v. Malone*, 1985). For example, in a resolution adopted in August 1983, the American Bar Association recognized "a correlation between children who suffer from the handicap of learning disability and children who are involved in the juvenile justice and the child welfare systems" and called upon attorneys, judges, and local bar associations to improve the handling of cases involving children with learning disabilities ("The Link," 1985).

Between 1976 and 1983 the authors and their colleagues, as part of the Learning Disabilities—Juvenile Delinquency (LD-JD) Project, sought to test the relationship between learning disabilities and juvenile delinquency and to provide at least partial answers to the question of what can be done to weaken the relationship. The LD-JD Project addressed three questions. First, is there in fact a link between learning disabilities (LD) and juvenile delinquency (JD)? Second, what is the nature of that link? And third, can it be broken or at least weakened by a program of remediation? In this chapter we consider the answers to those questions. We begin the chapter with a description of several theories linking learning disabilities with juvenile delinquency. The theories, which were tested by the LD-JD Project, invoke various learning characteristics, social traits, and environmental factors that are believed to make learning disabled youth more likely to commit crimes.

THE LINK BETWEEN LD AND JD

Theories and Hypotheses

Like all social programs (Glaser, 1980; Lewin, 1951), programs for delinquents with learning disabilities have had their genesis in an idea, articulated in terms of explicit and implicit theories and based on logic and observations. The essential idea in this case was that LD accounts for JD, albeit not entirely; and a number of theories and hypotheses were advanced. Most of these theories and hypotheses originated before the initiation of extensive research on the link between LD and JD, but some grew out of that research. They have been discussed extensively by the authors, their colleagues, and others over the last 10 years.[1] Three theories dominated the field and formed the basis upon which researchers and practitioners built intervention strategies: the school failure theory, the susceptibility theory, and the differential treatment theory.

Briefly stated, *the school failure theory* suggests that learning disabilities produce academic failure that, in turn, results in delinquent behavior (Murray, 1976; Post 1981). This theory implies a causal chain linking the learning and social characteristics of LD youth to school failure, dropout, and juvenile delinquency. Initially, as a result of school failure, LD children who are slow learners and disciplinary problems may be labeled problem students, perceived as socially awkward and unattractive, and grouped with other children who have behavior problems. Such negative labeling and association with delinquency-prone children may prompt LD youths to engage in socially troublesome behavior (Bazemore, 1985). A negative self-image and sense of frustration resulting from failure in school may motivate the LD student to strike back at society in anger. This kind of psychological reaction causes the LD delinquent to be especially violence-prone. Failure in school may also decrease attachment to school and to teachers as significant adults (Johnson, 1979). This withdrawal of attachment and commitment to socially accepted courses of action may be intensified by the active rejection or uncaring attitudes of teachers and administrators.

At this point social control theory predicts that delinquency will increase among LD students as their attachment and commitment to school diminish (Empey & Lubeck, 1971). LD teenagers may also experience economic incentives to commit crimes, especially theft, if they anticipate that their poor academic record will make it impossible for them to achieve their aspired levels of occupational prestige or income. Ultimately, LD may be associated

[1]See, for example, Bader, 1975; Bernstein & Rulo, 1976; Broder, Dunivant, Smith, & Sutton, 1981; Cox, 1981; Dunivant, 1982; Elliot & Voss, 1974; Keilitz & Miller, 1980; Keilitz, Zaremba, & Broder, 1982; Mauser, 1974; McCullough, Zaremba, & Rich, 1979; Murray, 1976; Podboy & Mallory, 1978; Ramos, 1978; Sawicki & Schaeffer, 1979; Smykla & Willis, 1981; Swanstrom, Randle, & Offord, 1981; Unger, 1978; Ungerleider, 1985; Zimmerman, Rich, Keilitz, & Broder, 1981. For bibliographies on the link between disability and crime, see Murray, 1976; Pointer & Kravitz, 1981.

with a general tendency to attribute to others the blame for negative events (Hirshi, 1969).

According to the second theory, *the susceptibility theory* (Murray, 1976; Post, 1981), children with LD possess certain cognitive and personality characteristics that predispose them to commit crimes. Such characteristics—which are components of or are caused by LD—may include lack of impulse control, inability to anticipate the future consequences of actions, poor perception of social cues, irritability, suggestibility, and a tendency to act out. Proponents of this theory argue that these disorders, which are frequently associated with LD, directly contribute to the development of delinquent behavior (Reilly & Bullock, 1979).

Both the susceptibility and school failure theories hold that LD, together with other factors, directly or indirectly produces delinquent behavior. Assuming that the probability of apprehension and arrest is a function of the frequency and seriousness of delinquent acts, the susceptibility and school failure theories predict a proportionate increase in the probability of LD youths coming into contact with the criminal justice system.

The third theory is *the differential treatment theory*. It holds that LD youth are treated more harshly by the criminal justice system even when LD and non-LD youth engage in the same types and degrees of delinquent behaviors (Dunivant, 1982; Keilitz, Zaremba, & Broder, 1981). This theory consists of three separate hypotheses that posit differential arrest, adjudication, and disposition of LD youths. The differential arrest hypothesis is that LD adolescents have a greater risk of being apprehended by the police than do their non-LD peers, even for comparable levels of delinquent activity. LD youths may be more likely than non-LD youths to be detected for the same offenses; they may lack the abilities necessary to plan strategies, to avoid being detected, to dissemble during encounters with police (i.e., to conceal their true thoughts), or to comprehend the questions and warnings of law enforcement officers. Police may also pick up, interrogate, and arrest LD adolescents disproportionately because LD teenagers may be awkward and abrasive in social interactions.

Based on similar reasoning, the second hypothesis suggests that LD youths have a higher probability of adjudication following arrest than do their non-LD peers who have committed the same offenses (Broder et al., 1981; Zimmerman et al., 1981). The differential adjudication hypothesis is that LD teenagers charged with a violation are at greater risk of adjudication than similarly charged non-LD adolescents. It may be that LD youths are treated differently by juvenile justice officials because of characteristics associated with LD, such as social abrasiveness, irritability, and lack of self-control. LD youths may also be at greater risk of adjudication because they lack certain cognitive and social skills. This differential treatment may come from any of several criminal justice officials—for example, intake or probation officers, defense or prosecuting attorneys, or judges.

The third hypothesis holds that LD adolescents have a greater risk of being committed to a training school or other correctional facility than non-

LD teenagers adjudicated on the same charge (Dunivant, 1982). Based on some of the same reasoning outlined for differential adjudication, this differential disposition hypothesis states that learning disabled youths have a higher probability of receiving a severe disposition from the court.

Research

Based on a review of the empirical evidence gathered through 1975, Murray (1976) concluded that the existing research was so deficient that it could not be used "even for rough estimates of the strength of the link" between LD and JD and it had not established "the existence of a causal relationship between learning disabilities and delinquency" (p. 65). Similar conclusions were reached in a study by the General Accounting Office (Comptroller General of the United States, 1977). In response, the Office of Juvenile Justice and Delinquency Prevention (OJJDP) of the U.S. Department of Justice funded a research and development project in 1976, the LD-JD Project, to provide empirical data upon which informed policy decisions could be made. The National Center for State Courts (NCSC) received a grant to undertake large-scale studies of the relationship between LD and JD and to carry out an extensive evaluation of the effectiveness of a remediation program for learning disabled delinquents. A second grant was awarded to the Association for Children with Learning Disabilities (ACLD) to design and conduct a remediation program to improve the academic skills and reduce the delinquency of learning disabled teenagers officially adjudicated as delinquents.

The research and development effort sponsored by OJJDP spanned more than 7 years, from 1976 to 1983, and involved a variety of grants, continuation grants, and subcontracts. The ACLD's Research and Development Project, under the direction of the Dorothy Crawford, designed and conducted a program of remedial instruction for LD-JD youths from 1977 to 1979. The research component was conducted by Keilitz and his colleagues at Creighton University until August 1978 and was continued thereafter by the authors and their colleagues at the National Center for State Courts in Williamsburg, Virginia.[2]

The research component of the LD-JD Project consisted of two empirical studies and a program evaluation. The studies were conducted to determine whether learning disability is related to delinquency and, if so, to examine the nature of that relationship. The first was an age cross-sectional study, which was based on a sample containing a cross section of age groups measured at a single point in time. The second study consisted of a longitudinal investigation of a subsample of youth from the cross-sectional sample who had no history of official delinquency prior to the outset of the research. The third part of the research component, which is discussed in detail later in this chapter, was an evaluation of the effectiveness of the ACLD

---

[2]For the purpose of classification of subsamples of LD and non-LD youths, NCSC contracted with the Educational Testing Service (ETS) to perform the diagnostic evaluations of the adolescents in the study.

remediation program in improving academic achievement and preventing or controlling future delinquency.[3]

The Cross-Sectional Study.   Participants in the age cross-sectional study were boys sampled from public schools, juvenile courts, training schools, and departments of corrections in the metropolitan areas of Baltimore, Indianapolis, and Phoenix during 1977 and 1978. The sample included 973 teenagers from the public schools who had *not* been adjudicated delinquent and 970 youths who *had* been officially adjudicated delinquent by juvenile courts.

Information from school records, standardized test scores, and behavioral observations was used to assess LD. The boys were classified as not being learning disabled if their records did not indicate the presence of learning problems or if any detected learning problems could be attributed to mental retardation, severe emotional disturbance, physical handicap, or use of a primary language other than English. The remainder of the sample was administered a battery of tests from which learning disabilities could be diagnosed (Dunivant, 1984, Appendix A). Tests included the Wechsler Intelligence Scale for Children—Revised, the Woodcock Reading Mastery Tests, the KeyMath Diagostic Arithmetic Test, and the Visual Motor Gestalt Test. In addition, hyperactivity, inattentiveness, and other signs of learning disabilities were noted during testing sessions. LD classification was determined by significant discrepancies between ability and achievement test scores and by the presence of perceptual and behavioral problems. In general, a 2-year difference between ability, as measured by the IQ test, and achievement in reading and arithmetic indicated learning disability. To increase the consistency and objectivity of LD diagnoses, the classification rules were incorporated into a computer program that processed the test scores and behavioral observation ratings. Any youth whose achievement test scores were at or above the expected grade level for his age or whose full-scale IQ score was less than 69 was automatically classified as non-LD. Examination of the test scores revealed that a large majority of these learning disabled adolescents had much better quantitative skills than verbal competence.

Each youth was interviewed to obtain information about his involvement in delinquent activities, prior encounters with the police, attitude toward school, tendency to give socially desirable responses, and sociodemographic characteristics. In addition, a search of the juvenile court records was made in each of the sample cities to gather information about each boy's official involvement with the juvenile justice system. Measures were then constructed of the frequency and seriousness of self-reported delinquent behavior, previous arrests, school attitude, tendency toward socially desirable response, and previous adjudications. Advanced statistical techniques, including causal modeling and logistic regression, were utilized to detect the

---

[3]The methods, results, and implications of these three components of the LD-JD Project are described in great detail in numerous project reports available from the authors at the National Center for State Courts and from the Research & Development Training Institute. Inc., P.O. Box 15112, Phoenix, AZ 85060.

presence of a relationship between LD and JD and to evaluate the theories and hypotheses described earlier.[4]

We found that the evidence for the existence of a relationship between LD and self-reported delinquency was statistically significant. In other words, the observed relationship was not likely to have been the product of chance events in sampling or measurement. The LD adolescents reported that they had committed an average of 266 delinquent acts during their lives. This is 81 more than the corresponding mean number of delinquent acts (185) reported by the non-LD participants. Although the mean difference in seriousness of general delinquent behavior between LD and non-LD groups was not significant, the groups did differ significantly in the frequency of violent acts (e.g., assault with a dangerous weapon and gang fighting), in the amount of marijuana and alcohol use, and in the number of school discipline problems.

Learning disabilities were also strongly related to official delinquency. The incidence of learning disabilities among the adjudicated delinquents was 36%, indicating that a substantial proportion of the population of official delinquents is handicapped by learning disabilities. Weighting the sample to make it representative of the U.S. youth population, we found that the probability of being officially adjudicated was .09 for LD boys, whereas the probability of adjudication was only .04 for their non-LD peers. Thus, on a national basis 9 of every 100 young males with learning disabilities are officially adjudicated delinquent. This contrasts with an adjudication rate of only 4 per 100 for boys who are not learning disabled. Therefore, the odds of being adjudicated are 220% greater for LD than for non-LD adolescents. The odds of being taken into custody by the police were similarly greater for the participants with LD.

The three theories explaining a positive causal relationship between LD and JD received support from these results. First, using negative attitude toward school as an indicator of school failure, the findings supported the theory that learning disability produces school failure, which leads, in turn, to delinquent behavior. However, even though our analysis demonstrated that the school failure theory was consistent with the data, there was insufficient information available to determine which specific causal processes (e.g., frustration/aggression or economic incentives) were the bases of this effect.

Second, the susceptibility theory was supported by results indicating that some of the effect of LD on delinquent behavior occurred directly, that is, without being mediated by school failure. This strongly suggests that characteristics associated with learning disabilities, such as irritability or inability to anticipate future consequences of actions, contributed directly

---

[4]With data gathered in a nonexperimental or survey research design, such as the one used for this cross-sectional study, it is impossible to *prove* cause and effect. The analytic methods that we employed provided a means of determining whether the data were *consistent with* a set of causal hypotheses. These methods also gave us the important capability to reject hypotheses about causal relations that were not consistent with the data. In general, however, data may be consistent with more than one set of causal hypotheses. Some caution, therefore, needs to be exercised when interpreting the results of the causal analysis. Causal analysis enabled us to determine which causal hypotheses were consistent and which were inconsistent with the data, but it could not be used to prove that any causal hypothesis that might have been consistent with the data was—in fact—true.

to delinquent behavior. Analyses were conducted to determine whether some groups of learning disabled adolescents were more susceptible to delinquency than others. No differences in degree of vulnerability were found for groups varying in age, ethnicity, or socioeconomic status.

Third, the results were consistent with two of the three hypotheses of the differential treatment theory. LD youths were more likely to have been arrested than were their non-LD counterparts who reported having committed offenses with equal frequency and seriousness. The available data did not permit us to ascertain the basis for this result. The differential adjudication hypothesis also received strong confirmation. Even when differences were statistically controlled in sociodemographic background, frequency and seriousness of self-reported delinquent behavior, and probability of arrest, the LD teenagers in the sample had a significantly higher probability of being officially adjudicated delinquent than did their non-LD peers. It is not clear which causal processes were at work. The differential disposition hypothesis was rejected. After officially adjudicated groups of LD and non-LD boys were equated statistically for differences in background characteristics and delinquent behavior, there was no evidence that the learning disabled delinquents had a greater likelihood of being confined to a corrections facility. For comparable offenses LD and non-LD youths received equally severe punishments.

The Longitudinal Study.   The sample for the longitudinal study comprised 351 boys from the group of 973 official *non*delinquents in the sample of the cross-sectional study. The boys were reinterviewed about their delinquent behavior and school attitude at 1- and 2-year intervals after initial testing. Court records were searched for information about any official contacts the boys had with a juvenile court during the 2-year period following the initial data collection. The sample contained 57 boys (16%) who were classified as learning disabled. The objective of the longitudinal study was to determine whether LD was related to JD by observing whether increases in delinquent behavior and adjudication were greater over time for the LD than the non-LD boys.

The results were generally consistent with those of the cross-sectional study. There was convincing evidence that learning disabilities were associated with increases in delinquent activities and official contacts with the juvenile justice system. This association was not explainable on the basis of sociodemographic characteristics or the tendency to respond in socially approved ways. In addition, in contrast to the results in the cross-sectional study, the LD and non-LD boys in the longitudinal sample did not differ in their attitudes toward school. Thus, the hypothesized indirect effect of LD posited by the school failure theory could not be confirmed.

Learning disabilities did make a significant direct contribution to increases in illegal activities over time, suggesting that the intellectual and personality impairments associated with LD may have been involved in producing delinquent behavior. The results also indicated that the effect of LD in fostering delinquency was more pronounced for some subgroups than others. White youths from families with more parental education and occupational prestige experienced relatively larger increases in delinquent behavior. Further, the probability of official contacts with the juvenile justice system for comparable offenses was higher for the LD youths than the non-LD participants. The results were statistically significant for the likelihood of being arrested and almost significant for the probability of being adjudicated. Whether these differences were due to the cognitive deficiencies of the LD adolescents and/or to the negative reactions of law enforcement and juvenile justice personnel to teenagers with LD could not be ascertained.

As we found in the cross-sectional study, LD boys were not at greater risk of severe dispositions following adjudication for comparable offenses. That is, the probability of confinement in a correctional institution did not differ significantly for LD and non-LD boys.

WEAKENING THE LINK

From 1977 to 1979 the Association for Children with Learning Disabilities (ACLD), as a part of the LD-JD Project, conducted a remediation program to demonstrate "the value of diagnosing and treating learning disabilties as an aid to the rehabilitation of juvenile offenders" (ACLD, 1978), as Murray had advocated in 1976. The major goals of the remediation program were to improve scholastic achievement, improve self-esteem and attitudes toward school, and prevent delinquency (Dunivant, 1984; Keilitz, Saks, & Broder, 1979).

For a full understanding of this research component of the LD-JD Project, it is important to note that even if learning disabilities cause delinquency, remediation will not necessarily prevent or reduce the delinquency of LD youths. Sustaining causes of delinquency (labeling by adults and peers, negative self-image, association with delinquents)—as opposed to precipitating causes (learning disabilities)—can render remediation ineffective (Lane, 1980). Likewise, it is possible for academic remediation to reduce delinquency even if learning disabilities were neither precipitating or sustaining causes of the delinquency in the first place. For example, delinquent behavior may be the result of a lack of attachments to significant adult figures in the family, school, or other social institutions. If a remediation program is structured so that a bond develops between the LD youth and a teacher, then academic remediation may effect a reduction in the delinquency (Greenwood & Zimring, 1985). Thus, answers to the program evaluation question of whether a program of remediation can weaken the link between LD and JD are not necessarily related to the scientific question of whether a link exists and what the nature of that link might be.

The Program

The ACLD remediation program was based on an academic treatment model that provided individual instruction in functional areas of greatest learning deficiency, for example, expressive language, reading, and arithmetic. According to the original design of the remediation program (Keilitz, Saks, & Broder, 1979), a teacher (i.e., a trained specialist in learning disabilities) was to meet with each participant in a conventient location—usually a public school, training school, or community center—for four 50-minute training sessions per week for 1 school year. The typical caseload was 10 students for each teacher. During the sessions teacher and student worked to improve academic skills and attitudes toward school with instructional materials that had been carefully selected to be compatible with the adolescent's strongest learning modality.

The major program evaluation and policy question was: Can academic interventions be designed that will rehabilitate learning disabled delinquents, that is, reduce their delinquency from what it would have been in the absence of treatment? This is a question of significant social import when one considers the extent and seriousness of juvenile crime and the percentage of adjudicated delinquents who are learning disabled (cf. Comptroller General, 1977). Great social and economic costs of crime and lost human potential could be avoided if remediation programs successfully prevented nonadjudicated LD children and teenagers from becoming delinquent and rehabilitated those LD adolescents who had already been adjudicated. Thus, the evaluation of the ACLD program carried significant implications for public policy in education and juvenile justice. If the ACLD treatment program proved successful, it would suggest that academic remediation should be included in comprehensive delinquency prevention programs for LD youths.

The school failure hypothesis furnished the rationale for the adoption of an academic treatment model. The program model was based on the premise that learning disabilities produce poor achievement; poor achievement creates strain; and the combination of LD, poor achievement, and strain results in juvenile delinquency (Crawford, 1978). The designers of the remediation program hypothesized that teaching basic academic skills to LD delinquents would reduce school failure, lessen strain and frustration, and diminish subsequent delinquent episodes (D. Crawford, personal communication, 1980). In the terminology of causal models, learning disabilities would exert indirect effects on juvenile delinquency.

Evaluation Methods

The remediation program operated through two 1-year cycles between September 1977 to July 1979 in the metropolitan areas of Baltimore, Indianapolis, and Phoenix. Approximately 400 officially delinquent boys and girls between and including the ages of 12 and 17 were recruited to receive remediation. These juvenile offenders were identified through the cooperation of local juvenile courts, training schools, and corrections departments. They were randomly assigned in approximately equal numbers to either a remediation group or a control condition (Cook & Campbell, 1979). The remediation sample was a subset of a larger sample of youths of the cross-sectional study drawn from the juvenile courts in Baltimore, Indianapolis, and Phoenix and from seven training schools in the vicinity of these cities.

Because of attrition pre- and posttest data were available for only 120 LD and 33 non-LD members of the remediation group and for 110 LD and 26 non-LD members of the control group. This sample consisted primarily of males (89%) and was ethnically diverse, with 45% white, 35% black, 10% Hispanic, 6% American Indian, and 1% "other" subjects. The average age of those in the sample at the beginning of the study was 15.2 years. Verbal IQ ranged from 55 to 108 with an average of 81; performance IQ had a mean of 93 with minimum and maximum scores of 60 to 133.

All members of the remediation and control groups were pretested with the KeyMath Diagnostic Arithmetic Test, the Woodcock Reading Mastery Test, and a scale measuring attitudes toward school. In addition, approximately 100 of the participants were administered a story-writing test designed to measure written language expression. In most cases these tests were given along with a battery of other tests used to determine the presence of LD, including the Wechsler Intelligence Scale for Children—Revised and the Bender Visual Motor Gestalt Test. Information about sociodemographic characteristics, family background, and involvement in delinquent activities was also obtained.

The extent of prior delinquent behavior was assessed in a self-report questionnaire. In addition, a survey of court records yielded information about the participants' previous official contacts with juvenile courts. The major delinquency measures employed in the evaluation included the following five indices: frequently of self-reported delinquency, scaled seriousness of self-reported delinquency, number of adjudicated charges, scaled seriousness of adjudicated charges, and scaled severity of dispositions.

How effectively was the remediation program implemented? Since treatment-as-delivered is seldom identical to treatment-as-planned, an important component of program evaluation is a description of the implementation and operation of the program (Leithwood & Montgomery, 1980). In addition, measurement of program processes and implementation can play a useful role in program modification.

Differences among members of the remediation group in total hours of instruction covered a wide range. On the average, participants in the treatment group received 32 total hours of remediation over a period of 6 months, which was the average duration of participation in the remediation program. Although 50% of the remediation group received 24 or fewer hours of remediation, 25% of the group received more than 40 hours of instruction. And although the interval between pre- and posttesting was approximately 10 months, most members of the remediation group participated for a much shorter time. Thus, the amount of remediation received was much less than had been planned originally. A variety of unanticipated constraints limited the number of hours of remediation that could be provided, despite great effort on the part of the ACLD program staff.

There was a significant tendency for participants to receive remediation in their areas of greatest deficit. Individuals with comparatively low verbal IQ scores received more remediation in expressive and receptive language, those with low Woodcock pretest scores received more reading and spelling remediation, and those with low KeyMath prescores were given more remediation in arithmetic.

Several analyses were undertaken to determine whether various group assignment or uncontrolled attrition processes threatened the validity or generalizability of the evaluation analyses. The results indicated that, with a few minor exceptions, there was no evidence of sampling bias. Futhermore, attrition did not appear to bias the random assignment process by which initially comparable treatment and control groups were created. Members of the remediation and control groups who were posttested did not differ significantly at pretesting on sociodemographic, academic, or deliquency indices.

Educational Change

Did the remediation program increase the academic skills of the LD delinquents, as compared with the control condition? The remediation group had higher mean scores of residual change than the control group on every test of educational achievement. In the subsample of 90 participants who had taken both the pre- and the posttest of written language, the remediation group's mean residual change scores were significantly greater than those of the control group for two indices of written language competency: average sentence length (or complexity) and grammatical usage. The effect of remediation on improvement in arithmetic skills, as reflected by the KeyMath residual change scores, depended on initial (pretest) skill level to a significant degree. Thus, remediation proved demonstrably more effective than control only for those teenagers who had high KeyMath scores at pretest. The remediation group's improvement in reading achievement also exceeded that of the control group; however, the mean difference in Woodcock residual change scores did not reach the level required for statistical significance.

In summary, the data indicate that the program of remedial instruction increased the basic academic skills of learning disabled juvenile delinquents. As is typically found in evaluation of instructional methods, the tests designed specifically to measure skills being taught in the program proved more sensitive to the effects of remediation than did the standardized tests. The remediation and control groups did not differ significantly in change of school attitude. However, further analyses qualify this result.

What was the form of the relationship between scholastic change and amount of remediation received? Was there a threshold effect? Several exploratory analyses were carried out to determine whether the degree of academic change increased in a smooth, incremental fashion as the number of hours of remediation increased, or whether there was a substantial increase (jump) in academic change after a certain level (threshold) of remediation. Evidence was found for significant threshold effects with the Woodcock test, with both measures of written langauge expression, and with school attitude. Basically, the results indicated that mean gains were zero below the threshold but were significantly greater than zero above the threshold, which was 67 hours for the Woodcock, 56 hours for written language expression, and 35 hours for school attitude. Although KeyMath gains were larger for those participants who received at least 69 hours of remediation than for those who received less, the threshold effect was only marginally significant. Thus, the overall form of the relationship between academic change and amount of remediation can be described as a step function, or as a forward-tilted S. A minimum of 55 to 65 hours of instruction was required before the beneficial effects of remediation on academic skills were clearly identifiable.

Several analyses were conducted to determine whether the effectiveness of remediation depended on the adolescent's age, ethnicity, IQ, or pretest achievement level. Subsamples that differed in those characteristics had significantly different residual change scores for both the KeyMath and the Woodcock test. Among teenagers with low performance aptitude (performance IQ scores from 64 to 88), remediation was most effective in raising the arithmetic and reading scores of those who were 12 through 15 years of age. For teenagers with high performance IQ (103 to 130), however, those who were 16 or older improved relatively more during remediation. Although there were slight variations in this pattern on the Woodcock test for different ethnic groups and for participants who differed in initial skill level, the same major pattern was evident for most ethnic and pretest subgroupings. The magnitude of the differences in mean change between remediation and control subgroups was large in several instances; for example, it was in excess of one grade equivalent unit on the KeyMath and one standard deviation on the Woodcock. Thus, remediation produced substantial gains for certain subgroups, which were distinguishable in terms of their age, IQ, ethnicity, and initial skill level.

The evaluation of the ACLD remediation program's effectiveness in improving educational growth leads to the following conclusions and implications. First, the program accurately identified members of the learning disabled population for which it was designed and provided remedial instruction in their functional areas of greatest deficiency. The amount of remediation actually provided by the program was considerably less than had been planned initially. Typically, the remediation program furnished two 50-minute periods of instruction during each week that the delinquent participated. Selection and attrition processes did not bias the composition of the samples. Second, modest overall gains in scholastic achievement were observed. Third, certain minimal, or threshold, levels of remediation seemed necessary to produce noticeable improvements in academic achievement. For various measures of educational growth the thresholds were estimated to lie in the range of 55 to 65 hours of remediation. Fourth, remediation worked more effectively for some subgroups than for others. Specifically, the beneficial effects of remediation were dependent on the age and IQ of the participant, the younger–low IQ and older–high IQ adolescents recording the greatest gains. Remediation was least effective for younger–high IQ and older–low IQ participants. Further research is required to ascertain the reliability of and the reasons for these differences.

Effects on Delinquency

Six questions addressed the effectiveness of remediation in preventing or reducing self-reported and official delinquency. In general, answers to the questions showed that deliquency was decreased and suggested how the reductions were produced.

First, to what extent did participation in the remediation program reduce the level of self-reported delinquent behavior, as compared with that of the control condition? The remediation group did not have significantly larger reductions in either frequency or seriousness of self-reported delinquency relative to the control group. Analyses that will be described further, however, revealed that the effects of remediation were significant for the subgroup of participants with low pretest scores of seriousness.

Second, was the recidivism of learning disabled juvenile delinquents lowered as a result of remediation? Although two of the indices of recidivism that were employed, mean charge seriousness and disposition severity, were lower for those who had received remediation than for those who had not, the differences were not statistically reliable. The effectiveness of remediation on the third index of recidivism, residual change in the number of charges on which the youth was adjudicated, depended on the pretest number of charges.[5] Specifically, remediation contributed to a relative reduction in the number of charges for those participants who had been adjudicated on fewer charges prior to the beginning of the study; however, no such beneficial effects were evident for those LD delinquents whose pretest records indicated several previous adjudications. As discussed later, remediation significantly reduced official delinquency for particular subgroups that differed in sociodemographic and intellectual characteristics.

Third, what was the form of the relationship between the degree of delinquency change and the amount of remediation received? That is, was there a threshold effect? A variety of exploratory analyses were conducted to determine how self-reported and official delinquency decreased as the number of hours of remediation increased. The results indicated that the relationship between the amounts of remediation and delinquency could best be described as a step-down function. That is, the effect of remediation on delinquency was nonexistent until a certain critical (threshold) level was reached, at which point a substantial decline in delinquency was observed. The threshold value was in the range of 35 to 40 hours for the self-reported measures of antisocial behavior; substantially less delinquent behavior was reported by those who received more than 38 hours of remediation than by those who received less. This step-down effect was also more pronounced for participants who had reported high levels of delinquent behavior at the outset. Similar step-down functions were observed for the measures of official delinquency. Here, however, the break occurred after 50 hours of re-

---

[5]A residual change score is the difference between the posttest score that was actually observed and the posttest score that would have been predicted on the basis of the observed pretest score.

mediation and held uniformly for all participants regardless of initial official delinquency scores. Thus, the threshold analyses indicated that remediation consisting of at least 40 to 50 hours of instruction was significantly effective in preventing or reducing future delinquency.

Fourth, was the remediation program especially effective in preventing delinquency among youths with particular characteristics? As discussed earlier, the evaluation of the remediation program's effectiveness in fostering educational achievement showed that remediation produced more successful results with certain types of youths than with others. Further analyses were carried out to determine whether the effects of remediation on delinquency also varied as a function of some of the participants' characteristics. Results indicated that the effectiveness of the remediation program in reducing both self-reported and official delinquency depended on the age, performance IQ, ethnicity, and pretest delinquency level of the participant. On measures of self-reported delinquency, remediation proved relatively more effective for those LD youths with low pretreatment delinquency scores.

In addition, remediation significantly reduced the official delinquency of several subgroups of the sample, as measured by the number of adjudicated charges, the seriousness of adjudicated charges, and the severity of dispositions. Among the ethnic groups, remediation was more effective in reducing the recidivism of blacks than of whites or other minorities. As with self-reported delinquency, remediation produced more beneficial outcomes for participants with low initial levels of official delinquency. However, when considering the joint effects of ethnicity and pretest delinquency, a more complicated pattern emerged. Remediation was effective in preventing further official delinquency for white participants who were younger (12 to 14 years of age) and had lower pretest scores, for other minority delinquents who were older (16 to 17 years of age) and had higher pretest scores, and for black youths at all age and pretest levels. The official delinquency of learning disabled youths with below-average performance IQ scores (less than 100) was also decreased by participation in the remediation program.

Fifth, was the remediation program differentially effective for LD and non-LD delinquents? There were 102 adjudicated adolescents who had learning problems but who did not satisfy the objective (discrepancy-based) criteria for being classified as learning disabled assigned to the remediation and control conditions. This serendipitous occurrence permitted an analysis that demonstrated that remediation was significantly more effective in preventing self-reported and official delinquency among LD than among non-LD adolescents. The greater effectiveness of remediation for the LD participants was significantly more pronounced for those delinquents who reported high levels of delinquent activity at pretesting. Remediation did not apear to be at all successful in reducing the self-reported delinquency of non-LD participants with high pretest scores.

With respect to measures of official delinquency, remediation was significantly more effective in reducing the charge seriousness and disposition severity experienced by LD rather than non-LD participants. This suggests that the type of remediation designed by ACLD may be particularly suited to the needs of learning disabled youths, that is, adolescents whose achievement profiles reveal significant discrepancies, and the beneficial effects of this remediation may not extend to all students with learning problems.

Sixth, to what degree was the effect of remediation on delinquency transmitted indirectly through changes in academic achievement and school attitude? With this question we sought to evaluate a major premise of the remediation program, namely, that the effect of remediation on change in delinquency resulted from the changes in academic performance and attitudes produced by remediation. Path analysis was used to examine this hypothesis (Hanushek & Jackson, 1977).

The results indicated that almost all of the total effect of remediation on delinquency reduction was direct in nature. That is, the reductions in self-reported and official delinquency could not be attributed to any improvements in educational achievement or school attitude resulting from remediation. The findings did show that school attitude exerted large positive effects on general self-reported delinquency; that is, as attitude toward school improved, self-reported delinquency decreased. However, remediation produced negligible enhancements in school attitude, and changes in achievement test scores could not account for changes in school attitude.

These results suggest that the major factor is the success of the program in preventing delinquency was *not* academic skill improvement per se. The findings do not provide support for the strain hypothesis, which had been the original rationale for the remediation approach. The most plausible explanation for the direct effect of remediation on delinquency reduction points to social control, or bonding, theory. That is, the beneficial effects of remediation could have been produced by the close interpersonal relationship established between the adolescent and the teacher. Interactions with the teacher may have had socializing influence that inhibited delinquent behavior; the relationship may have bonded the delinquent to the normative social order. This does not necessarily mean that the substance of their interaction, the teaching and learning, was unimportant. Remediation may have been precisely the kind of situation that was needed to facilitate socialization and attachment: one in which motivation was aroused, concern demonstrated, traits and values modeled, and hard effort expended.

Although the overall effect of remediation on change in self-reported and official delinquency was not significant, specific comparisons suggest the potential for remediation for reducing delinquency among certain subgroups. The effectiveness of remediation was dependent on certain of the adolescents' characteristics—for example, ethnicity, IQ, age, and pretreatment delinquency score. Furthermore, minimal levels of remediation were required before beneficial effects were noticeable. In addition, the type of remediation provided by the ACLD model seemed better suited to learning disabled juveniles; they were helped more by remediation than participants who were not learning disabled.

CONCLUSION

The findings of the LD-JD Project establish that a causal link between learning disabilities and delinquency exists and provide some information about how the link can be weakened, if not entirely broken. The strong evidence for a relationship between learning disabilities and delinquency should prove convincing to researchers, educational practitioners, juvenile justice officials, and policymakers.

The results of the cross-sectional and longitudinal studies carry important implications for future research and public policy. They indicate that the relationship between LD and JD is quite complex, reflecting such factors as school failure, susceptibility to delinquency, and differential arrest and adjudication. By and large, the data are consistent with causal theories—the school failure theory, the susceptibility theory, and the differential treatment theory—that describe the contribution learning disabilities and related social and environmental factors make to delinquent behavior. Of course, LD is only one among many causes of juvenile delinquency—like drug abuse, unemployment, poverty, chaotic home situations, and a host of genetic and constitutional factors (Wilson & Herrnstein, 1985). Only a relatively small proportion of the youth population is affected by LD. However, within this group learning disabilities appear to be one of the important causes of delinquency.

Adolescents handicapped by learning disabilities have learning and social characteristics that predispose them toward criminal behavior. They are a relatively high risk group for delinquency, and they comprise a substantial percentage of those who have been officially adjudicated, with most estimates falling in the 10% to 50% range. This fact implies that juvenile justice, human services, and educational agencies should design special prevention and rehabilitation programs for this population. Some rehabilitation programs, such as the ACLD remediation program, have been effective in remediating academic deficiencies and reducing future delinquency. Although further research is needed to identify the specific causal processes by which LD affects delinquency and to establish reliable prevalence estimates of LD among young offenders (Keilitz & Van Duizend, 1984), we should not wait until the locus of causation has been completely circumscribed before embarking on expanded prevention and rehabilitation programs (Greenwood & Zimring, 1985). The fact that remediation did, under certain circumstances, improve academic achievement and reduce delinquency implies that performance-based educational programs, which use direct instruction techniques, would help increase the educational achievement and decrease the delinquency of adolescents handicapped by learning disabilities. Therefore, this model should be integrated into the curricula of public schools, alternative educational programs, training schools, and tutorial projects that service delinquent teenagers with LD. Importantly, special remedial services should also be extended to a larger pool of learning disabled juveniles who are not yet seriously delinquent but who are clearly at risk. In order to carry out this recommendation, a great deal of training and program development must be undertaken. For example, information about LD assessment, curriculum materials, program management, teacher training, and interagency coordination is needed. Obviously, important questions remain concerning possible ways to enhance the effectiveness of remediation.

Compared with other investigations of the link between LD and JD, the LD-JD Project used the largest and most representative study sample, the most comprehensive assessments of learning disabilities and delinquency, the most systematic research design and procedures, and the most sophisticated statistical analyses. Unfortunately, in an era of diminishing resources to support research, it seems unlikely that similar experimental action research, which is difficult and costly to perform (Hackler, 1978; Cook & Campbell, 1979), will be undertaken to replicate or refute the results of the project for quite some time.

REFERENCES

Bader, B. W. (1975). *Social perception and learning disabilities.* Des Moines, IA: Moon Lithographing & Engraving.

Bazemore, G. (1985). Delinquent reform and labeling perspective. *Criminal Justice and Behavior, 12,* 131–169.

Bernstein, S., & Rulo, J. H. (1976). Learning disabilities and learning problems: Their implications for the juvenile justice system. *Juvenile Justice, 27,* 43–47.

Broder, P. K., Dunivant, N., Smith, E. C., & Sutton, L. P. (1981). Further observations on the link between learning disabilities and juvenile delinquency. *Journal of Educational Psychology, 73,* 838–850.

Comptroller General of the United States. (1977). *Learning disabilities: The link should be determined, but schools should do more now.* Washington, DC: General Accounting Office.

Cook, T. D., & Campbell, D. T. (1979). *Quasi-experimentation: Design and anlaysis issues for field settings.* Chicago: Rand McNally.

Cox, J. A. (Ed.). (1981). *The learning disabled delinquent: Issues and programming.* Pensacola, FL: Community Mental Health Center.

Crawford, D. (1978). *ACLD R&D revised workplan.* Phoenix: Association for Children with Learning Disabilities, Research and Development Project.

Dunivant, N. (1982). *The relationship between learning disabilities and juvenile delinquency.* Williamsburg, VA: National Center for State Courts.

Dunivant, N. (1984). *Improving academic skills and preventing delinquency of learning-disabled juvenile delinquents: Evaluation of the ACLD remediation program.* Williamsburg VA: National Center for State Courts.

Elliot, D. S., & Voss, H. L. (1974). *Delinquency and dropout.* Lexington, MA: Lexington Books.

Empey, L. T., & Lubeck, S. G. (1971). *Explaining delinquency: Construction, test, and reformation of sociological theory.* Lexington, MA: Lexington Books.

Glaser, D. (1980). The interplay of theory, issues, policy, and data. In M. W. Klein & K. S. Teilman (Eds.), *Handbook of criminal justice evaluation* (pp. 123–142). Beverly Hills, CA: Sage.

Greenwood, P. W., & Zimring, F. E. (1985). *One more change: The pursuit of promising intervention strategies for chronic juvenile offenders.* Santa Monica, CA: Rand Corporation.

Hackler, J. C. (1978). The dangers of political naïveté and excessive complexity in evaluating delinquency prevention programs. *Evaluation and Program Planning, 1,* 273–278.

Hanushek, E. A., & Jackson, J. E. (1977). *Statistical methods for social scientists.* New York: Academic Press.

Hirshi, T. (1969). *Causes of delinquency.* Berkeley: University of California Press.

Johnson, R. E. (1979). Are adolescent theft, vandalism, and assault due to the same causal processes? *International Journal of Comparative and Applied Criminal Justice, 49*(2), 106–109.

Keilitz, I., & Miller, S. L. (1980). Handicapped adolescents and young adults in the justice system. *Exceptional Education Quarterly, 2,* 117–126.

Keilitz, I., Saks, M. J., & Broder, P. K. (1979). *The evaluation of the learning disabilities/juvenile delinquency remediation program: Evaluation design and interim results.* Williamsburg, VA: National Center for State Courts.

Keilitz, I., & Van Duizend, R. (1984). *Youth and the justice system: Can we intervene earlier?* (Prepared statement presented in a hearing before the Select Committee on Children, Youth, and Families, House of Representatives, 98th Congress, 2d Session). Washington, DC: U.S. Government Printing Office.

Keilitz, I., Zaremba, B. A., & Broder, P. K. (1982). Learning disabilities and juvenile delinquency. In L. D. Savitz & N. Johnston (Eds.), *Contemporary criminology* (pp. 95–104). New York: Wiley.

Leithwood, K. A., & Montgomery, D. J. (1980). Evaluating program implementation. *Evaluation Review, 4,* 193–214.

Lewin, K. (1951). *Field theory in social science.* New York: Harper.

The link . . . undetected learning disabilities and juvenile delinquency. (1985). *Their World,* 52–56. (Available from Foundation for Children with Learning Disabilities, New York).

Mauser, A. J. (1974). Learning disabilities and delinquent youth. *Academic Therapy, 9,* 389–400.

McCullough, B. C., Zaremba, B. A., & Rich, W. D. (1979). The role of the juvenile justice system in the link between learning disabilities and delinquency. *State Court Journal, 3,* 2–47.

Murray, C. A. (1976). *The link between learning disabilities and juvenile delinquency: Current theory and knowledge.* Washington, DC: U.S. Government Printing Office.

Podboy, J. W., & Mallory, W. A. (1978). The diagnosis of specific learning disabilities in a delinquent population. *Federal Probation, 42,* 26–33.

Pointer, W. D., & Kravitz, M. (1981). *The handicapped offender: A selected bibliography.* Washington, DC: U.S. Department of Justice.

Post, C. H. (1981). The link between learning disabilities and juvenile delinquency: Cause, effect and "present solutions." *Juvenile & Family Court Journal, 32,* 58–68.

Ramos, N. P. (Ed.). (1978). *Delinquent youth and learning disabilities.* San Rafael, CA: Academic Therapy.

Reilly, T., & Bullock, L. (1979). Academic and intellectual functioning of adjudicated adolescents: A status report based on randomly selected case studies. *Behavioral Disorders, 4,* 246–250.

Rutherford, R. B., Nelson, C. M., & Wolford, B. I. (1985). Special education in the most restrictive environment: Correctional/special education. *Journal of Special Education, 19,* 59–71.

Sawicki, D., & Schaeffer, B. (1979). An affirmative approach to the LD/JD link. *Juvenile & Family Court Journal, 30,* 11–16.

School Board of Prince William County, Virginia v. Malone, No. 83–862–A (E.D. Va. March 5, 1984), *affirmed,* No. 84–1347 (4th Cir. May 24, 1985).

Smykla, J. O., & Willis, T. W. (1981). The incidence of learning disabilities and mental retardation in youth under the jurisdiction of the juvenile court. *Journal of Criminal Justice, 9,* 219–225.

Swanstrom, W. J., Randle, C. W., & Offord, K. (1981). The frequency of learning disability: A comparison between juvenile delinquent and seventh grade populations. *Journal of Correctional Education, 32,* 29–33.

Unger, K. V. (1978). Learning disabilities and juvenile delinquency. *Journal of Juvenile and Family Courts, 29*(1), 25–30.

Ungerleider, D. F. (1985). *Reading, writing, and rage: The terrible price paid by victims of school failure.* Rolling Hills Estates, CA: Jalmar Press.

Wilson, J. Q., & Herrnstein, R. J. (1985). *Crime and human nature.* New York: Simon & Schuster.

Zimmerman, J., Rich, W. D., Keilitz, I., & Broder, P. K. (1981). Some observations on the link between learning disabilities and juvenile delinquency. *Journal of Criminal Justice, 9,* 1–17.

Susan M. Egan

VIGNETTE   Walter, Hector, Damion, and Thomas

Is special education needed in corrections? What would these students have done without it?

Walter

A pleasant looking 19-year-old white male, Walt was in for rape. Outwardly quite extroverted, Walt concealed many of his worst fears by clowning around and exhibiting other manic behavior. Through his continual barrage of chatter it was only sometimes fleetingly observable that Walt had learning problems.

At age 4 Walt was sexually molested by his maternal grandfather. A stepfather continued this abuse while Walt was between the ages of 8 and 12. As Walt entered adolescence, not surprisingly he was confused about his own sexual identity.

Compounding this confusion was the growing isolation Walt felt as he fell further and further behind his classmates academically. Identified as educationally disadvantaged, Walt was placed in a noncategorical special education class in the sixth grade. Throughout his junior high and high school years he mingled with students who were mildly and moderately retarded as well as those who were seriously emotionally disturbed.

It was not until Walt's arrest, conviction, and commitment to his state's youth authority that all of Walt's secrets became known. The first comprehensive multidisciplinary study was completed, specifically targeting his learning disability as an auditory processing dysfunction. A total treatment program was initiated to help him deal with the abuse he had endured and to understand its negative effects on his own emotional development. This special program offered him the opportunity to put both his sexual and academic fears behind him. Eighteen months of hard work paid off for Walt; he left the youth authority a more mature and confident young man, with his GED certificate proudly in hand.

Hector

Hector was angry. He was usually angry. At 19 he was violence-prone and dangerous. A Mexican national, his dark, acne-scarred countenance was framed with stringy black hair, and a sinister black handlebar mustache draped over his mouth.

Years of incarceration had given Hector an acceptable level of English proficiency, but his violent outbursts and frequent assaults on staff and other students quickly sent him to our program. He was identified as a seriously emotionally disturbed youth, eligible for special education services. Though limited in academic skills, it was obvious that Hector was bright. He was an excellent mimic, and through his quick acquisition of English and the sparkle in his eye when he spoke of his infant daughter, we found a means to work with him. We placed him in a parenting and child development class, and Hector slowly began to emerge. In one emotional session about child abuse, he ran from the classroom in tears. Sobbing, he told his counselor of the physical and sexual abuse he had received from his father. It was the first he had ever spoken of these horrors, but he vowed his own children would never be subjected to such cruelty.

In Hector's remaining 2 months with us, he earned a position as a student aide, helping teachers assist students with limited English proficiency.

Smiles became his trademark.

With the continued support of family and friends Hector has managed to stay out of trouble for 2½ years. His goal is to be a working father at home to care for his daughter; perhaps he will attain it.

Damion

Damion was 18 when he entered our school. A tall, broad-shouldered, strong young black man, he consistently slumped and looked only at the floor as he walked and talked. He was moody, sullen, and frequently depressed. He had mood cycles that would leave him virtually catatonic; he would sit in one place and stare undistractedly for hours at a time.

Damion stopped attending school on any regular basis in the sixth grade. By the ninth grade he was known as a troublemaker: he picked fights, stole from other students, and was believed to be responsible for a school break-in resulting in vandalism to a classroom. He managed to parlay the theft of a schoolmate's bicycle into 3 years of incarceration. Though not retarded, Damion's teachers found him "not bright." His vacant expression, when you could get him to look at you, left the impression that little was going on inside him.

By way of the probation department and county detention facilities, Damion eventually arrived at the youth authority. The school records passed along with him described a seriously disturbed youth. He was diagnosed as being seriously depressed and was immediately served by a multidisciplinary team. The psychiatrist, school psychologist, and others set academic goals to coincide with his medication and therapy. Although the prognosis for Damion was not hopeful, the understanding of staff trained in special education techniques has made education possible for Damion. And the treatment staff on his living unit were trained to accept his reticence not as defiance but as part of his illness.

Thomas

Deaf from birth, Thomas, a 17-year-old black male, had been born to a fatherless family that refused to accept his handicap. Surviving on public assistance, his mother used the disability checks she received for his deafness to further her drug habit. Thomas was virtually raised on the streets and received little value from the special school in which he was placed. Erratic attendance, coupled with denial and rejection at home, left him with no method of communication and little socialization.

Small wonder that Thomas fell into the company of street gangs. He became a "somebody," a member of one of the strongest and most violent gangs. He flew his gang colors with pride, and they returned the loyalty, nurturing and protecting him. After his arrest Thomas was sent to a facility for younger boys because of his vulnerability. Through a special education team a staff counselor with signing skills was assigned to him. He was referred to a private school for the communicatively handicapped and was accepted there by the director, who was also severely hearing impaired. In what must have been the most unusual of correctional experiences, security personnel drove him to and from school each day in handcuffs and leg irons. Accompanied and supported by his counselor, he mastered both AmSlang and speech-reading. In 2 years of special education he managed to make more progress than he had made in his previous 12 years of schooling. His reading and math skills and especially his social skills increased significantly.

When he was discharged from parole a year after his release, his schooling stopped. Gang associates learned sign language to communicate with him although his mother continued to refuse to learn. A year and a half later Thomas was again in our waiting room; gang involvement had gotten him committed again. With a big smile of recognition he waved to me. Now 22, though, he is no longer eligible for special education funding. And with departmental resources being scarce, it does not bode well for his future.

The Behaviorally Disordered Offender

CHAPTER 7   *James E. Gilliam and Brenda K. Scott*

The students who are the subject of this chapter are given many labels. *Emotionally disturbed* (ED), *seriously emotionally disturbed* (SED), *emotionally handicapped* (EH), and *behaviorally disordered* (BD) are only a few examples. Professionals working in the area of corrections believe that many of their students are behaviorally disordered, and many special educators teaching the behaviorally disordered are concerned that many of their students engage in delinquent behavior and are potential candidates for incarceration. Although a number of students in correctional educational programs are described as emotionally disturbed or behaviorally disordered, relatively few correctional educators are aware of the accompanying characteristics and learning needs.

Knowledge about ED/BD offenders is limited for several reasons. The terms used, *emotional disturbance* and *behavioral disorders,* come from the fields of mental health and public school education. These terms have not been widely used in correctional systems. The mental health system relies on terms and nomenclature derived from psychiatric classification systems, principally the *Diagnostic and Statistical Manual* (DSM-III) (American Psychiatric Association, 1980). The terms used in education are promoted by state and federal regulations that define this subpopulation as handicapped. Criminal justice and corrections systems classify offenders according to age and the type of offense committed, as defined in the penal codes. The variety of terms used for various classification purposes has contributed to the paucity of information that is useful to correctional educators in describing the characteristics of ED/BD offenders, their incidence and prevalence rates, and recommended approaches to their education.

Just as the mental health, educational, and correctional systems have been separated, so, too, have their respective professional journals. There is little information about juvenile offenders in the special education literature and little about ED/BD students in the criminal justice literature. Recognizing that this separation has gone on too long, professionals in behavior disorders and correctional education are now starting to contribute to each other's professional literature, most notably in *Behavioral Disorders* and the *Journal of Correctional Education*. The publication of this text is another indication of the emerging interest within both fields to share information and strategies.

This chapter is designed to provide information about ED/BD students in correctional education programs. The limitations of space preclude a detailed discussion of all the topics that deserve attention. Our goal is to provide correctional educators with information to help them better understand and effectively teach ED/BD students in their programs. We address here the identification of this population, delineation of its characteristics, and the prevalence and assessment of behavior disorders in correctional programs. The chapter concludes with the description of a study conducted by the authors that involved juvenile offenders displaying emotional or behavioral difficulties.

Prior to discussion we want to clarify our use of the terms *emotionally disturbed* and *behaviorally disordered*. It is our contention that these two terms are equivalent and synonymous. Historically, the term *emotionally disturbed* has been used more frequently, but there is a growing trend to use the term *behaviorally disordered* to describe this population. We prefer the latter term and will use it to describe the students discussed here, except when citing specific information in which the term *emotionally disturbed* is used. Also, the terms *children, adolescents*, and *youth* will be used as they appear in the literature; however, the preferred term is *student*.

IDENTIFICATION OF THE BEHAVIORALLY DISORDERED

The behaviorally disordered are a unique subpopulation of handicapped students whose handicaps are not easy to define but profoundly affect everyone. These students are frequently described as withdrawn, depressed, isolative, in their own world, out of touch with reality, anxiety-ridden, oppositional, impulsive, asocial, antisocial, acting out. They are given many labels—for example, schizoid, overanxious, immature, conduct disordered, socialized aggressive. They often have academic difficulties, achieve below their potential, and are behind their peers in most subject areas.

The behavior problems of these students are a constant concern to their teachers, parents, and peers. They frequently experience difficulty both in and out of school, causing people to react negatively toward them or to avoid them as much as possible. Frequently they come into contact with authorities in the fields of education, mental health, or criminal justice (sometimes all three), usually resulting in the assignment of a diagnostic label and placement for treatment of their behavioral problems. The problems exhibited by behaviorally disordered students are complex and multifaceted. Paul (1982) points out that these students do not have a single, simple condition but manifest various problems of inappropriate behavior, faulty thinking, excessive variations in mood, depressed intellectual functioning, symptoms of physical illness, developmental lags in social and emotional maturity, and/or underachievement.

The determination of which students are behaviorally disordered is a source of considerable disagreement among diagnostic personnel. Differences in personal concepts of deviance, the terminology used, and the purpose for making a diagnosis are variables that affect who is identified as behaviorally disordered. Authorities are in general agreement, however, on three fundamental factors that should be considered: (1) the perceived departure of the behavior from acceptable standards; (2) the degree of that deviation; and (3) the length of time the behavior has continued. Coleman (1986) identifies the three factors as chronicity, frequency, and severity. Algozzine (1980) cautions, however, that it is not simply the level and type of behavior that the student exhibits that causes him or her to be viewed as disturbed but also the fact that certain characteristics are disturbing to others. Quay (1979) notes that the behavior problems of students labeled behaviorally disordered differ in quantity but not in quality from those who are not labeled. The difference, then, is in the degree of the behavioral excess or deficit. The question of how much or how little behavior is enough to be considered disturbed or disordered has never been satisfactorily answered. In the final analysis there is no single test or absolute criterion for determining what a behavior disorder really is.

CHARACTERISTICS OF BEHAVIORAL DISORDERS

Even though disagreement exists as to who is behaviorally disordered, there are certain behavior characteristics repeatedly noted in studies describing this population. Quay (1979) states, "There is now overwhelming evidence that the application of multivariate statistical techniques has demonstrated that, excluding psychosis, the vast majority of deviant behaviors of children and adolescents can be subsumed under four major patterns: conduct disorder, anxiety-withdrawal, immaturity, and socialized aggression" (p. 36). Students described as conduct disordered are aggressive, noncompliant, quarrelsome, interpersonally alienated, and they act out against adults and peers. Anxiety-withdrawal is a pattern of behavior characterized by anxiety, depression, fear of failure, social inferiority, and self-concern reflecting subjective distress and what Quay (1979) describes as "neuroticism." Immaturity reflects problems in concentration, perseverance, impulsivity, and following directions and leads to a deficient ability to come to grips with the demands of home and school. Socialized aggression represents a dimension of acting out and aggression, but these students do establish and maintain relationships with others. Their aggression is usually focused on rejection of authority and the norms of the larger society. This group is often described as socialized delinquents. The behavioral characteristics frequently observed in each of the four patterns are listed in Table 7.1.

A student evaluated in a mental health agency and diagnosed as behaviorally disordered will probably be assigned a diagnostic label listed in the American Psychiatric Association's *Diagnostic and Statistical Manual of Mental Disorders* (DSM-III) (1980). The DSM-III is the standard diagnostic manual for the majority of mental health agencies and is used by some professionals in the correctional and public school educational systems. The DSM-III suggests that disorders of childhood and adolescence can be grouped under five major headings: intellectual, behavioral, emotional, physical, and developmental. Listed in Table 7.2 are these five headings and some examples of specific disorders under each heading.

The DSM-III manual provides information about each disorder's essential features, associated features, age of onset, sex ratio, prevalence, usual course, familial pattern, impairment, complications, predisposing factors,

Table 7.1   Patterns of Deviant Behavior of Children and Adolescents

Conduct Disorder
Fighting, hitting, assaultive
Temper tantrums
Disobedient, defiant
Destructiveness
Impertinent, impudent
Uncooperative, resistive
Disruptive, interrupting
Negative, noncompliant
Restless, hyperactive
Boisterous, noisy, "showing off"
Bullies, threatens, dominates
Untrustworthy, dishonest, lying
Profanity, abusive language
Quarrels, argues, teases
Irresponsible, undependable

Anxiety-Withdrawal
Anxious, fearful, tense
Shy, timid, bashful
Withdrawn, seclusive, friendless
Depressed, sad, disturbed
Hypersensitive, easily hurt
Self-conscious, easily embarrassed
Feels inferior or worthless
Lacks self-confidence
Easily flustered
Aloof
Cries frequently
Reticent, secretive

Immaturity
Short attention span, poor concentration
Daydreaming
Clumsiness, poor coordination
Preoccupied, staring into space, absentminded
Passive, lacking initiative, easily led
Sluggish, drowsy, inattentive
Lacking interest, bored
Lacks perseverance, fails to finish things
Messy, sloppy

Socialized Aggression
Has "bad" companions
Steals in company of others
Loyal to delinquent friends
Belongs to a gang
Stays out late at night
Truant from school
Truant from home

Source: Based on "Classification" by H. C. Quay in *Psychopathological Disorders of Childhood* (2nd ed., pp. 17–21), by H. C. Quay and J. S. Werry (Eds.), 1979. New York: Wiley.

Disorders of Childhood and Adolescence   Table 7.2

Intellectual	Physical
Mental retardation	Eating disorders
Behavioral	Anorexia nervosa
Attention deficit disorder	Bulimia
With hyperactivity	Pica
Without hyperactivity	Rumination disorder of infancy
Residual type	Atypical eating disorder
Conduct disorder	Stereotyped movement disorders
Undersocialized aggressive	Transient tic disorder
Undersocialized nonaggressive	Chronic motor tic disorder
Socialized aggressive	Tourette's disorder
Socialized nonaggressive	Atypical stereotyped movement disorder
Atypical	Other disorders with physical manifestations
Emotional	Stuttering
Anxiety disorders of childhood or adolescence	Functional enuresis
Separation anxiety disorder	Functional encopresis
Avoidance disorder of childhood or	Sleepwalking disorder
adolescence	Sleep terror disorder
Overanxious disorder	**Developmental**
Other disorders of infancy, childhood, or	Pervasive developmental disorders
adolescence	Infantile autism
Reactive attachment disorder of infancy	Childhood onset pervasive developmental
Schizoid disorder of childhood or adolescence	disorder
Elective mutism	Atypical
Oppositional disorder	Specific developmental disorders
Identity disorder	Developmental reading disorder
	Developmental arithmetic disorder
	Developmental language disorder
	Developmental articulation disorder
	Mixed specific developmental disorder
	Atypical specific developmental disorder

Source: From *Diagnostic and Statistical Manual of Mental Disorders* (3rd ed., p. 15) by the American Psychiatric Association, 1980, Washington, DC: American Psychiatric Association.

and criteria for diagnosis. DSM-III has been criticized because the disorders are not defined well enough to be verified by direct observation and measurement (Apter & Conoley, 1984), and it provides little in the way of recommendations for educational services or interventions (Coleman, 1986). Nevertheless, DSM-III will likely continue to be the source of diagnostic labels assigned to offenders with behavioral disorders. Therefore, correctional educators and others need to be aware of these labels and have some understanding of what they mean in terms of student behavior.

Labeling and Defining the Behaviorally Disordered

As stated earlier, students with behavior disorders are given many labels and descriptors. The term *emotional disturbance* has been the most frequently used descriptor (Wood & Lakin, 1979). According to Coleman (1986), "Since its appearance more than 50 years ago, *emotional disturbance* has been an umbrella term used for such varied conditions as schizophrenia, autism, psychosomatic disorders, phobias, withdrawal, depression, anxiety, elective mutism, aggression, and a host of other pathologies" (p. 2). Although this label has gained widespread usage, it is by no means universally accepted and is currently being criticized by professionals (Grosenick & Huntze, 1979; Huntze, 1985).

Numerous definitions of emotional disturbance/behavioral disorders have been proposed, but no single definition has been found to be adequate. To illustrate the scope of the problem, a sampling of definitions is presented here.

> Children with behavior disorders are those who chronically and markedly respond to their environment in socially unacceptable and/or personally unsatisfying ways but who can be taught more socially acceptable and personally gratifying behavior. (Kauffman, 1977, p. 23)

> Behavior disorders of a pupil are behavior characteristics that (1) deviate from educators' standards of normality and (2) impair the functioning of that pupil and/or others. These behavior characteristics are manifested as environmental conflicts and/or personal disturbances, and are typically accompanied by learning disorders. (Cullinan, Epstein, & Lloyd, 1983, p. 149)

> Psychological disorder is said to be present when a child emits behavior that deviates from an arbitrary and relative social norm in that it occurs with a frequency or intensity that authoritative adults in the child's environment judge, under the circumstances, to be either too high or too low. (Ross, 1980, p. 9)

Although having validity and serving the particular purposes of individual authors, none of these definitions have found widespread acceptance in the field. The definition used in Public Law 94–142 is the only definition that has attained national acceptance and has had significant impact on public policy (Kauffman, 1985). Its impact can be seen in the fact that it has been adopted in some form by the majority of state departments of education.

> Seriously emotionally disturbed is defined as follows:
> (i) The term means a condition exhibiting one or more of the following characteristics over a long period of time and to a marked degree, which adversely affects educational performance:
>   (a) An inability to learn which cannot be explained by intellectual, sensory, or health factors;
>   (b) An inability to build or maintain satisfactory relationships with peers and teachers;
>   (c) Inappropriate types of behavior or feelings under normal circumstances;
>   (d) A general pervasive mood of unhappiness or depression; or

(e) A tendency to develop physical symptoms or fears associated with personal or school problems.

(ii) The term includes children who are schizophrenic. The term does not include children who are socially maladjusted, unless it is determined that they are seriously emotionally disturbed. (*Federal Register*, 1977)

This definition is essentially derived from one constructed by Bower (1969), which describes characteristics of disturbed behavior that are observable in school and other settings and requires that these behaviors be exhibited over a long period of time and to a marked degree. Emphasis is placed on educational performance and problems in learning due to these behavioral and/or emotional characteristics. According to Bower (1982) problems in learning and educational performance are perhaps the most significant aspects of the emotionally disturbed student's handicap.

Problems with the PL 94–142 Definition

Even though there is much to recommend it, this definition has been frequently criticized. Kauffman (1985) points out that it does not easily enable one to determine whether a particular child is or is not emotionally handicapped because of the latitude in interpretation of the phrases "to a marked extent" and "over a long period of time." Kauffman also criticizes the definition because the addendum (ii) specifically cites schizophrenia as being included in the definition when any psychosis would clearly qualify under the five characteristics. Exclusion of the socially maladjusted is also illogical, according to Kauffman, because the behavior of these students would fit within one or more of the characteristics to a marked degree and over a long period of time. Kauffman concludes that the definition lacks the precision necessary to take much of the subjectivity out of the decision making. But he adds, "In the final analysis, the definition of behavior *disorder* or emotional *disturbance* is unavoidably a subjective matter" (p. 16).

Grosenick and Huntze (1980) have focused on the term *seriously emotionally disturbed* as one of the major shortcomings of the PL 94–142 definition. They attack the definition on the basis that the label seems to focus on psychiatrically defined disturbances, which represent only a small percentage of school behavior problems. Also, the label may be stigmatizing because of the negative implications of blame and guilt for parents. In addition, because the definition uses the qualifier *seriously*, it seems unclear whether the definition applies only to the most severe range of emotional disturbances or is meant to cover the full spectrum of behavioral disorders. Grosenick and Huntze note that the term *seriously* is not used to define any other handicapping conditions. Important to correctional educators is the fact that the distinction between emotional disturbance and social maladjustment demanded by the definition is difficult to determine. Given what we know about the socially maladjusted, most socially maladjusted students would seem to meet one or more of the criteria of the behaviorally disordered.

Grosenick and Huntze propose that the term *seriously emotionally disturbed* be changed to *behavior disorders* in the PL 94–142 definition, but at present the definition has not been revised.

The Socially Maladjusted

Juvenile offenders are frequently referred to as socially maladjusted. In the minds of many people social maladjustment and juvenile delinquency are synonymous terms.

Who Are the Socially Maladjusted?   This question cannot be answered directly because little information is available describing this condition. As Neel and Rutherford (1981) state, "Although frequently used to describe children whose behavior is considered socially inappropriate, *social maladjustment* has seldom been defined" (p.79). They indicate that the term is used to identify students whose antisocial and frequently illegal behavior conforms to the norms of their deviant cultural or peer group. Although the socially maladjusted are often referred to as disobedient, disruptive, defiant, and incorrigible, little information is available to differentiate this group of students from other behaviorally disordered students.

Historically, an informal and erroneous assumption has developed that equates social maladjustment and juvenile delinquency. Delinquency, however, is a legal term designating children who have been adjudicated for violating laws, and not all socially maladjusted youth are adjudicated delinquent. As public school educators and juvenile justice system professionals readily attest, many socially maladjusted students repeatedly violate societal standards and laws but are not adjudicated. Thus, adjudication is not a sufficient criterion for labeling someone socially maladjusted. A major question remains as to whether the socially maladjusted can be accurately distinguished from the behaviorally disordered; perhaps a more important question is whether such a distinction should be attempted.

How Are the Socially Maladjusted Defined?   Defining social maladjustment is fraught with the same difficulties encountered in defining emotional disturbance or behavioral disorders. The issue frequently is debated on the basis of personal opinion, but little data and few generally accepted parameters exist to guide assessment or classification systems. The following are just two examples of the many definitions of social maladjustment.

> Social maladjustment refers to children who are antisocial—children who *could* but *will not* conform to the expectation of society. (Apter & Conoley, 1984, p. 15)

> Social maladjustment may be described as behavior that violates laws or unwritten standards of the school or community, yet conforms to the standards of some social subgroup. Common patterns of social maladjustment include vandalism, stealing, fighting, truancy, substance abuse, sexual precocity, bullying and threatening, and other antisocial acts that occur in the context of or at least are generally supported and

encouraged by adolescent peers. (Cullinan, Epstein, & Lloyd, 1983, p. 140)

The problem that results from excluding social maladjustment from the definition of emotional disturbance was noted earlier. This exclusion is particularly significant to the juvenile justice system and to correctional education programs because most of the students served are considered to be socially maladjusted; they have been adjudicated for committing some type of criminal offense. There seems to be no support for this exclusion on the grounds of logic, semantics, or need. And there is no clear-cut evidence in the field that distinguishes between behaviorally disordered and socially maladjusted youths.

Beyond the characteristics presented earlier, what is known about the socially maladjusted population? Socially maladjusted students demonstrate many behaviors that are considered characteristic of the behaviorally disordered—for example, learning problems, difficulties establishing and maintaining interpersonal relationships, and inappropriate behaviors (Kauffman, 1985; Quay, 1979). There is little information in the literature addressing differentiation between the behaviorally disordered and the socially maladjusted. It has been suggested that the socially maladjusted can be identified by lower anxiety levels, lack of concern about the negative consequences of their behavior, and locus of control (Smith, 1979). Even though these claims have been accepted by many as valid, there is no compelling body of research to support them. Most socially maladjusted students meet one or more of the criteria underlying the label *seriously emotionally disturbed*, and it seems illogical to exclude this group from the behaviorally disordered.

PREVALENCE OF BEHAVIORALLY DISORDERED JUVENILE OFFENDERS

How many students in correctional education programs are diagnosed as behaviorally disordered or emotionally disturbed? No one knows. Few comprehensive surveys have been conducted on a national scale, and those that have been completed have been criticized for biases that make the results suspect. In one national survey Morgan (1978) sent questionnaires to state juvenile correctional administrators in the 50 states and 5 U.S. territories. He reported that emotional disturbance is the most prevalent handicap among residents of juvenile correctional institutions, affecting 16.2% of the population. Eggleston (1984) also conducted a survey of correctional education systems across the United States. In response to questions regarding the percentage of identified handicapped students, the results indicated that in the systems surveyed 35.5% of the students were identified as emotionally disturbed. In a national needs analysis of behavior disorders, Grosenick and Huntze (1980) reported that the youth services personnel they interviewed estimated that 10% to 50% of adjudicated youth had been labeled handicapped prior to their commitment, and of this group it was estimated that one-half had been labeled as behaviorally disordered. The remainder were usually labeled mentally retarded or learning disabled. Even though Grosenick and Huntze's findings are only estimates, they support the general conclusion that a sizable number of behaviorally disordered students are in correctional facilities.

Why is there a lack of prevalence data for behaviorally disordered juvenile offenders? A large proportion of disturbed juvenile offenders are not identified because comprehensive psychological and psychiatric evaluations are conducted only on a limited basis. Generally, such evaluations are conducted only when parents, probation officers, or correctional facility personnel request them, and the results of these evaluations are not included in correctional agencies' annual reports. In general, most correctional agencies are concerned with statistics related to juvenile referrals, criminal offenses, and detention. The data collected regarding student characteristics are usually demographic in nature or relate more to educational achievement.

Nelson, Rutherford, and Wolford (1985) point out that large variations exist across states with regard to the estimated percentage of handicapped juvenile offenders (ranging from 4% to 99%). They suggest that possible litigation against those states not providing education to handicapped incarcerated persons may have encouraged underestimation of the number of handicapped offenders.

Following federal regulations and recent court decisions, juvenile correctional systems are being required to increase their efforts to identify and serve handicapped youthful offenders in their facilities (Warboys & Shauffer, 1986). The result should be an increase in the identification of all handicapped students, particularly the emotionally disturbed or behaviorally disordered offender.

ASSESSMENT

The education and treatment of juvenile offenders depend heavily on the results of the assessment process. Diagnostic personnel play a pivotal role in determining what will happen to a student committed to a correctional facility. The results of psychological and educational evaluations are critical in identifying students in need of special education services. A number of problems currently exist in the assessment process, including the selection and use of assessment instruments, the qualifications and skills of assessment personnel, and the diagnostic labels assigned.

For most youthful offenders the assessment process begins along with their incarceration. In most states the juvenile correctional system has a diagnostic reception center, where offenders are placed for a given amount of time (usually 2 to 4 weeks but sometimes longer) for purposes of determining their individual physical, mental, educational, and behavioral status, which ultimately leads to program placement. While in the reception center, offenders are evaluated by assessment personnel and are given various tests. A common test battery consists of an achievement test, an individual intelligence test, and a test of personality. The Wide Range Achievement Test is the most commonly administered achievement test, but additional norm-referenced achievement tests such as the Metropolitan Achievement Test or the Iowa Test of Basic Skills may also be used. Frequently administered intelligence tests include the Wechsler Intelligence Scales for Children—Revised (WISC-R) and the Wechsler Adult Intelligence Scales—Revised (WAIS-R). Personality tests vary according to the preferences of the examiner, but the Rorschach test, the Minnesota Multiphasic Personality Inventory (MMPI), and/or a projective drawing test are frequently used. Vocational aptitude and interest tests may also be given. The intent is to provide placement information concerning the facility and/or educational program best suited for the student.

In most correctional facilities the diagnosis of emotional disturbance is also based on the results of the test batteries just listed, resulting in a variety of problems. Achievement and intelligence tests are not designed or normed for personality assessment or identification of emotional disturbance/behavioral disorders. And personality tests have been criticized for their poor reliability and questionable validity. Direct, systematic observation of behavior under varying conditions is seldom done. Therefore, most diagnostic decisions are based on clinical judgments. However, because assessment personnel vary in their level of training, licensure, and diagnostic expertise, their clinical judgments vary also, resulting in a variety of diagnostic problems. For example, educational diagnosticians and associate psychologists, with proper training, are qualified to administer and score the tests previously mentioned but generally are unqualified to diagnose emotional disturbance. They must report their findings to a licensed psychologist, who confers the diagnosis, often without having seen the student. Thus, unqualified clinical opinions are used by a qualified professional to render a critical diagnostic decision.

Another problem related to the assessment process concerns the labels used for classifying the type of emotional disturbance. Some DSM-III diagnoses, such as attention deficit disorders and conduct disorders, are listed as a type of emotional disorder but do not result in a student's being certified as eligible for special education as a handicapped student. These disorders are not viewed as "seriously" emotionally disturbed. The result is that many students who demonstrate significant adjustment and behavioral problems are excluded from special education services.

Once placed in a correctional educational program, a student is unlikely to be referred by educational personnel for comprehensive assessment to determine whether a handicap exists. The reasons for this are many. Correctional educators often see little difference in the behavior of students labeled emotionally disturbed or behaviorally disordered and the behavior of their unlabeled students. And because most correctional education programs do not have segregated special education programs, both labeled and unlabeled students will, in all probability, continue to be in one classroom anyway. In addition, the paperwork involved in the formulation of an IEP is viewed as tedious and is not required if the student is not in special education. Thus, correctional educators are reluctant to refer students for special education assessment.

Nonetheless, the assessment process is critical in the identification of emotionally disturbed/behaviorally disordered students. The problems noted here deserve attention to ensure that all students in correctional education programs receive appropriate services that will enhance their education and ultimately their postcorrectional life.

THE RELATIONSHIP OF BEHAVIOR DISORDERS TO JUVENILE DELINQUENCY

For many reasons the relationship between behavior disorders and juvenile delinquency has never been satisfactorily described. First of all, the incidence of behavior disorders in youth has not been determined with any acceptable level of accuracy. And although statistics are available to describe the incidence of adjudicated juvenile delinquents, a substantial number of juveniles commit offenses that are not detected and are therefore not included in the statistics regarding juvenile offenders. Furthermore, because of the differences in the services provided by the educational, mental health, and correctional systems, no uniform classification system has been used to identify and record the common characteristics of the students served by these systems. Additionally, if a student is clearly identified in a correctional facility as behaviorally disordered, he or she will often be transferred to the state mental health system for care and treatment. Thus, limited information is available to describe the characteristics of the behaviorally disordered served in correctional facilities. This is a curious but interesting fact because data are available to describe the incidence and characteristics of learning disabled and mentally retarded offenders (e.g., Dunivant, 1981; Santamour & Watson, 1982).

A Descriptive Study of Incarcerated Juvenile Offenders

To provide some descriptive information about the characteristics of behaviorally disordered juvenile offenders, the authors collected data on the behavioral problems and social skills of a sample of 82 juvenile offenders in two correctional institutions. Sixty of the students were diagnosed as emotionally disturbed by correctional psychologists; the other 22 students were not known to be emotionally disturbed but were described by their teachers as demonstrating behavioral problems. The students' scores on Quay and Peterson's Revised Behavior Problem Checklist (RBPC) (1983) and The Teacher Skill Checklist (TSC) (McGinnis, Goldstein, Sprafkin, & Gershaw, 1984) were analyzed to determine whether there were any significant differences between these groups. Records were available describing the characteristics of the emotionally disturbed sample but were unavailable for the behavioral problem (BP) group; only their similarity in age and IQ scores were recorded. Table 7.3 provides descriptive information about the emotionally disturbed sample.

Particularly interesting in these data is the significant difference in intelligence quotients between the males and females. There is no explanation for this difference, and interviews with staff from the correctional educational program involved confirmed the accuracy of the scores. Furthermore, the staff members reported that females admitted to that correctional facility usually score lower on intelligence tests, and their performance in the school program is commensurate with their intellectual ability. Even though the number of females in the sample is small, this finding raises some interesting questions. Do incarcerated females in other correctional facilities also score lower than males on intelligence tests? If so, why? Is the determining factor in this case the fact that these females have been diagnosed emotionally disturbed? Do incarcerated emotionally disturbed females in other correctional facilities score lower on intelligence tests than their male counterparts? More research is clearly needed about the characteristics of incarcerated offenders.

Table 7.4 provides information about the DSM-III diagnostic classifications of this same group of emotionally disturbed students. As might be expected, the largest diagnostic group was classified as conduct disordered.

Characteristics and Offenses of a Sample of Incarcerated Emotionally Disturbed Juvenile Offenders (N = 60) — Table 7.3

Age (Year-Month)	Sex	Ethnicity	
Mean = 14-3 Range = 11-0 to 17-0	Males = 42 (70%) Females = 18 (30%)	Anglo = 43 (72%) Black = 9 (15%) Hispanic = 8 (13%)	
Mean IQ Scores	Males	Females	Total Sample
Verbal	112	84	102
Performance	124	94	114
Full scale	113	88	105
Offenses	Males	Females	Total Sample
Runaway/truancy	6	10	16
Involuntary manslaughter	1	0	1
Theft	1	1	2
Auto theft	4	1	5
Burglary	11	4	15
Prostitution	0	1	1
Criminal mischief	1	1	2
Sexual abuse of child	3	0	3
Unclassified	15	0	15

Table 7.4   **DSM-III Classifications of a Sample of Incarcerated Emotionally Disturbed Juvenile Offenders**

Classification	Males	Females	Total Sample
Major depression	2	1	3
General anxiety disorder	1	0	1
Dysthymic disorder	1	0	1
Borderline personality	3	2	5
Posttraumatic stress	1	0	1
Adjustment disorder	1	1	2
Conduct disorders			
Undersocialized aggressive	6	1	7
Socialized aggressive		1	1
Undersocialized nonaggressive	2	4	6
Socialized nonaggressive	4	4	8
Overanxious disorder	1	0	1
Oppositional disorder	1	0	1
Identity disorder	1	0	1
Mixed specific developmental disorder	2	2	4
Two or more classifications			7

That classification included students who repeatedly and persistently broke rules and violated societal standards. Undersocialized conduct disorders was the classification applied to youths who had not developed any meaningful, caring interpersonal relationships with others, whereas youths with socialized conduct disorders had developed meaningful relationships with at least a few persons, usually peers.

The students' teachers rated each student on the Revised Behavior Problem Checklist (RBPC) and the Teacher Skill Checklist (TSC). The RBPC is comprised of 89 items describing various behavior problems and is based on a number of factor analytic studies on the deviant behavior of children and adolescents. The original Behavior Problem Checklist, on which the revised version is based, has been widely used for a variety of purposes, including a screen for behavior disorders in schools, an aid in clinical diagnosis, and part of a battery of instruments for the classification of juvenile offenders (Quay & Peterson, 1983). The RBPC uses weighted scoring with 0 as the rating for no problem, 1 for a mild problem, and 2 for a severe problem. Scoring results in four major scale scores: conduct disorder, socialized aggression, attention problems—immaturity, and anxiety—withdrawal. There are also two minor scale scores: psychotic behavior and motor tension—excess. Table 7.5 presents the results of assessing the sample of emotionally disturbed offenders and the sample of juvenile offenders with behavioral problems, using the RBPC.

Revised Behavior Problem Checklist Scores for a Sample of Incarcerated Emotionally Disturbed Juvenile Offenders and a Behavior Problem Sample

Table 7.5

Subscales (Number of Items)	Emotionally Disturbed Sample ($N = 60$)		Behavior Problem Sample ($N = 22$)	
	Mean	Standard Deviation	Mean	Standard Deviation
Conduct disorder (22)	18.85	12.38	28.95**	7.21
Socialized aggression (17)	33.75**	31.41	11.77	14.29
Attention problems—immaturity (16)	7.42	5.20	9.82*	2.56
Anxiety—withdrawal (11)	9.20	5.83	10.05	4.11
Total score (89)	90.87	42.44	89.77	28.71

* $p > .05$.
** $p > .01$.

The Teacher Skill Checklist, a component of the *Skillstreaming the Elementary School Child* (McGinnis, Goldstein, Sprafkin, & Gershaw, 1984) curriculum, is comprised of 60 items describing social skills that students may be more or less proficient in using. The teacher rates the student on a Likert-type scale, ranging from 1 (almost never) to 5 (almost always), depending on the student's proficiency in using the social skills. The checklist items are grouped according to the following skills: classroom survival skills (13 items); friendship-making skills (12 items); skills for dealing with feelings (10 items); skill alternatives to aggression (9 items); and skills for dealing with stress (16 items). Table 7.6 presents the results of assessing both samples using the TSC.

The results of both checklists suggest that only minimal differences exist between these two groups of students in terms of behavior problems and social skills. The significant difference on the conduct disorder scale indicates that the behavior problem group may be more interpersonally alienated than the emotionally disturbed group. The significant difference on the socialized aggression scale indicates that the emotionally disturbed sample differs from the behavior problem sample in displaying more acting-out, externalized behavior. This scale represents a dimension in which an individual has developed interpersonal bonds with others, and the finding is supported by the significant difference found in the friendship-making skills of the emotionally disturbed students on the TSC. Significant differences were also observed between the two groups on the attention problems—immaturity subscale of the RBPC, with the behavior problem group displaying greater difficulty than the emotionally disturbed group. This scale reflects problems in concentration, perseverance, impulsivity, and following directions, which may explain why teachers identify these students as demonstrating serious

Table 7.6   **Teacher Skill Checklist Scores for a Sample of Incarcerated Emotionally Disturbed Juvenile Offenders and a Behavior Problem Sample**

Skill Grouping (Number of Items)	Emotionally Disturbed Sample ($N = 60$)		Behavior Problem Sample ($N = 22$)	
	Mean	Standard Deviation	Mean	Standard Deviation
Classroom survival skills (11)	37.25	9.08	35.00	8.17
Friendship-making skills (12)	34.68*	7.11	28.00	8.46
Skills for dealing with feelings (10)	25.03	7.15	22.23	6.03
Skill alternatives to aggression (9)	21.05	7.09	18.95	6.37
Skills for dealing with stress (16)	38.95	11.97	36.27	11.78
Total score (60)	156.97	37.40	140.45	33.92

*$p. > .01$.

behavior problems. With the exception of friendship-making skills, there is little difference between the social skills of the emotionally disturbed sample and the behavior problem sample, as measured by the TSC. Because there are no norms for comparison, no conclusions can be drawn as to how these correctional education students differ from their nonincarcerated peers.

Although this analysis is only descriptive and is limited by the small number of behavior problem students and the lack of information about this group, it does provide some information about the behavioral problems and social skills of juvenile offenders known to be emotionally disturbed and those described as behaviorally problematic. The results suggest that both groups of students sampled in these correctional facilities demonstrated behaviors serious enough to be considered emotionally disturbed. It is interesting to note that the behavior problems of the undiagnosed group were rated significantly more serious in two of Quay's classification categories than those of the offenders diagnosed as emotionally disturbed. The reasons for this are unclear. The study suggests that few reliable differences exist between these groups. The differences that did appear do not support the assumption that socially maladjusted youths (i.e., the behavior problem sample) are more socialized, less neurotic, or more socially skilled. If there truly are differences between the socially maladjusted and the emotionally disturbed, more studies of this type are needed to discover their nature.

CONCLUSION

Traditional interventions have been unsuccessful in producing lasting change in the behavior patterns of delinquent youths. For this reason we need to consider alternative approaches that address deficiencies not only in the students, but also in their families and schools. Such interventions must be implemented early, before patterns of deviant behavior are firmly ingrained.

Behaviorally disordered offenders present unique problems and challenges to special educators and correctional educators. Existing problems were noted here regarding definitions and terms, identification criteria and procedures, and lack of information describing these students. These problems were discussed in the hope that professionals from special and correctional education will focus their attention on these problems and begin to share information and resources. By combining our efforts, we can meet the challenge of providing these students with an appropriate and beneficial education.

REFERENCES

Algozzine, B. (1980). The disturbing child: A matter of opinion. *Behavioral Disorders, 5,* 112–115.

American Psychiatric Asociation. (1980). *Diagnostic and statistical manual of mental disorders (3rd ed.).* Washington, DC: Author.

Apter, S. J., & Conoley, J. C. (1984). *Childhood behavior disorders and emotional disturbance.* Englewood Cliffs, NJ: Prentice-Hall.

Bower, E. M. (1969). *Early identification of emotionally handicapped children in school (2nd ed.).* Springfield, IL: Thomas.

Bower, E. M. (1982). Defining emotional disturbance: Public policy and research. *Psychology in the Schools, 19,* 55–60.

Coleman, M. C. (1986). *Behavior disorders: Theory and practice.* Englewood Cliffs, NJ: Prentice-Hall.

Cullinan, D. C., Epstein, M. H., & Lloyd, J. W. (1983). *Behavior disorders of children and adolescents.* Englewood Cliffs, NJ: Prentice-Hall.

Dunivant, N. (1982). *Causal analysis of the relationship between learning disabilities and juvenile delinquency.* Williamsburg, VA: National Center for State Courts.

Eggleston, C. R. (1984). *Results of a national correctional/special education survey.* Paper presented at the Correctional/Special Education National Conference, Arlington, VA.

Federal Register, vol.42, p.42,478. (1977). Amended in *Federal Register,* vol 46, p.3,866. (1981).

Grosenick, J. K., & Huntze, S. L. (1980). *National needs analysis in behavior disorders: Adolescent behavior disorders.* Columbia: University of Missouri Department of Special Education.

Huntze, S. L. (1985). A position paper of the Council for Children with Behavioral Disorders. *Behavioral Disorders, 10,* 167–174.

Kauffman, J. M. (1977). *Characteristics of children's behavior disorders.* Columbus, OH: Merrill.

Kauffman, J. M. (1985). *Characteristics of children's behavior disorders* (3rd ed.). Columbus, OH: Merrill.

McGinnis, E., Goldstein, A. P., Sprafkin, R. P., & Gershaw, J. (1984). *Skillstreaming the elementary school child: A guide for teaching prosocial skills.* Champaign, IL: Research Press.

Morgan, D. I. (1978). Prevalence and types of handicapping conditions found in juvenile correctional institutions: A national survey. *Journal of Special Education, 13,* 283–295.

Neel, R. S., & Rutherford, R. B. (1981). Exclusion of the socially maladjusted from services under P.L. 94–142. In F. Wood (Ed.), *Perspectives for a new decade: Education's responsibility for seriously disturbed and behaviorally disordered children and youth* (pp. 79–84). Reston, VA: Council for Exceptional Children.

Nelson, C. M., Rutherford, R. B., & Wolford, B. I. (1985). Special education for handicapped offenders. In J. E. Gilliam & B. K. Scott (Eds.), *Topics in emotional disturbance* (pp. 311–316). Austin, TX: Behavior Learning Center.

Paul, J. L. (1982). Emotional disturbance in children. In J. L. Paul & B. C. Epanchin (Eds.), *Emotional disturbance in children* (pp. 4–34). Columbus, OH: Merrill.

Quay, H. C. (1979). Classification. In H. C. Quay & J. S. Werry (Eds.), *Psychopathological disorders of childhood* (2nd ed., pp. 1–42). New York: Wiley.

Quay, H. C., & Peterson, D. R. (1983). *Interim manual for the Revised Behavior Problem Checklist.* Unpublished manuscript.

Ross, A. O. (1980). *Psychological disorders of children: A behavioral approach to theory, research, and therapy* (2nd ed.). New York: McGraw-Hill.

Santamour, M. B., & Watson, P. S. (Eds.). (1982). *The retarded offender*. New York: Praeger.

Sarri, R. C. (1980). Alternative residential programs. In J. B. Jordan, D. A. Sabatino, & R. C. Sarri (Eds.), *Disruptive youth in school* (pp. 183–150). Reston, VA: Council for Exceptional Children.

Warboys, L. M., & Shauffer, C. B. (1986). Legal issues in providing special education services to handicapped inmates. *Remedial and Special Education, 7,* 34–40.

Wood, F. H. (1979). Defining disturbing, disordered or disturbed behavior. In F. H. Wood & K. C. Lakin (Eds.), *Disturbing, disordered or disturbed? Perspectives on the definition of problem behavior in educational settings* (pp. 3–16). Minneapolis: University of Minnesota, Advanced Training Institute.

Bruce I. Wolford

The Whiz

VIGNETTE

The Whiz, as the young man in this story came to be known in the correctional institution where I was working as an educational counselor, gained his prison nickname as a result of his near wizardry in the assembly, disassembly, and repair of electronic equipment. None of the school's audiovisual equipment was left unexamined. Although this self-trained technician could quickly repair nearly any malfunctioning gadget, one was never sure what added component the machine might have gained while upon the Whiz's workbench. During his 18-month stay at a medium security prison he managed to adapt every piece of the school's audio equipment so it could be quickly converted into a speaker for his beloved electric guitar.

The Whiz was clearly an individual with talents and capability for contributing to our society. So why did I meet him in a prison where he was serving a 3- to 10-year sentence for a variety of theft- and drug-related convictions? The Whiz could not make it in a public school; despite his measurable potential he continued to fail. His home and family, though neither affluent nor overly supportive, were not characterized by abuse as is the case for so many institutionalized offenders.

I believe the Whiz could have been classified as behaviorally disordered and/or emotionally disturbed although no formal assessment of such a condition was ever made. He failed in public school, not from a lack of capacity to learn, but rather because of behaviors that were disruptive to the process of learning and the educational system. The Whiz was a youth of excess. His behavior, like his zeal for electronics, was intense, and he exhibited wide swings in mood and behavior.

I recall a story told to me by a co-worker in charge of the prison's recreational services. The Whiz was the leader of an inmate rock group patterned after The Who—a band known as much for its flamboyant stage antics as for its hard-driving music. The Whiz, demonstrating his excessive behaviors, during long rehearsal sessions tutored his band not in playing the songs but in practicing the intricacies of jumping off the stage at the close of their concert.

To match his excesses were deficits in behavior and personal social development. The Whiz had little sense of appropriate social distance and would routinely invade the space of others around him. He had not acquired the skills of social interaction that one would expect of someone his age. He had not been able to learn from appropriate models, or had not been exposed

This vignette has been taken from Wolford, B. I. (1983), "Correctional Education and Special Education—An Emerging Partnership; or 'Born to Lose'." In R. B. Rutherford, Jr. (Ed.), *Severe Behavior Disorders of Children and Youth*, 6, pp. 13–19. Copyright © 1983 by the Council for Children with Behavior Disorders. Reprinted by permission.

to them. He also exhibited many self-abusive behaviors, and his body was marred by cigarette burns, needle tracks, and crudely applied tattoos.

The Whiz did not finish his freshman year of high school. He turned to the streets. He began to experiment with drugs. The idle time, his developing drug addiction, and his circle of acquaintances helped to lead him to crime.

I have stated that the Whiz was poorly served by three very important groups—the public schools, the criminal justice system, and correctional education. The public schools labeled him a failure and helped to develop in him an image of himself as a reject, as someone who did not have a place in "normal" society. So he left school without the skills needed to succeed in life and, more importantly, without a sense of direction or purpose.

The juvenile and adult criminal justice systems—through courts, probation programs, and prisons—continued the lead of the public schools. The Whiz was never diagnosed as having a problem other than his criminal behavior and drug addiction. He was not recognized as having failed in life for a particular reason or set of reasons, but rather as being a criminal who was in need of punishment and correction.

Then came the correctional educational system, which did not consider what had led to the Whiz's failures. The correctional education program felt this youth needed an education and enrolled him in Adult Basic Education and General Equivalency Diploma prep. He also needed a trade, so the system helped to get him into a correspondence electronics program and a vocational training course in office machine repair.

At the school he found a safe harbor from the stormy climate of the prison. In this small and highly structured environment he was accepted and able to function as part of a unit. Although this niche assisted him in mental and physical survival in the prison, it is questionable whether the long-term effects of such an experience were in his best interests.

Never in his progression through public schools, the criminal justice system, or correctional education had the real needs of the youth been identified. No one had really considered what had made it difficult for him to succeed.

The Whiz got his GED, dropped out of vocational school, and finished his correspondence program. Soon thereafter he was released on parole. Because of his obvious talents correctional educators helped him line up a job interview with an electronics firm upon his release. By some measures the Whiz was a parolee with a bright future: he had an education, a trade, and the possibility of a job.

Some who knew him were surprised when he never showed up for the job interview, and when he called the prison 8 months after his release and 6 months after he had been declared a parole violator to ask for a letter of reference and tell us how well he was doing. Some were even surprised when they heard he had been arrested and charged with another series of drug offenses coupled with violent crimes.

No one should have been surprised. The Whiz left with the same problems he had when he dropped out of public school and when he entered the criminal justice system. He lacked the life skills needed to make it on the streets. He neither understood nor had the skills necessary to control his own behavior.

For correctional educators, unlike many in the business of public education, our failures, not our successes, come back to visit. When a correctional educator sees an alum, he or she has a new institutional number (in most cases). We rarely see or hear about those who make it on the streets.

The Whiz was not unique; to the contrary, he is all too typical of offenders found in the criminal justice system. There are thousands of young people and adults like the Whiz who are among the 2.2 million Americans under correctional supervision. The Whiz did not make it. He exemplifies the individual with problems that we know require a great deal of attention to resolve. What made the Whiz memorable to me was not only his unique skills and special needs but also the tattoo on his arm. Tattoos adorn the shoulders and forearms of many men and women who inhabit our correctional institutions. The Whiz had a tattoo. He had identified himself as "Born to Lose," and he had been willing to announce it to the whole world. The irony of the situation was that the Whiz, through his statement of hopelessness, had inadvertently made an even more telling statement. He had not been able to communicate even this most basic message. The Whiz, or his tattoo artist,

had misspelled *lose*. He will forever pronounce to the world that he is "Born to Loose."

I am hopeful that through cooperative efforts between special education and correction education many individuals with special needs in our nation's prisons and under other forms of correctional supervision will not reenter society with the belief that they were BORN TO LOSE.

PART III

Implementing Correctional Special Education

INTRODUCTION   *Robert B. Rutherford, Jr.*

In chapter 1 Nelson identified the essential components of effective correctional special education programs. These components are (1) providing functional assessments; (2) providing a functional curriculum; (3) offering vocational training; (4) providing transition services; (5) providing a comprehensive system of services; and (6) providing effective training for teachers in correctional special education. The five chapters in part III describe these components in detail.

In chapter 8 Howell describes functional evaluation in correctional settings. He presents specific assessment procedures designed to assist educators in planning and delivering instruction to handicapped offenders in correctional classrooms.

Chapters 9 and 10 deal with functional, prevocational, and social curriculum components of correctional special education. In chapter 9 Fredericks and Evans present a functional curriculum designed to prepare youthful offenders for adult living and the world of work. They define functional curriculum, describe its scope, and discuss how to teach a functional curriculum. In chapter 10 Goldstein points out the relationship between social skill deficiency and delinquency. He describes structured learning procedures for teaching prosocial skills to antisocial adolescents.

Chapters 9 and 10 contain some degree of overlap in that social skills training (the topic of chapter 10) is one component of a functional curriculum, described in chapter 9. We elected to preserve this overlap because the discussion of a functional curriculum would be incomplete without consideration of social skills training. Furthermore, Fredericks and Evans provide many practical suggestions for teaching a social skills curriculum, such as that designed by Goldstein, in the context of training in daily living and vocational skills.

In chapter 11 Edgar, Webb, and Maddox deal with issues in the transition of youthful offenders from correctional facilities to the public schools. They discuss transition in general and then describe the Juvenile Corrections Interagency Transition Model.

In chapter 12 Leone describes the role of teachers in correctional special education programs. He discusses the types of programs and settings in which correctional educators teach; the streetwise skills, professional competencies, and political abilities necessary for effective correctional special education teachers; and the nature of teaching in the criminal justice system.

Together, these chapters describe current "best practices" in correctional special education. Each is based on professional experience with the topic discussed. Again, differences in those experiences and in the programs being described, in addition to personal biases, contribute to variety in focus and format. We believe these chapters will provide readers with an understanding of what should go into effective correctional special education programming, as well as an indication of how far this new field has yet to go.

Functional Assessment in Correctional Settings

CHAPTER 8   *Kenneth W. Howell*

This chapter presents information on the functional evaluation of clients in correctional settings. The term *functional* is used here to indicate an interest in procedures that can be used by teachers to plan and deliver instruction. The chapter is broken into two parts, the first of which covers issues related to evaluation, treatment, and corrections. The second part of the chapter describes procedures for carrying out functional evaluation activities.

The term *evaluation* subsumes a host of procedures and activities that range in complexity and purpose and vary to some extent with the characteristics of clients and settings. However, the basic principles of evaluation apply to all programs in essentially the same ways. Therefore, a discussion of evaluation in correctional settings will share a lot of common wording with discussions of evaluation in public schools, in the workplace, and/or in everyday life. Thus, it isn't necessary for correctional educators to develop a view of evaluation that is new. Instead, they are faced with the need to extend what is currently known about evaluation into correctional settings.

The past isolation of corrections, coupled with current interest in it, has put correctional educators in a unique position. They are able to shop around for things that work. This chapter is meant to provide guidelines that will enable those educators to pick the best available evaluation practices and thereby avoid recycling errors made elsewhere (Howell, 1985).

CLARIFYING PURPOSE

Most evaluative activities can be understood in terms of a few core concepts that provide a base from which decisions can be made and to which an evaluator can retreat when things start to get confusing. These concepts begin with the idea that an evaluator's purpose affects the assessment outcome.

Consequently, it is necessary for each of us to clarify our own interest in evaluation; differences in purpose can lead to different understandings of this presentation. Just as race drivers, commuters, delivery persons, and police officers all make different use of automobiles, so administrators, teachers, paraprofessionals, and psychologists all make different use of evaluation procedures. Let's take a moment to consider our own individual orientation.

Evaluation is meant to facilitate decision making, and the characteristics of an evaluation are determined to some extent by the size of the unit to which these decisions will be applied. Programmatic decisions to be applied to entire institutions require certain procedures, whereas decisions about individual treatment require others. For example, program evaluation characteristically makes use of relatively broad measures of performance that are summarized infrequently. Evaluation of individuals tends to depend on more specific measures that are administered more frequently. Our focus here is individual treatment assessment, and the reader will need to maintain this perspective.

The following anecdote illustrates how a shifting focus can confuse discussions of evaluation. In speaking once to a group of correctional educators about the evaluation of individuals, the author commented negatively on an achievement test commonly used by members of the audience. The test's superficial coverage of critical content was being criticized when someone objected. This person complained that there was little benefit in criticizing the instrument because no alternative was available. The author replied by describing an alternative procedure that provides thorough content coverage but does not yield normative standard scores, such as grade level equivalencies. The audience member then complained that such a test required too much time to administer and was useless without normative scores because her vocational education program required a documented sixth grade achievement score as a prerequisite for attendance. At this point the source of disagreement became obvious. The author was describing procedures for guiding treatment, but the audience member was interested in procedures for determining program eligibility. It was the classic polemic of educational evaluation: the confusion between treatment and classification.

Decision Making

We evaluate in order to make decisions. There are two general categories of decisions that we need to make regarding the education of handicapped clients: classification decisions and treatment decisions. Classification can be characterized as a sorting activity designed to assure the placement of students in appropriate program components. In the illustration just given, the audience participant's concern about the assignment of students to prevocational and vocational programs was a classification issue. Classification decisions determine whether a client will receive special education services by virtue of being either handicapped or gifted. Treatment decisions determine what kind of educational treatment a student will receive once placed in special education. These two types of decisions are related but different and should not be confused.

Classification in the special educational context ultimately is based on evidence of unusual (either inadequate or exceptional) student progress or performance in an academic or social skills curriculum. Instructional programs in regular classes are geared to meet the learning needs of the majority of students. An expected level of progress is illustrated in Figure 8.1. The solid line in the figure represents the rate at which a typical student is expected to move through a curriculum (approximately 1 year's growth for each year in school). Because even "normal" clients do not all behave in the same way, some variability in progress must be tolerated within regular classes. The acceptable range of variability in regular classes is represented by the broken lines that parallel the expected progress line. When a student's performance falls outside the shaded area, regular class procedures are not practical or effective, and exceptional (special) education must be employed. Obviously, the acceptable range varies according to program curriculum and teacher skill; it is group defined, and normative criteria are traditionally used to decide whether a student needs additional educational services.

In Figure 8.2 the dots represent repeated performance measures of one student. After about 4 years, when the student's progress falls below the acceptable minimum and therefore outside the range of normal instruction, the student is referred, classified as handicapped, and placed in special education. At this point, which is represented by the hooked line in the figure, a process of educational decision making is begun, focusing on treatment. The idea is simple. If orthodox approaches to instruction are not working for the client, modifications must be made. However, before a new instructional program can be begun, a treatment evaluation must answer two questions: (1) what does the student need to be taught, and (2) how should the student be taught? These questions relate not only to curriculum, but also to the stu-

Progress Expectations   Figure 8.1

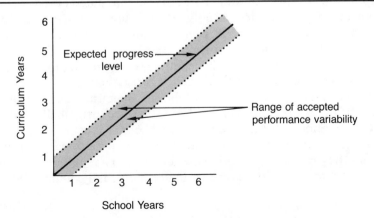

School Years

Figure 8.2   Treatment Change and Effect on Progress

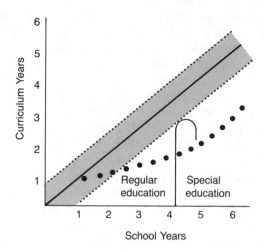

School Years

dent's personal response to treatment. They are idiographic questions and are best answered with nonnormative procedures. If the modifications employed in special education are appropriate, the client's progress will be altered and should eventually reenter the range of acceptable variability addressed by regular education programs.

Treatment Versus Classification

The field of special education has had a long-standing preoccupation with classification stemming primarily from efforts to assign clients to disability categories such as the mentally retarded, the learning disabled, and the behaviorally disordered. The need to label students in this fashion developed out of early attempts to understand and describe the conditions preventing certain individuals from leading normal lives. However, this goal became confused by the advent of funding policies that mandated classification prior to reimbursement for services (Hobbs, 1975). Changing theories of deviance soon combined with administrative and financial expedience to create the muddled classification schemes in place today.

As stated earlier, the focus of this chapter is treatment, not classification. However, in order to maintain this focus, it is necessary to discount the treatment implications of classification attempts. Specific disability labels lack treatment utility for several reasons. First, they are historically tied to quasi-medical ideas about the causes, or sources, of student failure. Procedures for isolating and measuring these causes lack instructional utility because the factors they recognize either occurred in the past and are not currently active or are medical in nature and are not easily addressed through instruction.

A second limitation of disability labels is their inadequate descriptive power. Because not all mentally retarded students are the same, they do not all require the same treatment. The same is true of the populations identified as learning disabled and emotionally disturbed. These specific disability labels do not describe heterogeneous populations any more accurately than labels derived from students' racial, ethnic, or social/economic status.

A final limitation of labels, and the reason the classification-treatment dichotomy is an important one, is that the labels say as much or more about those who give them as about those who receive them. For example, the highest placement per capita in classrooms for the behaviorally disordered is in the state of Utah, whereas the lowest is in Washington, DC (Huntze & Grosenick, 1980). The disparity is apparently a result of the different levels of tolerance for deviant behavior that are found in the two settings: when a more conservative definition is employed, a larger proportion of the population becomes defined. Thus, labels often tell about the labeler rather than the labelee.

THE NATURE OF TREATMENT EVALUATION

Evaluation is a comparative activity. Deno and Mirkin (1977) have presented a simple and useful device for illustrating evaluation that clarifies its comparative nature. Their model is called the discrepancy model and is presented in Figure 8.3. According to this model evaluation takes place through the process of comparing a student's behavior to a predetermined standard. If the student does not behave as expected, a performance discrepancy is noted. That discrepancy will be meaningful if the content is appropriate, the standard is appropriate, and the behavior sample is reliable and valid. When the comparison of the student's behavior to a standard does yield a mean-

The Discrepancy Model of Evaluation   **Figure 8.3**

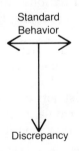

Standard
Behavior

Discrepancy

ingful discrepancy, then an instructional intervention must be devised to eliminate the discrepancy. Because instruction is not needed if a discrepancy is not found and because the quality of instruction is reflected in its capacity to reduce the discrepancy, evaluation and treatment are definitionally linked. There are many important factors crowded into this simple model, and a thorough analysis is well beyond the scope of this chapter. However, the three prerequisites for meaningfulness deserve some elaboration.

Appropriate Content

The first prerequisite for a meaningful evaluation, which hinges on the recognition of a meaningful discrepancy, is appropriate content. Things seem to be appropriate if they match a particular purpose or agenda, and although the whole topic of schooling in correctional facilities is complex, for now let's just assume that the school's agenda is to move students successfully through the curriculum. A curriculum is a set of prespecified learning outcomes or objectives (Johnson, 1967) derived from an analysis of social demands. Progressing through these objectives should lead to higher levels of social competency. In special education the sequence, grouping, and complexity of these objectives are varied to accommodate a student's particular needs. An evaluation will have meaning if it results in information related to curriculum decisions and facilitates the student's mastery of specified objectives.

The idea that the quality of a treatment evaluation depends on its linkage to curriculum has certain implications for practice. The clearest of these is that evaluation cannot be carried out until curriculum has been defined. Unfortunately, this most basic tenet of treatment evaluation is often missing within correctional settings, where the curriculum grows piecemeal out of the intersection of vocational education, adult literacy programs, graduate equivalency tests, and available instructional programming. Evaluation procedures should be selected because they match the curriculum. In programs without a specified curriculum, testing devices themselves often supplant the curriculum; passing a particular test may become the only recognized instructional outcome. Such a situation is reversed. Tests should be selected because they match what is being taught; they should not determine what is being taught.

A treatment evaluation can tell teachers what a student needs to be taught only if the evaluation procedures complement the curriculum. The degree to which tests and curriculum match can be determined only if a curriculum exists. Most states and school districts have established elementary, secondary, and even adult literacy curricula, although these vary considerably in their sophistication and their impact within correctional settings.

Appropriate Standards

The second prerequisite for a meaningful evaluation is the existence of valid standards. Standards, or criteria, are essential for evaluation because comparison cannot take place without them. Noting what is occurring is a useless task without also noting what should be occurring. In addition, standards must be valid, which for our discussion means that they should represent a functional level of student behavior. The two types of standards used in educational evaluation are norms and behavioral criteria. Norms tell how students compare to other students, whereas behavioral criteria tell how they measure up to the demands of certain tasks.

Norms. The normative standards most familiar to educators, unfortunately, are the least valuable for treatment evaluations. A norm-referenced test (NRT) references, or compares, performance on a test to previously established descriptions of group performance. The norm is established by giving the test to a representative sample of students and summarizing the distribution of their scores. That distribution is then segmented through standard statistical procedures. Later, when other students take the test, their performances are summarized by identifying the parts of the distribution into which their scores fell.

The primary treatment limitation of NRTs is that they compare students to other students rather than to levels of desired skill performance. To accomplish this comparison, an NRT must separate students from one another; it must assure that the scores of students taking the test do in fact vary. If all students taking an NRT got the same score, the test's descriptive power would be reduced to zero; it would be impossible to distinguish the performance of one student from that of another. Therefore, NRTs are constructed in ways that provide a guaranteed range of scores.

NRT test authors characteristically employ three techniques. First, they include a wide range of curriculum on the test so that students working at higher levels of complexity have the opportunity to score some points that students at lower levels do not. Second, the populations used for the norming samples are selected randomly with respect to skill levels to assure that the work of both skilled and unskilled students are represented in the norms. And third, test authors pick items for the test on the basis of their ability to discriminate between students.

This third technique dramatically reduces the instructional utility of the test. Items that most students pass and/or fail are purged from the pool, and only items that some students pass and others fail eventually wind up on an NRT. As it turns out, the items that most students pass are the ones that most students are taught, because most teachers agree that they are important. When NRT authors eliminate such items, they are throwing out the instructional core that most teachers teach in favor of marginal items that some teach and others do not. Obviously, this lowers the value of the test for teachers.

The first technique, assuring variable performance by covering a wide range of material, also limits the instructional utility of NRTs. It is common to find normative achievement tests with items that range in difficulty from 1st to 12th grade curriculum levels. Thus, for any individual taking the test, only a small proportion of the items are currently relevant. The majority of the items are either too easy or too hard. However, to provide insight into a student's instructional needs, a test must present items at the student's current functional level; items above that level only promote random responses, and items below it only document what the student has already learned.

One other problem with norms deserves our attention. Norms derived from populations that differ from the tested student in meaningful ways may distort the interpretation of the test scores. Most educators are familiar with the idea that normed tests can be biased against minority students. However, many do not realize how this bias can distort the portrayal of a student's skills. Any score is thought to reflect two elements: truth, the magnitude of the thing the score was designed to summarize; and error, the portion of the score reflecting things other than what the score was designed to measure. Error can contribute to a score through things like broken pencils, practice effect, noise in the room, coincidental learning, or any number of other phenomena. In some cases, error can be contributed through factors associated with population characteristics, such as age, race, wealth, or geographic location. For example, in the case of a math test, the math scores of students who differ from the norming population may seem to be systematically high or low because of nonmathematic factors, such as economic bias found in the wording of the test items. Obviously, this limits the usefulness of the test as a measure of math skill. Because few NRTs are normed on adults and because the population of incarcerated youth varies so dramatically from the orthodox samples used to norm tests, this problem, along with the other limitations described, severely restricts the use of NRTs in guiding treatment decisions in correctional settings.

Behavioral Criteria.   Behavioral criteria, sometimes called criteria for acceptable performance (CAP), differ from norms in a variety of respects. Interestingly, behavioral criteria do what misinformed people think norms do: they represent functional levels of proficiency. It is important for evaluators to understand that normative concepts like "above average" lack these functional implications, particularly in correctional settings, where the mean performance is characteristically lower than that of the general population.

Objectives are commonly required to have statements of content (what the student will learn), behavior (what the student will do to demonstrate what has been learned), conditions (under what circumstances the student will exercise the behavior), and CAP. The behavior portion of an objective is included because functional skill/knowledge cannot be operationally defined without having something to measure. However, in order for measurements to be reliable, they must have observable targets, and so an emphasis on overt behavior becomes a by-product of a general need for instructional accountability. Although it is necessary for objectives to have statements of behavior, evaluators always need to remember that these behaviors are only indicators of learning and are seldom completely valid.

Because the behavior statement in objectives has been given the mission of representing what is taught, gradations of behavior are assumed to indicate different levels of instructional effectiveness or learner proficiency.

The two most common proficiency dimensions are accuracy and rate of response. *Accuracy,* which is summarized in terms of percent correct, is the most familiar proficiency dimension. It can be assumed that two students who obtain different accuracy scores on the same task are not equally proficient at the task. Similarly, two tasks that require different levels of accuracy for successful completion are thought to vary in difficulty. However, even students and tasks that demonstrate or require 100% accuracy can vary in proficiency and difficulty. In other words, people who are 100% accurate can improve—by maintaining their level of accuracy while increasing their rate of response.

Rate of response is an important proficiency dimension for several reasons. First of all, rate, like accuracy, is a sensitive indicator of student knowledge and task difficulty. The person who adjusts a carburetor with 100% accuracy and twice as fast as others is said to know carburetor adjustment better. In addition, rate of response has implications for generalization, retention, and acquisition of more complex skills. The fluid use of subskills is often a prerequisite for success in later tasks. For example, students who decode slowly are not well prepared to comprehend what they are reading because they encounter fewer ideas per minute than they would if they decoded faster. And finally, rate of response is an indicator of automaticity. When a skill becomes automatic, it does not require the individual to be aware of using it—which is critical to functional performance. Driving a car is a good example to describe automaticity. A person first learning to drive has to concentrate on each operation. During this stage of learning student drivers have instructors in the car with them to watch for potential difficulties because the students are not sufficiently proficient at steering and accelerating and braking to concentrate on these skills and still be aware of approaching tractor trailer trucks. Such students may perform these operations with great accuracy if they can devote total attention to the tasks at hand. In contrast, experienced (automatic) drivers can perform just as accurately but without any awareness of the individual operations. Automatic performance is so proficient that application of a skill takes place without conscious thought (Wagner & Sternberg, 1984).

The idea that behavior indicates learning and that gradations of behavioral proficiency indicate levels of learning is important for persons interested in functional evaluation. However, specialists in social behavior have recognized a further principle with special application to learning in correctional facilities: *behavior is situational* (Mehan, 1981). We all understand that behaviors appropriate in one setting are inappropriate in others and that individuals who can function adequately in one setting may not be able to do so in others. As a result, behavioral proficiency in one setting (e.g., a prison) may not adequately indicate the level of functioning in other settings (e.g., outside the prison). This becomes a bigger problem as the differences between the two settings become more extreme. Correctional educators, who work in the most atypical of all educational settings, need to be aware of situational gradations when defining performance. Functional criteria for acceptable performance depend as much on the conditions specified in the objectives as on the behaviors. For example, levels of functional skill might best be indicated by holding behavioral proficiency constant and introducing conditional gradations, as shown in Table 8.1.

Behavioral criteria should be determined through some sort of *standardization* procedure. Standardization does not apply specifically to norming; it means that the criteria specified for a criterion-referenced test (CRT) must be supported by some sort of technical rationale and that the authors should provide evidence of this rationale (and the procedures used to establish it) in a technical manual. Unfortunately, educational evaluation currently is in a transitional stage, and many consumers are not sufficiently knowledgeable about CRTs. Interest in CRTs has increased (Berk, 1984), but popular knowledge about them has not; and as a result, the educational testing market is flooded with instruments of varying quality. A CRT should include a technical manual providing the source of the test's criteria as well as information on the test's reliability and validity. These basic requirements are outlined in the American Psychological Association's Standards for Tests (American Psychological Association, 1985), but some of the most popular CRTs in use today do not comply with these guidelines.

Behavioral criteria are established in several ways. The most common way is to consult with experts and/or review available research literature. Many criteria levels are already established, particularly in basic skills. When a criterion is not available, the easiest procedure for establishing it is to employ a sampling technique. This technique differs from norming in that it involves the intentional selection of a population of experts, rather than the randomly selected population used in norming.

Behavioral criteria can be conceptualized as the level of performance at which active instruction on an objective is no longer needed. This means that students below task criterion need instruction on the skill but those above it require only monitoring (to be sure their performance does not deteriorate).

Table 8.1   **Objectives with Conditional Gradations**

Content	Behavior	Conditions	CAP
		Academic Example	
Addition	Write answers	On worksheet	100% accuracy
Addition	Write answers	On GED	100% accuracy
Addition	Write answers	In checkbook	100% accuracy
		Social Example	
Opinions	Express aloud	Role playing	Without disrupting conversation
Opinions	Express aloud	With familiar company	Without disrupting conversation
Opinions	Express aloud	With strangers	Without disrupting conversation

Task criterion must represent a level of proficiency typical of those who have mastered the task. Therefore, only masters of the task are selected for the CRT standardization process.

Behavioral criteria may be expressed in terms of performance or progress. Performance standards tell how proficient a student should be at the end of instruction. Progress standards tell how quickly a student is expected to advance toward a performance criterion. Both types of standards are illustrated in Figure 8.4. The figure shows that on the third week of instruction, Student A is reading 100 words per minute (wpm), whereas Student B is reading 50 wpm. Because the standard is 150 wpm, both students have negative performance discrepancies. Student A's discrepancy in absolute terms is -50 wpm (-33% in proportional terms); Student B's discrepancy is -100 wpm (-67% wpm). However, Student B is progressing faster than the progress standard whereas Student A is progressing more slowly. The existence of performance and progress standards allows us to recognize that both students need to be taught this reading skill (to raise their performance) but only Student A requires a modification in treatment. Student B is progressing rapidly enough to reach the performance criterion by the aim date.

Appropriate Behavior Samples

In order for the results of a treatment evaluation to be meaningful, the evaluator must assure that it is based on appropriate measures. So far, it has been asserted that the measured content should be what the student needs to learn and the criteria should represent functional levels of proficiency.

Performance and Progress Standards　　　　　　　　　　　　　　　**Figure 8.4**

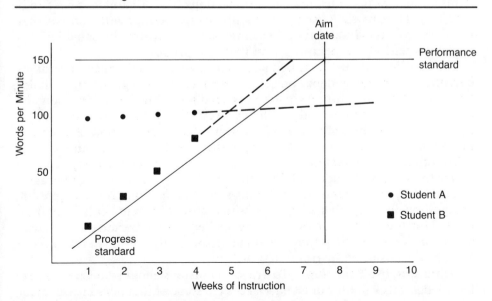

The third prerequisite for meaningful evaluation is a reliable and valid behavior sample. In education, behavior typically is obtained by testing or observing a student. Many educators seem to believe that testing is synonymous with evaluation, but it is not. A test is simply a format devised for collecting a behavior sample. In order for an evaluator to be assured that a discrepancy is meaningful, the behavior sample must allow useful comparisons to the standard. Thus, a test provides an appropriate behavior sample if it matches the curriculum in critical ways. Most of these critical dimensions have already been discussed and are listed in checklist form in Table 8.2. Two particular indicators of sample quality that appear on the list but have not been discussed in sufficient detail are curriculum match and representative sampling. In addition, sampling rate requires further discussion.

Curriculum Match.   Earlier in this chapter, evaluation was linked to decision making, and decision making was broken into classification and treatment. As indicated during that discussion, classification and treatment are separate evaluative activities, both of which require the guidance of good measurement. However, because they have different aims, they require the application of different measurement techniques and standards. For treatment decisions, the evaluator must be sure to select an instrument that was designed to yield treatment, not classification, information. For the most part, such instruments will be criterion-referenced rather than norm-referenced.

Treatment evaluation has the purpose of guiding instruction within an area of curriculum. Curriculum is composed of objectives that are made up, in part, of statements of content and behavior. In order for a test to provide adequate treatment guidance, it must be clearly linked to these content and behavior domains. Ideally, this link is accomplished by cross-referencing items (or groups of items) to instructional objectives. Evaluators need to be sure that the tests they use require students to interact with content their teachers have taught and that these interactions involve the same kinds of behaviors teachers expect to see in their classrooms.

The conflict between test behavior and instructional expectation is exemplified by the dependence on select-response items (e.g., multiple choice, true/false, matching) for group-administered tests. The behavioral domains of identifying a response and producing a response are as different from one another as many areas of content. This means that using multiple choice items to evaluate areas of content like computation can be as misleading as using subtraction items to test multiplication. As a rule, select (identify) items are easier than supply (produce) items. In some cases, they are not only easier, but they actually summarize different skills. In spelling, for example, the recognition of misspelled words seems to require different skills from those needed for the production of correctly spelled words. Because select items allow for easier grading, they are popular for group-administered tests, in spite of their limited instructional utility.

Representative Sampling.   To draw conclusions about someone's skill or knowledge, an evaluator must have access to some of that person's behavior. Obviously, the reliability of the conclusions is limited not only by the kind

Test Problems and Solutions Table 8.2

Problem	Recommended Solution
Tests are not easy to use.	Make sure there are directions and scoring procedures. Make the test easy to follow, transport, and interpret.
Tests do not have clearly defined purposes.	Know the purpose and limitations of the instrument being used. Determine whether it is a placement or a treatment test and whether it is a norm- or criterion-referenced test.
Most tests and test items do not measure defined content and behavioral domains.	Be able to cross-reference items and procedures to content and behavioral domains. These may include subskills, theoretical domains, response domains, stimulus-response domains, and proficiency domains.
Most test items are not keyed to objectives.	Develop a test plan that includes objectives. This may take the form of a table of specifications. Write or select items for each square (objective) in the table and code the items for cross-reference.
Tests that are keyed to objectives are seldom standardized.	Decide on the appropriate type of data (accuracy or rate) for the content to be tested. Set standards by reviewing the literature, asking experts, or sampling a standardization population.
Few tests permit examination of strategic behavior.	Decide whether product evaluation is sufficient. If not, devise a way to make the process observable, usually through the use of error analysis or actual process examination.
Many tests do not permit evaluators to collect an adequate sample.	Decide how consolidated the content is. Write adequate items (usually 10) for each strategic element of highly consolidated content or for each instance of unconsolidated content.
Many tests feature stimulus formats that are inappropriate.	Examine the context to which the results will be generalized. Also consider the proficiency dimension to be employed. Decide whether rate is called for or whether the test will be used for repeated measure.
Tests use inappropriate scoring procedures.	Use measurement rules that assign points to the smallest educationally relevant unit.

Source: Adapted from *Curriculum-based Evaluation for Special and Remedial Education* by K.W. Howell and M.K. Morehead, 1987, Columbus, OH: Merrill. Copyright 1987 by Merrill Publishing Co.

of behavior sampled (as was just explained), but also by the amount of behavior on which the conclusions are based. Consider how we might feel if someone were to form an opinion about our social or academic competence based on a 10-minute sample of behavior taken at 4:15 A.M. on an average morning. Most of us would complain that a sample of behavior taken at that hour misrepresents us. However, to what hour would we move it? A 10-minute sample, regardless of its placement in the day, will inadequately summarize our status because it is not representative. This lack of representativeness is not just a function of the total time involved; ten 1-minute samples spaced throughout the day would be more representative than the one 10-minute sample.

Adequacy of sampling is dependent on both the content coverage and the amount of behavior obtained. Many tests obtain such a limited sample of behavior that conclusions based on their results must be considered suspect. However, the ideal amount of behavior actually required for reliable evaluation is hard to specify. It is normally recommended that tests require students to engage in targeted skills at least 10 times in order to obtain an adequate sample. However, 10 instances may be too many if the test covers a large sample of highly related skills, or 10 may be too few if it is attempting to sample from curriculum domains composed of isolated facts.

Sampling Rate.   The importance of rate as a proficiency measure dictates the use of measures that yield rate data. Rate tests are typically constructed differently from accuracy tests so that a student's fluency of response will not be inhibited by the test format. Rate formats are characterized by repeated presentations of unambiguous items that require brief responses. Thus, rate measures are used for curricula in which students must achieve automaticity. Rated tests make sense for basic skills like decoding or computation or for basic knowledge like topic specific vocabulary or symbols; rated measures do not make sense for higher level content like theme writing.

Rate tests are not the same as other timed tests. Timed tests and rate tests have radically different formats and should not be confused. Timed tests typically present a series of items ordered from easy to difficult, which must be worked within a fixed time period. This time limit is imposed in order to decrease variability in individual student performance and therefore raise the test's reliability. However, because such tests present wide ranges of items, it is impossible to set performance standards on them that have functional implications. On the other hand, rate tests cover narrow bands of curriculum and are designed to summarize how quickly students can make one well-defined response. Thus, the timing of traditional achievement tests does not provide important information about rate proficiency.

FUNCTIONAL EVALUATION

Correctional facilities are now required to provide programs for handicapped students (Rutherford, Nelson, & Wolford, 1985). As part of this service, teachers are expected to develop an individualized treatment plan for each student in their programs. These treatment plans should include statements about where the student currently is, where the student is going, and what will be done to get the student there. The quality of these statements hinges on the quality of the evaluative information used to develop them.

So far our discussion has centered on appropriate evaluations. Before turning to the actual procedures employed during such evaluations, we need to focus on tasks because it is task performance that is examined in functional evaluation.

Task Analysis

As presented earlier, the curriculum can be conceptualized as a grouping of objectives (or tasks) arranged in a more or less sequential order on the basis of their complexity. During a treatment evaluation the educational evaluator attempts to locate the student within this sequence. Although it is common to describe this process as a student evaluation, it is equally accurate, and in some ways more useful, to view the process as an evaluation of tasks.

Tasks and objectives are the same things; they are composed of content, behavior, conditions, and criteria. Students who succeed in performing a particular task are thought to have achieved functional command of each of these elements. Students who are not successful at that task are thought to lack command of one or more of these elements. Because one goal of treatment evaluation is the specification of tasks in which the student should be instructed, the evaluator attempts to find the curricular boundary between known and unknown tasks. This boundary represents the narrow slice of curriculum with which the student can be expected to interact with optimum learning. Tasks below this band have already been learned, so studying them will probably bore the student and will certainly waste time. Tasks far above the band are too difficult, and attempts to teach them may promote frustration.

The example in Figure 8.5 illustrates the characteristics of a task. Failure on a task can be attributed to a lack of skill within one or more of the essential components of the task. There are two types of components: subtasks and strategies. Subtasks are the prerequisite tasks that a person must have learned in order to perform a larger task. The subtask/task relationship is defined by the prerequisite status of the subtask; all tasks are subtasks of some higher level skill. And all tasks and subtasks have the same basic elements and components. If a student cannot succeed at the task of subtracting two-digit numbers requiring borrowing, one explanation for that

---

Subtask and Strategy Components of a Subtraction Problem   **Figure 8.5**

Task: Subtract 2-digit number from 2-digit number when borrowing is required.

Subtask Component	Strategy Component
4. Subtract 2-digit numbers not requiring borrowing	5. Record answer in correct location
3. Borrow from 10's place	4. Subtract
2. Know subtraction facts (0–20)	3. Make the 2 a 12 by borrowing
1. Know operational signs	2. Recognize the need to borrow
	1. Recognize the need to subtract

failure may be the lack of competency on a subtask, such as subtracting without borrowing.

If subtasks are thought of as the raw materials that one assembles during task completion, then strategies can be thought of as the blueprints used to guide the assembly. Strategies are the procedures, rules, and processes for combining subtasks. Obviously, a student who lacks an essential subtask will not be able to carry out the procedures involving it and will therefore fail at the larger task. However, competency on all subtasks does not assure automatic success with the task, because a student who has mastered all of the subskills still needs to know what to do with them. If the strategy for subtask combination is not known, an otherwise knowledgeable student may fail to complete the task.

The task analytical approach to curriculum can be used to understand both evaluation and instruction. Instruction is thought to be most effective if it targets curriculum at the correct level of student difficulty. Thus, a primary outcome of treatment evaluation is the accurate and appropriate specification of what to teach, selection of an objective that is neither too easy nor too difficult for the student. Difficulty in this instance is not determined by the absolute complexity of a particular task but by the student's prior knowledge of the components of the task; an objective that is very hard for one student may be quite easy for another. A teacher presenting information at the correct level of difficulty focuses on the presentation of task strategies that enable students to combine what they already know in new ways to succeed on new objectives.

Conducting a Treatment Evaluation

An Overview.   Figure 8.6 presents a flow chart of the task analytic model of evaluation (Howell & Morehead, 1987). The squares and rectangles represent evaluator activities designed to provide information to answer the questions presented in the diamonds. This model is based on the premise that students fail at tasks because they are missing one or more of the essential components of the task. Treatment evaluation is carried out to find these unknown components. The evaluation involves four stages of activity: fact finding, hypothesizing, validating, and decision making. The evaluator first finds out what the student cannot do, then thinks of an explanation for the student's failure, and checks to see whether the explanation is correct. The final stage of the evaluation is to decide what to do about it. This is a straightforward, common-sense approach to treatment evaluation.

Stage 1: Fact Finding.   In this stage the evaluator finds out what is wrong with the way a student is behaving. Fact finding is carried out to pare down the curriculum to a few areas of primary concern. The pivotal activity in this stage is survey level assessment, which collects a general sample of the student's behavior. Assessment can involve the use of achievement tests, class assignments, observations, client interviews, or interviews with previous instructors. These procedures lack the task-related specificity needed to actual-

The Task Analytical Model of Educational Diagnosis

Figure 8.6

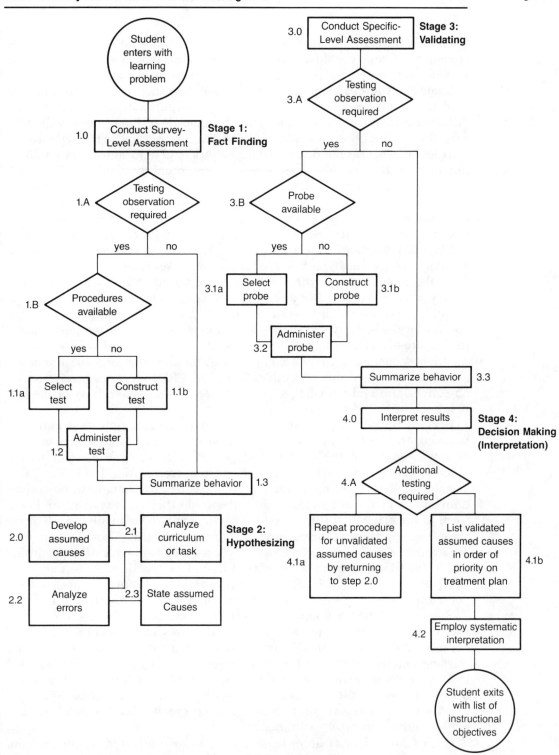

Source: From *Curriculum-based Evaluation for Special and Remedial Education* by K.W. Howell and M.K. Morehead, 1987, Columbus, OH: Merrill. Copyright by Merrill Publishing Co. Reprinted by permission.

ly guide treatment, but they are adequate to identify problematic areas of student performance. Most of the tests available today should be considered survey tests, particularly if they are norm-referenced tests.

Stage 2: Hypothesizing.   Once the fact finding stage determines what the student cannot do, the evaluator must try to figure out why. In this stage differences in evaluator sophistication become clear. Functional evaluators generate explanations for student failure that can actually be treated through instruction, whereas nonfunctional evaluators tend to form hypotheses about unalterable factors like cognitive or perceptual disabilities. The task analytical evaluator restricts assumptions about causes of failure to curricular components, such as subtasks and strategies. In doing so, the evaluator exhausts every educational explanation for the failure before exposing the client to more theoretical, and often less practical, procedures.

Stage 3: Validating.   An evaluator's explanations of student failure should always be treated as hypotheses, or *assumed* causes. The explanations come from the evaluator—not the client—and are based on an interpretation of survey level test results. Because survey procedures lack sufficient specificity to guide instructors, their results must be confirmed in a process called specific level testing, which supplies the kind of focused information required to validate or reject a hypothesis. A specific level test is always a CRT. As mentioned earlier, a CRT is composed of an objective and the materials needed to carry out that objective. By basing CRT objectives on curricular objectives, the evaluator helps to guarantee the content validity of the test results.

Because the only hypotheses generated in the task analytic model are subtask and strategy hypotheses, tests that measure subtasks and strategies must be employed during the validation stage. Few achievement tests supply the kind of content or behavioral specificity required at this level. The CRTs selected or developed must adequately measure the short-term objectives on which students are working. In order to do this, such tests should conform to the criteria outlined earlier, particularly those involving adequate sampling, appropriate formats, and validated standards. These instruments are available in program placement tests, as well as in education programs that subscribe to a competency-based line of instruction. Some currently available published CRTs are also appropriate, and more of these are expected to appear on the market as consumer demand for them increases.

Stage 4: Decision Making.   After specific test results have been collected, the evaluator decides whether the assumed causes advanced in Stage 2 were correct. If they were, an essential task component has been found to be missing, and that component must be targeted for instruction. If the assumed causes were not correct, the evaluator must return to Stage 2 and generate another hypothesis. This process is not as bad as it sounds; assumed causes are drawn from known skill sequences, and specific level tests often take only a minute or two to administer.

Once a subtask or strategy component has been targeted for instruction, repeated administrations of the CRT can be used to generate data about the effectiveness of instructional treatments. The same procedures used to determine *what* is taught can be employed to determine *how* it is taught.

An Academic Example

Suppose a student who is assigned to a particular educational program reports that he has had a lot of trouble in school but his school records have long since been lost. Policy requirements may dictate that such a student first be evaluated for classification purposes, to determine into which program tract he is placed. If that is the case, the classification agenda should be addressed as quickly as possible, and its results should *not* be used to formulate treatment recommendations.

Treatment recommendations are derived from a functional evaluation beginning with survey assessment. If previous school records are not available, general testing covering many curriculum areas and levels of complexity needs to be carried out to find the student's current range of functioning. Arithmetic placement tests, samples of written work such as letters or assignments, oral reading inventories, and client interviews should be used to narrow the focus to a set of tasks that are not hopelessly above the student's current skill capacity. After a general impression of the student's functioning is obtained, assumed causes related to subtasks and strategies should be developed in one of two ways. The regular way is to examine the array of student responses to a skill sequence (to be functional, such a sequence must be correct and in behavioral terms). Skills clearly mastered or failed can be marked on the sequence, whereas questionable skills can be targeted for specific level testing. The second option is to analyze errors made by the student, to see whether they form patterns that indicate missing skills.

Let's assume that the client in this case fails to understand material typically found in fourth grade science books. A review of reading comprehension reveals that his comprehension depends on the areas of skill shown in Table 8.3. Of these skills some can be ruled out as potential hypotheses on the basis of competency demonstrated in survey testing and interviews. These tasks are marked *pass*. Of those that cannot be ruled out, some (such as reading rate and knowledge of technical vocabulary) can be checked immediately by returning to the original passage and using it as a specific test. Critical reading skills are less well defined, and validation may require selection of a test to assess general reading comprehension. Such a test can be found among the subtests in currently available instruments.

A Social Behavior Example

A different student may have problems getting along with others. For social behavior problems the best survey procedures are often observations of and interviews with the client and/or her acquaintances. In this case survey procedures indicate that one of this student's problem areas is initiating and maintaining conversations. From a communication skills curriculum the list of subtasks in Figure 8.7 is selected for assessment in a sequence of situa-

Table 8.3   **A Sample Status Sheet for Comprehending a Passage from a Fourth Grade Science Book**

Tasks	Status	Specific Level Test Needed
Decodes passage		
Reads accurately	Pass	
Reads fluently	Unsure	Test rate on target passage
Knows vocabulary		
General vocabulary	Pass	
Technical vocabulary	Unsure	Test knowledge of science terms
Has language competence		
Receptive	Pass	
Expressive	Pass	
Has adequate prior knowledge of content		
General	Pass	
Specific to passage	Unsure	Test knowledge of science concepts
Has critical reading skills		
Recognizes missing information	Unsure	Test
Uses content clues	Unsure	Test
Uses other resources	Unsure	Test

Figure 8.7   **Table of Specifications**

Subtasks	Conditions		
	Role-Playing	Class	Exercise Periods
Monitors what others are saying			
Recognizes points deserving elaboration			
Relates points to personal experience			
Obtains attention of others			
Presents comments			

tions relevant to the student. The specific assessment procedure may be as simple as asking the client and knowledgeable acquaintances to rate her performance of each subtask in each situation. If interviewing seems impractical, observations of her conversation within each of the targeted conditions may need to be carried out.

From the examples it should be clear that the task analytic approach is not necessarily cumbersome and/or time-consuming. The biggest problem that most correctional educators have with it results from their comparative naïveté about task components. Obviously, if an evaluator must search out skill sequences for each student, an otherwise brief evaluative exercise becomes prohibitively time-consuming. This problem is magnified by the ill-defined curricular expectations and the situational isolation that characterize correctional settings. However, it is important to remember that subtasks and strategies come from tasks, not from individual students. As a result, a task sequence obtained during the examination of one student is valid for any other student experiencing failure on that same task.

In the past, educational programs in correctional settings have been somewhat immune to the various mandates to which public school programs are routinely subjected. Consequently, many correctional programs do not have a curriculum of sufficient specificity to facilitate functional evaluation. However, such curricula are probably available from local school districts, state departments of education, and/or other correctional educational programs.

CONCLUSION

It is important to remember that students are viewed as special because they do not learn adequately under typical treatment conditions. The education of such students will not necessarily be advanced by the application of more sophisticated, but less practical, evaluation procedures. Such procedures frequently have the unfortunate effect of drawing attention away from the curriculum and toward ill-defined ideas about personal disabilities. The functional evaluator keeps evaluation activities firmly bound to the curriculum that will ultimately be used to reflect a student's competence. By maintaining this curricular focus and employing task specific procedures for sampling behavior and establishing standards, evaluators can set the stage for immediate and positive changes in student learning.

REFERENCES

American Psychological Association. (1985). *Standards for educational and psychological testing.* Washington, DC: Author.

Berk, R. A. (Ed.). (1984). *A guide to criterion referenced test construction.* Baltimore, MD: Johns Hopkins Press.

Deno, S. L., & Mirkin, P. K. (1977). *Data based program modification: A manual.* Reston, VA: Council for Exceptional Children.

Hobbs, N. (1975). *Issues in the classification of children.* San Francisco: Jossey-Bass.

Howell, K. W. (1985). Selecting special education treatments. *Journal of Correctional Education, 36,* 26–29.

Howell, K. W., & Morehead, M. K. (1987). *Curriculum-based evaluation for special and remedial education.* Columbus, OH: Merrill.

Huntze, S. L., & Grosenick, J. K. (1980). *National needs analysis in behavior disorders: Human resource issues in behavior disorders.* Columbia: University of Missouri, Department of Special Education.

Johnson, M. (1967). Definitions and models in curriculum theory. *Educational Theory, 7,* 127–140.

Mehan, H. (1981). Social constructivism in psychology and sociology. *Quarterly Newsletter of the Laboratory of Comparative Human Cognition, 3,* 71–77.

Rutherford, R. B., Nelson, C. M., & Wolford, B. I. (1985). Special education in the most restrictive environment: Correctional special education. *Journal of Special Education, 19,* 60–71.

Wagner, R. K., & Sternberg, R. J. (1984). Alternative conceptions of intelligence and their implications for education. *Review of Educational Research, 54,* 179–223.

Andrea Piercy

Teaching in a Medium-Security Prison   VIGNETTE

I am the special education teacher at Maryland Correctional Institution—Jessup. This correctional facility is a medium-security institution housing approximately 1200 men (original capacity was 500). It was designed to house first-time felons between the ages of 18 and 24 with intermediate sentences. The average sentence length is approximately 18 months; the average stay in this institution is 6 months. The prison population is predominantly young; in jail slang it is made up of "hoppers." Hoppers are young men with short sentences, usually given for property-related crimes. The population as a whole views itself as passing through. There is little settling in or looking at time and deciding how to productively do one's "bit." Older inmates view these hoppers as real nuisances who clutter up their home or as objects of amusement.

One of my job descriptions as the education teacher is to meet the educational needs of these hoppers, should they be identified as educationally handicapped. But that is just one of my job descriptions; the role of the special education teacher in correctional education is generally one of covering the waterfront.

The special education teacher does much more than teach: he or she screens, tests, is the case manager, provides emotional support, writes (constantly—IEPs, schedules, anecdotal records, educational assignments, psychological and medical consultations, review notices, parental notifications, student consent forms, and more), negotiates (between and/or among students, "regular" teachers, vocational teachers, principals, central office specialists, security personnel), plans, modifies plans, and does any other task that might crop up during the day. It sometimes seems as if one's first priority—teaching—is constantly reshuffled to the bottom of the desk.

However, assembling 12 special education students for the morning resource classes brings home plainly and sometimes painfully the necessity of planning and teaching. Having no plan is a sure way to achieve instant chaos. Every minute must be structured for things to go well, and the structuring must be according to what each student needs if the plan is to produce meaningful learning. Special education is not an excuse to be academically sloppy. Structuring is difficult, yet it is the special education teacher's real priority.

There is no typical day. I do set up a pattern, a structure, but then I am invariably forced to change or depart from it. The short-term population of the jail adds to the challenge of my job. I do not have the same stable, well-known group making progress on IEP objectives for an entire semester or two. And each referral to special education requires assessment, legal and emotional counseling, written reports, and a negotiated IEP in addition to individualized instruction. In my current group I have had one student for 2 years, another for 3 months, and the other 10 are brand new—brand new hoppers just passing through, not terribly interested in learning and probably doubting that they can learn to read or do math any better. Their needs are many—academic and social deficiencies that have been years in the making and need years to correct. And there are certain needs that can only be adequately met on the other side of the prison fence—vocational training, developing economic self-sufficiency, using community resources, and learning to live in a socially responsible manner.

All of this can make my job very bleak—and some days it is. Why do I do it? I'm not sure at times. It's a job, but I could earn more money in other jobs. A long time ago I realized that I actually enjoyed teaching: sitting with a student, determining what he or she did or didn't know, figuring out how to hook that together in a new pattern, and seeing that student learn something—borrowing in subtraction, getting over that mystical hump in decoding, or just excitedly sharing some news item with classmates and having them respond with enthusiasm. Those experiences made me happy.

That happy feeling doesn't come every day. Sometimes it doesn't come for weeks at a time. But it always comes again, often when I least expect it. And in jail that happy feeling seems happier. Sometimes a student feels the excitement, too, and makes a commitment to learning.

That is what I do and why I do it. Where I do it seems incidental—I am an educator in corrections more than a correctional educator. The impact of the jail, of course, is far more than incidental. Its effect on the student and the teacher is pervasive. But teaching is teaching. And when learning reflects a positive change, it creates in me a positive feeling.

In October 1986, Andrea Piercy passed away after a long illness. She had taught for eight years in the correctional systems of Maryland and Virginia. In 1986 she was honored by the Maryland Correctional Education Department with an award for excellence in teaching.

Functional Curriculum

CHAPTER 9   *Bud Fredericks and Vicki Evans*

This chapter describes the nature, benefits, and use of a functional curriculum for students who are mildly retarded, learning disabled, and severely behavior disordered. Such a curriculum also has benefit for students who perceive school as irrelevant, who are poor students, or who are potential dropouts. In addition, a functional curriculum is frequently necessary for both handicapped and nonhandicapped youth who are incarcerated (Rutherford, Nelson, & Wolford, 1985).

A functional curriculum is a curriculum that prepares a student for adult living. It encompasses three major domains: independent living skills, social skills, and vocational skills. A functional curriculum is an alternative to the traditional high school curriculum that focuses more on abstractions and includes subject matter that a special education student may find irrelevant. For instance, a special education student may have difficulty understanding, or even relating to the need to understand, the organization of city and state government as it is presented in the traditional high school social studies class. The subject matter does not clearly relate to that student's life. However, that same student may have little difficulty learning the process for obtaining a driver's license, which is issued by the state, or a dog license, which is issued by a city or municipality, and may well understand the difference between the city police and the county sheriff.

ELIGIBILITY FOR A FUNCTIONAL CURRICULUM

The decision to place a student in a functional curriculum in lieu of a traditional secondary curriculum is one that should be made carefully, taking into account the potential of the student to learn, current performance levels, and the student's potential to remain in school. Any student who is seriously considering dropping out of school or who dropped out before being incarcerated should be considered a candidate for a functional curriculum. If a student will not be completing public school education, the school should offer a program to help that student survive. A functional curriculum is such a program.

Students who exhibit severe behavior problems and disrupt the school environment to such an extent that they are frequently suspended are also candidates for placement in a functional curriculum. Frequently, such students perceive the school program to be irrelevant or too difficult. This perception causes them not to participate seriously in academic activities, a form of rebellion or withdrawal that brings criticism. That criticism triggers further rebellion, now directed at authority figures—teachers and administrators. More criticism, more rebellion, and the cycle accelerates. Students in this situation should be considered for an alternative or functional curriculum.

Students functioning four reading grade levels below their grade placement by the ninth grade should also be considered for placement in a functional curriculum. A reading level so impaired will cause extreme difficulty for students trying to cope with the abstract concepts presented in most coursework at the secondary level and will usually result in continuing academic frustration and failure. These negative feelings, in turn, may cause students to initiate or accelerate inappropriate behaviors or may cause them to consider leaving school. Students can frequently be diverted from this failure syndrome by being placed in a functional curriculum and gradually reintroduced to more traditional academic subjects.

Finally, those youth who are incarcerated, both handicapped and nonhandicapped, often require instruction in a functional curriculum. The Bureau of Justice Statistics (1983) reported demographic data that indicate considerable deficits in daily living skills among inmates. Administrators of the Oregon State Penitentiary, in information shared with the principal author, reported large deficits in independent living skills among the learning disabled/mildly retarded population of adult offenders. Rutherford et al. (1985) advocate for instruction in a functional curriculum for incarcerated juvenile and adult offenders. Hazel, Schumaker, Sherman, and Sheldon-Wildgen (1981) found that one domain of a functional curriculum (i.e., social skills training) reduced the number of subsequent offenses that released youth committed.

A functional curriculum need not replace all traditional academic coursework. The decision as to which subject it replaces depends on the functional abilities and needs of the individual student. Certainly courses such as physical education, home economics, and shop can be appropriate additions to a functional curriculum. And for students well-versed in math, for example, but having a great deal of trouble with reading skills, a partial functional curriculum can replace coursework in language arts and social studies while allowing them to continue in the traditional math program.

A major problem that arises from moving students into a functional curriculum is removal of the opportunity to meet specified graduation requirements. Therefore, the decision to place students in a functional curriculum needs to be made carefully. Schools should be encouraged to provide alternative diplomas that indicate completion of high school coursework rather than traditional graduation requirements. The regular diploma has primary importance for students going on to advanced academic study. For students seeking employment, the alternative diploma can show that they have finished a specified course of high school study and have graduated. Such a diploma is often sufficient and generally does not negatively impact their employment.

SUPPORT FOR A FUNCTIONAL CURRICULUM

Is there really a need for a functional curriculum as part of a secondary special education program in corrections? Many correctional and special education teachers do not include a functional curriculum in their programs, and few teachers of students with learning and behavioral disabilities have been trained to provide it. Thus, a functional curriculum is not routinely offered in most programs for mildly handicapped learners.

However, in a recent survey conducted among 24 resource room teachers of learning disabled secondary students in Oregon, teachers identified 10% to 23% of their students as severely behaviorally disordered. Inevitably these students were reading at least four grade levels below the ninth grade level, with many of them reading at only second and third grade levels. All the teachers admitted having difficulty managing this population and indicated that most of these students had experienced either out-of-school or in-school suspension. The teachers knew of students who had dropped out of school and believed that the underlying reasons were the school's inability to manage the students or to provide a meaningful education for them. All of the teachers also admitted that their training had not prepared them to cope with this population. (This need for preservice teacher training is also supported by Davies in a 1983 survey of 420 resource room teachers, 87.4% of whom listed "knowledge of and skill in a variety of pupil management techniques" as one of the most important competencies to possess.) The Oregon survey suggests that a population of students exists that is not being adequately served by established special education programs. Brozovich and Kotting (1984) report that 64% of the 87 resource teachers they surveyed indicated that their educational program did not include a specific component designed to promote students' personal growth, social/emotional development, or mental health.

In a separate study of secondary special education programs in Oregon, Halpern and Benz (1984) gathered data about the curriculum taught in secondary special education programs. Ten curriculum clusters were identified as being particularly appropriate for students in secondary special education; the clusters included such areas as traditional academics, prevocational and vocational education skills for independent living, and interpersonal skills. Teachers and administrators agreed that instruction was available in most of these curricular areas to students with disabilities in more that 90% of Oregon's high schools. However, according to the parents of these pupils, fewer than 50% of their children actually received instruction in such areas as vocational preparation, functional academics, home living skills, and community living skills. Half of the teachers cited vocational preparation and community living instruction as areas in need of improvement, and nearly 40% of the parents also indicated dissatisfaction with the content of these two areas when they were offered as part of the curriculum. In the words of one of the parents who participated in the study,

> I am very concerned about the present push for "excellence" which is stressing increased pressure for college as being the ultimate goal after high school. I see it as a "put down" to those who are either unable or not wanting to go to college. As a result of increased academic requirements, the vocational type programs are being cut. These programs meet the needs of a lot of students who are not college-bound. John Gardner said that "if a society respects the philosophers, but not the plumbers, then neither the philosophy nor the pipes will hold water."

The need for a functional curriculum, as defined here, is also supported by the literature in this area. Vetter (1983) conducted a follow-up study of students who were mildly retarded/learning disabled. The results indicated that two major needs were demonstrated—social skill training and functional skill training. Vetter's follow-up study further emphasized that learning disabled students who had left school judged a daily living skill curriculum more important than a traditional academic curriculum.

White, Schumaker, Warner, Alley, and Deshler (1980) studied the personal, social, and vocational success of 47 learning disabled (LD) and 57 non-LD young adults. The individuals studied had been out of school from 1 to 5 years. In the area of vocational adjustment, the LD adults were found to have lower status jobs and to be less satisfied with their employment. In the area of socialization, the LD adults were less involved in social organizations and leisure activities. The adults with learning disabilities also reported lower levels of parent support and less satisfaction with school experiences as well as higher incidence of criminal convictions. In response to these finding, the researchers indicated that "the schools have neither adequately prepared the young LD adults for the social/affective facets of adult life nor taught them what to expect when they leave school" (p. 18).

A functional curriculum, as defined in this chapter, includes three domains: independent living skills, social skills, and vocational skills. There is a real need for independent living skills for students in corrections who have severe behavioral, intellectual, and/or learning disorders. Perhaps the most dramatic evidence of such a need was provided by a special project at the Oregon State Penitentiary. The state of Oregon, in response to pressure from the state Developmental Disabilities Council, the Association of Retarded Citizens, and the state Mental Health Division, segregated offenders whom they classified as mentally retarded from the general prison population. In reality, many of these offenders were severely learning disabled. The segregated unit received a special rehabilitation program, and the staff of the program quickly learned that many of these prisoners were deficient in basic skills, such as using the telephone, following up on want ads in newspapers, filling out employment applications, and adding and subtracting sums of money. They were also deficient in many social skills essential for survival in a job situation. Because of these deficiencies, the special unit of the state penitentiary developed a functional curriculum, including independent living skills, as a necessary part of the prisoners' rehabilitation program.

The need for the social skills domain of the functional curriculum has also been well documented in the special education literature (Wallace & McLoughlin, 1979). Goldstein (see chapter 10) suggests that social skills should be a major component in the correctional education curriculum and Wood (1982) emphasizes that socioemotional development should be one of the primary concerns of every teacher.

Certain assumptions concerning the behavior of adjudicated youth have led to social skills training programs for these individuals. One assumption is that these youth may be mildly retarded, learning disabled, or behaviorally disordered and are often at a disadvantage in schools, the community, and recreation and job settings because they do not have the necessary skills to interact appropriately with others. Whether they exhibit inappropriate behaviors (e.g., throwing tantrums, sulking, pouting, yelling) engage in illegal activities, or exhibit behavior deficits (e.g., an inability to greet other people, answer or ask questions, carry on a conversation), this lack of appropriate social skills can make these individuals easily discernible, cause them to be labeled or rejected, and bring them into repeated contacts with the juvenile justice system (Hazel, Schumaker, Sherman, & Sheldon-Wildgen, 1983). Hazel et al. (1981) developed a training program called ASSET, based on these assumptions. Their results showed that 80% of the youth in their program were offense-free 1 year after the program was terminated. Only 61% of the youth in two matched comparison groups were offense-free at that time. The authors concluded that social skills training may have an impact on the number of future offenses youth commit.

Friedman, Quick, Mayo, and Palmer (1983) describe the implementation of a social skills training procedure within the context of an intensive day-treatment program for multi-problem adolescents. Their program focused primarily on social skills training in combination with other therapeutic measures; however, their training did not include a functional curriculum. They reported data for their first 22 clients and showed a reduction from 14 to 4 in foster care placements and from 22 to 3 in temporary shelter care placements after social skills training. The number of psychiatric placements for this group also decreased. During a 1-year follow-up period none of the students were committed to training schools or other programs for delinquents. Among those who participated in the program, 54% spent at least 80% of their time constructively involved. Goldstein, Sprafkin, Gershaw, and Klein (1980) also developed a social skills training approach called structured learning (see chapter 10).

LeCroy (1983) identifies four components of social skills training models currently in use.

1. Selecting goals; that is, assisting youth in identifying specific goals toward which they need to work.
2. Modeling of appropriate social skills by the therapist or group members or viewing of modeling in films.
3. Role-playing, the heart of most social skills training, in which youths are asked to try on new modes of verbal and nonverbal behavior. Their responses are practiced and shaped to meet criteria for acceptable performance in natural settings.
4. Prompting before or during a role-play performance to cue certain behaviors. Many social skills training programs stress practice in the natural environment through homework assignments. For instance, after role-play practice, youths may be asked to go up and start talking with persons they would like to know better outside the training group.

Frosh (1983) suports the concept that social skills training assists students in adaptive functioning in a community. He mentions several cautions, however, including the fact that the sources of youths' problems are often multiple, chronic, intractable, and outside the professional range of even the most capable worker. Thus, social skills training may not be a panacea for all of a youth's problems. Another caution concerns the issue of generalization—the maintenance of treatment gains across time and settings. Not only must students manifest the learned social behaviors in school settings other than those where the social skills were learned, but those learned behaviors must also be exhibited in out-of-school settings.

The third domain of the functional curriculum is vocational training. Since almost 25% of an adult's life is spent in a vocational endeavor, the preparation of students for that portion of their lives is extremely important. For the correctional population employment is generally a major concern following return to the community. For the incarcerated student employment training becomes mandatory. Platt, Tunick, and Wienke (1982) describe a program of vocational training for an incarcerated special needs population. Not only are job skills taught, but emphasis is also placed on adjustment to work.

The importance of vocational education for incarcerated personnel is highlighted by the National Advisory Council on Vocational Education (1981). This report indicates that parolees who had received vocational education had significantly fewer arrests while on parole and fewer parole violations than parolees who had not received vocational training. Platt (1986) makes the case that a correctional institution has many vocational training opportunities and challenges educational programmers to provide effective vocational programs to juvenile offenders who are handicapped. For the student who is contemplating dropping out of school, employment is an immediate need.

Even though many students with mild learning, intellectual, and behavioral disorders have little difficulty learning the tasks necessary to perform specific jobs, their employment histories are frequently poor. Cronis and Justen (1975) found that individuals with handicaps failed on the job not because of their inability to perform job tasks, but because of their inability to adjust to the social demands of the work environment. Pagel and Whitling (1978) reported that maladaptive behavior was the principal reason for the community placement failure of persons with handicaps. Nickelsburg (1973) studied the productivity of workers with handicaps and reported the differences between 16 successful and 16 unsuccessful trainees. The major difference was the inappropriate social behavior displayed by the unsuccessful trainees. For example, the unsuccessful trainees spent more time standing idle, talking, joking, playing with others, laughing on the job, and being away from their assigned work stations. Greenspan and Shoultz (1981) also found social reasons for the involuntary termination from competitive employment of 30 individuals with mild and moderate handicaps: deficits in temperament, character, and social awareness.

Social skills cannot be taught solely in the classroom; they must be generalized in the community and, in the case of vocational social skills, in the vocational setting itself (Langone & Westling, 1979). Yet employers do not have the time, nor do they consider it part of their responsibility, to train new employees in social or associated work skills (Egan et al., 1984). This training must be accomplished during the school years, under close supervision, and with adequate feedback to students.

HOW TO TEACH A FUNCTIONAL CURRICULUM

The scope of the three domains of a functional curriculum is detailed in Figure 9.1.

The Need for Generalization

A student may demonstrate the ability to pick out the best buy among food items on a paper-and-pencil test in the classroom but may not be able to accomplish that same task in the supermarket, where price labels appear below the items and computation must be done on the spot with a calculator. Another student may be able to verbalize what it means to interact positively with other people in the environment but may not be able to do so in an actual situation. Certain skills can be practiced or role-played in the classroom, but they must eventually be generalized in real situations in the community. For instance, a job interview can be practiced in a classroom, but those skills

Figure 9.1   **The Scope of a Functional Curriculum**

Independent Living Skills	Social Skills
Telephone skills	Human awareness
Newspaper skills	Self-esteem
Transportation skills	Personal rights
Public transportation utilization	Relationships
Car ownership and management	Feelings
Money skills	Problem solving
Budgeting	Sexual knowledge
Bill paying	Communication
Banking	Compliments
Shopping skills	Assertiveness
Food	Listening skills
Clothes	Speaking skills
Other	**Vocational Skills**
Menu planning	Applying for a job
Cooking skills	Learning how to interview for a job
Home and yard maintenance	Performing on the job
Survival reading	Using correct social skills on the job
Use of the calculator	
Measurement skills	
Leisure time skills	

must actually be demonstrated in a bona fide job interview. The use of a calculator can best be taught in a classroom, but calculating the costs of items in stores, totaling the balance in a checkbook, or budgeting one's money must eventually be demonstrated in the real world. There are *no* functional living skills, social skills, or vocational skills that can be learned solely in a classroom environment. Each must be practiced in the actual setting or situation in which the skill will be used. Many published curricula provide paper-and-pencil exercises, but few have put together a system that allows the student to generalize functional skills in the community. Without that generalization a teacher can never be sure that the student has adequately learned the skills taught.

Curriculum

We have examined the majority of curricula purporting to teach functional skills and have found most of them deficient in several respects. Some are inadequately sequenced; in other words, essential steps are missing for students who have difficulty learning, or the curriculum has not been task-analyzed into fine enough steps. Frequently, the sequence either is not logically ordered or is not arranged in an order that will maximize student learning.

Although we have not examined and tried all of the currently published curricula, we have examined the majority. In addition, we have been able to try some of these in a classroom environment. As a result of that examination and trial, we have determined a number of curricula to be satisfactory for the special needs population. They are sequenced with learning steps small enough for the slow learner and in an order that moves from the least to the most difficult. Most have assessment instruments and allow for review of material. A list of these curricula is given in the Curriculum Resource List for Functional Academics, beginning on page 211, immediately in front of the end-of-chapter references.

The Instructional Paradigm

For the past 6 years Teaching Research of Monmouth, Oregon, has managed a public school resource center for students who are mildly retarded or learning disabled and severely behavior disordered. Youth in this classroom come not only from the five high schools in the school district but also from a local group home managed by Teaching Research. The group home serves children and youth within the state who have a history of being serially placed in foster care, who have failed in public school settings, or who come from an institutional setting. Teaching Research has used a functional curriculum in the resource room and has developed a teaching paradigm. The model provides instruction in the following sequence:

1. The student's current functional abilities are assessed.
2. Skills that can be taught in the classroom setting are taught there.
3. Student progress in the classroom setting is assessed. If progress is not satisfactory, the skill is retaught in the classroom setting. If progress is satisfactory, the student moves on to the next stage of instruction.
4. Skills that cannot be taught in the classroom are taught in the community.

As a matter of convenience, teachers generally prefer to teach a subject in the classroom environment. However, the acquisition of most functional skills can be demonstrated only in a community environment. An alternative for incarcerated students is to create a situation in the classroom as much like that in the community as possible. For instance, research by McDonnell, Horner, and Williams (1984) indicated that a combination of slides of an actual supermarket, practice in the classroom, and then generalization in the market provided more expeditious learning than just teaching in the market. Thus, well-designed classroom instruction can, in some circumstances, be more efficient in achieving the generalization of functional skills. The research of Horner and his associates (Horner & McDonald, 1982; Horner, Sprague, & Wilcox, 1982; Horner, Williams, & Steveley, 1984; Horner, James, & Williams, 1985) in teaching functional skills to a severely handicapped population can be adapted for less severely handicapped students because the principles of learning, specifically generalization, are similar for both populations.

Assessment

An assessment process is needed to determine not only what should be taught to the student, but also in what order it should be taught. Setting priorities is a difficult task, but the immediate needs of each student must be dealt with first; longer-range needs can be considered later. When assessing and setting priorities, the following factors should be considered.

□   the age of the student
□   the immediate functional living needs of the student
□   the long-range functional living needs of the student

Determination of long-range needs requires some predicting. Some students may not be able to live completely independently but may need some form of supported living environment. In such instances, the requirements of those environments must be determined. Students need to be taught the skills that will allow them to survive in their environments.

A process for conducting assessment has been developed by Evans et al. (1983). Assessing and determining the type of functional academic curriculum appropriate for individual students involves the following steps:

1. Complete an environment characteristics form for all curicular areas.
2. Determine the student's long-range placement in residential and vocational settings.
3. Determine the skills required for present and future environments.
4. Assess the student in skill areas required for present and future environments.
5. Determine the setting in which each skill will be trained and the setting in which each skill will be maintained or practiced.
6. Prioritize skills to be instructed and develop IEP objectives if appropriate.
7. Present skill programs according to the priorities list and the IEPs.

Complete Environment Characteristics Form.   The environment characteristics form is used to determine the skills required for success in a variety of residential and vocational settings that are typically used by individuals with mild or moderate developmental disabilities. These settings include foster care, adult group homes, semi-independent and independent community living arrangements, public schools, sheltered workshops, and supported and competitive community vocational placements. Although most offenders are capable of living independently, the environmental checklist may be necessary for some who do not have the necessary intellectual or behavioral capabilities. Use of the form may involve interviews with staff members of the various facilities, independent completion by a representative from each facility, or direct observations by the educator in charge. Figure 9.2 shows how such a form might be completed for the curricular area of money management. An environment characteristics form is not completed for each student, instead, it is completed for each geographic area and each curricular area.

Determine Long-Range Goals.   The second step in developing a functional academic curriculum is to determine the student's future environments. This determination is based on the student's age, skill level, parental input, personal preference, and available community resources. For example, a 17-year-old student who will be living independently after release from a correctional facility may require a program emphasizing independent living skills and vocational training. Figure 9.3 shows how the present and future residen-

Environment Characteristics Form

Figure 9.2

ENVIRONMENT CHARACTERISTICS FORM

Community Salem   Date of Assessment September 9, 1987   Curricular Area Money management

Skills	Residential						Vocational			
	Foster Care	Adult Group Home	Semi-Ind. Community Living	Independ. Community Living	Other		Public School	Sheltered Workshop	Supported Community	Competi-tive Community
Receives weekly or monthly paycheck	X	X	X	X				X	X	X
Calculates weekly or monthly income	X	X	X	X				X	X	X
Identifies budget priorities for month	X	X	X	X						
Allots needed money for items on budget sheet			X	X						
Balances budget according to priorities list			X	X						
Makes savings account withdrawals/ deposits		X	X	X						
Makes checking account withdrawals/deposits		X	X	X						
Endorses checks correctly	X	X	X	X						
Purchases/pays bills according to budget sheet	X	X	X	X						
Pays bills on time			X	X						
Obtains change for purchases if applicable	X	X	X	X			X		X	X
Safely keeps/carries money	X	X	X	X			X	X	X	X
Borrows when appropriate	X	X	X	X						
Purchases money order				X						
Purchases and uses traveler's checks										
Opens savings account			X	X						
Opens checking account			X	X						

Figure 9.3   Student Priorities Cover Sheet

STUDENT PRIORITIES COVER SHEET

Student   Jane Doe   Date   9/9/87

Birthdate   6/3/70   Age   17   Sex   F

Environment:

	Present	Placement Date
Residential	Foster care	6/7/87
Vocational	Sprague High School	9/7/87

	Future	Projected Placement Date
Residential	Semi-independent living	September 1988
Vocational	Supported community	June 1988

Involved Agencies/Persons

	Name	Role
1.	Chris Hadden	Teacher
2.	Kirk Hendrickson	Vocational trainer
3.	Debbi Kraus	Foster parent
4.		
5.		

Skill Priorities List:

Skill Program	Date Started	Date Completed	Home	Voc	Other
1. Social/sexual	9/15/87	10/20/87		Ⓣ	
2. Money management	9/15/87		M	T	
3. Personal hygiene	9/20/87		Ⓣ		
4. Community mobility	9/20/87		M	T	
5. Vocational	9/15/87			M	Kirk Ⓣ
6. Calculator math	10/20/87			Ⓣ	
7. Communication				Ⓣ	
8. Leisure activities				Ⓣ	P.E.
9. Newspaper			M	T	
10. Menu planning					
11. Food preparation					
12. Telephone skills					

Code: T = Training   M = Maintenance   Ⓣ = Training and maintenance tial and vocational settings might be indicated on a student priorities cover sheet. The lower portion of the form is completed at a later time.

Determine Skills Required for Present and Future Environments. The skills in each curricular area required for present and future environments are transferred to a student assessment form from the environment characteristics form. These skills are shown as required (see Figure 9.4).

Assess Student in Skill Areas Required for Present and Future Environments. The student assessment form is also used to record a student's skill level in each required skill. Assessment is based on information obtained from observations of the student, samples of student work, interviews with parents and other involved persons, and individual testing procedures. The items listed for each curricular area are written to accommodate a variety of commercial and teacher-made materials. Each skill should be demonstrated at an appropriate criterion level to ensure its successful application in the student's present and future environments. Determination of this criterion is at the discretion of the educator. Figure 9.4 shows an example of how skill assessment is indicated on the form; the student either has the skill or needs training in it.

Determine Setting in Which Skill Will Be Trained. The setting for training and/or maintenance of each instructed skill is indicated on the student assessment form. School, home, or other relevant setting may be identified. Again, Figure 9.4 gives an example of how this information is represented on the form.

Prioritize Skill Programs. The student priorities cover sheet (See Figure 9.3) summarizes the skills requiring instruction for each student and lists them according to priority level of need. Skills that are considered high priority include those that

□ ensure the personal safety of self or others
□ are required for both present and future environments
□ ensure student success in the present environment

All skills that fall within these categories should be placed near the top of the priorities list. Other factors also influence the order of priority for skill programs; for example, preferences of parents, limitations of training facilities, and specialized needs of the student.

After assessment has been completed and a student's immediate and long-range needs have been determined, the IEP (if required) is prepared with all necessary professionals, the parents, and the student participating.

Independent Living

The teaching strategy used for functional independent living skills follows this sequence: teach what is appropriate to be taught in the classroom environment; test; generalize to the natural environment; observe and keep data. If a student fails to achieve criterion in either the classroom or the natural environment, instruction continues until the criterion is reached.

Figure 9.4   **Student Assessment Form**

				Location		
Skills	Required	Has Skill	Needs Training	School	Home	Other
Receives weekly or monthly paycheck	X	X				
Calculates weekly or monthly income	X		X		ⓣ	
Identifies budget priorities for month	X		X		ⓣ	
Allots needed money for items on budget sheet	X		X		ⓣ	
Balances budget according to priorities list	X		X		ⓣ	
Makes savings account withdrawals/deposits	X		X	T	M	
Makes checking account withdrawals/deposits	X		X	T	M	
Endorses checks correctly	X	X				
Purchases/pays bills according to budget sheet	X		X		ⓣ	
Pays bills on time	X		X		ⓣ	
Obtains change for purchases if applicable	X		X	T	M	
Safely keeps/carries money	X	X				
Borrows when appropriate	X	X				
Purchases money order						
Purchases and uses traveler's checks						
Opens savings account	X		X	T	M	
Opens checking account	X		X	T	M	

STUDENT ASSESSMENT FORM

Name Jane Doe   Date of Assessment September 19, 1987

Curricular Area Money management   Evaluation Team Debbie Kraus and Jim Johnson

Code: T = Training   M = Maintenance   ⓣ = Training and maintenance

Before any functional skill is taught, a task analysis should determine the steps of the skill. As previously mentioned, the lack of such an ordered list constitutes the major deficit of many published curricula. Figure 9.5 shows an example of a task analysis for the task of using a local telephone book for functional information (Evans et al., 1984). Such a task analysis ensures that the subject is comprehensively covered and also provides the basis for maintaining data on the student's progress.

Task Analysis for Telephone Book Skills   **Figure 9.5**

Telephone Book Usage

Terminal Objective: Use local telephone book to locate functional information
Prerequisite Skills: 1. Alphabetize words to 3-letter discrimination
                        2. Read following words:
                            a. fire department
                            b. police department
                            c. ambulance
                            d. repair service
                            e. time of day
                        3. Understand concepts of city, state, in-state, and out-of-state
                        4. Read and write numbers 0 to 9

Worksheets 2A and 2B: Emergency Numbers
Phase I;   Locate emergency and other business numbers in telephone book
            a. Emergency number: police   d. Other business number: police
            b. Emergency number: fire department e. Other business number: fire
            c. Emergency number: ambulance
Phase II: Describe at least one situation in which emergency and other business numbers
            should be used
            a. Emergency number: police   d. Other business number: police
            b. Emergency number: fire department e. Other business number: fire
            c. Emergency number: ambulance

Worksheets 3A and 3B: Telephone Service Numbers
Phase III: Locate telephone service numbers in phone book
            a. In-state directory assistance number   d. Telephone repair number—residence
            b. Out-of-state directory assistance   e. Time
                number
            c. Telephone repair number—business
Phase IV: Describe function of telephone service number
            a. In-state directory assistance number   d. Telephone repair number—residence
            b. Out-of-state directory assistance   e. Time
                number
            c. Telephone repair number—business

Worksheets 4A and 4B: White Pages
Phase V: Locate telephone numbers and addresses in white pages (higher level students
            may be introduced to guide words)
            a. Given city and person's last name   c. Given city and person's first name,
            b. Give city and person's first and last   last name, and middle initial
                name   d. Given city and person's last name
                                                           and address

Worksheets 5A and 5B: Yellow Pages
Phase VI: Locate sections in yellow pages
            a. Beauty salons   d. Restaurants
            b. Churches   e. Department stores
            c. Physicians
Phase VII: Locate telephone numbers and addresses in yellow pages
            a. Beauty salon   d. Restaurant
            b. Church   e. Department store
            c. Physician

Worksheets 6A and 6B: Brand Names and Service Numbers
Phase VIII: Locate sections for service of brand name items in yellow pages
            a. Appliance service   d. Rental service
            b. Automobile towing service e. Automotive repair service
            c. Plumbing service

Figure 9.5
continued

Phase IX: Locate phone numbers and addresses for service of brand name items
  a. Appliance service   d. Rental service
  b. Automobile towing service   e. Automotive repair service
  c. Plumbing service

Teaching Notes
1. It is recommended that phases be taught in the order presented. However, each phase should be evaluated to determine suitability for meeting student needs. The teaching sequence may be changed and/or phases eliminated if necessary to meet student skill needs.
2. All steps accompanying each phase should be taught before a student is advanced to the next phase.
3. Worksheets covering the same information are written on two levels, with level A being less difficult than level B. Students need to demonstrate competency on either worksheet to advance. The teacher should determine which worksheet is appropriate for each student.
4. Telephone books should be used during baselining, instruction, and assessment.

Most independent living skills eventually must be demonstrated in the natural environment to verify that learning has occurred. For instance, a shopping list can be planned in the classroom, and the use of a calculator, in addition to basic money skills and budgeting, can be taught there. Then, in a correctional setting, shopping for commissary items can provide practice in each of these skills. In the commissary the student can practice functional reading—that is, reading the signs over the different shelves to learn where items are located, determining with a calculator the best selection for an item on the shopping list, and determining whether there is enough money to pay for all the items selected. Paying for the items and determining that correct change was given are two other skills that can be demonstrated. In addition, since many students with mild to moderate developmental disabilities have a history of poor behavior, appropriate social behavior can be practiced.

If incarcerated youth return to school after they are released, it is imperative that their special education programs continue this type of community-based training. Shopping in a supermarket has to be taught. And similar shopping expeditions can be arranged for clothes. Finding correct sizes and desired styles and determining the quality of clothing that can be bought in various stores are skills to be learned. Field trips can ensure that students are generalizing learned skills. Trips to banks, public amusement places, and variety stores expose students to a variety of shopping experiences and present opportunities to use functional reading skills; they also permit students to experience different forms of transportation and to practice social skills in a variety of situations.

Social Skills Training

The ultimate goal of social skills training is to teach students to effectively cope with the social demands of their living and work environments. These demands may be as simple as making everyday purchases from a store clerk, accepting compliments from a close friend, or conversing with a co-worker at break time. They may be as complex as building a long-term marital relationship. Included in the overall goal is teaching students to understand themselves and their own needs; to assume responsibility for fulfilling their living and work needs in ways that are acceptable to society; and to communicate effectively with a variety of people, including family, neighbors, supervisors, waiters, and landlords. Students need to learn to cope with a wide range of social situations involving both familiar and unfamiliar settings, circumstances, and the people. Some of these situations can be predicted and addressed during a training process, but many are unpredictable and unique to the circumstances of each student's life. Therefore, it is critical that students be able to generalize learned social behaviors in a variety of different circumstances. They must be able to identify the goal of each social situation, choose an appropriate course of action to meet that goal, and evaluate the effectiveness of their actions, determining an alternative approach if necessary. From that perspective the complexity of social skills training seems enormous.

Instruction within the classroom should provide students with a knowledge base of the topics in a comprehensive social skills curriculum. Training within the community should emphasize generalization of learned behaviors to a variety of different situations, settings, and people. Community training should also address the need for students to respond appropriately to the reinforcers and punishers typically found in the community. Incarcerated students can practice social skills by responding appropriately to others, developing friendships, and coping with aversive situations, among other activities.

Instruction of Social Skills in a Positive Classroom Setting.   There are many reasons for teaching social skills within a classroom setting. First, classroom settings provide the opportunity for instruction in aspects of human awareness that cannot be taught in a natural setting—for example, self-esteem, personal rights, relationships, feelings, and problem solving. Second, classroom instruction allows students to learn and practice communication skills in a supportive setting without the anxiety and distracting events that are often present in the natural environment. In addition, social skills training in a classroom group provides students with the opportunity to interact and share values and beliefs with peers and significant adults. Group programs allow students to gain support from the knowledge that other people are faced with their same fears and needs.

The daily schedule for each student placed in an alternative functional curriculum should include 1 hour of social skills instruction, encompassing a wide array of topics. Human awareness topics were highlighted earlier. Sexuality issues should also be presented so that students have a better understanding of internal changes and can make responsible decisions regarding premarital sex, birth control, marriage, and procreation. Communication skills should teach students effective methods of responding to both positive and negative situations. Making small talk, giving compliments, and active listening need to be included. In short, a comprehensive social skills curriculum teaches the skills necessary for effectively coping with the interpersonal demands of everyday living.

Several factors influence the effectiveness of social skills teaching in correctional classrooms. Teachers need to arrange students for effective behavior management. Individual desks are useful in giving students their own space and in permitting varied classroom arrangements. A chalkboard should be available so that information can be presented visually as well as orally; the chalkboard visually organizes materials for students, thereby increasing the likelihood that the materials presented with be understood and used in the future.

Instructional strategies that prove successful in teaching social skills are those that motivate and reward the student for active participation in the learning process and for personal growth. A traditional lecture approach is not recommended. Instead, group discussion may be useful in presenting information to students. This strategy demands that students be involved in the lesson and provides opportunities to teach group interaction, problem-solving, listening, and communication skills. Group discussion is also effective in preparing students for the social demands of mainstream classrooms that use this strategy.

Role-playing is another useful strategy for encouraging students to participate in the lesson and for practicing communication skills in a supportive setting. After students understand the skills required to participate in role-play, teachers can ask them to act out a variety of situations. Role-play situations should be carefully selected and should reflect circumstances the student may encounter in the natural environment. To serve as a reference for students during the role-play, a list of simple steps clearly outlining what is expected should be written on the chalkboard. If students are to role-play being assertive, for example, these steps might be listed.

1. Look person in the eye
2. Stand at appropriate distance
3. Talk in clear, calm voice
4. Use "I" statements
5. Tell person what you want

Other students can be encouraged to give role-play participants supportive praise or recommendations, using the list of steps written on the chalkboard as a guide so that suggestions are relevant. Role-plays should be organized so that students participate with different people, including both peers and adults. This strategy is an excellent tool for allowing students to practice skills in a supportive setting.

For effective classroom instruction it is most important to establish a positive environment that will support students in the learning process. A critical factor in this effort is the amount of positive feedback provided for each student. Experience indicates that students require 80% positive feedback (i.e., 4 positive to 1 negative response) in their classroom setting to feel supported and positive about school. Students who receive less than this proportion may be adversely affected; those receiving as little as 50% positive feedback may be discouraged by the negative environment. Establishing a history of positive interactions with every student in the class is important. Social skills training presents topics that many students find embarrassing and uncomfortable to discuss. A positive learning environment that emphasizes students' strengths will enhance their ability to participate in and benefit from the social skills curriculum.

Practice of Learned Skills Within Natural Community Environments. The training of social behaviors outside the classroom setting is critical to the optimum success of a social skills program. One of the most important goals of this curricular area is to teach students to act in an appropriate social manner when in the mainstream of the school, institution, or community. To achieve effective transition from the correctional classroom to the community setting, there must first be active programming within the natural environment, including a variety of different settings, people, and situations.

One method of conducting this training is to give students specific social assignments reflecting situations that would normally occur in their lives. Examples might include inviting a friend to a sports activity, confronting a person who frequently calls the student names, or asking a supervisor for extra help in a job setting. The procedure for the student to follow is first to understand the goal or assignment, to identify a number of possible solutions to meet the goal, evaluate the solutions for their probable effectiveness, and choose one solution to use. The next step is to role-play the interaction required by the selected solution; the student needs to be clear about the social behaviors that should occur. Role-playing should also help reduce the student's anxiety level. The student should then complete the social assignment outside the classroom. The final step for the teacher is to give the student supportive feedback as soon after the incident as possible.

Another useful strategy is to present the student with an unexpected social situation, perhaps asking someone to give the student a compliment. Observations should determine whether the student accepts the compliment appropriately, using previously learned social skills. This strategy usually entails the recruitment of familiar and unfamiliar persons to interact with the student in a variety of ways, ranging from giving a pleasant greeting or making a simple request to bossing the student around inappropriately. An appropriate response should be reinforced; an inappropriate response should prompt feedback and additional role-playing until the student responds correctly. This strategy can be an effective means of training students in the natural environment; however, recruiting persons and setting up situations can be time-consuming.

It is important that the situations selected for social skills training reflect typical occurrences in the student's life. It is also important to include situations in which the student should *not* act—for example, when the boss looks too busy to talk, when two strangers are talking together and make no eye contact with the student, or when the student is working in a vocational setting in which talking is discouraged. Again, it is important that feedback be immediate and consistent and that the student role-play correctly any inappropriate response.

To adequately track student social behaviors, a precise data system is necessary. One that is easy to use and is designed for social skills monitoring in the natural environment is described in detail in Egan et al. (1984). This data system is useful not only for tracking the acquisition of social behaviors, but also for specifying a complete system of program design, data keeping, and program alteration in the remediation of inappropriate behaviors.

Vocational Domain

The best vocational training takes places in the community and certainly should be part of most released students' programs. However, our experience with vocational programs also argues for probationary vocational programs for adjudicated students scheduled for incarceration. Many students who have exhibited severe behavior disorders in a school setting do not exhibit nearly as many or as severe behaviors in a vocational setting. Although no data have been gathered to document this as a suitable probationary alternative, Meers (1983) also advocates a vocational alternative to incarceration. He outlines a plan whereby continued successful performance in a job setting forms an alternative to juvenile detention or adult incarceration.

We have experimented with various types of vocational programs over the past 6 years. We started with a program that was school-based and provided job training around the school. Although this approach measured how well students adjusted to work placements in lieu of academic placements, it did not provide us with sufficient opportunities to put students into situations requiring on-the-job social skills. We have termed these skills *associated work skills* and have listed many that are appropriate for this population.

Demonstrates work-associated skills in classroom
Completes simple application form
Has work permit
Understands interview process
Follows classroom schedule
Uses free time in socially appropriate way
Applies for structured vocational job
Interviews for structured vocational job
Demonstrates work-associated skills in vocational setting
Wears clothing appropriate for work setting
Maintains satisfactory personal hygiene
Observes basic rules of setting
Follows established routine/schedule
Works independently on specified tasks
Works cooperatively in group setting
Remains on-task during work period
Works at appropriate rate/speed

Produces finished work of satisfactory quality
Arrives at work on time
Takes break appropriately
Returns from lunch/break on time
Uses time clock/card
Follows safety procedures of setting
Uses safety gear
Responds to emergency situations
Notifies supervisor when sick/injured
Notifies supervisor of planned absences
Transports self to work setting
Locates essential sites at work setting (e.g., bathroom)
Engages in appropriate conversation
Interacts with co-workers without affecting work
Accepts constructive feedback from supervisor
Asks for assistance when needed
Complies with supervisor's requests
Does not display self-indulgent behavior
Does not display aggressive behavior
Works in two or more vocational areas
Applies for competitive job
Demonstrates work-associated skills in competitive job
Demonstrates satisfactory work performance
Understands and reads paycheck

Obviously, a number of these skills require that the vocational program be moved into the community. Initially, our Teaching Research project maintained an in-school vocational program to prepare students to go into the community. However, our data indicated that this preparatory period had little value; the more practice students got in the community with designated associated work skills, the better prepared they were for the job market. Consequently, our vocational program at this time is totally community-oriented.

In our program a paraprofessional vocational trainer locates jobs in the community in which students can be placed for 8 to 10 hours a week, usually during school hours. Placements are sought for all targeted students, aged 13 and older. Nonpaid positions are sought for the younger students. The vocational trainer finds the jobs, assures the employers that they have no obligation for training, and guarantees that the jobs will get done. Then the vocational trainer works with the students, not only teaching them the jobs but also shaping associated work skills. The trainer gradually fades out until students gain full independence on the job. Students are maintained in this position until they have learned their jobs and have done reasonably well with the associated work skills. Because some students have associated work skill problems across job sites, our policy is not to maintain students in a single job merely to improve these skills. Rather, we attempt to improve their work skills across a variety of job settings. When students have mastered a job, they are moved to a new job unless the old one expands or changes so that they must acquire new skills.

We view these job placements as an educational program in two respects. First, students acquire a variety of work experiences that allow them to be more selective about the types of work they are capable of doing and like to do. Second, their associated work skills can continue to be improved over time.

For the older students, those who will graduate within 18 months, we seek paid positions, even if they are only part-time. We believe that a number of part-time jobs of 6 to 15 hours a week can provide a high quality of life, especially if a student has the capability of doing only repetitive work. And of course, some part-time jobs can grow into full-time positions. Our goal is to have students move into independence with at least two part-time jobs. Here is a sample of the part-time jobs in which we have placed students.

□   Veterinary hospitals: cleaning cages and feeding animals
□   Food service: bus boy, dishwasher, salad person
□   Plumbing shop: restocking parts
□   Soft drink bottling: sorting recycled bottles
□   Supermarkets: sorting recycled bottles
□   Custodial jobs in a variety of settings
□   Rental agencies: washing campers and trucks
□   Motels: laundry work and room maid

We are not suggesting that these are the only types of jobs that our students can get. We are suggesting that these jobs may be readily available even in depressed economies for students who need to experience the world of work.

Within the correctional setting a variety of job sites are also available that can be used for part-time jobs. Food service, grounds keeping, custodial work, laundry, and clerical jobs are all potential vocational areas within the institution. Placement of incarcerated youth in those job settings, following the model outlined earlier, is not only possible but desirable. Data also indicate a high degree of cost benefit because parolees who had received vocational education demonstrated less recidivism (National Advisory Council on Vocational Education, 1981).

CONCLUSION

We suggest that a functional curriculum is a viable and preferred alternative for at least a portion of the adjudicated handicapped population. Students who are reading four grade levels behind their peers when they reach junior high school are candidates for such a curriculum, as are students who have dropped out of school or who exhibit severe behavior problems. The functional curriculum consists of three major domains: independent living, social, and vocational skills. We have given suggestions for assessment and teaching and have emphasized the need for community training in all skills.

CURRICULUM RESOURCE LIST FOR FUNCTIONAL ACADEMICS

Teaching Research Publications

The Teaching Research Curriculum for Adolescents and Adults with Mild and Moderate Handicaps, 1984, Teaching Research Publications, Monmouth, OR 97361. Published titles include "Taxonomy and Assessment" and "Telephone Skills"; draft titles include "Newspaper Skills," "Banking Skills," and "Budgeting Skills for the Home"; topics being developed include sex education, social relationships and communication, menu planning and shopping, and community mobility.

Independent Living Skills

I Think I Can Learn to Cook or I Can Cook to Think and Learn by Jean S. Triebel, and Mary Carol Manning, 1976, Academic Therapy Publications, 1539 Fourth Street, San Rafael, CA 94901.

Let's Eat by Nancy Hedstrom, 1971, Matex Associates, Inc., 90 Cherry Street, Box 519, Johnstown, PA 15907.

On Your Own, 1981, Janus Book Publishers, 2501 Industrial Parkway West, Hayward, CA, 94545. Titles in the series include "Caring for your Car," "Getting Help: A Guide to Community Services," "Need a Doctor?" and "Sharing an Apartment."

Phone Sense by Roger E. Kranich and Jerry L. Messee, 1980, One Press, Inc., P.O. Box 61688, Sunnyvale, CA 94088.

Planning for Your Own Apartment by Virginia Sweet Belina, 1975, Fearon Publishers, Inc., 6 Davis Drive, Belmont, CA 94002.

Your Homemaker at Work, 1974, Fearon Pitman Publishers, Inc., 6 Davis Drive, CA 94002. Titles in the series include "Planning Meals and Shopping," "Getting Ready to Cook," and "The Young Homemakers Cookbook."

Survival Reading

Basic Skills in Reading and Understanding Newspapers by Joseph Sanacre, 1979, Cebco Standard Publishing, 9 Kulick Road, Fairfield, NJ 97006.

Practice in Survival Reading, 1977, New Readers Press, Publishing Division of Laubach Literary International, Box 131, Syracuse, NY 13210. Titles in the series include "Machine Age Riddles," "Swing Around Town," "Label Talk," "Read the Instructions First," "Your Daily Paper," "It's on the Map," "Let's Look It Up," and "Caution: Fine Print Ahead."

Read On/Write On, 1981, Janus Book Publishers, 2501 Industrial Parkway West, Hayward, CA 94545. Titles in the series include "The Big Hassle and Other Plays," "The Put Down Pro and Other Plays," "The Promise and Other Stories," "The Choice and Other Stories," "The Last Good-Bye and Other Stories," and "Time and Change and Other Stories,"

Reading for Survival in Today's Society, 1978, Goodyear Publishing Company, Inc., Santa Monica, CA 90401.

Survival Guides, Janus Book Publishers, 2501 Industrial Parkway West, Hayward, CA 94545. Titles in the series include "Becoming a Driver," "Finding a Good Used Car," "Getting Around Cities and Towns," "Help! First Steps to First Aid," "Reading and Following Directions," "Reading a Newspaper," "Reading Schedules," "Using the Phone Book," and "Using the Want Ads."

Survival Skills Duplicating Master Activity Books, Media Materials, Inc., 2936 Remington Avenue, Baltimore, MD 21211. Titles in the series include "Getting a Job," "Keeping a Job," "Buying What You Need," "Getting the Groceries," "Paying Your Bills," "Taking a Trip," "Reading Your Newspaper," "The Media and You," "Using the Telephone Directory," and "Making Informed Decisions."

Survival Vocabularies, Janus Book Publishers, 2501 Industrial Parkway West, Hayward, CA 94545. Topics include banking language, credit language, clothing language, entertainment language, drugstore language, restaurant language, supermarket language, job application language, driver's license language, and medical language.

Reading and Language Skills

Getting It Together by Herman R. Goldberg and Bernard Greenbryer, 1973, SRA, Chicago.

The Learning Skills Series, 1978, Webster Division, McGraw-Hill, Inc., New York. Titles in the series include "Acquiring Language Skills," "Building Language Skills," "Continuing Language Skills," and "Directing Language Skills."

Reading and Understanding, 1969, SRA, Chicago.

Writing Skills Kit, Developmental Learning Materials, 7440 Natchez Avenue, Niles, IL 60648.

Money Management and Math Series

Banking and Budgeting, and Employment by Art Lennox, 1979, Frank E. Richards Publishing Company, Inc., Phoenix, NY 13135.

Learning About Measurement by Raymond J. Bohn, John Mersur, and John D. Wool, 1969, Frank E. Richards Publishing Company, Inc., Phoenix, NY 13135.

Money Matters Guide, Janus Book Publishers, 2501 Industrial Parkway West, Hayward, CA 94545. Titles include "Make Your Money Grow," "Insure Yourself," "Be Credit-Wise," "Know Your Rights," "Be Ad-Wise," "Master Your Money," "More for Your Money," and "Pay by Check."

Pacemaker Practical Arithmetic Series, 1980, Pitman Learning, Inc., 6 Davis Drive, Belmont, CA 94002.

Survival Guides, Janus Book Publishers, 2501 Industrial Parkway West, Hayward, CA 94545. Titles in the series include "Using Dollars and Sense," "Working Makes Sense," and "Buying with Sense."

Survival Skills Duplicating Master Activity Books, Media Materials, Inc., 2936 Remington Avenue, Baltimore, MD 21211. Titles in the series include "Personal Mathematics," "Income and Expenses," "Household Mathematics," "Shopping Mathematics," "Travel Mathematics," "Mathematics for Car Owners," "Career Mathematics," "Mathematics for Banking," "Insurance and Mathematics," and "Mathematics for Taxes."

Social Relationships and Sex Education

Chemical Abuse Prevention by Rebecca E. Strandland and Mitchell E. Kusy, 1979, Minneapolis Public Schools, 254 Upton Avenue South, Minneapolis, MN 55405.

Facts About Sex for Today's Youth by Sol Gordon, 1979, Wadsworth ED-U Press, Box 583, Fayetteville, NY 13066.

Facts About VD for Today's Youth by Sol Gordon, 1979, Wadsworth ED-U Press, Box 583, Fayetteville, NY 13066.

Finding Solutions: Learning How to Deal with Life's Problems and Decisions by James Cisek, 1980, Life Skills Training Associates, Box 48133, Chicago, IL 60648.

Human Sexuality for Junior High Students with Special Needs by Rebecca E. Strandland and Mitchell E. Kusy, 1978, Minneapolis Public Schools, Special Education Service Center, 254 Upton Avenue South, Minneapolis, MN 55405.

Personal Development and Sexuality, Planned Parenthood of Pierce County, Tacoma, Washington 98402.

Personal Hygiene by Rebecca E. Strandland and Mitchell E. Kusy, 1979, Minneapolis Public Schools, 254 Upton Avenue South, Minneapolis, MN 55405.

Sex Education, Planned Parenthood of Santa Cruz County, 212 Laurel Street, Santa Cruz, CA 95060.

The Sexual Adolescent and Communication with Teenagers About Sex by Sol Gordon, 1973, Wadsworth ED-U Press, Box 583, Fayetteville, NY 13066.

Vocational Skills

Career Awareness Plus, Janus Book Publishers, 2501 Industrial Parkway West, Hayward, CA 94545. Titles in the series include "Restaurant Job," "Restaurant Words," "Restaurant Word Cards," "Hospital Jobs," "Hospital Words," "Hospital Word Cards," "Hotel/Motel Jobs," "Hotel/Motel Words," "Hotel/Motel Word Cards," "Store Jobs," "Store Words," and "Store Word Cards."

Career Education Materials, 1978, Janus Book Publishers, 2501 Industrial Parkway West, Hayward, CA 94545. Titles in the series include "Don't Get Fired," "Get Hired!" "Janus Job Interview Guide," "Janus Job Interview Kit," "Janus Job Planner," and "My Job Application File."

Jobs: From "A" to "Z" by Yvette Doylin, Frank E. Richards Publishing Company, Inc., Phoenix, NY 13135.

People Working Today, Janus Book Publishers, 2501 Industrial Parkway West, Hayward, CA 94545. Titles in the series include "Alex on the Grill," "Bob the Super Clerk," "Janet the Hospital Worker," "Jester the Bellhop," "Johnny at the Circuits," "Julie at the Pumps," "Kenny Drives a Van," "Larry the Logger," "Laura Cares for Pets," and "Tony the Night Custodian."

REFERENCES

Brozovich, R., & Kotting, C. (1984). Teacher perceptions of high school special education programs. *Exceptional Children, 50,* 548–549.

Bureau of Justice Statistics. (1983). *Report to the nation on crime and justice: The data.* Washington, DC: U. S. Department of Justice.

Cronis, G., & Justen, E. (1975). Teaching work attitudes at the elementary level. *Teaching Exceptional Children, 7,* 103–105.

Davies, W. (1983). Competencies and skills required to be an effective resource education teacher. *Journal of Learning Disabilities, 16,* 596–598.

Egan, I., Fredericks, H., Peters, J., Hendrickson, K., Bunse, C., Toews, J., & Buckley, J. (1984). *Associated work skills: A manual.* Monmouth, OR: Teaching Research.

Evans, V., Fredericks, H., Toews, J., Hadden, C., Moore, W., & Dooley, M. (1984). *The Teaching Research curriculum for adolescents and adults with mild and moderate handicaps: Telephone skills.* Monmouth, OR: Teaching Research.

Friedman, R., Quick, J., Mayo, J., & Palmer, J. (1983). Social skills training within a day treatment program for emotionally disturbed adolescents. In C. LeCroy (Ed.), *Social skills training for children and youth* (pp. 31–45). New York: Haworth.

Frosh, S. (1983). Children and teachers in schools. In S. M. Spence & G. Shepherd (Eds.), *Developments in social skills training* (pp. 134–140). New York: Academic.

Goldstein, A. P., Sprafkin, R. P., Gershaw, N. J., & Klein, P. (1980). Social skills through structured learning. In G. Cartledge & J. F. Milburn (Eds.), *Teaching social skills to children* (pp. 25–30). New York: Pergamon.

Greenspan, S., & Shoultz, B. (1981). Why mentally retarded adults lose their jobs: Social competence as a factor in work adjustment. *Applied Research in Mental Retardation, 2,* 23–38.

Halpern, A., & Benz, M. (1984). *Toward excellence in secondary special education: A statewide study of Oregon's high school programs for students with mild disabilities.* Unpublished manuscript, University of Oregon.

Hazel, J. S., Schumaker, J. B., Sherman, J. A., & Sheldon-Wildgen, J. (1981). *ASSET: A social skills program for adolescents.* Champaign, IL: Research Press.

Hazel, J. S., Schumaker, J. B., Sherman, J. A., & Sheldon-Wildgen, J. (1983). Social skills training with court-adjudicated youths. In C. LeCroy (Ed.), *Social skills training for children and youth* (pp. 24–31). New York: Haworth.

Horner, R., James, D., & Williams, J. (1985). A functional approach to teaching generalized street crossing. *Journal of the Association for Persons with Severe Handicaps, 10,* 71–78.

Horner, R., & McDonald, R. (1982). A comparison of single instance and general case instruction in teaching a generalized vocational skill. *Journal of the Association for the Severely Handicapped, 7,* 7–20.

Horner, R., Sprague, J., & Wilcox, B. (1982). Constructing general case programs for community activities. In B. Wilcox & G. T. Bellamy (Eds.), *Design of high school programs for severely handicapped students* (pp. 61–98). Baltimore, MD: Brookes.

Horner, R., Williams, J., & Steveley, J. (1984). *Acquisition of generalized telephone use by students with severe mental retardation.* Manuscript submitted for publication.

Langone, J., & Westling, D. (1979). Generalization of prevocational and vocational skills: Some practical tactics. *Education and Training of the Mentally Retarded, 14,* 216–221.

LeCroy, C. (1983). Social skills training with adolescents: A review. In C. LeCroy (Ed.), *Social skills training for children and youth* (pp. 91–116). New York: Haworth.

McDonnell, J., Horner, R., & Williams, J. (1984). Comparison of three strategies for teaching generalized grocery purchasing to high school students with severe handicaps. *Journal of the Association for Persons with Severe Handicaps, 9,* 123–133.

Meers, G. D. (1983). Vocational teachers' role in serving juvenile offenders. *Journal of Vocational Special Needs Education, 5,* 31–33.

National Advisory Council on Vocational Education. (1981). *Vocational education in correctional institutions.* Washington, DC: U. S. Department of Education.

Nickelsburg, R. (1973). Time sampling of work behavior of mentally retarded trainees. *Mental Retardation, 11,* 29–40.

Pagel, S., & Whitling, C. (1978). Readmissions to a state hospital for mentally retarded persons: Reasons for community placement failure. *Mental Retardation, 16,* 164–168.

Platt, J. (1986). Vocational education in corrections: A piece of a bigger pie. *Remedial and Special Education, 7,* 48–55.

Platt, J., Tunick, R., & Wienke, W. (1982). Developing the work and life skills of handicapped inmates. *Corrections Today, 44,* 66–73.

Rutherford, R. B., Nelson, C. M., & Wolford, B. I. (1985). Special education in the most restrictive environment: Correctional/special education. *Journal of Special Education, 19,* 59–71.

Vetter, A. (1983). *A comparison of the characteristics of learning disabled and non-learning disabled young adults.* Unpublished doctoral dissertation, University of Kansas.

Wallace, G., & McLoughlin, J. A. (1979). *Learning disabilities: Concepts and characteristics* (2nd ed.). Columbus, OH: Merrill.

White, W., Schumaker, J., Warner, M., Alley, G., & Deshler, D. (1980). *The current status of young adults identified as learning disabled during their school career* (Research Report). Lawrence: University of Kansas, Institute for Research in Learning Disabilities.

Wood, F. H. (1982). Affective education and social skills training: A consumer's guide. *Teaching Exceptional Children, 14,* 212–216.

Teaching Prosocial Skills
to Antisocial Adolescents

CHAPTER 10   *Arnold P. Goldstein*

Until the early 1970s three major clusters of psychotherapies dominated efforts to alter the behavior of aggressive, unhappy, ineffective, or disturbed individuals: psychodynamics/psychoanalysis, humanistic/nondirective therapy, and behavior modification. Each of these diverse orientations provided specific therapeutic interventions for aggressive adolescents. The psychodynamic approach was manifested in psychoanalytical individual psychotherapy (Guttman, 1960), activity group therapy (Slavson, 1964), and the varied array of treatment procedures developed by Redl and Wineman (1957). Humanistic/nondirective therapies found expression in applications of client-centered psychotherapy (Rogers, 1957) to juvenile delinquents (e.g., Truax, Wargo, & Silber, 1966), the alternative educational programs offered by Gold (1978), and Dreikurs, Grunwald, and Pepper's (1971) approach to school discipline. A wide variety of behavior modification interventions also developed, reflecting the systematic use of contingency management, contracting, and the training of teachers and parents as behavior change managers (O'Leary, O'Leary & Becker, 1967; Patterson, Cobb, & Ray, 1973; Walker, 1979). Though each of these therapeutic philosophies differed from the others in several major respects, one of their significant commonalities was the shared assumption that somewhere within the client were as yet unexpressed, effective, satisfying, nonaggressive, or healthy behaviors, whose expression was among the goals of therapy. All three approaches expected such latent potentials to be realized by the client if the interventionist was sufficiently skilled in reducing or removing obstacles to this goal. The psychoanalyst sought to do so by calling forth and interpreting unconscious material blocking progress-relevant awareness. The nondirectivist sought to free the client's inner potential for change by providing a warm, empathic, maximally accepting therapeutic environment. And the behavior modifier, by means of one or more contingency management procedures, attempted to see to it that the client received contingent reinforcement when desirable behaviors or their approximations did occur, thus increasing the probability that these behaviors would recur. All three approaches assumed that somewhere within the individual's repertoire resided the desired, effective, sought-after behaviors.

In the early 1970s an important new intervention approach began to emerge—psychological skills training—which rested upon rather different assumptions. Viewing the helpee more in educational, pedagogic terms rather than as a patient in need of therapy, the psychological skills trainer assumed that the individual was lacking, deficient, or, at best, weak in the skills necessary for effective and satisfying interpersonal functioning. The task of the skills trainer became, therefore, not interpretation, reflection, or reinforcement, but the active and deliberate teaching of desirable behaviors. Rather than an intervention between a patient and a psychotherapist, what emerged was training between a trainee and a psychological skills trainer.

The roots of the psychological skills training movement lay within both education and psychology. The notion of teaching desirable behaviors has often, if sporadically, been a significant goal of the U.S. educational system. The character education movement of the 1920s and more contemporary moral education and values clarification programs are but a few of several historical examples. Added to this institutionalized educational interest were the hundreds of interpersonal and planning skills courses taught in community colleges and the hundreds of self-help books oriented toward skill-enhancement goals available to the public. The formal and informal educational establishment in the United States provided fertile soil and explicit stimulation for the psychological skills training movement.

Much the same can be said for psychology, as its prevailing philosophy and concrete interests also laid the groundwork for the development of this new movement. The learning process had been the central theoretical and investigative concern of U.S. psychology since the late 19th century. It assumed major therapeutic form in the 1950s, as psychotherapy practitioners and researchers alike came to view psychotherapeutic treatment more and more in learning terms. The healthy and still-expanding field of behavior modification grew from this joint learning-clinical focus and provided the immediately preceding context in which psychological skills training developed. In combination with the growth of behavior modification, psychological thinking increasingly shifted from a strict emphasis on remediation to one that was equally concerned with prevention. The bases for this shift included movement away from a medical model concept toward a psychoeducational perspective, which also gave strong impetus to the viability of the psychological skills training movement.

Perhaps psychology's most direct contribution to psychological skills training came from social learning theory and in particular from the work Albert Bandura both conducted and stimulated. Bandura (1973) describes three basic components of his approach.

The method that has yielded the most impressive results with diverse problems contains three major components. First, alternative modes of response are repeatedly modeled, preferably by several people who demonstrate how the new style of behavior can be used in dealing with a variety of. . .situations. Second, learners are provided with necessary guidance and ample opportunities to practice the modeled behavior under favorable conditions until they perform it skillfully and spontaneously. The latter procedures are ideally suited for developing new social skills, but they are unlikely to be adopted unless they produce rewarding consequences. Arrangement of success experiences particularly for initial efforts at behaving differently, constitute the third component in this powerful composite method. . . . Given adequate demonstration, guided practice, and success experiences, this method is almost certain to produce favorable results. (p. 253)

Other events and factors of the 1970s provided still further stimulation for the growth of the skills training movement. Relevant supportive research, the incompleteness of operant approaches, large client populations of grossly skill-deficient individuals in mental hospitals and elsewhere, and the paucity of useful interventions for a large segment of U.S. society—namely low income clients—all, in the context of historically supportive roots in both education and psychology, came together in my thinking and that of others as demanding a new intervention, something prescriptively responsive to these several needs. Psychological skills training was the answer, and a movement was launched.

Our involvement in this movement, a psychological skills training approach we have termed Structured Learning, began in the early 1970s. For several years our studies were conducted in public mental hospitals with long-term, highly skill-deficient, chronic patients. As our research demonstrated with regularity successful skill-enhancement effects (Goldstein, 1982), we shifted our focus from teaching adult, psychiatric inpatients a broad array of interpersonal and daily living skills to a more explicit concern with skill training for aggressive individuals. Our trainee groups have included spouses engaged in family disputes violent enough to warrant police intervention (Goldstein, Monti, Sardino, & Green, 1978), child-abusing parents (Solomon, 1978; Sturm, 1979; Goldstein, Keller, & Erne, 1985), and, most especially, overtly aggressive adolescents (Goldstein, Sprafkin, Gershaw, & Klein, 1980).

SKILL DEFICIENCY AND JUVENILE DELINQUENCY

A substantial body of literature has demonstrated that delinquent and other aggressive young persons display widespread interpersonal, planning, aggression-management, and other psychological skill deficiencies. Freedman, Rosenthal, Donahoe, Schlundt, and McFall (1978) examined the comparative skill competence levels of a group of juvenile delinquents and a matched group (in age, IQ, and social background) of nonoffenders in response to a series of standardized role-play situations. The offender sample responded in a consistently less skillful manner. Spence (1981) constituted comparable offender and nonoffender samples and videotaped individual interviews with a previously unknown adult. The offender group displayed significantly less eye contact, appropriate head movements, and speech, as well as significantly more fiddling and gross body movement. Conger, Miller, and Walsmith (1965) added further to this picture of skill deficiency and concluded that juvenile delinquents, as compared to nondelinquent cohorts,

> had more difficulty in getting along with peers, both in individual one-to-one contacts and in group situations, and were less willing or able to treat others courteously and tactfully, and less able to be fair in dealing with them. In return, they were less well liked and accepted by their peers. (p. 422)

Not only are adjudicated delinquents discriminable from their nondelinquent peers on a continuum of skill competence, but much the same is true for youngsters who are merely chronically aggressive.

> The socialization process . . .[is] severely impeded for many aggressive youngsters. Their behavioral adjustments are often immature and they do not seem to have learned the key social skills necessary for initiating and maintaining positive social relationships with others. Peer groups often reject, avoid, and/or punish aggressive children, thereby excluding them from positive learning experiences with others. (Patterson, Reid, Jones, & Conger, 1975, p. 4)

As Patterson et al. (1975) suggest, the social competence discrepancy between delinquent or aggressive youngsters and their nondelinquent, nonaggressive peers has roots in early childhood. In a longitudinal study Mussen, Conger, Kagan, and Gerwitz (1979) observed that boys who became delinquent were appraised by their teachers as early as third grade as less well adjusted socially than their classmates. They appeared less friendly, responsible, or fair in dealing with others and more impulsive and antagonistic to authority. Poor peer relations—being less friendly toward classmates, less well liked by peers—were further developmental predictors of later delinquency. Thus, psychological skill deficiencies (especially interpersonal) of diverse types characterize the early development of both delinquent and aggressive youngsters. The remediation of such deficits looms as an especially valuable goal. Our attempts in this area during the past decade have used a skill training intervention termed Structured Learning.

STRUCTURED LEARNING PROCEDURES

Assessment

As with all approaches to psychological skills training, Structured Learning begins with assessment of the trainees' levels of proficiency in the skills comprising the Structured Learning curriculum. We have found it useful to employ, alone or in combination, four methods of assessment: interviews, direct observation, behavioral testing, and skill checklists.

Interviews. Since youngsters' behavior impacts on peers, family, relatives, employers, and school personnel, these persons are prime sources of information about the youths' skills. Thus, in addition to skill-relevant interviewing of the youngsters themselves, useful information can be obtained, with the adolescents' permission, from interviews with these real-life figures.

Direct Observation. Intentionally or otherwise, important discrepancies often exist between what people say they do, or would do, in a given situation and how they actually behave. Valuable information about social skills can be obtained by actually observing youngsters functioning in school, at home, or elsewhere in their environment. What do they actually *do* when peers tease them, parents discipline them, employers point out errors, or teachers ask them to volunteer for an activity? Clearly, such behavioral information is an especially valuable piece of the assessment picture.

Behavioral Testing. One weakness of direct observation is that circumstances that allow youths to show whether they possess a given skill and are willing to use it may not occur during observation. For example, while the tester or observer is present, peers, parents, employers, and others may be on their best behavior or may otherwise act unrepresentatively. When direct observation of skills is not by itself sufficient for adequate skill assessment, an alternative is behavioral testing. This approach to assessment involves creating—by role-play, stimulation, play acting, or in imagination—the types of situations that in real life would require competent skill use for solution and then observing what adolescents do. Although the artificial nature of behavioral testing is a drawback, it can be applied to all potential trainees in a standardized manner. If the situations are well chosen and realistically portrayed, this method can elicit important information about skill proficiency and deficiency.

Skill Checklists. We have consistently found skill deficiency information obtained directly from youngsters to be a particularly worthwhile part of assessment. Self-report instruments not only tell us in which skills adolescents see themselves as strong or weak, but in sharing this information with us also reveal a bit about their motivation to change. Reliable instruments for this purpose include the Structured Learning Skills Inventories (Goldstein, Sprafkin, Gershaw, & Klein, 1980), the Social Behavior Assessment (Stephens, 1978), the Walker Social Skills Curriculum Scale (Walker, McConnell, Holmes, Todis, Walker, & Golden, 1983), the Progress Assessment Chart of Social Development (Gunzberg, 1980), the Kohn Social Competence Scale (Kohn, Parnes, & Rosman, 1979), and the Matson Evaluation of Social Skills with Youngsters (Matson, Esveldt-Dawson, & Kazdin, 1983).

Training Procedures

Following assessment to establish skill proficiency/deficiency, the Structured Learning approach consists of the didactic procedures recommended by Bandura (1973). Based on social learning research, these procedures consist of

(1) modeling, (2) role-playing, (3) performance feedback, and (4) transfer training.

Modeling.   Structured Learning requires first that trainees be exposed to expert examples of the behaviors we wish them to learn. The 6 to 12 trainees constituting a Structured Learning instructional group are selected on the basis of their shared skill deficiencies. Each potentially problematic behavior is referred to as a skill, and each skill is broken down into four to six different behavioral steps. The steps constitute the operational definition of the given skill. Using either live acting by the group's trainers or audiovisual modeling displays, actors portray the skill steps being used expertly in a variety of settings relevant to the trainee's daily life. Trainees are told to watch and listen closely to the way the actors in each vignette follow the skill's behavioral steps.

Role-Playing.   A brief, spontaneous discussion almost invariably follows the presentation of a modeling display. Trainees comment on the steps, the actors, and often the occurrence of the situation or skill problem in their own lives. Because our primary goal in role-playing is to encourage realistic behavior rehearsal, a trainee's statements about individual difficulties using the skill can often develop into material for the first role-play. To enhance the realism of the portrayal, the main actor is asked to choose a second trainee (co-actor) to play the role of the significant other person in his or her life who is relevant to the skill problem. It is important that the main actor seek to enact the steps just modeled.

The main actor is asked to briefly describe the real skill-problem situation and the real person(s) involved in it. The co-actor is called by the name of the main actor's significant other person during the role-play. The trainer then instructs the role-players to begin. It is the trainer's main responsibility, at this point, to be sure that the main actor keeps role-playing and attempts to follow the behavioral steps in so doing.

The role-playing is continued until all trainees in the group have had an opportunity to participate—even if all the same steps must be carried over to a second or third session. However, even though the framework (behavioral steps) of each role-play in the series remains the same, the actual content can and should change from role-play to role-play; the skill-deficiency problem as it actually occurs in each trainee's real-life environment should be the content of each role-play. When the role-plays are completed, each trainee should be better armed to act appropriately in real situations.

Performance Feedback.   Upon completion of each role-play, a brief feedback period ensues. The goals of this activity are to let the main actor know how well he or she followed the skill's steps or in what ways departed from them, to explore the psychological impact of the enactment on the co-actor, and to provide the main actor with encouragement to try out the role-play behaviors in real life. In these critiques the behavioral focus of Structured Learning is maintained. Comments must point to the presence or absence of specific, concrete behaviors and must not take the form of general evaluative comments or broad generalities.

Transfer of Training. Several components of Structured Learning sessions have, as their primary purpose, augmentation of the likelihood that learning in the training setting will transfer to the trainee's actual real-life environment. The first component consists of providing instruction in general principles of learning that govern successful or competent performance of the training and criterion tasks. This procedure has typically been operationalized in laboratory contexts by providing subjects with the organizing concepts, principles, strategies, or rationales that explain or account for the stimulus-response relationships operative in both the training and application settings. Structured Learning trainees receive in verbal, pictorial, and written form the appropriate information governing skill instigation, selection, and implementation.

The second transfer of training component, overlearning, is a procedure whereby learning is extended over more trials than are necessary to produce initial changes in the trainee's behavior. The repetition of successful skill enactment in the typical Structured Learning session is quite substantial. The target skill taught and its behavioral steps are (1) modeled several times; (2) role-played one or more times by the trainee; (3) observed by the trainee in every other group member's role-plays; (4) read by the trainee from a blackboard and skill card (a 3" × 5" card on which the skill's name and steps are printed); (5) written by the trainee in a notebook; (6) practiced in real life one or more times as part of the trainee's formal homework assignment; and (7) practiced one or more times in response to skill-oriented, intrinsically interesting stimuli introduced into the trainee's real life.

The third component used to facilitate transfer of training is the use of training stimuli that are identical to those found in the trainees' natural environments. In perhaps the earliest experimentation with transfer enhancement, Thorndike and Woodworth (1901) concluded that the facilitative effect of one habit on another was due to shared identical elements. Ellis (1965) and Osgood (1953) also emphasize the importance of the similarity in various aspects of the training and the application tasks. The greater the similarity of physical and interpersonal stimuli in the Structured Learning setting and those in the home, school, or other setting in which the skill is to be applied, the greater the likelihood of transfer.

The real-life nature of Structured Learning is operationalized in a number of ways: (1) the representative, relevant, and realistic content and portrayal of the models and situations in the live modeling or modeling tapes, all of which are designed to be highly similar to what trainees are likely to face in their daily lives; (2) the physical props used in and the arrangement of the role-playing setting to be similar to real-life settings; (3) the identification of significant other persons and their enactment by the co-actors to portray real-life situations; (4) the manner in which the role-plays themselves are conducted to be as responsive as possible to the real-life interpersonal stimuli to which the trainees will eventually respond with the given skill; (5) the real-life homework; and (6) the training of living units (e.g., all the members of a given ward or group home as a unit).

The fourth component involves the variation of stimuli used in training. Callentine and Warren (1955), Duncan (1958), and Shore and Sechrest (1961) have demonstrated that positive transfer is greater when a variety of relevant training stimuli are employed. Stimulus variability is implemented in our Structured Learning studies by (1) rotating group leaders across groups; (2) rotating trainees across groups; (3) having trainees repeat role-plays of a given skill with several co-actors; (4) having trainees role-play a given skill across relevant settings; and (5) using multiple homework assignments for each given skill.

The fifth component consists of real-life reinforcement of demonstrated skills. Even with successful implementation of both appropriate direct instruction procedures and transfer enhancement procedures, positive transfer may fail to occur. As Agras (1967), Gruber (1971), Tharp and Wetzel (1969), and many other investigators have shown, stable and enduring performance of newly learned skills in applied settings is at the mercy of real-life reinforcement contingencies.

We have found it useful to implement several supplemental programs outside the Structured Learning setting that can help provide the reinforcement needed to maintain new behaviors. These programs include provision for both external social reward (provided by people in the trainees' natural environments) and self-reward (provided by the individual trainee). In several schools, juvenile detention centers, and other agencies, we have actively sought to identify and develop environmental or external support by holding orientation meetings for staff and for the relatives and friends of trainees (i.e., the real-life reward and punishment givers). The purpose of these meetings is to acquaint significant others in the trainees' lives with Structured Learning theory and process. An important feature of these sessions is the presentation of procedures whereby staff, relatives, and friends can encourage and reward trainees as they practice their new skills. We consider these orientation sessions to be of major value in the transfer of training. Frequently, however, environmental support is insufficient to maintain newly learned skills, and in actuality many natural environments actively resist the trainees' efforts at behavior change. For these reasons we have found it useful to include in our transfer efforts a program of self-reinforcement. Trainees can be instructed in the nature of self-reinforcement and are encouraged to "say something and do something nice for yourself" if they practice their new skill well.

The five transfer-enhancement procedures described here do not exhaust the range of techniques employed. A complete listing of these strategies, along with citations of our research program investigations of their efficacy, are listed in Figure 10.1 (Goldstein, 1981).

Successful Transfer-Enhancing Procedures

Figure 10.1

1. Overlearning (Lopez, 1977)
2. Helper-role structuring (Litwack, 1977; Solomon, 1978)
3. Identical elements (Wood, 1977; Guzzetta, 1974)
4. Coping modeling (Fleming, 1976)
5. Stimulus variability (Hummel, 1977)
6. General principles (Lopez, 1977; Lack, 1975)
7. Programmed reinforcement (Gutride, Goldstein, & Hunter, 1973; Greenleaf, 1977)
8. Real-life feedback (Goldstein & Goedhart, 1973)
9. Teaching skills in tandem (reciprocal benefits) (Hummel, 1977)
10. Mastery induction (Solomon, 1977)

Note: All of these demonstrated transfer-enhancing techniques, as well as a substantial number of other potentially fruitful strategies, are examined at length in a small number of recent writings devoted to this all-important concern with generalization and endurance of treatment effects (Epps, Thompson, & Lane, 1985; Galassi & Galassi, 1984; Goldstein & Kanfer, 1979; Karoly & Steffen, 1980).

AGGRESSION-RELEVANT PSYCHOLOGICAL SKILLS

With the four procedures just described, we have taught several aggression-relevant skills to disputant spouses, abusive parents, delinquent adolescents, and other highly aggressive individuals. The skills and their component behavioral steps are listed here.

Asking for help
1. Decide what the problem is.
2. Decide whether you want help with the problem.
3. Identify the people who might help you.
4. Make a choice of helper.
5. Tell the helper about your problem.

Giving instructions
1. Define what needs to be done and who should do it.
2. Tell the other person what you want him or her to do and why.
3. Tell the other person exactly how to do what you want done.
4. Ask for the other person's reaction.
5. Consider that reaction and change your direction if appropriate.

Expressing affection
1. Decide whether you have warm, caring feelings about another person.
2. Decide whether the other person would like to know about your feelings.
3. Decide how you might best express your feelings.
4. Choose the right time and place to express your feelings.
5. Express affection in a warm and caring manner.

Expressing a complaint
1. Define what the problem is and who is responsible.
2. Decide how the problem might be solved.
3. Tell that person what the problem is and how it might be solved.
4. Ask for a response.

5. Show that you understand the other person's feelings.
6. Come to agreement on the steps to be taken by each of you.

Persuading others
1. Decide on your position and predict what the other person's is likely to be.
2. State your position cleary, completely, and in a way that is acceptable to the other person.
3. State what you think the other person's position is.
4. Restate your position, emphasizing why it is the better of the two.
5. Suggest that the other person consider your position for a while before making a decision.

Following instructions
1. Listen carefully while the instructions are being given.
2. Give your reactions to the instructor.
3. Repeat the instructions to yourself.
4. Imagine yourself following the instructions and then do it.

Responding to the feelings of others (Empathy)
1. Observe another person's words and actions.
2. Consider what the other person might be feeling and how strong the feelings are.
3. Decide whether it would be helpful to let the other person know that you understand his or her feelings.
4. If appropriate, tell the other person in a warm and sincere manner how you think he or she is feeling.

Responding to a complaint
1. Listen openly to the complaint.
2. Ask the person to explain anything you don't understand.
3. Show that you understand the other person's thoughts and feelings.
4. Tell the other person your thoughts and feelings, accepting responsibility if appropriate.
5. Summarize the steps to be taken by each of you.

Responding to persuasion
1. Listen openly to another person's position.
2. Consider the possible reasons for the other person's position.
3. Ask the other person to explain anything you don't understand about what was said.
4. Compare the other person's position with your own, identifying the pros and cons of each.
5. Decide what position to support, based on what will have the greatest long-term benefit.

Responding to failure
1. Decide whether you have failed.
2. Think about both the personal reasons and the circumstances that have caused you to fail.
3. Decide how you might do things differently if you tried again.

4. Decide whether you want to try again.
5. If it is appropriate, try again, using your revised approach.

Responding to contradictory messages
1. Pay attention to those body signals that help you know you are feeling trapped or confused.
2. Consider the other person's words and actions that may have caused you to have these feelings.
3. Decide whether that person's words and actions are contradictory.
4. Decide whether it would be useful to point out any contradiction.
5. If appropriate, ask the other person to explain any contradiction.

Responding to anger
1. Listen openly to the other person's angry statement(s).
2. Show that you understand what the other person is feeling.
3. Ask the other person to explain anything you don't understand about what was said.
4. Show that you understand why the other person feels angry.
5 If it is appropriate, express your thoughts and feelings about the situation.

Preparing for a stressful conversation
1. Imagine yourself in the stressful situation.
2. Think about how you will feel and why you will feel that way.
3. Imagine the other person(s) in that stressful situation. Think about how that person(s) will feel and why they will feel that way.
4. Imagine yourself telling the other person(s) what you want to say.
5. Imagine the response that your statement will elicit.
6. Repeat the above steps, using as many approaches as you can think of.
7. Choose the best approach.

Determining responsibility
1. Decide what the problem is.
2. Consider possible causes of the problem.
3. Decide which are the most likely causes of the problem.
4. Take actions to test which are the actual causes of the problem.

Setting problem priorities
1. List all the problems that are currently pressuring you.
2. Arrange this list in order, from most to least urgent.
3. Take steps (delegate, postpone, avoid) to temporarily decrease the urgency of all but the most pressing problem.
4. Concentrate on solving the most pressing problem.

Dealing with being left out
1. Decide whether you're being left out (ignored, rejected).
2. Think about why the other people might be leaving you out of something.
3. Consider how you might deal with the problem (wait, leave, tell the other people how their behavior affects you, talk with a friend about the problem).
4. Choose the best way and do it.

Dealing with an accusation
1.   Think about what the other person has accused you of (whether it is accurate, inaccurate, said in a mean way or in a constructive way).
2.   Think about why the person might have accused you (have you infringed on that person's rights or property?).
3.   Think about ways to answer the person's accusations (deny, explain your behavior, correct the other person's perceptions, assert, apologize, offer to make up for what has happened).
4.   Choose the best way and do it.

Dealing with group pressure
1.   Think about what the other people want you to do and why (listen to the other people, decide what their real intent is, try to understand what is being said).
2.   Decide what you want to do (yield, resist, delay, negotiate).
3.   Consider how to tell the other people what you want to do (give reasons, talk to one person only, delay, assert).
4.   If appropriate, tell the group or other person what you have decided.

DEALING WITH MANAGEMENT PROBLEMS AND RESISTIVE BEHAVIOR IN STRUCTURED LEARNING GROUPS

As in all training or psychotherapy interventions, group members may actively resist participation (e.g., missing sessions, being late, refusing to role-play, walking out), may participate but inappropriately (e.g., displaying excessive restlessness, inattention, inability to remember procedures), display one or another form of inactivity (e.g., apathy, minimal participation, falling asleep), or hyperactivity (interrupting, monopolizing, digressing, jumping out of a role). To deal effectively and rapidly with this array of group or individual management problems, we have used one or more resistance-reducing techniques.

1.   *Empathic encouragement.* This intervention consists of (a) offering the trainee the opportunity to explain in greater detail his or her difficulty with participation as instructed and listening nondefensively; (b) clearly expressing your understanding of the trainee's feelings; (c) if appropriate, responding that the trainee's view is a viable alternative; (d) presenting your own view in greater detail, including supporting reasons and probable outcomes; (e) expressing the appropriateness of delaying a resolution of the trainee-trainer difference; and (f) urging the trainee to tentatively try to participate.
2.   *Reinstruction and simplification.* This approach may be implemented in one or more of the following ways: (a) have the trainee follow one behavioral step, rather than a series of steps; (b) have the trainee play a passive (co-actor or nonspeaking) role in the role-play prior to playing

the role of the main actor; (c) cut the role-play short; (d) instruct the trainee in what to say in the role-play (either prior to the role-play or through coaching during the role-play); and/or (e) reinforce the trainee for improvement over prior performance rather than requiring performance at the standards set for other members.

3. *Threat reduction.* For trainees who find some aspect of the Structured Learning session threatening or anxiety-producing, we recommend a series of procedures designed to help the trainee calm down sufficiently to attend to the task at hand. Some threat-reduction methods include (a) having one of the trainers model a particular task before asking the threatened trainee to to try the task; (b) reassuring the trainee with remarks such as "Take your time," "I know it's hard," or "Give it a try and I'll help you through it"; and (c) clarifying any aspects of the trainee's task that are still unclear.

4. *Elicitation of responses.* This set of strategies is called for in cases where the group is being unresponsive to efforts to get trainees involved. Methods include (a) calling for volunteers; (b) introducing topics for discussion; (c) asking a specific trainee to participate, preferably someone who has shown some signs of interest or attention (i.e., eye contact, gestures).

5. *Termination of responses.* Trainers should take a direct stand in situations that divert the attention of the group from the task at hand. Some termination methods include (a) interrupting ongoing behavior; (b) withholding social attention from trainee behavior; (c) ceasing interaction with resistive trainee and asking others to participate; and (d) urging trainees to get back on the correct topic.

RESEARCH EVALUATION

Since 1970 our research group has conducted a systematic program of evaluating and improving the effectiveness of Structured Learning. Approximately 60 investigations have been conducted, involving a wide variety of trainee populations. These include chronic adult schizophrenics (Goldstein, 1973; Goldstein, Sprafkin, & Gershaw, 1976; Goldstein et al., 1980; Liberman, 1970; Orenstein, 1973; Sutton-Simon, 1973), geriatric patients (Lopez, 1977; Lopez, Hoyer, Goldstein, Sprafkin, & Gershaw, 1980), child-abusing parents (Solomon, 1977; Sturm, 1980), young children (Hummel, 1980; Swanstrom, 1978), change-agent individuals such as mental hospital staff members (Berlin, 1977); Goldstein & Goedhart, 1973; Lack, 1975; Robinson, 1973; Schneiman, 1972), police (Goldstein, Monti, Sardino, & Green, 1979), persons employed in industrial contexts (Goldstein & Sorcher, 1973, 1974), and in recent years aggressive and other behaviorally disordered adolescents (Goldstein et al., 1980; Goldstein, Glick, Reiner, Zimmerman, Coultry, & Gold, 1985; Greenleaf, 1977; Litwack, 1976; Spatz-Norton, 1984; Trief, 1976; Wood, 1977; Zimmerman, 1985).

With regard to adolescent trainees, Structured Learning has been success-ful in enhancing such prosocial skills as empathy, negotiation, assertiveness, following instructions, self-control, and perspective taking (i.e., seeing things from another's viewpoint). Beyond demonstrating that Structured Learning works with youngsters, these studies also have highlighted other aspects of the teaching of prosocial behaviors. In an effort to capitalize on adolescent responsiveness to peer influence, Fleming (1976) demonstrated that gains in negotiating skills are as great when the Structured Learning group leader is a respected peer as when the leader is an adult. Litwack (1976), more con-cerned with the skill-enhancing effects of an adolescent's anticipation of later serving as a peer leader, showed that such helper-role expectation increases the degree of skill acquired. Trief (1976) demonstrated that successful use of Structured Learning to increase perspective-taking skill also leads to con-sequent increases in cooperative behavior. The significant transfer effects both in this study and in the Golden (1975), Litwack (1976), and Raleigh (1977) investigations have been important signposts in planning further research on transfer enhancement in Structured Learning.

As in earlier efforts with adult trainees, the value of teaching certain skill combinations has also been examined. Aggression-prone adolescents often get into difficulty when they respond with overt aggression to authority figures with whom they disagree. Golden (1975) successfully used Structured Learning to teach such youngsters resistance-reducing behavior, a combina-tion of reflection of feeling (the authority figure's) and assertiveness (a forth-right but nonaggressive statement of one's own position). Jennings (1975) was able to use Structured Learning successfully to train adolescents in several of the verbal skills necessary for satisfactory participation in more tradi-tional, insight-oriented psychotherapy. Guzzetta (1974) was successful in us-ing Structured Learning to teach empathic skills to parents in an effort to help close the gap between adolescents and their parents. Investigations conducted by Spatz-Norton (1984) and Zimmerman (1985) combined Structured Learn-ing with complementary interventions and demonstrated substantial effects on adolescent trainee prosocial behaviors, beyond the effects of either inter-vention employed singly.

The overall conclusions that may justifiably be drawn from these several empirical evaluations of our work with adolescents as well as other trainees are threefold.

1. *Skill acquisition.* Across diverse trainee populations (clearly including aggressive adolescents in urban secondary schools and juvenile deten-tion centers) and diverse target skills, skill acquisition is a reliable train-ing outcome, occurring in well over 90% of Structured Learning trainees. Although pleased with this outcome, we are acutely aware of the ease with which therapeutic gains demonstrable in the training context are accomplished, given the potency, support, encouragement, and low threat value of trainers and therapists in that context. The more consequential outcome by far is trainee skill performance in real-world contexts (i.e., skill transfer).

2. *Skill transfer.* Across diverse trainee populations, target skills, and applied (real-world) settings, skill transfer occurs with approximately 45%
to 50% of Structured Learning trainees. Goldstein and Kanfer (1979), as
well as Karoly and Steffen (1980), have indicated that across several dozen
types of psychotherapy involving many different types of psychopathol-
ogy, the average transfer rate is between 15% and 20% of patients seen
in follow-up. The 50% rate consequent to Structured Learning is a significant improvement on this collective base rate, though it must immediately
be underscored that this finding also means that the gains shown by half
of our trainees were limited to in-session acquisition. Of special importance, however, is the consistently clear manner in which skill transfer
in our studies was a function of the explicit implementation of laboratory-
derived transfer-enhancing techniques, such as those described earlier.

3. *Prescriptiveness.* A prescriptive research strategy is, at heart, an effort
to conceptualize, operationalize, and evaluate potentially optimal matches
of trainer, trainee, and training method. Prior to constituting such combinations, trainer, trainee, and training characteristics that may be active contributors to such matches must be examined singly and in combination. In other words, active and inert contributors to skill acquisition and transfer must be identified. A continuing series of multiple
regression investigations have begun to point to state, trait, cognitive,
demographic, and sociometric predictors to high levels of skill acquisition and transfer (Anderson, 1981; Hoyer, Lopez, & Goldstein, 1982). More
research concerning prescriptive ingredients seems worthy of pursuit.

Concurrent with or following our development of the Structured Learning approach to psychological skills training, a number of similar programmatic attempts to enhance social competency emerged. Those that focused
in large part on aggressive youngsters and their prosocial training include
Life Skills Education (Adkins, 1970, 1974); Social Skills Training (Argyle,
Trower, & Bryant, 1974); AWARE: Activities for Social Development (Elardo & Cooper, 1977); Relationship Enhancement (Guerney, 1977); Teaching
Conflict Resolution (Hare, 1976); Developing Human Potential (Hawley &
Hawley, 1975); ASSET (Hazel, Schumaker, Sherman, & Sheldon-Wildgen,
1981); Interpersonal Communication (Heiman, 1973); and Directive Teaching
(Stephens, 1978). The instructional techniques that constitute each of these
skill training efforts derive from social learning theory and typically consist of instructions, modeling, role-playing, and performance feedback—with
ancillary use, in some instances, of contingent reinforcement, prompting,
shaping, or related behavioral techniques.

Other Research Involving Skill Training of Aggressive Adolescents

Developing in part out of the empirical tradition of behavior modification,
psychological skills training efforts came, not surprisingly, under early and
continuing research scrutiny. The existing body of psychological skills training investigations that involve aggressive adolescent and preadolescent sub-

jects is outlined in the Summary of Psychological Skills Training Research with Adolescent and Preadolescent Trainees, beginning on page 237, immediately preceding the end-of-chapter references. The 31 investigations in the summary are essentially all of the psychological skills training studies conducted with aggressive youngsters to date. Two-thirds represent multiple-group designs; the remainder are single-subject studies. As noted earlier, psychological skills training is operationally defined in an almost-identical manner across all of these investigations; that is, as a combination of instructions, modeling, role-playing, and performance feedback. Study subjects are adjudicated juvenile delinquents, status offenders, or chronically aggressive youngsters studied in secondary school settings. Although target skills have varied across the investigations, for the most part they have concerned interpersonal behaviors, prosocial alternatives to aggression, and aggression-management or aggression-inhibition behaviors. As Spence (1982) correctly notes, single-case studies have tended toward microskill training targets (e.g., eye contact, head nods), whereas multiple-group studies have sought to teach more macroskill competencies (e.g., coping with criticism, negotiation, problem solving).

Results, in terms of skill acquisition, have been consistently positive. Aggressive adolescents have been able to learn a broad array of previously unavailable interpersonal, aggression-management, affect-relevant, and related psychological competencies via the training methods examined here. Evaluation for maintenance and transfer of acquired skills yields a rather different outcome, however. Many studies tested for neither; the rest combine to report a mixed result. As noted earlier, our own investigative efforts in this regard (Goldstein, 1981) point to the not-surprising conclusion that generalization of skill competency across settings (transfer) and time (maintenance) is a direct function of the degree to which the investigator/trainer implemented, as a part of the training effort, procedures explicitly designed to enhance transfer and/or maintenance.

To summarize our view of empirical efforts to date, psychological skills training with aggressive adolescents rests on a firm investigative foundation. A variety of investigators, designs, subjects, settings, and target skills is continuing to provide a healthy examination of the effectiveness of such training. Skill acquisition is a reliable outcome, but the social validity of this consistent result is tempered substantially by the frequent failure—or indeterminancy—of transfer and maintenance.

FUTURE DIRECTIONS

A Systems Perspective

Our view of psychological skills training—or of any psychological intervention—is that its components, optimally, will perpetually evolve and never reach completion or closure. The modest success of skill training with regard to transfer and maintenance effects is by itself sufficient basis for dissatisfaction with current parameters. What might profitably be added to or deleted from the basic foursome of constituent techniques, is best tested by what Kazdin (1980) describes as constructive and dismantling treatment designs.

> With the constructive approach, the investigator usually begins with a basic treatment component that is relatively narrow or circumscribed in focus. Research is conducted that adds various ingredients to the basic treatment to determine what enhances treatment effects. As research continues, effective components are retained and a large treatment package is constructed. (p. 87)

> The dismantling treatment strategy refers to analyzing the components of a given treatment. . . . Once a treatment package has been shown to "work," research may begin to analyze the precise influence of specific components. . . . To dismantle a given technique, individual treatment components are eliminated or isolated from treatment. Comparisons usually are made across groups that receive the treatment package or the package minus the specific components. (p. 84)

Skillful use of combinations of constructive and dismantling designs reflects what we consider to be the optimal experimental design strategy at this stage in the development of psychological skills training. In implementing such designs, we believe that two planes exist—one horizontal and the other vertical—along which potentially viable treatment components may be experimentally added and deleted. Along the horizontal plane are the treatment components used with individual trainees. In this regard our current Structured Learning research (e.g., Goldstein et al., 1985; Spatz-Norton, 1984; Zimmerman, 1985) is seeking, by a constructive design strategy, to discern whether the potency of our basic psychological skills training package (modeling, role-playing, performance feedback, and transfer training) will be significantly increased if, in addition to our direct teaching of prosocial behavior, we seek to simultaneously teach prosocial values (by means of Kohlberg's, 1986, moral education techniques) and aggression-inhibitors (by means of relaxation and self-statement disputation training). In other words, we would be teaching not only what to do instead of aggression (prosocial values and behaviors), but also how to manage or reduce the aggression itself. These few horizontal components are mere examples of the potential array of existing or yet-to-be-developed techniques that can be meaningfully tested as possible additions to existing operational definitions of psychological skills training.

But skills training does not occur in an environmental vacuum. There are always several other players in the game of interpersonal competency—parents, peers, employers, siblings, friends, teachers, strangers, antagonists—and they appear along the vertical plane. Rather than simply seeking to train the main player (the trainee), we can also intervene vertically and seek to impact directly on any and all of those figures in the trainee's real world whose behavior may significantly influence the trainee's skill competency. With reference to aggressive adolescents, our recent monograph *School Violence* (Goldstein, Apter, & Harootunian, 1984) presents such an example of a systems, or vertical, intervention research strategy. School violence, we contend, will yield most fully when, in addition to the several suggested interventions targeted directly for aggressive youngsters, equally energetic attention is directed to the teachers involved, the school's administration, the youngsters' parents, the school board, and other relevant persons, even at the broader state and federal levels. We have not yet tested this particular comprehensive implementation of a constructive treatment design but share it here as an extended example of a research strategy that may be particularly fruitful in a psychological skills training context.

Prescriptive Use

The efficacy of psychological skills training may also be enhanced by adherence, in both its investigation and implementation, to a prescriptive, tailored, or differential-ingredients strategy. Here the effort is made to be responsive to trainee learning styles, group-relevant behaviors, and personality characteristics when defining the specific training procedures to be used and deciding how they will be implemented—the spacing, duration, and pacing of the group's sessions; the trainers to be employed; the skills to be taught and their difficulty, sequencing, and relevance to trainee motivation; and other training factors. In short, prescriptive use of psychological skills training seeks to discern and employ optimal characteristics of the training endeavor for *particular* trainees. This research and practice strategy parallels analogous viewpoints productively advanced earlier with regard to education (Cronbach, 1967; Harootunian, 1978; Hunt, 1972; Stern, 1970) and psychotherapy (Goldstein, 1978; Goldstein & Stein, 1976; Magaro, 1969). However, we wish to highlight here a number of aspects of psychological skills training as especially heuristic targets of this prescriptive viewpoint, that is, dimensions of skill training in which individualization seems most likely to enhance trainee skill competency. All of these suggestions are speculative products of skill training experiences and are in need of direct empirical scrutiny.

There is, first, the nature of trainees' skill deficiencies. It is not enough—as Michelson and Wood (1980) and others have argued—to employ multilevel, multimodel deficit assessment techniques to seek to reliably identify in *which* skills youngsters are deficient. It is also necessary, we propose, to be prescriptively responsive in our remedial efforts to the fact that there are three different ways in which an individual can be deficient in any given skill.

> First, children may lack knowledge or concepts of appropriate social behavior . . . or they may possess concepts atypical of their peer group. . . . At least three forms of social knowledge may be represented in a skill concept, each of which is viewed as necessary for effective social functioning: (a) knowledge of appropriate goals for social interac-

tion, (b) knowledge of appropriate strategies for reaching a social goal, and (c) knowledge of the context(s) in which specific strategies may be appropriately applied. . . . Second, children may lack, perhaps as a result of insufficient practice of the skills, actual behavioral abilities. . . . Finally, some children may be deficient in giving themselves feedback about their interpersonal encounters. Specifically, these children may lack the ability (a) to monitor and evaluate their own behavior and its effects on others . . . and (b) to make inferences or attributions about their interpersonal successes and failures that are conducive to continued effort, adaptation, and self-confidence in social interactions. (Ladd & Mize, 1983, pp. 129–130)

It follows that selection of target skills might optimally reflect not only such typical parameters as the skill(s) in which the trainee is deficient, the degree of deficiency, and the interpersonal and environmental contexts in which the deficiency manifests itself, but also the particular nature of the deficit (knowledge, behavior, feedback). The selection of target skills that are functional for the adolescent has clear and direct implications for the prescriptive specification of just what is to be taught. It is relevant to note that recently, in addition to Ladd and Mize (1983), other psychological skills trainers and researchers have increasingly conceptualized and operationalized the skill training process as a multistage intervention requiring different training procedures and goals for each stage (Asher & Renshaw, 1981; Dodge, 1983; Goetz & Dweck, 1980; Hazel et al., 1981; McFall, 1976; Rathjen, 1984; Scandura, 1977).

Our decade-long experience with Structured Learning, across a variety of trainee populations, has provided a lengthy series of additional leads for studying the prescriptive individualization of the skill training process. In all instances our basic procedures have been modeling, role-playing, performance feedback, and transfer training. Yet also in all instances we have energetically sought to adapt these four training components to the particular receptivity channels and learning styles of the trainees involved. Depending in large measure on such trainee qualities, our modeling displays have been audio, video, or live; role-playing has varied in length, simplicity, and repetitiveness; performance feedback has been directive, especially gentle, or lengthy; and transfer training has been a function of the trainee's available community resources, homework opportunities, and capacity for abstraction. A more concrete sense of what we mean by such prescriptive implementation is captured in the following excerpts from our trainers manual for Structured Learning with adult psychiatric inpatients (Goldstein, Sprafkin, & Gershaw, 1976).

With long-term hospitalized patients—whose attention span is short and whose motivation for skill enhancement is low—we have adapted the procedures set forth earlier in this manual by (1) having the trainers be more active and participate more directly in role playing, (2) having the trainers offer social (and token or material) reinforcement more frequently and for lesser skill increments, (3) having the trainers begin thinning of reinforcements later, (4) having shorter and more repetitive group sessions, (5) having fewer trainees per group, (6) paying more relative attention to simpler levels of a given skill, (7) allowing more total time per skill, and (8) requiring less demanding homework assignments. (p. 16)

Similarly, with aggressive adolescents we have prescriptively evolved toward (1) groups no larger than five or six; (2) briefer initial structuring of group procedures; (3) live modeling by the trainers; (4) use of two or three *different* vignettes when modeling; (5) heightened levels of trainer activity, directiveness, and control; (6) increased use of token or material reinforcers; (7) employment of visual depictions of target skill steps; (8) added reliance on preannounced rules for group management; (9) certain of the same modifications noted for adult psychiatric patients; and, of course, (10) adolescent-relevant target skills and (11) adolescent-experienced skill trainers.

There is one additional and perhaps especially important way in which psychological skills training is best employed in a prescriptive manner. The next generation of psychological skills training interventions will, we believe, possess many of the features described in the final sections of this chapter. Psychological skills training of the future will, in addition, find such training offered as part of a larger intervention package into which it is meaningfully integrated. An example of such a multifaceted intervention is our own aggression-replacement training (Goldstein, Glick, Zimmerman, Reiner, Coultry, & Gold, 1985), in which the Structured Learning approach to skill training (a behavioral intervention) is offered on an extended basis simultaneously with trainee participation in anger-control training (an affective intervention) and moral education (a cognitive intervention), in a prescriptive effort to treat chronically aggressive incarcerated adolescents.

Trainee Motivation

We believe that psychological skills training research and practice have not given sufficient attention to the relevance of trainee motivation and its development. It is important that future investigative efforts in this domain seek to redress this imbalance and thus examine means to substantially enhance skill competency motivation—a matter often of special relevance for aggressive adolescents. In addition to appropriate contingent reinforcement, trainee motivation can be enhanced in conjunction with three different events that unfold sequentially during the skill training process: (1) establishment of the trainer-trainee relationship, (2) selection of appropriate target skills, and (3) establishing certain motivation-relevant group parameters.

Trainer-Trainee Relationship.   It is a truism in such interpersonal contexts as psychotherapy, counseling, and education that client or student motivation to do "the work" of the process is, in part, driven by the force of a positive relationship with the change agent involved.

As in any pedagogical undertaking, it is likely that the success of a social skill training program also depends on the quality of the relationship established between the child and the instructor. Even the most-well-designed and all-inclusive training program may be rendered ineffective if it is conducted in an overly didactic, mechanical, and uninviting manner. Rarely, however, have previous social skill training investigators alluded to instructor characteristics or the instructor-child relationship as important aspects of the skill training process. (Ladd & Mize, 1983, p. 153)

But all truisms are not necessarily true. In fact, a host of clinicians have speculated that therapeutic progress of diverse sorts will be advanced with aggressive adolescents by a very different kind of helper-helpee relationship (especially initially); namely, one characterized by low empathy, high impersonality, and careful avoidance of emotional exploration (Dean, 1958; Goldstein, Heller, & Sechrest, 1966; Redl & Wineman, 1957; Schwitzgebel, 1961; Slack, 1960). Edelman and Goldstein (1984) examined this proposition empirically and, indeed, found quite substantial support for the prescriptive utility of low empathy (plus high genuineness) in helper behavior. Thus, we support the generalization that trainee motivation and consequent skill acquisition are likely influenced substantially by the quality of the trainer-trainee relationship. But precisely what kind(s) of relationships are optimal in this context remains an open question.

Skill Selection.   Which skills will be taught, and who will select them? This is as much a motivational as a tactical question, for to the degree that youngsters are enabled to anticipate learning skill competencies *they* think they need, which *they* discern as presently deficient but of likely utility in their real-world relationships, to that degree their motivation is correspondingly enhanced. We have operationalized this perspective in Structured Learning by means of a process we call "negotiating the curriculum." First, we avoid the option of serving as unilateral skill selector for the trainee. In doing so, we concur with Schinke (1981).

Seldom recognized in interpersonal skills training with adolescents is how values influence client referral and problem definition. Decisions about desirable skills are weighted by personal preferences, moral judgments, and ethical constraints. (p. 81)

We similarly avoid the cafeteria-like option that denies our skill-relevant expertise and knowledge, lays out the entire skill curriculum, and simply ask trainees to select those they wish. Either approach is inadequate. Instead, we use a strategy that allows both parties to participate actively. We begin by having the trainer (who knows the trainee well) and the trainee independently complete their respective versions of the Structured Learning Skills Inventory (Goldstein, Sprafkin, Gershaw, & Klein, 1980). Then much the same as a meeting between an academic advisor and a student to plan a program of studies, the skill trainer and trainee compare, contrast, examine, and select from their Skills Inventories content that reflects both the trainer's beliefs about what the trainee needs and the trainee's beliefs about his or her own deficiencies and desired competencies. We believe this applied procedure enhances motivation. However, whether it in fact serves this important function is an investigative question worth careful examination.

Group Procedures.   Our concern with trainee participation in the skill selection process stems from our intent to enhance the trainee's task-associated intrinsic motivation. But extrinsic task characteristics can also be mobilized to maximize inducements for active, on-task trainee participation. Although there is as yet little empirical evidence in support of the group procedure recommendations that follow, they appear to us to be reliable.

The first consideration is where the group sessions are held. In most schools and institutions we try to find a special place, associated in the trainees' thinking with particular privileges or opportunities (e.g., a teacher's lounge, student center, recreation area), and yet not a place so removed in its characteristics from the trainees' typical real-life settings as to reduce the likelihood of skill transfer.

A second consideration is when the group will meet. If it is not judged to be too great an academic sacrifice, we attempt to schedule skill training sessions when youngsters will miss an activity they do not especially enjoy (including certain academic subjects), rather than free play, lunch, gym, or the like.

Third, who will lead the group? For our first program-initiating groups, in particular, we seek as trainers persons who are the most stimulating, most tuned to the needs and behaviors of aggressive adolescents (but not the most overtly empathic, for reasons described earlier), and in general most able to capture and hold the attention of participating youngsters. These trainers include teachers, cottage parents, institutional staff members, and so on. Because the impact of the initial group meeting(s) bears on not only the motivation and performance of trainees in that group, but also on the interest, motivation, and eventual performance of youngsters in subsequently formed groups, the group leadership skills of the first trainers can have far-reaching motivational consequences.

Fourth, which skill will be taught first? This is a crucial decision, one of special relevance to trainee motivation. In addition to reflecting the give and take of the negotiated skill curriculum, the first skill taught should be one likely to yield immediate, real-world reward for the trainees. It must work; it must pay off. Although some trainers prefer to begin with the simpler conversation skills, as a sort of warm up or break in, our preference is to try to capture both simplicity and reward potential. The self-perceived need of the trainees for the near-future value of a given skill, therefore, weighs heavily in our initial skill selection decisions.

Prevention.   Almost all applications of psychological skills training, including those targeted to children and adolescents, have been remedial and not preventive. Our collective efforts, investigative and applied, have been directed toward accurately identifying and effectively training youngsters with demonstrable skill deficits. Exceedingly little attention has been directed toward children and adolescents at risk who are not manifestly deficient in psychological skills. Exceedingly little attention has also been directed toward very young children or youngsters *in anticipation* of skill needs requisite to mastering the formidable array of developmental hurdles over which all must pass—in school, at play, at home, in the community, with peers or family or authority figures.

> Love, sex, and peer relationships are likely to require social skills (e.g., having a conversation, listening, joining in), skills for dealing with feelings (e.g., dealing with fear, expressing affection, understanding the feelings of others), and skills useful for dealing with stress (e.g., dealing with embarrassment, preparing for a stressful conversation, responding to failure). School-related tasks demand proficiency at yet other skills, in particular, planning skills (e.g., dealing with group pressure) and authority figures (e.g., following instructions). Similarly, work settings are also multifaceted in their task demands and, hence, in their requisite skills, especially those requiring planning and stress management. For many youngsters, whether at school, at work, or elsewhere, the skill demands placed upon them will frequently involve the ability to deal satisfactorily with aggression, either their own or someone else's. In these instances, skills to be mastered may include self-control, negotiation, and dealing with group pressure. (Goldstein et al., 1980, pp. 5–6)

Thus, it can be seen that normal developmental hurdles are both high and numerous. Deficit prevention research and application seems to be an especially valuable future path.

SUMMARY OF PSYCHOLOGICAL SKILLS TRAINING RESEARCH WITH ADOLESCENT AND PREADOLESCENT TRAINEES

Bornstein et al. (1980)
Design: Single case; multiple baseline
Treatment: Instructions, modeling, role-play, and feedback
Trainees (N): Aggressive adolescent inpatients (4)
Setting: Psychiatric hospital
Target skill(s): Assertiveness
Outcome(s): Increase in skill performance contingent on training; decrease in aggression, maintained at 6 months

Braukmann et al. (1973)
Design: Single case; multiple baseline

Treatment: Instructions, modeling, role-play, and feedback
Trainees (N): Juvenile delinquents (2)
Setting: Family group home
Target skill(s): Heterosexual interaction skills (head nods, attending, etc.)
Outcome(s): Increase in skill performance contingent on training; increase in heterosexual contact at parties

Braukmann et al. (1974)
Design: Single case; multiple baseline
Treatment: Instructions, modeling, role-play, and feedback

Trainees (N): Juvenile delinquents (6)
Setting: Family group home
Target skill(s): Interview skills (posture, eye contact, etc.)
Outcome(s): Increase in skill performance contingent on training

De Lange et al. (1981)

Design: Multiple group; training, no training control
Treatment: Modeling, role-play, and feedback
Trainees (N): Juvenile delinquents (50)
Setting: Residential institution
Target skill(s): Assertiveness
Outcome(s): No significant between-condition differences

Elder et al. (1979)

Design: Single group; multiple baseline
Treatment: Instructions, modeling, role-play, and feedback
Trainees (N): Aggressive adolescents (4)
Setting: Psychiatric hospital
Target skill(s): Assertiveness and anger control
Outcome(s): Increase in skill performance contingent on training; decrease in aggression, maintained at 6 months

Greenleaf (1977)

Design: Multiple group; training (present v. absent), transfer programming (present v. absent), attention control, brief instructions control
Treatment: Modeling, role-play, and feedback
Trainees (N): Aggressive adolescents (43)
Setting: Secondary school
Target skill(s): Helping others
Outcome(s): Training > controls on study skill acquisition and maintenance

Gross et al. (1980)

Design: Single group; multiple baseline
Treatment: Instructions, modeling, role-play, and shaping
Trainees (N): Juvenile delinquents (10)
Setting: Group home
Target skill(s): Prosocial responsiveness (responding to criticism, responding to teasing)
Outcome(s): Increase in skill performance contingent on training; reduced truancy at postcheck, 2 months, and 1 year

Hazel et al. (1981)

Design: Multiple group; training, no training control
Treatment: Instructions, discussion, modeling, role-play, and feedback
Trainees (N): Juvenile delinquents (24)
Setting: Probation office
Target skill(s): Giving feedback, negotiation, resisting peer pressure, etc.
Outcome(s): Training > controls on study skills, maintained at 2 months

Hollin & Courtney (1983)

Design: Multiple group; training for 8 weeks, training for 4 days, no training control, or nonreferred control
Treatment: Instructions, modeling, role-play, and feedback
Trainees (N): Juvenile delinquents (15)
Setting: Residential institution
Target skill(s): Conversations skills (eye contact, listening, initiating); conflict avoidance skills
Outcome(s): No significant between-condition differences

Hollin & Henderson (1981)

Design: Multiple group; training, no training control
Treatment: Instructions, modeling, role-play, and feedback
Trainees (N): Juvenile delinquents (14)
Setting: Residential institution
Target skill(s): Conversation skills, nonverbal communication skills
Outcome(s): No significant between-condition differences

Hummel (1980)

Design: Multiple group; training (single or combined skills), varied or constant stimulus conditions
Treatment: Modeling, role-play, and feedback
Trainees (N): Aggressive adolescents (47)
Setting: Secondary school
Target skill(s): Negotiation, self-control
Outcome(s): All training under varied stimulus conditions > all training under constant stimulus conditions

Kifer et al. (1974)

Design: Single case; multiple baseline
Treatment: Instructions, role-play, and feedback

Trainees (N): Juvenile delinquents and their parents (3)
Setting: Family group home
Target skill(s): Negotiation skills (expressing opinion, reaching agreement)
Outcome(s): Increase in skill performance contingent on training

Lee et al. (1979)
Design: Multiple group; training, attention control, no training control
Treatment: Instructions, modeling, and role-play
Trainees (N): Aggressive adolescents (30)
Setting: Secondary school
Target skill(s): Aggression-control skills, assertiveness
Outcome(s): Training > controls on assertiveness, no significant between-condition differences on aggression-control skills

Litwack (1976)
Design: Multiple group; training and anticipation of serving as a trainer, training, brief instructions control
Treatment: Modeling, role-play, and feedback
Trainees (N): Aggressive adolescents (40)
Setting: Secondary school
Target skill(s): Following instructions, expressing a compliment
Outcome(s): Both training conditions > controls on both study skills, training & helper role structuring training

Long & Sherer (1984)
Design: Multiple group; training, discussion control, no training control
Treatment: Modeling, role-play, and feedback
Trainees (N): Juvenile delinquents (30)
Setting: Probation counseling
Target skill(s): Affective and aggression-relevant communication
Outcome(s): Significant increase in internality of training and discussion groups

Maloney et al. (1976)
Design: Single case; multiple baseline
Treatment: Role-play and contingent reinforcement
Trainees (N): Juvenile delinquents (4)
Setting: Family group home
Target skill(s): Conversation skills (posture, volunteering answers)

Outcome(s): Increase in skill performance contingent on training by peers or by teaching parents

Matson et al. (1980)
Design: Single group; multiple baseline
Treatment: Instructions, modeling, role-play, feedback, and contingent reinforcement
Trainees (N): Aggressive adolescent inpatients (4)
Setting: Residential institution
Target skill(s): Conversation skills (eye contact, choosing content, etc.)
Outcome(s): Increase in skill performance contingent on training, maintained at 3 months

Minkin et al. (1976)
Design: Single case; multiple baseline
Treatment: Instructions, modeling, and role-play
Trainees (N): Juvenile delinquents (4)
Setting: Family group home
Target skill(s): Conversation skills (asking questions, giving feedback)
Outcome(s): Increase in skill performance contingent on training

Ollendick & Hersen (1979)
Design: Multiple group; training, discussion control, no training control
Treatment: Instructions, modeling, role-play, and feedback
Trainees (N): Juvenile delinquents (27)
Setting: Residential institution
Target skill(s): Interpersonal accommodation skills, verbal and nonverbal
Outcome(s): Training > controls on study skills, reduction in anxiety, increase in internal locus of control

Pentz (1980)
Design: Multiple group; brief instructions control, no training control; training by teacher, parent, or peer; aggressive v. passive trainees
Treatment: Modeling, role-play, and feedback
Trainees (N): Aggressive and unassertive adolescents (90)
Setting: Secondary school
Target skill(s): Assertiveness
Outcome(s): All training conditions > controls on study skill acquisition and transfer by teacher, parent, or peer trainers

Robin (1981)
Design: Multiple group; training, family therapy, wait-list control
Treatment: Instructions, modeling, role-play, and feedback
Trainees (N): Adolescents from conflicted families (33)
Setting: Clinic
Target skill(s): Problem-solving communication skills
Outcome(s): Training > control on all study skills, training therapy on behavioral skills maintained at 10 weeks

Robin et al. (1977)
Design: Multiple group; training, wait-list control
Treatment: Instructions, discussion, modeling, role-play, and feedback
Trainees (N): Adolescents from conflicted families and their parents (24)
Setting: Clinic
Target skill(s): Problem-solving communication skills
Outcome(s): Training > control on study skills, no transfer to home

Sarason & Ganzer (1973)
Design: Multiple group; training, discussion control, no training control
Treatment: Modeling, role-play, and feedback
Trainees (N): Juvenile delinquents (192)
Setting: Residential institution
Target skill(s): Prosocial problem solving
Outcome(s): Training > control on study skills

Sarason & Sarason (1981)
Design: Multiple group; training with live modeling, training with video modeling, no training control
Treatment: Instructions, modeling, role-play, and feedback
Trainees (N): Adolescents in school with high dropout and delinquency levels (127)
Setting: Secondary school
Target skill(s): Job interview, resisting peer pressure, asking for help, dealing with frustration
Outcome(s): Training with live modeling > controls on job interview skills, training (both types) > controls on problem-solving skills, no

significant between-condition differences on other study skills

Shoemaker (1979)
Design: Multiple group; training, discussion control, no training control
Treatment: Instructions, discussion, role-play, feedback, and contingency reinforcement
Trainees (N): Juvenile delinquents (30)
Setting: Residential institution
Target skill(s): Assertiveness
Outcome(s): Training > controls on study skills, no generalization to interview situation

Spence & Marzillier (1979)
Design: Single case; multiple baseline
Treatment: Instructions, modeling, role-play, and feedback
Trainees (N): Juvenile delinquents (5)
Setting: Residential institution
Target skill(s): Conversation skills (eye contact, head movement, listening)
Outcome(s): Increase in nonverbal skill performance contingent on training, maintained at 2 weeks

Spence & Marzillier (1981)
Design: Multiple group; training, attention placebo control, no training control
Treatment: Instructions, modeling, role-play, and feedback
Trainees (N): Juvenile delinquents (76)
Setting: Residential institution
Target skill(s): Coping with criticism and teasing, inviting friendships
Outcome(s): Training > controls on study skills

Spence & Spence (1980)
Design: Multiple group; training, attention control, no training control
Treatment: Modeling, role-play, and feedback
Trainees (N): Juvenile delinquents (44)
Setting: Residential institution
Target skill(s): Nonverbal skills (e.g., eye contact), interaction skills (e.g., dealing with teasing)
Outcome(s): Training > controls on study skills, no maintenance at 6 months

Thelen et al. (1976)
Design: Multiple group; training, didactic control, baseline control

Treatment: Modeling, role-play, and feedback
Trainees (N): Juvenile delinquents (6)
Setting: Group home
Target skill(s): Conflict resolution skills (coping with accusations, expressing positive feelings)
Outcome(s): Increase in skill performance contingent on training, not maintained at 2 weeks

Trief (1976)
Design: Multiple group; training (cognitive, affective, or combined aspects of skill), attention control, brief instructions control
Treatment: Modeling, role-play, and feedback
Trainees (N): Juvenile delinquents (58)
Setting: Residential institution

Target skill(s): Perspective taking
Outcome(s): All training conditions > controls on study skills acquisition and transfer

Werner et al. (1975)
Design: Multiple group; training, no training control
Treatment: Instructions, modeling, role-play, and feedback
Trainees (N): Juvenile delinquents (6)
Setting: Family group home
Target skill(s): Prosocial communication with police officers (eye contract, cooperation, expression of reform)
Outcome(s): Pre- and posttraining increase in study skills for training and control groups

REFERENCES

Adkins, W. R. (1970). Life skills: Structured counseling for the disadvantaged. *Personnel and Guidance Journal, 49,* 108–116.
Adkins, W. R. (1974). Life coping skills: A fifth curriculum. *Teachers College Record, 75,* 507–526.
Agras, W. S. (1967). Behavior therapy in the management of chronic schizophrenia. *American Journal of Psychiatry, 124,* 240–243.
Anderson, L. (1981). *Role playing ability and young children: The prescriptive question.* Unpublished masters thesis, Syracuse University.
Argyle, M., Trower, P., & Bryant, B. (1974). Explorations in the treatment of personality disorders and neuroses by social skill training. *British Journal of Medical Psychology, 47,* 63–72.
Asher, S. R., & Renshaw, P. D. (1981). Children without friends: Social knowledge and social skill training. In S. R. Asher & J. M. Gottman (Eds.), *The development of children's friendships.* New York: Cambridge University Press.
Bandura, A. (1973). *Aggression: A social learning analysis.* Englewood Cliffs, NJ: Prentice-Hall.
Berlin, R. (1977). *Teaching acting-out adolescents prosocial conflict resolution through structured learning training of empathy.* Unpublished doctoral dissertation, Syracuse University.
Bornstein, M., Bellack, A. S., & Hersen, M. (1980). Social skills training for highly aggressive children. *Behavior Modification, 4,* 173–186.
Braukmann, C. J., & Fixsen, D. L. (1975). Behavior modification with delinquents. In M. Hersen, R. M. Eisler, & P. M. Miller (Eds.), *Progress in behavior modification* (Vol. 1, pp. 191–231). New York: Academic Press.
Braukmann, C. J., Fixsen, D. L., Phillips, E. L., Wolf, M. M., & Maloney, D. M. (1974). An analysis of a selection interview training package for predelinquents at Achievement Place. *Criminal Justice and Behavior, 1,* 30–42.
Braukmann, C. J., Maloney, D. M., Phillips, E. L., & Wolf, M. M. (1973). The measurement and modification of heterosexual interaction skills of predelinquents at Achievement Place. Unpublished manuscript, University of Kansas, Lawrence.
Callantine, M. F., & Warren, J. M. (1955). Learning sets in human concept formation. *Psychological Reports, 1,* 363–367.
Conger, J. J., Miller, W. C., & Walsmith, C. R. (1965). Antecedents of delinquency: Personality, social class, and intelligence. In P. H. Mussen, J. J. Conger, & J. Kagen (Eds.), *Readings in child development and personality.* New York: Harper & Row.
Cronbach, L. J. (1967). How can instruction be adapted to individual differences? In R. M. Gagne (Ed.), *Learning and individual differences.* Columbus, OH: Merrill.
Dean, S. I. (1958). Treatment of the reluctant client. *American Psychologist, 13,* 627–630.
DeLange, J. M., Lanham, S. L., & Barton, J. A. (1981). Social skills training for juvenile delin-

quents: Behavioral skill training and cognitive techniques. In D. Upper & S. M. Ross (Eds.), *Behavioral group therapy, 1981: An annual review.* Champaign, IL: Research Press.

Dodge, K. A. (1983). *A social information processing model of social competence in children.* Unpublished manuscript, Bloomington, IN.

Dreikurs, R., Grunwald, B. B., & Pepper, F. C. (1971). *Maintaining sanity in the classroom.* New York: Harper & Row.

Duncan, C. P. (1958). Transfer after training with single versus multiple tasks. *Journal of Experimental Psychology, 55,* 63–72.

Edelman, E. M., & Goldstein, A. P. (1984). Prescriptive relationship levels for juvenile delinquents in a psychotherapy analog. *Aggressive Behavior, 10,* 269–278.

Elardo, P., & Cooper, M. (1977). *AWARE: Activities for social development.* Reading, MA: Addison-Wesley.

Elder, J. P., Edelstein, B. A., & Narick, N. N. (1979). Adolescent psychiatric patients: Modifying aggressive behavior with social skills training. *Behavior Modification, 3*(2), 161–178.

Ellis, H. (1965). *The transfer of learning.* New York: Macmillan.

Epps, S., Thompson, B. J., & Lane, M. P. (1985). *Procedures for incorporating generalization programming into interventions for behaviorally disordered students.* Unpublished manuscript, Ames, IA.

Fleming, D. (1976). *Teaching negotiation skills to pre-adolescents.* Unpublished doctoral dissertation, Syracuse University.

Freedman, B. J., Rosenthal, R., Donahoe, C. P., Schlundt, D. G., & McFall, R. M. (1978). A social behavioral analysis of skill deficits in delinquent and nondelinquent adolescent boys. *Journal of Consulting and Clinical Psychology, 46,* 1448–1462.

Galassi, J. P., & Galassi, M. (1984). Promoting transfer and maintenance of counseling outcomes: How do we do it? How do we study it? In S. D. Brown & R. W. Tent (Eds.), *Handbook of counseling psychology.* New York: Wiley.

Goetz, T. E., & Dweck, C. S. (1980). Learned helplessness in social situations. *Journal of Personality and Social Psychology, 39,* 246–255.

Gold, M. (1978). Scholastic experiences, self-esteem, and delinquent behavior: A theory for alternative schools. *Crime and Delinquency, 7,* 290–309.

Golden, R. (1975). *Teaching resistance-reducing behavior to high school students.* Unpublished doctoral dissertation, Syracuse University.

Goldstein, A. P. (1973). *Structured learning therapy: Toward a psychotherapy for the poor.* New York: Academic Press.

Goldstein, A. P. (Ed.). (1978). *Prescriptions for child mental health and education.* New York: Pergamon Press.

Goldstein, A. P. (1981). *Psychological skill training.* New York: Pergamon Press.

Goldstein, A. P., Apter, S., & Harootunian, B. (1984). *School violence.* Englewood Cliffs, NJ: Prentice-Hall.

Goldstein, A. P., Glick, B., Reiner, S., Zimmerman, D., Coultry, T. A., & Gold, D. (1985). Aggression replacement training: A comprehensive intervention for the acting-out delinquent. *Journal of Correctional Education, 27,* 120–126.

Goldstein, A. P., & Goedhart, A. (1973). The use of structured learning for empathy-enhancement in paraprofessional psychotherapist training. *Journal of Community Psychology, 1,* 168–173.

Goldstein, A. P., Heller, K., & Sechrest, L. B. (1966). *Psychotherapy and the psychology of behavior change.* New York: Wiley.

Goldstein, A. P., & Kanfer, F. H. (Eds.). (1979). *Maximizing treatment gains.* New York: Academic Press.

Goldstein, A. P., Keller, H., & Erne, D. (1985). *Changing the abusive parent.* Champaign, IL: Research Press.

Goldstein, A. P., Monti, P.J., Sardino, T. J., & Green, D. J. (1979). *Police crisis intervention.* New York: Pergamon Press.

Goldstein, A. P., & Sorcher, M. (1973, March). Changing managerial behavior by applied learning techniques. *Training and Development Journal,* 36–39.

Goldstein, A. P., & Sorcher, M. (1974). *Changing supervisor behavior.* New York: Pergamon Press.

Goldstein, A. P., Sprafkin, R. P., & Gershaw, N. J. (1976). *Skill training for community living: Applying structured learning therapy.* New York: Pergamon Press.

Goldstein, A. P., Sprafkin, R. P., Gershaw, N. J., & Klein, P. (1980). *Skillstreaming the adolescent.* Champaign, IL: Research Press.

Goldstein, A. P., & Stein, N. (1976). *Prescriptive psychotherapies.* New York: Pergamon Press.

Greenleaf, D. (1977). *Peer reinforcement as transfer enhancement in structured learning therapy.* Unpublished masters thesis, Syracuse University.

Gross, A. M., Brigham, T. A., Hopper, C., & Bologna, N. C. (1980). Self-management and social skills training. *Criminal Justice and Behavior, 7,* 161–184.

Gruber, R. P. (1971). Behavior therapy: Problems in generalization. *Behavior Therapy, 2,* 361–368.

Guerney, B. G., Jr. (1977). *Relationship enhancement.* San Francisco: Jossey-Bass.

Gunzberg, H. C. (1980). *Progress Assessment Chart of Social Competence.* London: SEFA Publications.

Gutride, M. E., Goldstein, A. P., & Hunter, G. F. (1973). The use of modeling and role playing to increase social interaction among asocial psychiatric patients. *Journal of Consulting and Clinical Psychology, 40,* 408–415.

Guttman, E. S. (1970). Effects of short-term psychiatric treatment for boys in two California Youth Authority institutions. In D. C. Gibbons (Ed.), *Delinquent behavior.* Englewood Cliffs, NJ: Prentice-Hall.

Guzzetta, R. A. (1974). *Acquisition and transfer of empathy by the parents of early adolescents through structured learning training.* Unpublished doctoral dissertation, Syracuse University.

Hare, M. A. (1976). *Teaching conflict resolution simulations.* Paper presented before the Eastern Community Association, Philadelphia.

Harootunian, B. (1978). Teacher training. In A. P. Goldstein (Ed.), *Prescriptions for child mental health and education.* New York: Pergamon.

Hawley, R. C., & Hawley, I. L. (1975). *Developing human potential: A handbook of activities for personal and social growth.* Amherst, MA: Education Research Associates.

Hazel, J. S., Schumaker, J. B., Sherman, J. A., & Sheldon-Wildgen, J. (1981). *ASSET: A social skills program for adolescents.* Champaign, IL: Research Press.

Heiman, H. (1973). Teaching interpersonal communications. *North Dakota Speech and Theatre Association Bulletin, 2,* 7–29.

Hollin, C. R., & Courtney, S. A. (1983). A skill training approach to the reduction of institutional offending. *Personality and Individual Differences, 4,* 257–264.

Hollin, C. R., & Henderson, M. (1981). The effects of social skills training on incarcerated delinquent adolescents. *International Journal of Behavioral Social Work, 1,* 145–155.

Hoyer, W. J., Lopez, M., & Goldstein, A. P. (1982). Predicting social skill acquisition and transfer by psychogeriatric inpatients. *International Journal of Behavioral Geriatrics, 1,* 43–46.

Hummel, J. (1980). *Session variability and skill content as transfer enhancers in structured learning training.* Unpublished doctoral dissertation, Syracuse University.

Hunt, D. E. (1972). Matching models for teacher training. In B. R. Joyce & M. Weil (Eds.), *Perspectives for reform in teacher training.* Englewood Cliffs, NJ: Prentice-Hall.

Jennings, R. L. (1975). *The use of structured learning techniques to teach attraction enhancing skills to residentially hospitalized disturbed children and adolescents: A psychotherapy analogue investigation.* Unpublished doctoral dissertation, University of Iowa.

Karoly, R., & Steffen, J. J. (Eds.). (1980). *Improving the long-term effects of psychotherapy.* New York: Gardner Press.

Kazdin, A. (1980). *Research design in clinical psychology.* New York: Harper & Row.

Kifer, R. E., Lewis, M. A., Green, D. R., & Phillips, E. L. (1974). Training predelinquent youths and their parents to negotiate conflict situations. *Journal of Applied Behavior Analysis, 7,* 357–364.

Kohlberg, L. (1986). The just community approach to corrections. *Journal of Correctional Education, 37,* 54–58.

Kohn, M., Parnes, B., & Rosman, B. L. (1979). *Kohn Social Competence Scale.* New York: Martin Kohn.

Lack, D. Z. (1975). *Problem-solving training, structured learning training and didactic instruction in the preparation of paraprofessional mental health personnel for the utilization of contingency management techniques.* Unpublished doctoral dissertation, Syracuse University.

Ladd, G. W., & Mize, J. (1983). A cognitive-social learning model of social-skill training. *Psychological Review, 90,* 127–157.

Lee, D. Y., Hollbery, E. T., & Hussard, H. (1979). Effects of assertion training on aggressive behavior of adolescents. *Journal of Counseling Psychology, 26,* 459–461.

Liberman, B. (1970). *The effect of modeling procedures on attraction and disclosure in a psychotherapy analogue.* Unpublished doctoral dissertation, Syracuse University.

Litwack, S. E. (1976). *The use of the helper therapy principle to increase therapeutic effectiveness and reduce therapeutic resistance: Structured learning therapy with resistant adolescents.* Unpublished doctoral dissertation, Syracuse University.

Long, S. J., & Sherer, M. (1984). Social skills training with juvenile offenders. *Child & Family Behavior Therapy, 6,* 1–11.

Lopez, M. A. (1977). *The effects of overlearning and prestructuring in structured learning therapy with geriatric patients.* Unpublished doctoral dissertation, Syracuse University.

Lopez, M. A., Hoyer, W. J., Goldstein, A. P., Gershaw, N. J., & Sprafkin, R. P. (1980). Effects of overlearning and incentive on the acquisition and transfer of interpersonal skills with institutionalized elderly. *Journal of Gerontology, 35*(3), 403–408.

Magaro, P. A. (1969). A prescriptive treatment model based upon social class and premorbid adjustment. *Psychotherapy: Theory, Research and Practice, 6,* 57–70.

Maloney, D. M., Harper, T. N., Braukmann, C. J., Fixsen, D. L., Phillips, E. L., & Wolf, M. M. (1976). Teaching conversation-related skills to pre-delinquent girls. *Journal of Applied Behavior Analysis, 9,* 371.

Matson, J. L., Esveldt-Dawson, K., Andrasik, F., Ollendick, T. H., Petti, T., & Hersen, M. (1980). Direct observational and generalization effects of social skills training with emotionally disturbed children. *Behavior Therapy, 11,* 522–531.

Matson, J. L., Esveldt-Dawson, K., & Kazdin, A. E. (1983). Validation of methods for assessing social skills in children. *Journal of Clinical Child Psychology, 12,* 174–180.

McFall, R. M. (1976). Behavioral training: A skill-acquisition approach to clinical problems. In J. T. Spence, R. C. Carson, & J. W. Thibaut (Eds.), *Behavioral approaches to therapy* (pp. 227–259). Morristown, NJ: General Learning Press.

Michelson, L., & Wood, R. (1980). Behavioral assessment and training of children's social skills. In M. Hersen, R. M. Eisler, & P. M. Miller (Eds.), *Progress in behavior modification* (Vol. 9, pp. 240–291). New York: Academic Press.

Minkin, N., Braukmann, C. J., Minkin, B. L., Timbers, G. D., Timbers, B. J., Fixsen, D. L., Phillips, E. L., & Wolf, M. M. (1976). The social validation and training of conversational skills. *Journal of Applied Behavior Analysis, 9,* 127–139.

Mussen, P. H., Conger, J. J., Kagan, J., & Gerwitz, J. (1979). *Psychological development: A life-span approach.* New York: Harper & Row.

O'Leary, K. D., O'Leary, S., & Becker, W. C. (1967). Modification of a deviant sibling interaction pattern in the home. *Behavior Research and Therapy, 5,* 113–120.

Ollendick, T. H., & Hersen, M. (1979). Social skills training for juvenile delinquents. *Behavior Research and Therapy, 17,* 547–555.

Orenstein, R. (1973). *Effect of teaching patients to focus on their feelings on level of experiencing in a subsequent interview.* Unpublished doctoral dissertation, Syracuse University.

Osgood, C. E. (1953). *Method and theory in experimental psychology.* New York: Oxford University Press.

Patterson, G. R., Cobb, J. A., & Ray, R. S. (1973). A social engineering technology for retraining the families of aggressive boys. In H. E. Adams & I. P. Unikel (Eds.), *Issues and trends in behavior therapy.* Springfield, IL: Charles C. Thomas.

Patterson, G. R., Reid, J. G., Jones, R. R., & Conger, R. E. (1975). *A social learning approach to family intervention* (Vol. 1). Eugene, OR: Castalia.

Pentz, M. A. (1980). Assertion training and trainer effects on unassertive and aggressive adolescents. *Journal of Counseling Psychology, 27,* 76–83.

Raleigh, R. (1977). *Individual versus group structured learning therapy for assertiveness training with senior and junior high school students.* Unpublished doctoral dissertation, Syracuse University.

Rathjen, D. P. (1984). Social skills training for children: Innovations and consumer guidelines. *School Psychology Review, 13,* 302–310.

Redl, F., & Wineman, D. (1957). *The aggressive child.* New York: Free Press.

Robin, A. L. (1981). A controlled evaluation of problem-solving communication training with parent-adolescent conflict. *Behavior Therapy, 12,* 593–609.

Robin, A. L., Kent, R., O'Leary, K. D., Foster, S., & Prinz, R. (1977). An approach to teaching parents and adolescents problem-solving communication skills: A preliminary report. *Behavior Therapy, 8,* 639–643.

Robinson, R. (1973). *Evaluation of a structured learning empathy training program for lower socioeconomic status home-aide trainees.* Unpublished masters thesis, Syracuse University.

Rogers, C. R. (1957). The necessary and sufficient conditions of therapeutic personality change. *Journal of Consulting Psychology, 21,* 95–103.

Sarason, I. G., & Ganzer, V. J. (1973). Modeling and group discussion in the rehabilitation of juvenile delinquents. *Journal of Counseling Psychology, 20,* 422–449.

Sarason, I. G., & Sarason, B. R. (1981). Teaching cognitive and social skills to high school students. *Journal of Consulting and Clinical Psychology, 49*(6), 908–918.

Scandura, J. M. (1977). Structural approaches to instructional problems. *American Psychologist, 32*, 33–53.

Schinke, S. P. (1981). Interpersonal-skills training with adolescents. In M. Hersen, R. M. Eisler, & P. M. Miller (Eds.), *Progress in behavior modification* (Vol. 11, pp. 66–115). New York: Academic Press.

Schneiman, R. (1972). *An evaluation of structured learning and didactic learning as methods of training behavior modification skills to lower and middle socioeconomic level teacher-aides.* Unpublished doctoral dissertation, Syracuse University.

Schwitzgebel, R. L. (1967). Short term operant conditioning of adolescent offenders on socially relevant variables. *Journal of Abnormal Psychology, 72*, 134–142.

Shoemaker, M. E. (1979). Group assertion training for institutionalized male delinquents. In J. E. Stumphauzer (Ed.), *Progress in behavior therapy with delinquents* (pp. 91–117). Springfield, IL: Charles C. Thomas.

Shore, E., & Sechrest, L. (1961). Concept attainment as a function of number of positive instances presented. *Journal of Educational Psychology, 52*, 303–307.

Slack, C. W. (1960). Experimenter-subject psychotherapy: A new method of introducing intensive office treatment for unreachable cases. *Mental Hygiene, 44*, 238–256.

Slavson, S. R. (1964). *A textbook in analytic group psychotherapy.* New York: International Universities Press.

Solomon, E. (1977). *Structured learning therapy with abusive parents: Training in self-control.* Unpublished doctoral dissertation, Syracuse University.

Spatz-Norton, C. (1984). *An evaluation of prosocial skill training plus aggression-control training with chronically aggressive children.* Unpublished doctoral dissertation, Syracuse University.

Spence, A. J., & Spence, S. H. (1980). Cognitive changes associated with social skills training. *Behavioral Research and Therapy, 18*, 265–272.

Spence, S. H. (1979). Social skills training with adolescent offenders: A review. *Behavioral Psychology, 7*, 49–57.

Spence, S. H. (1981). Differences in social skills performance between institutionalized juvenile male offenders and a comparable group of boys without offence records. *British Journal of Clinical Psychology, 17*, 24–29.

Spence, S. H. (1982). Social skill training with young offenders. In P. Feldman (Ed.), *Developments in the study of criminal behavior.* New York: Wiley.

Spence, S. H., & Marzillier, J. S. (1979). Social skills training with adolescent male offenders: Short-term effects. *Behavioral Research and Therapy, 17*, 7–16.

Spence, S. H., & Marzillier, J. S. (1981). Social skills training with adolescent male offenders—II: Short-term, long-term and generalized effects. *Behavioral Research and Therapy, 19*, 349–368.

Stephens, T. M. (1978). *Social skills in the classroom.* Columbus, OH: Cedars Press.

Stern, G. G. (1970). *People in context.* New York: Wiley.

Sturm, D. (1980). *Therapist aggression tolerance and dependency tolerance under standardized client conditions of hostility and dependency.* Unpublished masters thesis, Syracuse University.

Sutton-Simon, K. (1973). *The effects of two types of modeling and rehearsal procedures upon the adequacy of social behavior of hospitalized schizophrenics.* Unpublished doctoral dissertation, Syracuse University.

Swanstrom, C. R. (1978). *An examination of structured learning therapy and the children with conduct problems.* Unpublished doctoral dissertation, Syracuse University.

Tharp, R. C., & Wetzel, R. (1969). *Behavior modification in the natural environment.* New York: Academic Press.

Thelen, M. A., Fry, R. A., Dollinger, S. L., & Paul, S. C. (1976). Use of videotaped models to improve the interpersonal adjustment of delinquents. *Journal of Consulting and Clinical Psychology, 44*, 492.

Thorndike, E. L., & Woodworth, R. S. (1901). The influence of improvement in one mental function upon the efficiency of other functions. *Psychological Review, 8*, 247–261.

Trief, P. (1976). *The reduction of egocentrism in acting-out adolescents by structured learning therapy.* Unpublished doctoral dissertation, Syracuse University.

Truax, C. B., Wargo, D. G., & Silber, L. D. (1966). Effects of group psychotherapy with high accurate empathy and nonpossessive warmth upon female institutionalized delinquents. *Journal of Abnormal Psychology, 71*, 267–274.

Walker, H. M. (1979). *The acting-out child: Coping with classroom disruption.* Boston: Allyn & Bacon.

Walker, H. M., McConnell, S., Holmes, D., Todis, B., Walker, J., & Golden, N. (1983). *The Walker social skills curriculum.* Austin: Pro-Ed.

Werner, J. S., Minkin, N., Minkin, B. L., Fixsen, D. L., Phillips, E. L., & Wolf, M. M. (1975). Intervention packages: An analysis to prepare juvenile delinquents for encounters with police officers. *Criminal Justice and Behavior, 2,* 55–84.

Wood, M. (1977). *Adolescent acquisition and transfer of assertiveness through the use of structured learning therapy.* Unpublished doctoral dissertation, Syracuse University.

Zimmerman, D. (1985). *Enhancing perspective-taking and moral reasoning via structured learning therapy and moral education with aggressive adolescents.* Unpublished masters thesis, Syracuse University.

Gail Schwartz

VIGNETTE   A Success Story

Why do we do what we do? Why do I teach? In every teacher's career there is at least one student whose name and face and style conjure up great memories, reminding us of ourselves and why we do what we do. Bobby Wilson is one of those students, and this is his story.

Bobby was a resident of the maximum security juvenile facility where I taught social studies. Students arrived at the facility without public school transcripts or any other kind of information regarding their academic, social, or emotional needs. Consequently, the teaching process was pure trial and error. And with 20 students in my class, I was able to give only a limited amount of individual attention.

Bobby presented a real challenge. My efforts to engage him in classroom activities met with little success. Each day he came to class and sat in stony silence as I energetically tried to interest him and his classmates in American history. Bobby answered questions with cryptic responses and steadfastly refused to participate in the tasks at hand. He seemed ominous and succeeded in making me feel quite uneasy.

The tension between us increased. Nonetheless, armed with a minimal amount of in-house diagnostic information that indicated serious skill deficits in math and reading, I tried to motivate Bobby to lower his defenses and begin work on some of his academic problems. I sensed the existence of a learning disability that, combined with an emotional overlay, would make the task of breaking through a difficult one. I used *every* technique I knew to involve Bobby in class activities and assignments, but nothing worked.

Bobby's angry disposition was soon manifested in a series of violent outbursts in various areas of the facility: the cottage, dining hall, and classroom. He spent much of his time in isolation and began seeing a staff psychologist for individual counseling.

A few days before Bobby was scheduled to appear in court, I received notification that I had to testify at his hearing. That day came. As I approached the stand, I was apprehensive, knowing that I would have to tell the judge, as Bobby glared at me, about Bobby's lack of responsiveness in class, his verbally abusive episodes, and his poor test scores. I raised my right hand and swore to tell the truth, although I did not want to. I recounted my brief history with Bobby in accurate detail, even though I knew it would not help his case. And I looked directly at Bobby as I told the judge that although we had experienced some pretty stormy times, I was prepared to hang in there and continue our work together. I believed that behind all of Bobby's rage and pain were strength, determination, and potential for growth and change. I said that I would be there for Bobby if the judge decided that he should return to the institution.

Bobby did return. The next day he entered my classroom. I held my breath in anticipation of a fierce reaction to the previous day's events; but my fears were unfounded. Bobby sat quietly through the class, and when it came time for him to move on to his next class, instead he approached my desk. With a slight trace of a smile, he asked me what I thought about the hearing. I told him that I had been nervous and had frankly expected him to be angry about the information I gave the judge.

"You just told the truth," he said. "Did you really mean what you said about wanting to work with me?"

I told Bobby that I did, and we talked more about the hearing before he left for his other classes. From that time forward, he opened up a little more to me each day. Somehow, I had gained his trust. It may have been the combination of my not backing down but not giving up on him either. I'm not sure. But the important thing was that we could work together.

There were still difficult moments and hard times; but we established a relationship, with trust and confidence in each other, and that helped us work through the rough spots. Bobby's skills in reading and math improved; his violent outbursts diminished. His relationships with staff and peers grew more harmonious, too. By the time Bobby was released from the facility, he had learned to trust somewhat and to acknowledge his problems in a positive way. The original glare in his eyes became more often a shine, and self-confidence and self-respect replaced his former feelings of fear and insecurity.

I lost track of Bobby after his release. Although he promised to write, he never did. But he also did not return to the institution, so I simply crossed my fingers and hoped that his absence was a result of his functioning well outside the facility. I did not know for certain and thought I probably never would.

It was only a few years later, when I was shopping at a large flower and garden shop in town, that I found out what had really happened to Bobby. After wandering around the shop for a short while, I was approached by a young man clad in the bright orange jacket of the shop's employees. As he came closer, I recognized at once the familiar shine in his eyes. It was Bobby. We stood in the middle of the store and eagerly caught up on each other's lives. He told me had been involved in a few minor skirmishes with the law over the years but that he had been working steadily at the garden shop for the past year and was feeling good about his independence, his life, and his future. I remember how much he smiled when he spoke—and how much happier he seemed.

I had to leave to keep an appointment in town. But before we parted, Bobby looked at me seriously and told me that he would really like to help out, to come and talk to my students some time, to tell them what it really is like to be locked up, to be alone.

I smiled and said I would let him know. And as I left the store, I thought to myself how much Bobby had *already* helped me—much more than he could know.

Susan M. Egan

VIGNETTE   Observations on Special Education in Corrections

What has special education meant to corrections? Let's ask those most affected—the staff and the students.

Student: Hey man, what's so special about it? Don't every school work this way? How's it work? Well, we had this meeting, my teachers and my counselor and my therapist all sat down with me and they tell me how I did on all my tests and stuff. I don't like those tests—they think you're crazy. But this meeting they had, they told me I had something called a learning disability—that I get words confused when I read and stuff. I knew there must be something wrong. All my friends did much better than me in school. It was hard for me so I quit. Now? Well now school's still hard but my teachers help me a lot. I've got goals and stuff they gave me at the meeting so we're all in this together, you know what I mean?

Can I read now? Well—it's better, I found some neat books about bikes and I like that pretty much. I'm doing real good in math and may be able to take the GED next year. I'd really like to graduate though and get a real diploma. This special ed meeting said I maybe could graduate, they'd help me. I got it figured that if I'm gonna stay out I need a job and I need to graduate to get a good one. Would I have gone back to school without special ed? Probably not—it took them a long time to convince me to give it another try, but I'm glad I did.

Unit staff: What's special ed done for us? Well, when it first came around I thought, "Oh boy! Here we go again." You know it seems like every couple of years somebody tries something new. Then you've either got to drop what you were doing and do the new things, or worse, add them on top of what you're already doing. And you're supposed to take it out of your hide—there's never any more money and staff. Those of us who have been around a long time get real tired of every new program fad that comes along, and we don't like the education department telling us what to do. They can be ivory tower intellectuals, social worker types with bleeding hearts. They forget we're a lock-up facility and security comes first. Don't get me wrong, we've got treatment here, sure, but you can't treat 'em if they're out of control, right?

Well, anyway, special education was different. They included us right from the beginning in the training, and they listened to our suggestions about setting up the program. Then they had some laws they had to meet (I'm not real fond of the feds telling us what to do, but most of this made sense). We sit in on all the IEP metings, and the staffing reviews. It's great to know how the guys are doing in school. Used to be sometimes you'd think you were talking about two different people, the kids would act so different on the unit than what teacher's reports from school said. I guess I'd have to say the best part has been getting involved with teachers—they're not so bad. And these guys, they can't play games on us anymore because we're all in this together, right? You know I figured out, it wasn't just a new program to lay on top of what we were already doing but a process—a way to get the best of what we were all doing together.

Superintendent: I remember the first memo I got from Central Office about special ed. "Boy! Just what we need," I thought, "more consultants." See, there have been a lot of programs come and go around here, and most were some hotshot idea that some high-priced consultant had managed to sell our Central Office on. Most of those administrators have never had to run an institution day after day, and let's just say I was skeptical.

But from the beginning when the trainers came in to discuss the implementation plan with me, I could tell this was different. These people had information we could use. And they wanted to involve everybody on the grounds, not just teachers. You know, I have a real problem when the teachers are the only ones who get the funding to go to meetings and get training. That makes my other sections jealous. Well, I made everybody go to their first sessions—even the cooks and janitors. Hell—they supervise kids, too.

The trainers told us about the different kinds of handicaps, "impairments" they called them, and yeah—we've got a lot of kids who turned out to be eligible for IEPs—maybe a third at any given time. My staff learned how to work together. Hell—the reason we're here is to retrain these kids, and we were all headed in different directions. The special education process keeps everybody, staff and students, on target. And I like an efficient organization.

The payoff? Well, for us it's been the training. Each year they bring specialists in to update us. We've learned about language problems, and I've really seen a change in how everybody gives the kids instructions now. Instead of barking out six or eight orders in a row to a kid and then writing him up for not getting everything done right, they break down the orders and give the directions one or two at a time. And most of my staff are parents with school-aged children, so they were able to use this training at home, too. And phew! special ed really saved us when we got those three deaf kids all at once. We got signing interpreters and special teachers to help them, and there's no way we could have found the money to do that without special ed. Yeah, special ed has been a real boost to us—they're really a part of us now, and you'd really hear from me if you tried to take them away!

Teacher: What has special ed done for us? I'd say it gave us credibility or legitimacy in our institution. I think our education department was just bare- ly tolerated before. Some of it was our own fault. Many other staff don't have the college education we do and don't make as much money, so there was some jealousy. But honestly, I think we really did isolate ourselves with a sort of we're-better-than-you attitude.

Well, we're not. I was beginning to really burn out. It was always such a struggle getting kids to attend class. I had taken classes in special ed at the university as a requirement for my credential, but I never thought about applying it to corrections. I had mixed feelings. On the one hand, I didn't see any retarded kids or blind ones, so I never thought about our kids being handicapped. And because the kids were doing ok in my class, I thought why take on all the extra paper work? So I didn't bother making any referrals.

After I'd been through some of the awareness training, my thoughts began to shift to the other extreme—I had mostly remedial students and had com- pletely individualized my instruction. Maybe they were *all* special! I had a real hard time distinguishing those who were delayed because of disabilities from those who just hadn't had the exposure to education or had gaps in skills. Eventually, with the help of our school psychologist and resource specialist all the test results that had seemed like Greek to me (although I didn't want to admit that I didn't understand them!) began to make some sense. It became easier to separate the trees from the forest. One of my col- leagues had said, "When you're staring at a brick wall, how can you tell one brick from another?" But that's what the identification process is all about.

Sure, we don't always agree, but the IEP process has brought a lot more meaning to our education program. And the resources and supplementary materials that have been made available have really helped. I'd say special ed has helped correctional education finally get its act together.

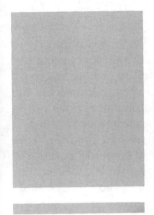

Issues in Transition: Transfer of Youth from Correctional Facilities to Public Schools

CHAPTER 11   *Eugene B. Edgar, Sharon L. Webb, Mary Maddox*

Large numbers of youth are involved with juvenile correction systems in the United States. The most recent data indicate that at least 33,190 youths under the age of 21 are currently incarcerated in state facilities (Rutherford, Nelson, & Wolford, 1985). Estimates of juvenile correctional programs indicate that between 28% (Rutherford et al., 1985) and 42% (Morgan, 1979) of these students are handicapped. Most youthful offenders are confined to detention or correctional facilities for relatively short periods of time (Smith, Ramirez, & Rutherford, 1984) and hence are likely to return to public schools after leaving a juvenile correctional facility. Some data indicate that successful completion of high school after contact with the juvenile justice system is a predictor of an adult life free of criminal activity (Needham & Grims, 1983). All juvenile offenders should have an opportunity to continue their education in a public school program that would enable them to acquire the social, academic, and work skills necessary to be productive citizens in our society.

The movement of adjudicated youth between the correctional and the public school systems is an example of transition between two separate agencies. This transition is difficult and complicated, even when the agencies involved have a high regard for their clients. The problems are even greater with handicapped adjudicated youth, who tend to be held in low esteem by agency staff. This chapter presents an overview of transition issues in general, followed by specific examples of strategies that have proven useful in transferring handicapped juvenile offenders from juvenile justice facilities to public school programs.

The authors acknowledge the contributions of Al Lynch, supervisor of the Division of Special Services in the Office of the Superintendent of Public Instruction and of Robert Thurton, supervisor of the Division of Juvenile Rehabilitation in the Department of Social and Health Services of the State of Washington.

Of course, substantial numbers of adjudicated youth do not return to public school programs. Some of these youth finish their high school requirements in the school program at the correctional facility, whereas others choose to drop out of school. These youth need effective transition from the correctional facility to work opportunities or job training situations in the community, and as with transition to public schools, careful procedures must be thoughtfully developed. Although this chapter focuses on transition from corrections facilities to public schools, many of the ideas and procedures also relate to the transition to work or job training opportunities. However, our procedures have developed from a careful probing of the professionals involved in the transition process and the designing of situation-specific strategies to resolve the identified problems. We have used this technique to develop strategies for transition between a number of human service agencies—from infant centers and Head Start programs to public school programs (Gallaher, Maddox, & Edgar, 1984); from secondary special education programs to community-based programs administered by developmental disabilities (Horton, Maddox, & Edgar, 1985) or vocational rehabilitation (Haynes, Maddox, & Edgar, 1985)—as well as for the delivery of concurrent services to handicapped children and youth by more than one agency (Egelston, Tazioli, Maddox, & Edgar, 1985). These projects have allowed us to design and field-test a process for developing transition strategies for *specific* populations. Thus, although we believe that many of the ideas from our work in juvenile corrections also relate to the transition to work or other situations, our approach demands the careful development and field-testing of procedures in *each* type of situation. We do believe our ideas will be found useful and encourage our readers to expand our procedures to other types of transition events.

TRANSITION IN GENERAL

A number of factors force people through transitions in the human service maze. These factors often relate to the system, not to the needs of clients, and result from an organizational approach that dissects clients into service pieces that can be paired with an agency or service provider. For example, a juvenile offender who is released from a juvenile justice facility may require both special education and mental health services but will have to go to separate agencies to receive those services because they are seldom provided jointly through one agency. Perhaps the most important of the operative factors is the absence of an overall plan for coordinating available services. We thought there was such a plan. As educators, we were most familiar with the range of educational services but were aware of other services (e.g., mental health, vocational rehabilitation, medicaid) and assumed that somewhere (probably in an office in Washington, DC) someone (probably a bureau chief, whatever that is) knew how the pieces of this vast puzzle fit together.

Undoubtedly, there was a wall chart somewhere depicting an integrated system. We were wrong.

Human service programs have developed haphazardly. Out of the concern of lawmakers, community leaders, and special interest groups driven by a vocal constituency or by observed need, programs have been created to respond to needs for health, education, and social services. In most instances the programs were developed for a specific clientele (e.g., Crippled Children's Services), and almost all human service programs have a target population to whom they provide services. The bureaucratic approach to identifying that population is eligibility criteria, which restrict the clientele that may receive services. Most agencies have definite entrance and exit criteria, often fixed by age, income level, and/or geography. Aging, income fluctuations, and changing residence are all factors that force clients into transition between agencies. In addition, various types of services are available only in specific locations. The rule is that the client goes to the services, seldom vice versa. Thus, client movement to and between services is a prerequisite to receiving them.

Describing Transition

The transition, or movement, of clients between two agencies can be described in terms of the sending agency, the receiving agency, and the client "handoff." These three components are present in any transition, and their careful analysis can lead to an improved transition.

The Sending Agency.   The sending agency has primary responsibility for clients before transition. In the case of handicapped adjudicated youth, correctional facilities or court programs are the sending agencies. The sending agency can improve transition by modifying its programs or treatments to better prepare clients for their new placements. For adjudicated youth this might mean adapting the correctional facility's vocational curriculum to reflect that found in the public school.

The Receiving Agency.   A receiving agency takes over primary service responsibility for a client from another agency. The schools often are the receiving agencies for youth leaving correctional facilities. Receiving agencies can improve transition for clients by modifying programs and services to build on the clients' previous programs. For example, local public schools might offer alternative programs and flexible scheduling for paroled youth with a history of failure in traditional programs.

Frequently, agencies serve as both receivers and senders. For example, a public school would be the sending agency when a youth is committed to a juvenile corrections facility and the receiving agency when the youth returns from the facility.

The Handoff.   The handoff is the process and procedures used to move the student or client from one agency to another. Handoff includes choosing a new placement, planning for it, communicating with parents, exchanging records, and handling the many other activities associated with the transfer of clients. In most cases the handoff is a no-man's land. Because it is not the clear responsibility of either the sending or the receiving agency, there are usually no systematic efforts to deal with critical handoff issues.

The handoff is the bridge between services, but it is not a static, frozen moment. It requires planning on both sides beforehand and systematic communication afterward. The absence of effective handoff procedures can negate the effects of exemplary services on either side of the bridge. Agreement on placement decisions, record transfer, and/or follow-up communication is critical to effective transition.

Fortunately, the handoff is the easiest element in transition services to change or improve if both sending and receiving agencies are willing to meet and agree on a process. Simple, low-cost procedures can ensure that important client information is exchanged, that clients are referred to appropriate services, and that parents are involved in important decisions.

Cautions for Working in Transition

Human service agencies have evolved complex organizational patterns that are not always consistent across agencies or states; what is true in one location may vary in another. A general rule of thumb is always to confirm perceptions before moving ahead. Although the general notions we present here probably have widespread applicability, the examples are setting-specific.

Territorial issues are common to human service programs. Agency staff often develop feelings of ownership regarding their services, their procedures, their definitions, and even their clients. Program details become closely guarded, are protected against change, and are seldom shared with outsiders. Rules, regulations, and daily routines evolve and are not easily understood by nonagency persons.

As a result, people in agencies typically communicate better internally than externally. It is much easier to take a problem to a superior or a subordinate within the agency than to confer with a counterpart in a different agency. Horizontal communication between agencies is inhibited by a number of factors. Varying organizational structures make it difficult to know which person to call in another agency; professionals face the same problems parents do in trying to contact human service providers. Agency policies also inhibit horizontal communication. Permission to cross agency boundaries may be required in one or both agencies. On the other hand, vertical communication within one agency is much easier. Unfortunately, it is not very effective in solving interagency problems.

Sending and receiving agencies can make only certain changes in the transition process—changes in their immediate programs or in the handoff. The staff of one agency cannot change the quality, approach, or variety of services offered in another agency. Despite this fact there is often much talk about the need to change the other agency to effect a better transition; senders point their fingers at receivers, and vice versa. Their energy is wasted.

PROCEDURAL GUIDELINES

The development of our transition model followed several philosophical guidelines. We conceptualized some of these early in the project; others evolved as we tried to solve difficult problems. All have proven useful as new and complicated issues have confronted us. To understand transition in a way that would lead to practical procedures, we defined three types of transition activities, all of which need to be pursued for successful transition plans.

Type I activities are those governed by formal interagency agreements at the federal or state level. These agreements need to be established because there is frequently an overlap of mandates, which results in duplicate services. Formal interagency agreements at the federal or state level can provide the top-down direction to bring order and rationality to a confusing situation. At present, confusion still reigns despite rather massive attempts to establish order.

Type II activities can best be called "grassroots" transition activities. They occur in a limited geographical or administrative region as individuals with decision-making power meet and agree to work together. When this type of interagency planning and service delivery occurs, the results are outstanding; agencies and services are molded to meet the needs of consumers. Type II efforts are generally thorough but require many hours over a long period of time. One key result can be the identification of statutory and regulatory barriers to coordination, information that is valuable to state and federal interagency planners (Type I). The critical element in any Type II activity is the personalities of the persons holding power—a variable not susceptible to models or outside intervention.

Type III activities are derived from the cookbook model. A series of recipes is developed, field-tested, and disseminated. Consumers peruse the list of recipes, select the ones they are interested in using, and try them out. If those work, they will try them again (and perhaps others). If the first recipes fail, because they were too expensive or too difficult, consumers are less likely to use them again. If several recipes fail, the entire cookbook is discarded. Recipes can be used by grassroots transition groups (Type II) to solve specific problems. And recipes, too, can result in the identification of statutory and regulatory barriers to coordination.

We have found that simple, step-by-step procedures give needed structure to agency interactions. *Simple* does not mean foolish or uneducated, but rather free of secondary complications and unnecessary elaborations. Although we acknowledge the need for detailed reviews of rules, regulations, laws, and theoretical points, meaningful collaborative relationships at the service delivery level require specific procedures.

Our task has been to develop recipes that are effective, easy, low-cost, and as foolproof as possible in dealing with real problems. There are four key ingredients in a successful recipe. The first is perceived need by the agencies and a desire to alter current practices. We must listen carefully to agency staff to understand the problems they are facing. Too often, those in planning positions develop solutions to problems that do not exist or at least are not perceived by the consumers of the proposed solutions. Second, procedures must be effective. Field-testing of all procedures in applied settings and precise evaluation must be the rule. Third, procedures must be easy, or at least possible, to implement. Procedures are preferable that require no extra money or staff and replace current activities rather than adding new ones. Finally, procedures must be detailed enough to facilitate implementation.

In searching for a structure that would provide direction for our activities, we were intrigued by the similarities in much of Bronfenbrenner's thinking on experimental ecology (Bronfenbrenner, 1977). Although our review of his ideas occurred after we had formulated our process, his notions do provide a theoretical base for our work. Certainly our focus on transition dovetails with the idea of ecological transition and the need for "investigations that go beyond the immediate setting containing the person to examine the larger contexts, both formal and informal, that affect events within the immediate setting" (Bronfenbrenner, 1977, p. 527). Clearly, understanding the movement of a handicapped youth from a correctional facility to a public school setting requires examining the structures of the correctional facility and the receiving school as well as the interactions between the two systems. The people within these systems, their knowledge, and the rules and regulations (formal and informal) that govern their behavior are the basis for "the ecological circumstances and events that determine with whom and how people (children, parents) spend their time" (Bronfenbrenner, 1977, p. 526).

Thus, our activities fall into the general class of ecological experiments. However, we are not conducting intervention research but are rather attempting to discover which system components make a difference in the lives of adjudicated youths. Our attempt to understand these systems and their interrelationships follows Professor Dearborn's advice to Urie Bronfenbrenner: "If you want to understand something, try to change it" (Bronfenbrenner, 1977, p. 517).

In order to really understand issues in transition, we have found it important to spend a lot of time talking to the people who are actually involved in transition activities. Further, we have found that the "line staff," rather than the agency heads or supervisors, are the best informants with regard to what should be changed and how. This process of starting with the hands-on staff and working back up the system has been defined as the backward mapping approach to policy implementation (Elmore, 1979). Instead of beginning with generalities and working toward specifics, backward mapping attempts to isolate critical points of interaction between agencies and describe what must happen at those points to solve related problems. Solutions are then developed into specific strategies and are implemented immediately, at those points in the service delivery system where the problems exist. After implementation, the procedures eventually become adopted by higher level administration and often become policy.

Issues in Transition

Scores of agencies, in addition to correctional facilities, have helped us define six important issues in transition. These issues can usually be easily addressed, often by elegantly simple solutions.

1. *Awareness.* Sending and receiving agencies need to know about one another's programs. Providers are part of a complex system of services that clients use both serially and concurrently. Client transitions can be greatly improved if companion agencies know what services are offered, what the staffing and facilities are like, what the philosophical approach is, what type of program planning is used (e.g., individualized education program, individual written rehabilitation plan, individual service plan). In rural areas there may be only one or two agencies to investigate. In more densely populated, service-rich areas, there are entire systems of agencies to explore. On-site visits, in-service training, and written materials can be exchanged to promote awareness among programs.

2. *Eligibility criteria.* Planning for new placements requires considering several possible alternatives. Sending agencies need to have a rough understanding of eligibility criteria to make valid and realistic referrals. Certainly, staff of one agency cannot be expected to make eligibility determinations for another agency. However, a working knowledge of eligibility criteria for other programs in the community greatly improves the sending agency's ability to identify realistic options.

3. *Exchange of information.* In order to prepare for new clients before their arrival, receiving agencies need information about them. Names, service needs and history, and assessment results can be exchanged between agencies with parent permission. An information exchange prior to transition helps to guarantee that a client is indeed eligible for referral to the receiving agency, allows the receiving agency to plan for the client, and ensures that client information gleaned in one placement can be used in another. Ongoing consultation between agencies can identify criteria to be used in the future for selecting students about whom information should be exchanged.

4. *Program planning before transition.* Assuming that every client has an educational or treatment history can help agencies to make transition planning a routine rather than a random event. Joint preplacement planning by sending and receiving agencies promotes continuity, thus preventing a gap in services. Piggybacking on an existing planning process is a convenient preplacement strategy.

5. *Feedback after transition.* Receiving feedback about what has happened to a former client serves many purposes for the sending agency. Information on client performance in new environments provides important data for program evaluation and alteration. Teachers in correctional institution schools need to know what happens to former students but usually know only about those who are resentenced to the institution. Follow-up information can be collected in a number of ways. Schools can

survey former students or their parents by telephone or mail, and parole counselors can provide feedback to institutional schools.

6. *Written procedures.* Formal procedures are needed to ensure that important handoff activities take place. Even single events, such as an exchange of pertinent information between agencies, need to be systematized. Formal written procedures improve client transition into new services in a number of ways. First, when procedures are codified, they are not easily overlooked or forgotten. A particular staff member may know informal, unwritten procedures well, but those procedures are lost when that person leaves the agency. Written procedures are also easier to evaluate and modify. In addition, they document responsibility and provide a vehicle for negotiations between agencies.

The issues discussed here can be addressed by agency staffs and incorporated into operating procedures without extra help, money, or resources. Procedures for client transfers can be built into routine staff activities without additional personnel. Our field tests of transition handoff procedures indicate that agencies do not incur significant additional costs. However, the initial investment of staff time in establishing transition procedures is, of course, greater than maintaining those same procedures once they are in place.

If formal planning for the transition of clients is not valued by the agencies involved, planning will not occur. And if planning for transition handoff events does not occur, critical steps will not be accomplished. It is not uncommon for service providers to marvel at their inability to accomplish such a simple task as records transfer. Yet if there is no planning for records exchange, those records will most assuredly not be transferred.

THE JUVENILE CORRECTIONS INTERAGENCY TRANSITION MODEL

The Juvenile Corrections Interagency Transition Model (Webb, Maddox, & Edgar, 1985) was developed to assist local school districts and agencies in coordinating their efforts as juvenile offenders (both handicapped and nonhandicapped) move from one school program to another. A juvenile is frequently transferred from a local public school to a detention center school, to a school at the correctional institution, to a group home, and then back to a community school. Frequently, schools and other public agencies have not been adequately prepared to place youths in their programs. Joint planning increases the chance that a student will remain in school.

In developing our model with a backward mapping approach, we first identified the types of professionals who were directly involved in transition activities. We were amazed (and overwhelmed) by the number of players who participate in moving a youth from a correctional facility to a public school: county court system personnel, regional juvenile parole or probation agency employees, corrections institution residential staff, corrections institution school staff, public school staff. These people work for different agencies, have separate bureaucracies, speak different jargons, follow varying treatment philosophies, and know little about each other's systems. At times there is even open conflict between the people in these different agencies; and even when there is good cooperation, the "system is slow to respond."

Being a third party—not related to the systems involved—made our task somewhat easier. On the other hand, being from a university made our task somewhat more difficult ("We've seen your type come, and we've seen them go"). Our task was to interview an adequate sample of the critical people involved in the transition process. We selected one correctional facility, one school district, and the county and state systems that served youth living within that area. We interviewed more than 75 individuals in all, including state and regional administrators. We asked how the transition procedure worked, what our informants thought were the major problems, and what they suggested to solve those problems. We were faced with an information overload. Sorting through the data was difficult because of conflicting and discrepant information, so we summarized the information and returned to our informants to sort out the discrepancies. After several rounds of interaction, we identified the problem areas (Maddox & Webb, 1986).

Problem Areas

Problems in the Institution. The residential and educational programs at the correctional institution, although functioning on the same campus, were managed by separate administrative units. Little systematic communication occurred between the two staffs. Specific problems included the following: scheduling a release date (done by the residential staff), notifying the institution's school staff of the student's release date (seldom done in a timely manner), preparing an educational report (often done after the student's release and not containing information needed by the receiving school), notifying the local school that the student is to be enrolled (seldom completed prior to the release of the student, often never completed), forwarding educational information to the public school (seldom done before enrollment), and preplanning for appropriate school placement (usually determined by the student's residential placement).

Public School Problems. Juveniles released from the five correctional facilities in Washington returned to 299 public school districts, with no systematic procedures to assist in the transfer. The position and job title of the contact person varied from one school district to the next; hence, institution staff did not know whom to contact about a returning student. Receiving schools complained that the educational information they were given lacked important details (e.g., grade level, classes completed, grading procedures, special education eligibility). Most important was the complaint that school districts were seldom notified until well after the student was enrolled.

Awareness Problems.   An overriding issue was the lack of accurate information about the other agencies and their procedures. Public school staff had little understanding of the operation, structure, or philosophy of correctional facilities. Parole officers did not understand school system procedures or policies. Institutional school teachers often had not visited a public school program in years. And there were no feedback loops that enabled an agency to know what happened to students after they left the agency. In general, the professionals in each system were honestly trying to do their best job, but in isolation. Lack of information and misinformation were the rule.

After the problem areas were identified, we asked our informants to suggest possible solutions. Their responses were used to develop specific strategies for the transition process. These strategies were then field-tested to determine their effectiveness.

Issues and Strategies

As we developed our model, we realized that the professionals using it would come from several different fields and would be familiar with different terminologies and procedures. We therefore tried to avoid the use of agency jargon and acronyms. We also realized that agencies were often unaware of information contained in a student's school records. For example, parole staff thought the only available educational information was a student's transcript; they did not know about attendance records, class schedules, immunization records, and special education records. Thus, describing the information available was an important component.

The Juvenile Corrections Interagency Transition Model contains 36 strategies in four areas (see Figure 11.1 for an outline): (1) awareness of other agency activities and missions; (2) transfer of records prior to entering or leaving an institution; (3) preplacement planning for transition before the youth leaves the institution; and (4) maintaining placement in the public school and ongoing communication between the juvenile rehabilitation and public school staffs about youth progress. For each strategy the model identifies who will participate in the strategy, when the strategy should be initiated, and what materials are required. The transition model also contains information and sample forms to help agency staff carry out the strategies.

Awareness.   Agencies share a lack of awareness about the philosophy, workscope, and procedures of other agencies serving the same population.

Figure 11.1   **Outline of the Juvenile Corrections Interagency Transition Model**

A. Awareness
    A.1. Interagency administrators meeting
        A.1.1. Develop and disseminate a list of roles and responsibilities of schools, regional division of juvenile rehabilitation (DJR), and institutions
    A.2. In-service education
        A.2.1 Conduct in-service training for selected staff from school district (SD), DJR, and correctional institution
        A.2.2. Conduct in-service training for institutional staff

    A.2.3. Conduct in-service training for SD principals, counselors, and staff regarding the juvenile justice rehabilitation system and/or the institutional education programs

  A.3. Institution and school district visits

    A.3.1. Visits to institutions by SD building teams or other SD representatives

    A.3.2. Visits by institutional administrators and staff to SD placement options

B. Transfer of records

  B.1. Establish and implement procedures for student's school records to be sent to institution

    B.1.1. Educational information requested and collected prior to juvenile's entering institution

    B.1.2. Institution's responsibility to obtain records if records have not been requested or have not arrived within 10 days after student's arrival

  B.2. Establish and implement procedures for transfer of student's records from institution to receiving school

    B.2.1. Educational information collected at institution and sent to juvenile parole counselor (JPC)

    B.2.2. With community residential placement (CRP) or short-notice placements, record collection expedited by institution

    B.2.3. Student withdrawal card developed and used to gather academic information prior to release

  B.3. Establish and implement procedures for transfer of student's records from one institution to another

    B.3.1. Receiving institution's responsibility to request school records when a student is moved from one institution to another

    B.3.2. Request for school records initiated by staff of CRP or group home (GH) when a juvenile is transferred from a CRP or state GH back to an institution

    B.3.3. Educational information collected prior to a juvenile's parole from a CRP or state GH

C. Preplacement planning and educational placement decision

  C.1. Develop a system to screen and assess youth for special education placement

    C.1.1. Identify students needing special education program at institution

    C.1.2. Use learning center in community (LC) for conducting assessment, making placement decisions, and preparing students for new placement

  C.2. Develop systematic placement procedures

    C.2.1. Define criteria for LC placement

    C.2.2. Identify potential in-district placement options and adaptations

    C.2.3. Develop criteria and systematic procedures for credit acceptance

    C.2.4. Prepare student for moving from LC to SD program

  C.3. Use all educational information collected to make school placement decision prior to time of release from institution

    C.3.1. School progress report from institutional school for use by JPC and SD in school placement planning

    C.3.2. Meeting of JPC with student, institutional school, and residential staff prior to student's release, to discuss educational goals after release

  C.4. Plan for placement prior to release

    C.4.1. Review all placement options within the SD and match to student needs

    C.4.2. Write education plan for each student, from which placement plan is developed

    C.4.3. Schedule and preregister student with receiving school staff prior to student arrival

    C.4.4. Hold school registration meeting with student and SD before entry into school program

    C.4.5. Form preplacement planning team

D. Maintaining placement and communication

  D.1. Cultivate parent or guardian involvement

    D.1.1. Develop communication between regional DJR staff and parents

    D.1.2. Develop communication between parents and receiving school

  D.2. Design school advocacy program for adjudicated youth

    D.2.1. Assign all adjudicated youth in each SD school building to one counselor

    D.2.2. Begin to form an advocacy network by assigning incoming paroled youth to SD staff advocate

    D.2.3. Place students in classes with supportive teachers

  D.3. Monitor attendance and behavior

    D.3.1. Monitor student's school progress and attendance at scheduled intervals

    D.3.2. Provide feedback to JPC regarding student attendance

  D.4. Develop direct communication between school and JPC for resource sharing and problem solving

    D.4.1. Develop communication system for contact between JPC and school

  D.5. Provide postplacement communication regarding student's educational placement

    D.5.1. Give postplacement feedback to institutional school about student's educational performance

Source: From *The Juvenile Corrections Interagency Transition Model* by S. Webb, M. Maddox, and E. Edgar, 1985, Seattle: University of Washington, Experimental Education Unit.

A number of issues have been identified within this area. First, institutional school personnel are not aware of educational alternatives available in local school districts. Therefore, strategies have been developed to conduct in-service training for institutional staff. Second, local public school staff do not understand the workings of institutional schools. Strategies include in-service training for local school staff at or with personnel from institutional schools. A third issue involves the juvenile parole counselor (or juvenile rehabilitation counselor), who is not fully aware of educational options in local school programs. Once again, systematic in-service sessions have been developed for these counselors, in addition to lists of local placement options. Figure 11.2 illustrates a developed strategy, complete with training agenda.

Figure 11.2 **Sample Strategy for In-Service Training**

Strategy and Activities

A.2.1. Conduct in-service training for selected staff from SD, DJR, and institution
   a. SD, DJR, and institution representatives identify participants, date, agenda, and responsibilities for implementation.
   b. In-service training is conducted.

Who Is Involved

   a. SD administrator or designee, DJR regional administrator or designee, institutional staff
   b. Agency administrators

When

Every 3 years

Materials

In-service training agenda
Lists of SD placement options
Evaluations

Interagency In-service Training Agenda

   I. Introduction
  II. Juvenile offenders: client characteristics
 III. Educational program at institution
       A. Basic education programs
       B. Special education programs
       C. Vocational education programs
  IV. Educational programs for students with special needs in the local school district
   V. Entry and exit procedures
       A. Institutional school
       B. Local school district
  VI. Reentry issues
       A. Parole counselor's goal and responsibilities
       B. Institutional school's goal and responsibilities
       C. Local school district's goal and responsibilities
 VII. Discussion of transition issues
       A. What can we do for you?
       B. What can you do for us?

Transfer of Records. Rarely do school records follow a student. Information about a student often is never transferred from the public schools to the correctional facility, or it never reaches the institutional school staff, or it arrives late. Strategies have been developed to facilitate the flow of records from public schools to institutions (see Figure 11.3 for a listing of related activities and materials). Each of the five institutions involved in testing our model also developed specific sequential steps to get school records to the appropriate local school prior to a youth's release. This strategy is critical in planning for special education students and in locating programs that will increase their chances for success.

Problems with records exchange may begin even within a single institution. For example, institutional school staff may not be informed that a student is being released (a decision often made by the institution's residential staff). That lack of information would obviously result in a delay in sending institutional school records to the local public school and the juvenile parole counselor. Strategies have been developed to facilitate the flow of information from the institution to local schools and juvenile parole counselors in a timely manner. Figure 11.4 details the activities and materials needed to transfer information from the institution to the parole counselor.

Preplacement Planning and Postplacement Communication. Other strategies of the model establish guidelines for school registration meetings. The adults serving the youth and the parents or guardian meet to discuss educational goals, expectations, and attendance; and they set times and procedures for further communication. This meeting establishes a positive communication base and avoids the pattern of parent and professional interaction only during times of crisis.

Transfer of Records   **Figure 11.3**

B.1.1. Educational information requested and collected prior to juvenile's entering institution

Required Activities
a. Diagnostic unit of division of juvenile rehabilitation examines student's records and determines school in which student was last enrolled.
b. Diagnostic worker contacts school, officially withdraws student, and obtains student's current placement and schedule.
c. Institution provides diagnostic worker with signed forms for mutual exchange of information and a letter of request for educational records.
d. Diagnostic worker requests school records by completing Education Records Request Checklist and institutional school consent-release forms.
e. Diagnostic worker requests information from detention school if juvenile has been detained for more than 1 week.
f. Diagnostic worker records school information in school section of form.
g. Diagnostic worker places copy of Education Records Request Checklist in school and residential sections of the legal file.

Materials
a. School information report form
b. Consent forms for release of information
c. Education Records Request Checklist
d. Detention school record sheet
e. Sample agenda for training diagnostic workers

Figure 11.4   **Records Exchange**

B.2.1. Educational information collected at institution and sent to juvenile parole counselor (JPC)

Required Activities
a. School progress report is requested.
b. School progress report and unofficial transcript are sent to JPC.
c. JPC identifies residential placement and contacts designated school official regarding need for student placement.
d. School district (SD) official calls institution if more information is needed for placement decision.
e. Using school progress report, JPC, parent, and SD reach placement agreement.
f. Institutional school and student are notified of SD placement recommendation.
g. Final transcript, grades, and records are sent to receiving school.

Materials
a. Sample school progress report
b. Unofficial transcript
c. Sample institutional school contact sheet
d. Sample list of SD placement options

It is important that communication continue between the public school and the institutional school after a student is released. One strategy requires the juvenile parole counselor to send a checklist to the institutional school at the end of the student's parole. The list indicates whether a student has a job or is in school; if in school, the checklist identifies the type of school placement. This information is very important to institutional school staff; it allows them to assess their procedures and makes them feel part of the juvenile's continuum of education. Figure 11.5 illustrates an end-of-parole checklist.

Evaluation Procedures

As we evaluated the transition model, we addressed four major issues: documentation that a specific activity has occurred; user satisfaction with materials or products; impact of strategies measured in quality, time, and cost; and cost of implementing model procedures.

Most projects evaluate their effectiveness by a direct measure of child or student performance. However, our desired outcome was to change the behavior of the adults responsible for providing services to handicapped youth, in order to improve the quality of these services. Benefits to the adjudicated youth and their families can be classified into two major areas of impact: (1) increased quality of services and (2) more efficient use of time. Major evaluation activities have addressed these impact issues. Additionally, a series of evaluation activities has centered on documenting the specific procedures and the satisfaction of the adults (professional staff) using them. One other crucial evaluation element has been calculation of the costs of each procedure. We have responded to the four major evaluation issues with a format that asks specific questions about each model procedure.

End-of-Parole Report Figure 11.5

Juvenile's name _____ Date parole ends _____
- ☐ Is not in school
- ☐ Is in school (Name of school _____
- School reports that _____
_____

Types of School Programs Since Release
- ☐ Learning center
- ☐ Alternative school
- ☐ Regular program
- ☐ Special education program
- ☐ GED program
- ☐ Vocational/technical training
- ☐ Community college

Current Place of Residence
- ☐ With parents
- ☐ Foster home
- ☐ Group home
- ☐ Friends or relatives
- ☐ On his/her own
- ☐ Whereabouts unknown
- ☐ Detained pending sentence
- ☐ Institutionalized (Name of institution _____)
- ☐ Employed (Name of employer _____)
  - ☐ Part-time
  - ☐ Full-time

Comments _____
_____

Report completed by _____ Date _____
SEND COMPLETED REPORT TO JUVENILE'S LAST INSTITUTIONAL ACADEMIC SCHOOL OFFICE

Documentation of Activities. Documentation of activities involves a specific description of the procedure; for example, a form is developed, records are transferred, the number of staff trained is listed, a report is generated, a checklist is developed. This is generally a quantitative evaluation that reports numbers, lists products, and/or notes events.

User Satisfaction. Satisfaction of users is a critical evaluation component. Regardless of the effectiveness of the procedures, if staff members are not satisfied with them or if they do not believe the procedures are important, staff are not likely to use them in the future. Therefore, all procedures are evaluated by probing user satisfaction.

Impact of Project and Model Procedures. The impact of the procedures is the most difficult aspect to evaluate. Part of the impact evaluation concerns the actual use of the procedures, which is considered under documentation. However, impact evaluation also measures the qualitative aspects of the procedures. Were more students placed promptly and appropriately in public schools as a result of record exchange? Did more paroled youths stay in school as a result of systematic placement procedures? Did prerelease school information arrive in the community in time for preplacement planning to occur? Did school records arrive at the institution sooner than in the past because they were requested before the student arrived at the institution? Did more youths stay in school longer when transition procedures were used?

Cost of the Procedures.   Field-test and project staffs collected data regarding the actual cost of implementing each specific model procedure. Staff time was documented for attending meetings and completing forms in addition to the costs of copying, postage, travel, and so on. Each strategy was evaluated for cost benefit and was adapted if necessary. The final model procedures included data on the implementation costs of each procedure, to assist users in selecting strategies.

Results

To date, all 36 strategies have been attempted in at least one setting in the state of Washington. Staff of all five correctional institutions have been trained in model procedures, as have some 200 other educational and correctional staff members throughout the state. Modifications in procedures have occurred, based on feedback from these field tests. The final product, the *Juvenile Corrections Interagency Transition Model* (Webb, Maddox, & Edgar, 1985), has now been completed.

Documentation.   The data support the conclusion that each of the proposed strategies is practical and can be implemented by field staff. Some strategies (e.g., the visit by public school staff to the institutional school) require considerable planning and expense (teacher release time), others require the development or modification of forms, and others simply require a process for the flow of information. Not all settings require the implementation of all strategies: "if it's not broken, don't fix it." However, for each of the listed strategies, support data indicate that the procedures have been successfully implemented by field staff.

Satisfaction.   Throughout the project user satisfaction was continually evaluated. As each strategy was field-tested, we obtained data that were used to modify the procedures in order to gain user approval. Many previously attempted procedures were discarded over the years because of user dissatisfaction with the activities. There were instances when the proposed solutions created more difficulty than the original problem. Several of the remaining strategies received some negative ratings; however, all of the 36 strategies were positively evaluated by direct-service staff using the specific procedures. Again, not all situations call for the use of all strategies, but we are confident that each strategy is appropriate in specific instances. Table 11.1 gives documentation numbers and satisfaction ratings for all 36 strategies.

Cost.   The cost of each strategy is important because most agencies are faced with limited budgets. All our procedures were designed to be as

Evaluation of Model Strategies   **Table 11.1**

Strategy	Trials	Satisfaction[a]
A.1.1. Develop and disseminate a list of roles and responsibilities of schools, regional division of juvenile rehabilitation (DJR), and institutions	3	3.7
A.2.1. Conduct in-service training for selected staff from school district (SD), DJR, and correctional institution	1	3.35
A.2.2. Conduct in-service training for institutional staff	5	3.0
A.2.3. Conduct in-service training for SD principals, counselors, and staff regarding the juvenile justice rehabilitation system and/or the institutional education programs	4	3.45
A.3.1. Visits to institutions by SD building teams or other SD representatives	6	3.55
A.3.2. Visits by institutional administrators and staff to SD placement options	1	3.4
B.1.1. Educational information requested and collected prior to juvenile's entering institution	16 (senders) 5 (receiving institutions)	3.9 2.9
B.1.2. Institution's responsibility to obtain records if records have not been requested or have not arrived within 10 days after student's arrival	5	2.0
B.2.1. Educational information collected at institution and sent to juvenile parole counselor (JPC)	5 (senders) 7 (receivers)	3.0 3.4
B.2.2. With community residential placement (CRP) or short-notice placements, record collection expedited by institution	5 (senders)	3.0
B.2.3. Student withdrawal card developed and used to gather academic information prior to release	1	3.0
B.3.1. Receiving institution's responsibility to request school records when a student is moved from one institution to another	1	Not reported
B.3.2. Request for school records initiated by staff of group home (GH) when a juvenile is transferred from a CRP or state GH back to an institution	3	Now being assessed
B.3.3. Educational information collected prior to a juvenile's parole from a CRP or state GH	3	Now being assessed
C.1.1. Identify students needing special education program at institution	4	Not reported
C.1.2. Use learning center (LC) in community for conducting assessment, making placement decisions, and preparing student for new placement	1	4.0
C.2.1. Define criteria for LC placement	1	3.0
C.2.2. Identify potential in-district placement options and adaptations	3	3.0
C.2.3. Develop criteria and systematic procedures for credit acceptance	3	3.0
C.2.4. Prepare student for moving from LC to SD program	1	2.0
C.3.1. School progress report from institutional school for use by JPC and SD in school placement planning	5	3.5

Table 11.1 *continued*

Strategy	Trials	Satisfaction[a]
C.3.2. Meeting of JPC with student, institutional school, and residential staff prior to student's release, to discuss educational goals after release	7	2.7
C.4.1. Review all placement options within the SD and match to student needs	3	2.7
C.4.2. Write education plan for each student, from which placement plan is developed	1	Not reported
C.4.3. Schedule and preregister student with receiving school staff prior to student arrival	2	3.0
C.4.4. Hold school registration meeting with student and SD before entry into school program	7	2.6
C.4.5. Form preplacement planning team	1	3.3
D.1.1. Develop communication between regional DJR staff and parents	1	4.0
D.1.2. Develop communication between parents and receiving school	1	3.0
D.2.1. Assign all adjudicated youth in each SD school building to one counselor	1	1.0
D.2.2. Begin to form an advocacy network by assigning incoming paroled youth to SD staff advocate	2	2.0
D.2.3. Place students in classes with supportive teachers	1	4.0
D.3.1. Monitor student's school progress and attendance at scheduled intervals	2	2.6
D.3.2. Provide feedback to JPC regarding student attendance	2	Not reported
D.4.1. Develop communication system for contact between JPC and school	4	2.7
D.5.1. Give postplacement feedback to institutional school about student's educational performance	5	2.6

[a]A numerical range of 1 to 4 was used: 1 = not satisfied, 4 = very satisfied. The rating given here is the mean.

inexpensive as possible; our desire was to develop procedures that could be used by existing staff without the expenditure of funds. Obviously the training of staff in the use of procedures had to be an expenditure, but we did not want to develop a new role (e.g., transition specialist) or necessitate the hiring of clerical or treatment staff. We believe we have been successful in the area of cost. During the initial phases of development we maintained cost records for each strategy, recording staff time, duplication, mailing, mileage, and other incidental costs. Some activities are costly (e.g., exchange of staff); however, we retained these strategies because user satisfaction indicated that the activities were worth the cost. On the whole, however, the basic strategies can be implemented with little financial outlay.

Impact.   The single most important evaluation is clearly impact: do these strategies make a difference? The positive impact of our strategies is illustrated with data from several areas.

One of our strategies was concerned with getting educational information sent from the institutional school to the public school prior to the release of the student from the institution. Prior to our intervention, a common complaint of receiving schools was that they seldom received educational information on a returning student prior to placement and often never received the information. Obviously, appropriate public school placement is facilitated by educational information prior to the placement decision. By analyzing the procedures, we discovered that the discharge date for institutional clients was most often determined by the residential staff. Therefore, in the flow of information the residential staff would need to inform the institutional education staff of a pending discharge to allow them time to prepare the educational report and mail it to the prospective receiving school. Strategies were developed to facilitate this flow. According to the strategies, the residential staff is to inform the institutional school staff 45 days in advance of a release date. Institutional school staff then have 10 days to prepare the report and mail it to the receiving public school, still 35 days prior to discharge.

Although the preintervention data indicated that all but one institution were usually mailing the reports at the time of or after release, the variance among institutions was large. After intervention a clear improvement was observed in the number of days prior to release that the reports were required. However, in one institution a more detailed analysis was needed in that the reports continued to be late. Careful analysis located the problem in the amount of time the institutional school staff was taking to prepare the reports. A more detailed analysis of the process resulted in the discovery that secretarial staff members were not typing the reports until 1 or 2 weeks after they had received them from the school staff. Once identified, the problem was rapidly and easily resolved.

This example is documentation of impact—the procedures did affect the transmittal of records in a positive manner. However, the larger question is, do the procedures in general assist the reentry of adjudicated youth into the community? We are currently tracking more than 150 youths who have been discharged over the past 2 years and will have data on those who have exited juvenile correctional facilities using the transition procedures. Preliminary data on the first seven youths affected by our procedures indicate a high success rate (see Table 11.2). Although these data represent only a small sample of the students we are now tracking, we are confident that other students are also demonstrating similar school progress.

An analysis of juveniles paroled during the first four months of 1985 (Guthmann, 1985) also reveals some positive findings. First, as compared to a similar study in 1981, when 21% of the youths released from juvenile correctional facilities were enrolled in school 6 months after release, the 1985 study found 48.6% of paroled youths enrolled in school 6 months after release. In

Table 11.2   **Preliminary Follow-up Results of First Seven Students Completing Formal Transition from Correctional Facility to Public School**

Student No./ Gender	Age at Discharge	Dis-ability	Current Status	Current Age	Months Since Discharge
1/M	14	None	Alternative vocational school	16	21
2/F	15	None	Alternative school	17	20
3/M	16	None	Public high school	17	19
4/M	14	None	Incarcerated	16	19
5/M	14	None	Public high school	16	18
6/F	16	LD	Public high school, special education	17	18
7/F	17	BD	Graduated, taking classes at public high school	19	15

the region where most of our transition procedures were field-tested and implemented, 62.8% of the paroled youths were in school 6 months after release. Undoubtedly, a number of factors account for the later data (e.g., better reporting methods, attention to school placement after the 1981 study); however, the author of the report notes our transition procedures as a positive factor. And, of course, the more significant issue is, does school enrollment indicate a successful outcome for the student? We believe it is one indication of success.

Need for a "Driver"

Transition from a correctional facility to public school is an important event in the life of an adjudicated youth. However, there is no agency responsible for assuring that transition activities are implemented. Thus, the most crucial issue in transition is to identify the "driver," the source of energy that assures systematic transition activities.

Who should be this driver? The most logical response is that the system should ensure appropriate transition activities; procedures and policies should be built into the system structure (in this case the structures of both juvenile correctional and public school systems). However, the truth of the matter is that few procedures are currently geared toward transition. The purpose of our backward mapping approach was to develop system policy, but even in our state, after 3 years of major effort, few formal procedures specifically oriented toward transition are preserved in agency policy. It may be a long while before the system takes over.

The idea of a third party driver has intriguing possibilities. In this instance a new group (agency) would be formed with the responsibility of assuring that transition procedures are developed and implemented. In essence, our project has served this role. The obvious problem with the third party approach is continuity when the third party funding ends—as it always must. Secondary problems with a third party driver include the believability of the third party and several factors discussed previously—turf, interagency politics, and the difficulty of outsiders changing internal procedures.

The notion of a critical (or vital) person as the driver is often quietly eliminated. However, vital persons do make a difference. We have found that the bottom line with regard to effective transition is that transition planning must be valued by decision makers. Administrators need first to recognize the problems and then the consequences of not solving them. After that they must make a commitment to do something about the problems. In the absence of assigned responsibility for transitional services, we must rely on the commitment of agency managers to ensure planned transitions. Those individuals must become vital persons in the transition process.

CONCLUSION

Transitions are not easy times, for either adjudicated handicapped youths or professionals. The lack of a designated responsible person in charge of transition, the myriad agencies involved, the problems of cross-agency communication and planning, the continued pressure of "not enough time"—all contribute to the difficulty. We believe the ideas presented in this chapter provide a road map for understanding transition issues. More specifically, the Juvenile Corrections Interagency Transition Model provides specific recipes for responding to many of the issues that make transition difficult. But in the end someone must assume the responsibility for carrying them out. We hope this chapter has presented information and motivation to do the things necessary to improve the transition process for youthful offenders.

REFERENCES

Bronfenbrenner, U. (1977). Toward an experimental ecology of human development. *American Psychologist, 32,* 513–531.

Coleman, J. (1974). *Youth: Transition to adulthood.* Chicago: University of Chicago Press.

Eggelston, C. R., Tazioli, P., Maddox, M., & Edgar, E. B. (1985). *Concurrent services model.* Seattle: University of Washington, Experimental Education Unit.

Elmore, R. (1979). Backward mapping: Implementing research and policy decisions. *Political Science Quarterly, 94,* 601–616.

Gallaher, J., Maddox, M., & Edgar, E. B. (1984). *Early childhood interagency transition model.* Bellevue, WA: Edmark.

Guthmann, D. R. (1985). *An analysis of community transition among juveniles paroled in Washington state.* Olympia, WA: Division of Juvenile Rehabilitation, Department of Social and Health Services.

Haynes, M., Maddox, M., & Edgar, E. B. (1985). *The community services transition model.* Seattle: University of Washington, Experimental Education Unit.

Horton, B., Maddox, M., & Edgar, E. B. (1984). *The adult transition model.* Bellevue, WA: Edmark.

Maddox, M., & Webb, S. (1986). The juvenile corrections interagency transition model: Moving students from institutions into community schools. *Remedial and Special Education, 7,* 56–61.

Morgan, D. J. (1979). Prevalence and types of handicapping conditions found in juvenile correctional institutions: A national survey. *Journal of Special Education, 13,* 293–295.

Needham, M. J., & Grims, M. (1983). *1982-83 Youth in Transition Project* (Chapter 1). Denver: Colorado Department of Education and Colorado Division of Youth Services.

Rutherford, R. B., Nelson, C. M., & Wolford, B. I. (1985). Special education in the most restrictive environment: Correctional/special education. *Journal of Special Education, 19,* 51–71.

Smith, B. J., Ramirez, B. A., & Rutherford, R. B. (1983). Special education in youth correctional facilities. *Journal of Correctional Education, 34,* 108–112.

Walker, H. M., McConnell, S., Holmes, D., Todis, B., Walker, J., & Golden, N. (1983). *The Walker social skills curriculum: The Accepts program.* Austin, TX: Pro-Ed.

Webb, S., Maddox, M., & Edgar, E. B. (1985). *The juvenile corrections interagency transition model.* Seattle: University of Washington, Experimental Education Unit.

Will, M. (1984). Bridges from school to working life. *Programs for the Handicapped, 2,* 1–5.

Kathy Fejes and Lois Foxall

The Westbank Educational Center   VIGNETTE

The prevention of delinquency among nonadjudicated adolescents at risk is an objective of many community programs within the criminal justice system. Another area of prevention focuses on reducing the recidivism of adolescents who have already encountered the legal system. To these ends, the Westbank Educational Service Center in Marrero, Louisiana, provides an alternative to incarceration through day-care treatment for adjudicated juveniles with special needs. Referrals are made by probation officers in concert with the recommendation of an assessment team.

The educational program is considered a special school "alternative to regular placement" and, as such, offers highly individualized coursework leading to a Certification of Achievement, GED, return to regular school, or vocational program placement in the community. In addition to special education classrooms organized around basic academics, several other facets make up the treatment program. Enrichment education classes meet daily and focus on life skills, such as sewing, safety, general repair, auto maintenance, health, cooking, gardening, and social manners. All students, both male and female, participate in each of these skill development areas. Community volunteers (including a juvenile court judge) provide additional instruction in the enrichment program. Classes in art, music, dance, and even scuba diving are available to students. Field trips are scheduled three times each month: one is a recreational trip, and two are of an educational nature.

Vocational counseling is geared toward learning good work habits, acquiring job interviewing skills, completing employment applications, and exploring career opportunities. In addition, an in-house staff conducts computerized vocational interest and aptitude assessments. Results afford students a concrete base for vocational planning.

Behavioral counseling and family therapy are also integral components of the program. Throughout the day behavioral counselors help students maximize appropriate behaviors and manage inappropriate ones (through time out and detention, for example). Mandatory family therapy of no less than 1 hour each week is provided by the in-house staff.

An incoming student experiences approximately 4 weeks of assessment and goal setting, after which an individualized service plan (ISP) is developed. The ISP is broken down into nine steps with varying goals and objectives designed to meet the needs of the student. A progress meeting of the student, counselor, therapist, teachers, and other staff as needed is conducted every 4 weeks to determine movement to the next step.

Perhaps the most unique aspect of the Westbank Educational Service Center is program flexibility. The majority of students attending the center live with their families and commute on a daily basis. However, for students whose families may be in a state of disintegration, the option is available to live on the center grounds in nonsecure cottages staffed by full-time personnel. Space exists for 16 males and 16 females in two separate cottages designed specifically to optimize the students' sense of self-worth. The facilities include fireplaces, family rooms, and gourmet kitchens. A third on-campus option currently nearing completion is a secure, self-contained facility for adjudicated juveniles who require a highly structured environment and are in need of special education services. The center allows student mobility between these program options without disruption of the educational process.

The bottom line of this program is its effect on recidivism. Center statistics based on the 139 students who have been released from the facility for longer than 6 months since July 1983 reveal that 72% have committed no repeat offenses. That seems a good beginning to the solution of a complex problem.

Teaching Handicapped Learners in Correctional Education Programs

CHAPTER 12   *Peter E. Leone*

Adjudicated youths receive services in a range of community-based programs, training schools, and prisons in the United States. In public and private facilities secure custody is provided for more than 80,000 incarcerated adolescents (McGarrell & Flanigan, 1985), whereas a much greater number receive services in nonrestrictive settings in the community. Educational services provided to handicapped youth in these facilities and programs vary in their adequacy and comprehensiveness. Often the structure of the educational program is related to the restrictiveness of the facility or placement. Not surprisingly, large programs and facilities are much more likely to have specialized services for youth than are small ones (Hughes & Reuterman, 1982).

Only recently have programs been developed to train correctional education teachers and correctional special education teachers (Sutherland, 1985; Leone, 1986). Many teachers in correctional education programs were trained in elementary or secondary education and learned on the job how to adapt their instructional skills to working with incarcerated adolescents and young adults. Some correctional educators, especially those teaching in vocational areas, were not trained as educators at all but received provisional certification in order to teach youths in correctional facilities. Overall, the past decade has witnessed improvement in the educational levels of staff serving adjudicated youth in juvenile correctional facilities (Reuterman & Hughes, 1984).

This chapter covers a range of topics related to teaching mildly handicapped learners in correctional education programs. It discusses the various settings in which correctional education programs are located and the competencies for teachers of handicapped adjudicated and incarcerated youth. The chapter concludes with a discussion of correctional education classrooms and administrative arrangements unique to the field.

In discussing handicapped learners in correctional education programs, this chapter takes an applied perspective. Much of the information presented and many of the generalizations made about special education programs and the criminal justice system are based on observations at a number of juvenile and adult facilities serving handicapped youth, experience in staff development in correctional facilities, and discussions with correctional education teachers and administrators across the country. The dearth of professional literature, especially empirical and field-based research on adjudicated handicapped youth, and the methodological problems associated with conducting research with correctional populations (Reppucci & Clingempeel, 1978) warrant an applied perspective. The lack of empirical research also presents a challenge to teacher trainers and researchers concerned with the educational and social development of adjudicated handicapped youth.

CORRECTIONAL EDUCATION PROGRAMS

Adjudicated youth are a heterogeneous group. Likewise, the educational programs serving these youths differ within states and local jurisdictions and across the country. Consequently, it is difficult to describe a *typical* correctional educational program; they vary with the facilities and institutions that house them. One way of describing the range of educational services is to discuss the types of programs and facilities that exist within the criminal justice system. Broadly speaking, they include diversion, probation, and alternative educational programs; juvenile halls, training schools, and reform schools; camps and ranches; and programs for juveniles incarcerated in adult facilities. Although these programs and facilities have traditionally been operated by the criminal justice system, in recent years there has been an increase in the number of private agencies providing services (McGarrell & Flanagan, 1985).

Diversion, Probation, and Alternative Education Programs

Diversion, probation, and placement of youth in alternative education programs are community-based responses by juvenile courts to the delinquent acts committed by minors. Diversion programs, often administered by social service or youth service agencies, involve rehabilitation, counseling, restitution, arbitration, or victim negotiation (Severy, Houlden, Wilmoth, & Silver, 1982; Shichor, 1983). Many youths involved in diversion programs are young, first-time offenders. Diversion programs are designed to protect or divert youngsters from the potentially negative effects of incarceration or further involvement with juvenile courts. Youths receiving services in diversion programs often are enrolled in alternative school programs administered by the public schools, mental health, or social service agencies. Handicapped youths enrolled in diversion programs typically do not receive specialized services from the diversion program itself but may be enrolled in a special education program or an alternative program with a special education component administered by the public schools or another agency.

Probation is a system of monitoring the behavior of delinquent youth in the community. Under the auspices of the court, probation officers supervise youths and work with public schools and social service agencies in rehabilitative efforts. Like diversion programs, probation programs typically do not offer educational services but work with other agencies that do. Frequently, the terms of a youngster's probation include satisfactory attendance and progress in school.

When initially placed on probation, some youths are enrolled in alternative school programs operated by the juvenile court or a mental health agency. Although many youths enrolled in these programs are adjudicated, alternative programs also serve adolescents who have substance abuse problems, who are abused or neglected, or who have dropped out of traditional public school programs. Alternative school programs are usually quite small in comparison to comprehensive high school programs. The staff may include three or four teachers with at least one holding special education teaching credentials. Some alternative education programs are used in conjunction with group or foster home placement for adjudicated youth. After a period of time ranging from a few weeks to a few months, most youths remaining on probation are reintegrated into public school programs.

One widely adopted community-based program for delinquents is the Teaching Family Model developed by behavior analysts at the University of Kansas in the late 1960s (Braukmann, Fixsen, Phillips, & Wolf, 1975). Adjudicated youths served by this model (earlier known as Achievement Place) live with five to eight other troubled youth in a house with a young married couple. These "teaching" parents are responsible for clinical and administrative aspects of the program, and the youths attend public schools in the neighborhoods where their group homes are located.

Evaluation of the Teaching Family Model programs indicates that they are less expensive to operate than similar community programs. On measures of deviant behavior at time of exit from the program and at follow-up, however, adolescents enrolled in Teaching Family Model programs are no different from delinquent peers in similar programs (Weinrott, Jones, & Howard, 1982).[1]

Juvenile Halls, Training Schools, and Reform Schools

In contrast to diversion programs and probation, juvenile halls, training schools, and reform schools are large, restrictive residential settings. As juvenile correctional institutions, juvenile halls or court schools have existed in the United States since the founding in 1846 of the Lyman School for Boys in Massachusetts (Coffey, 1974). Most often, youths waiting for preliminary

---

[1]See Rothman (1980), Sarri (1980), and Schutjer (1982) for descriptions of other community-based programs.

hearings and youth ordered to spend time in secure custody are found in these facilities. A challenge faced by educators providing services to youths in juvenile halls, training schools, and reform schools is the indeterminant amount of time that youths spend in these institutions.

Educational programs in juvenile halls are modeled, for the most part, after secondary school programs (Roush, 1983). Instruction in reading and computational skills is typically emphasized, and in some programs vocational training is provided. Many educational programs in juvenile halls and training schools are designed to assist students in passing the GED (general education development) exam. One problem that interferes with continuity of educational programming for adjudicated youth in juvenile halls and detention centers is the relative mobility of the youth (Bullock, Arends, & Mills, 1983; Leone, Price, & Vitolo, 1986; Roush, 1983). Many adolescents spend time in two or more centers during the course of a year. In addition, youths are often moved from one facility to another on very short notice; it is not uncommon for staff to discover, when checking on a youngster's absence from class, that he or she was transferred to another facility or was released. Under these conditions it is difficult to provide appropriate instructional or transitional services.

If the mobility of youth in juvenile halls and detention centers makes educational programming in general rather difficult, it makes the provision of special education and related services a very challenging task. Among other things the mobility of youth makes it difficult to provide due process protections to those suspected of being handicapped and to their parents. The least restrictive environment provision of PL 94–142 is a moot point when security, not educational concerns, governs placement and movement of youth within the criminal justice system.

Assessment of special needs students is also affected by this mobility. As the authors of earlier chapters have indicated, records from a youngster's previous school are often difficult to obtain. Many incarcerated youths have not regularly attended school just prior to their detention; and even when records are available, by the time they arrive from the school district, the delinquent youth has already been assessed (in accordance with PL 94–142 timelines), has been released from the facility, or has been moved to another institution.

In spite of some of these problems, special education services are provided at most juvenile halls, training schools, and reform schools. However, in a number of jurisdictions, programs do not adequately meet the needs of handicapped adolescents (General Accounting Office, 1985; Hagerty & Israelski, 1981; Rutherford, Nelson, & Wolford, 1985).

Camps, Ranches, and Specialized Treatment Facilities

In contrast to juvenile halls and detention centers, camps, ranches, and specialized treatment facilities are much smaller, and they usually confine juveniles for longer periods of time. Camps and ranches provide services to adjudicated youth at locations far from metropolitan areas. Youths who are ordered to spend time at camps or ranches are typically involved in work related to the operation of the facility.

Educational services at camps and ranches are often conducted like distributive education programs, in which students spend half of their time in school and the balance of their time working. Whereas the mobility of students in juvenile halls and detention centers is an impediment to providing educational services, so the relatively small size of many camps and ranches makes the provision of special education services difficult. Like public school programs in rural areas, many camps and ranches located in sparsely populated sections of states have difficulty attracting qualified staff.

Two types of juvenile correctional facilities similar to camps and ranches are private programs and treatment facilities for special populations. Like camps and ranches these institutions are relatively small, but they provide services in urban as well as rural areas. At the present time approximately 1,800 private juvenile correctional facilities provide services in the United States (McGarrell & Flanagan, 1985).

At some camps, ranches, and specialized treatment facilities, educational services for all students are individualized (Bobal, 1984; James & Granville, 1984). More often than not, however, individualized programming for handicapped youth is not provided at these types of correctional centers.[2]

Programs for Juveniles in Adult Correctional Facilities

In recent years there has been a trend within the criminal justice system toward treating juveniles involved in violent or serious crimes as adults (Shichor, 1983). Although most juveniles involved with the justice system are enrolled in diversion or probation programs or are confined in juvenile halls, court schools, or camps and ranches, a number of youth are confined in adult facilities. In some states 10% of the population in adult correctional facilities is under 21. At the national level an estimated 117,000 youth 21 years of age and younger are sentenced to adult correctional institutions (Gerry, 1983).

Educational programs for juveniles in adult prisons and correctional facilities are generally less adequate than programs in juvenile institutions. The curriculum available for juveniles in adult institutions includes adult basic education classes, GED programs, vocational programs, and post-secondary education programs. However, not all of these programs are available at all facilities, and incarcerated youth are typically assigned to prisons for security reasons rather than educational needs. Special education services are occasionally provided to youth in prisons (Rutherford et al., 1985), but educational services in general are rarely, if ever, provided to youth in jails or detention centers (Children's Defense Fund, 1976).

---

[2]See Lindner and Wagner (1983) for a description of a private juvenile facility and Bobal (1984) and James and Granville (1984) for a discussion of specialized programs for violent juvenile offenders.

A problem facing many handicapped youth in adult prisons is the internal disciplinary system. Preliminary investigation (Buser, 1985) suggests that handicapped youth are more likely to be cited for disciplinary violations than are their nonhandicapped peers; and when assigned to isolation in prison, disabled youth spend substantially more time segregated from their peers than do their nonhandicapped age-mates.

Problems associated with rule-violating behavior in prisons are similar to the problems associated with the suspension and expulsion of handicapped youth from public school programs (Leone, 1985a). However, suspension or expulsion from high school often triggers a review of the appropriateness of a handicapped adolescent's educational program and a determination of any relationship between a handicapping condition and misbehavior. Incarcerated youth are not afforded these safeguards. In community-based programs and juvenile halls adolescents who break the rules may be excluded from classes and given the opportunity to complete academic tasks on their own. In prison most youths sentenced to solitary confinement for disciplinary infractions are not permitted to work on school material and are effectively barred from receiving any educational services. Special education teachers in prisons typically do not have the time or are not allowed by the security staff to provide educational services to those in isolation.

COMPETENCIES FOR CORRECTIONAL SPECIAL EDUCATION TEACHERS

Handicapped youth in the criminal justice system receive educational services in the range of settings just discussed. Another way of discussing the provision of special education services to adjudicated youth is to describe the competencies needed by correctional special education teachers. During the past few years special educators have begun to recognize the need to provide special education services to adjudicated youth (Johnson, 1980; Mesinger, 1977; Nelson & Kauffman, 1977; Smith, Ramirez, & Rutherford, 1983). However, few teacher training programs exist that combine corrections and special education (Sutherland, 1985).

Generic competencies for teachers of youth with learning and behavior problems have been developed (Blackhurst, McLoughlin, & Price, 1977) but little attention has been devoted to the identification of essential skills for teachers of adjudicated and incarcerated handicapped youth (Scott, 1980; Valletutti & Mopsick, 1973; Paulson & Allen, 1986). Given the diverse nature of the correctional education programs discussed earlier and the heterogeneous nature of delinquent youth, competencies for teaching special education within the criminal justice system should include generic instructional skills as well as skills specific to the settings or institutions in which disabled or handicapped students are receiving services.

The C/SET Survey

In April 1984 the Corrections/Special Education Training (C/SET) Project at Arizona State University convened a national conference of state directors and consultants in special education and correctional education. One of the tasks accomplished at this conference was a survey to identify preservice and in-service training competencies for special educators working with adjudicated youth (Leone, 1984). The 34 state directors and coordinators of special education and the 51 state directors and coordinators of correctional education (serving both juveniles and adults) who completed the survey were asked to identify and rank order the knowledge, information, and skills needed by teachers working with incarcerated handicapped youth and to identify in-service topics and concerns.

Responses of correctional educators and special educators were very similar. Both groups identified instructional methods and classroom management skills as high priorities. Correctional educators rated knowledge of the criminal justice system and knowledge of correctional institutions among their top preservice priorities. Special educators identified skills in individualizing instruction and assessment as their top priorities. Communication and interpersonal skills, knowledge of materials and curricular development, and knowledge of service delivery systems, agencies, and support networks were also highly ranked by both groups. Figures 12.1 and 12.2 list preservice competencies ranked from most to least important by correctional and special educators, respectively.

With regard to practicum, both correctional and special educators felt that prospective teachers should be involved in a wide range of field-based experiences, including internships in public school and correctional settings. Many respondents also believed that training should involve work with dis-

Figure 12.1 Rank Ordering of Knowledge, Information, and Skills Identified by Correctional Educators for Preservice Training

1. Instructional methods
2. Classroom management
3. Criminal and juvenile justice systems
4. Correctional institutions
5. Communications and interpersonal skills
6. Assessment and test interpretation
7. Service delivery systems and networks of support
8. Characteristics of handicapped youth
9. Characteristics of incarcerated youth
10. Materials and curricular development
11. Counseling strategies
12. Individualizing instruction and IEPs
13. Classroom planning and decision making
14. Security and custody
15. Adapting instruction and modifying materials

Figure 12.2 Rank Ordering of Knowledge, Information, and Skills Identified by Special Educators for Preservice Training

1. Assessment and test interpretation
2. Instructional methods
3. Classroom management
4. Individualizing instruction and IEPs
5. Correctional institutions
6. Characteristics of handicapped youth
7. Counseling strategies
8. Communication and interpersonal skills
9. Materials and curricular development
10. Service delivery systems and networks of support
11. Special education regulations
12. Vocational and career education
13. Characteristics of incarcerated youth
14. Criminal and juvenile justice systems
15. Self-assessment

advantaged youth in recreational, social service, or other community-based programs.

In-service topics and concerns identified by the C/SET survey respondents paralleled the preservice competencies that were identified. Major areas of concern—behavior management and instructional strategies—are similar to the in-service concerns frequently raised by public school teachers. Furthermore, the training competencies listed by these state directors and consultants in special education and corrections are very similar to the training needs identified in a survey of educators in secure detention facilities (Paulson & Allen, 1986).

After reviewing the results of the C/SET survey (Leone, 1984) and reflecting on experiences in staff development with correctional education programs (Leone, 1986), the author developed three broad categories of competencies needed by teachers of adjudicated handicapped youth: streetwise skills, professional competencies, and political skills.

Streetwise Skills

We should begin by acknowledging that incarceration is an experience that most educators have never had. Thus, many troubled youths who are sent to juvenile halls, training schools, camps, and ranches have had very different public school and community experiences from those of the correctional educators who teach them. Educators who are streetwise attempt to understand the culture of the troubled youth with whom they work. It is imperative that special educators recognize that many adjudicated and incarcerated handicapped youth, like others in corrections, are economically and socially disadvantaged. Thus, in addition to experiencing the adverse effects of a disability or learning handicap, special needs youth in correctional education programs exhibit the characteristics of disadvantaged youth.

For correctional educators being streetwise means being able to effectively communicate with adjudicated youth and understand their world. The informal social rules that govern behavior among disadvantaged youth affect the ability of teachers to provide effective instruction. Differences between the youths' informal social structure and the formal organizational structure of the institution or program can subvert well-developed educational programs (Fuller & Rapoport, 1984).

Streetwise educators who understand adjudicated or incarcerated youth and their subcultures are more likely to design effective instructional services than are educators who naively model their classrooms or programs after secondary special education classes. Streetwise skills, a difficult set of competencies to define, include the following:

□ ability to determine and understand the rules that govern behavior among disadvantaged youth in a particular setting
□ ability to communicate effectively with incarcerated youths, using both listening and speaking skills

□ ability to design instructional plans that capitalize on positive aspects of the disadvantaged youth subculture (e.g., sense of identity, allegiance to the group) without compromising the integrity of the educational program
□ ability to maintain professional standards without being manipulated by troubled youth

To special educators with a behavioral perspective, these streetwise skills might appear to involve primarily the identification of potentially reinforcing events and contingencies that shape the behavior of disadvantaged youths. However, the cultural perspective associated with streetwise skills suggests that other factors and characteristics of incarcerated handicapped youths play an important role in determining how to provide special education services within the criminal justice system. Moreover, many of the streetwise skills listed here, in contrast to the generic professional competencies that follow, are specific to particular institutions and geographic locations.

Professional Competencies

Professionally competent educators possess a range of instructional and managerial skills that assist them in individualizing instruction and promoting the learning of their students. Professional competencies for teachers working with adjudicated and incarcerated handicapped youths are similar to the competencies needed by special educators in other settings.

Correctional educators who are professionally competent keep abreast of current instructional technology and critically scrutinize instructional methods. They do not automatically adopt existing methods without assessing their effectiveness with students (Howell, 1985).

With regard to special education competencies, teachers of incarcerated handicapped youths should be conversant with the laws and regulations affecting the education of handicapped and incarcerated individuals. Teachers should recognize the characteristics of handicapped learners, emphasizing instructional skill deficits rather than psychoeducational or etiological characteristics that provide little instructionally relevant information. Teachers should also have well-developed skills in identification, assessment, instruction, and classroom management.

Skills in identification and assessment should clearly differentiate formal standardized assessment for classification purposes from informal criterion- or curriculum-based assessment for instructional decision making (Tucker, 1985). Instructional procedures—the *how* of teaching—should emphasize direct instruction (Becker, Engelmann, Carnine, & Rhine, 1981) and other practices associated with achievement gain among disadvantaged and low-achieving youth (Stallings, 1980). Strategies such as data-based instruction (Deno & Mirkin, 1978; Leone, 1985b) that actively involve the learner in monitoring his or her progress acknowledge adjudicated youth as independent learners and help them assume responsibility for their own learning.

Professional competencies related to classroom management include having a good grasp of behavioral principles and counseling techniques. Teachers of adjudicated handicapped youth need to be able to consistently deliver the consequences of behavior and judiciously enforce reasonable classroom or program rules.

In general terms professional competencies associated with being an effective correctional special education teacher include

□ ability to apply knowledge of legislation and regulations governing the education of the handicapped in correctional education settings
□ ability to screen and assess students suspected of being handicapped
□ ability to develop appropriate instructional goals and objectives for individual students
□ ability to use a range of instructional strategies for presenting material, teaching concepts and skills, and providing review and follow-up activities
□ ability to monitor student progress through the curriculum and adjust instruction appropriately
□ ability to teach students how to monitor their own academic performance and assume greater responsibility for their learning
□ ability to design and modify instructional materials to meet the needs of handicapped learners
□ ability to effectively deliver the consequences of student behavior and use behavioral strategies to promote prosocial behavior

Political Skills

The political skills associated with being an effective special educator working within the criminal justice system involve understanding the organizational context in which programs operate. Like the streetwise skills discussed earlier, some political skills needed by correctional special educators are specific to the institutions or programs in which they teach. Just as youth subcultures have certain implicit rules and expectations, so organizations have implicit purposes that may or may not be related to their explicit purposes. Current policies in juvenile justice are just as likely to be driven by ideological positions as by evidence suggesting that a particular treatment is effective in rehabilitating delinquents or in reducing crime (Shichor, 1983).

In various jurisdictions correctional education programs are administered by departments of juvenile services, social services, or corrections. Similarly, teachers may be employed by local school districts, social service or correctional agencies, or a state department of education. Teachers with well-developed political skills understand working relationships among agencies and, as advocates for the adjudicated youths they teach, strive to improve the quality of the services they provide. Political skills associated with being an effective correctional special education teacher include

□ ability to understand the interagency agreements between programs, institutions, and school systems and their effect on service delivery

□ ability to advocate within the system for adequate program resources and materials
□ ability to advocate for handicapped students within the correctional education program
□ ability to understand and respect other professionals and staff within an institution or program as well as the parents of adjudicated students

Being politically savvy does not imply that teachers attempt to subvert the system within which they teach. Rather, understanding the system allows one to avoid being co-opted by other divisions of the organization whose purposes are not educational (e.g., security, maintenance). Many correctional special education teachers develop competency in political skills while on the job. However, prospective correctional special education teachers can begin during their training to develop an understanding of the political contexts within which programs operate by discussing these issues with their supervising or cooperating teachers and by visiting and observing programs.

TEACHING IN THE SYSTEM

Special education as a service delivery system is relatively new to the criminal justice system. Most public school systems in the United States, at the time PL 94–142 was passed, had existing special education programs in their schools. Although those programs may not have met the standards specified in the new legislation, the schools were meeting the needs of some handicapped students. In contrast, educational programs operated by the criminal justice system did not at that time assess or identify students suspected of being handicapped. Consequently, correctional education programs have had to develop systems for screening, identification, assessment, and instruction of handicapped youth. And because many provisions of the law were designed for the public schools, implementation has been difficult in the criminal justice system (Leone, Price, & Vitolo, 1986).

The heterogeneous nature of adjudicated handicapped youths and the diversity of programs serving them make it difficult to find or describe typical administrative arrangements and classrooms. Like their counterparts in the public schools, correctional special education teachers have a great deal of latitude in how they structure their classrooms and, in some cases, what curriculum they adopt. On the surface many correctional education classrooms resemble alternative education programs or remedial programs in public schools. And some of the demands placed on educators in community-based programs for adjudicated youth are similar to those experienced by teachers who work with behaviorally disordered adolescents. Educators who teach in juvenile halls, camps, and adult prisons, however, work in an environment in which discipline and maintenance of order are high priorities. Teachers in locked facilities often have responsibilities related to the security of the institution in addition to their pedagogical duties. In general, the higher the level of security in a given institution or program, the greater the level of structure within the classrooms in that institution.

Administrative Arrangements

Teachers who work with adjudicated handicapped youth are employed by the range of agencies discussed earlier—public schools; departments of social service, juvenile justice, and corrections; and private agencies that operate programs under contract with the criminal justice system. Because of the number of different agencies involved in providing correctional education, many different administrative arrangements govern the delivery of educational services to handicapped youth.

Correctional education programs usually operate on a year-round basis, and teachers typically receive less vacation time than their colleagues in the public schools. One problem common to both correctional education programs and other educational programs not operated in the public schools is a lack of substitute teachers. When teachers are ill or have to attend meetings, many correctional education programs cancel or combine classes for the duration of the absence.

In correctional education programs with a limited number of classes and students, one senior teacher with a relatively light teaching load may assume the administrative responsibilities associated with the office of the principal or assistant principal in a secondary school program. Other programs and agencies employ principals or administrators, whose responsibilities include supervision of classrooms and teachers in several different correctional institutions or community-based programs. Special educators working with adjudicated youth may report to a principal for the day-to-day operation of their classrooms but may also receive assistance and support from a special education consultant.

Occasionally, classes in institutions are canceled for security reasons. Prisoner counts, lockdowns, and other disruptions associated with maintaining order sometimes interfere with scheduled classes. These disruptions are rare in most facilities but are generally more likely to occur in large institutions than in small community-based programs.

The administrative support and resources available to correctional educators vary with the source of funding and the public perception of the criminal justice system within that state. In states with well-developed educational systems and a strong commitment to rehabilitation, the correctional education programs are likely to provide more support for teachers than do programs in states where this is not the case.

Students

Students enrolled in special education programs in correctional settings do not fit any stereotypic notions that one might have of handicapped juvenile delinquents. The characteristics and educational skill deficits of handicapped juvenile offenders are similar to those of other adjudicated youth not identified as handicapped or disabled (Cheek, 1984; Reilly, Wheeler, & Etlinger, 1985). Most juveniles, whether placed on probation or incarcerated, are not adjudicated for violent offenses. Although a certain amount of bravado may be exhibited by students new to the classroom, other students ignore this type of behavior. Students are often quite loyal to their teachers and communicate appropriate expectations for classroom behavior to others.

In some juvenile facilities competition between rival gangs presents problems for security staff. Many institutions prohibit the wearing or display of any insignia or "colors" or the exchange of salutes associated with a gang. Although gang activity per se does not pose problems for correctional educators, the institutional climate is certainly affected by their presence.

Many incarcerated youth take their studies seriously and apply themselves in class. Others resist attending school or attend only as a means of passing time. However, as reluctant students discover the incentive structure of the institution or program (e.g., attending classes results in "good time" or points, and a sufficient amount of good time or a large enough number of points can result in earlier release), they are more likely to apply themselves to their studies.

Many students in correctional education programs experience a positive feeling about teachers and learning for the first time in their school careers, in response to small class sizes and the empathy exhibited by their teachers. In classes where appropriate instructional methods are used, correctional educators report that many of their students show tremendous educational growth in the first few months in the program. For many adjudicated youth the instruction they receive in the criminal justice system is the most continuous and structured educational programming they have received since their elementary school years.

Vocational Education

Vocational programs in the criminal justice system are not typically designed to accommodate special needs learners. In some facilities a minimal reading or computational level is required for participation, which effectively bars many handicapped adolescents from participating. In other programs vocational classes are available to all youth, regardless of prerequisite academic skills.

Some vocational programs serving adjudicated youth have developed strong ties to local businesses (James & Granville, 1984). In addition to providing an extension of the classroom for on-the-job training, local businesses can assist incarcerated youth in making successful transitions back into the community.

At the Charles H. Hickey School, a training school administered by the Juvenile Services Administration of the state of Maryland, vocational education is an important component of the curriculum. In addition to receiving academic instruction, all students at Hickey School, including those identified as handicapped, are enrolled in 6-week courses in an employability skills center and in different vocational skill areas. This instructional arrangement introduces students to occupational areas such as carpentry, small appliance repair, health, and auto maintenance and repair and fits into the relatively short stay of most juvenile offenders at the school.

Materials

Materials available in the correctional education classroom are variable. Although some programs have current texts and resources, in many programs books and other instructional media and equipment are worn and dated. Typically, materials are vocationally oriented with a high interest format.[3] Some programs use social skills curricula to teach basic literacy. In many correctional education programs materials are designed to assist students in completing their GED exams.

The Classroom

A visitor to a special education classroom in a correctional facility is likely to find class sizes smaller than those in public school programs. Students are likely to be working independently on workbooks or worksheets with occasional assistance from the teacher or a student aide. Work stations and small-group areas can often be found at one side of the room, and samples of students' work or displays of students' progress are likely to be posted on the walls. In some classes students may be found working independently at a microcomputer.

Many classrooms serving incarcerated youth resemble remedial classes in the public schools. Although alternative or community-based programs for adjudicated youth may occasionally be disrupted by inappropriate student behavior, serious acts of misbehavior are rare within correctional institutions. For many incarcerated youth the correctional education classroom is a place far removed from the hostile world of the prison or juvenile hall.

Teachers in correctional education programs use a range of behavioral techniques to motivate their students, including certificates of achievement, "student of the week" recognition, and cooperative learning strategies. Many correctional educators use contingency contracting and other similar strategies that explicitly specify expected student performance and teacher responses.

CONCLUSION

Handicapped youth are found in a wide range of correctional programs and settings, including diversion, probation, and alternative education programs; juvenile halls, training schools, and reform schools; camps, ranches, and

---

[3]See, for example, materials published by Globe Book Company, Prentice-Hall Media, and Steck-Vaughn Company

specialized treatment facilities; and prisons. One problem common to many correctional education programs is the mobility of the students. The relatively short period of time that adolescents spend in some programs makes it difficult to provide continuity in instruction.

Most handicapped youth in the criminal justice system receive the special education and related services to which they are entitled. However, the mobility of adjudicated youth makes it difficult to assess students suspected of being handicapped, in accordance with PL 94–142 timelines.

Teachers working in the criminal justice system need to possess streetwise skills, professional competencies, and political skills. Streetwise skills enable correctional educators to understand the subculture of the adjudicated youths they teach and communicate more effectively with them. Professional competencies are those skills that involve assessment, instruction, materials development, and behavior management of handicapped youth. Political skills within the criminal justice system involve understanding the context within which the program operates and using that knowledge to effectively advocate for improvement in educational services for adjudicated youth.

Teaching handicapped youth within the criminal justice system is a challenging task. Teachers typically work on a year-round basis and may be employed by any one of a number of different agencies. Rewards associated with teaching in the criminal justice system include working with adolescents who may not have received appropriate educational services for years and who consequently exhibit a great deal of academic growth in a relatively short period of time.

REFERENCES

Becker, W. C., Engelmann, S., Carnine, D. W., & Rhine, W. R. (1981). Direct instruction model. In W. R. Rhine (Ed.), *Making schools more effective: New directions from Follow Through*. New York: Academic Press.

Blackhurst, A. E., McLoughlin, J. A., & Price, L. M. (1977). Issues in the development of programs to prepare teachers of children with learning and behavior disorders. *Behavioral Disorders, 2,* 157–168.

Bobal, C. M. (1984). An unconventional approach to providing educational services to violent juvenile offenders. In R. Mathias, P. DeMuro, & R. Allinson (Eds.), *Violent juvenile offenders: An anthology* (pp. 273–281). San Francisco: National Council on Crime and Delinquency.

Braukmann, C. J., Fixsen, D. L., Phillips, E. L., & Wolf, M. M. (1975). Behavioral approaches to treatment in the crime and delinquency field. *Criminology, 13,* 299–331.

Bullock, T., Arends, R. I., & Mills, F. (1983). Implementing educational services in a youth detention facility. *Juvenile and Family Court Journal, 34*(3), 21–29.

Buser, C. (1985). *The relationship between educational handicaps and disciplinary infractions in an adult male prison setting.* Unpublished master's thesis, University of Maryland, College Park.

Cheek, M. C. (1984). The educational and sociological status of handicapped and non-handicapped incarcerated female adolescents (Doctoral dissertation, University of Maryland, 1983). *Dissertation Abstracts International, 45,* 954A.

Children's Defense Fund. (1976). *Children in adult jails.* Washington, DC: Author.

Coffey, A. R. (1974). *Juvenile justice as a system.* Englewood Cliffs, NJ: Prentice-Hall.

Deno, S. L., & Mirkin, P. K. (1978). *Data-based program modification: A manual.* Reston, VA: Council for Exceptional Children.

Fuller, B., & Rapoport, T. (1984). Indigenous evaluation: Distinguishing the formal and informal organizational structures of youth programs. *Evaluation Review, 8,* 25–44.

General Accounting Office. (1985). *Implementation of Public Law 94–142 as it relates to handicapped delinquents in the District of Columbia.* Washington, DC: Author.

Gerry, M. H. (1983). *Monitoring the special education programs of correctional institutions.* Washington, DC: U.S. Department of Education.

Hagerty, G., & Israelski, I. (1981). The challenge of adjudicated and incarcerated handicapped youth. *Counterpoint, 2*(1), 18.

Howell, K. W. (1985). Selecting special education treatments. *Journal of Correctional Education, 36,* 26–29.

Hughes, T. R., & Reuterman, N. A. (1982). Juvenile detention facilities: Summary report of a second national survey. *Juvenile and Family Court Journal, 33*(4), 3–14.

James, T. S., & Granville, J. M. (1984). Practical issues in vocational education for serious juvenile offenders. In R. Mathias, P. DeMuro, & R. Allinson (Eds.), *Violent juvenile offenders: An anthology* (pp. 337–345). San Francisco: National Council on Crime and Delinquency.

Johnson, J. L. (1980). Helping incarcerated youth: An organizational approach. *Behavioral Disorders, 5,* 86–95.

Leone, P. E. (1984, April). *Preservice and inservice training for teachers of incarcerated handicapped youth.* Paper presented at the Correctional/Special Education Training Conference, Arlington, VA.

Leone, P. E. (1985a). Suspension and expulsion of handicapped pupils. *Journal of Special Education, 19,* 111–121.

Leone, P. E. (1985b). Data-based instruction in correctional education. *Journal of Correctional Education, 36,* 77–85.

Leone, P. E. (1986). Teacher training in corrections and special education. *Remedial and Special Education, 7*(3), 41–47.

Leone, P. E., Price, T., & Vitolo, R. K. (1986). Appropriate education for all incarcerated youth: Meeting the spirit of P.L. 94–142 in youth detention facilities. *Remedial and Special Education, 7* (4), 9–14.

Lindner, C., & Wagner, B. R. (1983). The Ocean Tides experiment: Treatment of serious juvenile offenders in an open residential setting. *Federal Probation, 47,* 26–32.

McGarrell, E. F., & Flanagan, T. J. (Eds.). (1985). *Sourcebook of criminal justice statistics—1984* (U.S. Department of Justice, Bureau of Justice Statistics). Washington, DC: U.S. Government Printing Office.

Mesinger, J. F. (1977). Juvenile delinquents: A relatively untapped population for special education professionals. *Behavioral Disorders, 2,* 95–101.

Nelson, C. M., & Kauffman, J. M. (1977). Educational programming for secondary school age delinquent and maladjusted pupils. *Behavioral Disorders, 2,* 102–113.

Paulson, D. A., & Allen, D. A. (1986). Training needs of educators and support personnel in correctional facilities. *Teacher Education and Special Education, 9*(1), 37–43.

Reilly, T. F., Wheeler, L. J., & Etlinger, L. E. (1985). Intelligence versus academic achievement: A comparison of juvenile delinquents and special education classifications. *Criminal Justice and Behavior, 12,* 193–208.

Reppucci, N. D., & Clingempeel, W. G. (1978). Methodological issues in research with correctional populations. *Journal of Consulting and Clinical Psychology, 46,* 727–746.

Reuterman, N. A., & Hughes, T. R. (1984). Developments in juvenile justice during the decade of the 70s: Juvenile detention facilities. *Journal of Criminal Justice, 12,* 325–333.

Rothman, E. P. (1980). From the desk of the principal: Perspectives on a school based community treatment program for disruptive youth. In J. B. Jordan, D. A. Sabatino, & R. C. Sarri (Eds.), *Disruptive youth in school* (pp. 102–117). Reston, VA: Council for Exceptional Children.

Roush, D. W. (1983). Content and process of detention education. *Journal of Offender Counseling Services & Rehabilitation, 7,* 21–36.

Rutherford, R. B., Nelson, C. M., & Wolford, B. I. (1985). Special education in the most restrictive environment: Correctional/special education. *Journal of Special Education, 19,* 59–71.

Sarri, R. C. (1980). Alternative residential programs. In J. B. Jordan, D. A. Sabatino, & R. C. Sarri (Eds.), *Disruptive youth in school* (pp. 138–150). Reston, VA: Council for Exceptional Children.

Schutjer, M. (1982). Day treatment for delinquent youth: An alternative to residential care. *Children Today, 6,* 20–23, 77.

Scott, J. (1980). A training model for correctional educators. *Journal of Correctional Education, 34,* 4–7.

Severy, L. J., Houlden, P., Wilmoth, G. H., & Silver, S. (1982). Community receptivity to juvenile justice program planning. *Evaluation Review, 6,* 25–46.

Shichor, D. (1983). Historical and current trends in American juvenile justice. *Juvenile and Family Court Journal, 34*(3), 61–75.

Smith, B. J., Ramirez, B., & Rutherford, R. B. (1983). Special education in youth correctional facilities. *Journal of Correctional Education, 34,* 108–112.

Stallings, J. (1980). Allocated academic learning time revisited, or beyond time on task. *Educational Researcher, 9*(10), 11–16.

Sutherland, D. (1985). Training programs for correctional/special educators. *Journal of Correctional Education, 36,* 64.

Tucker, J. A. (1985). Curriculum-based assessment: An introduction. *Exceptional Children, 52,* 199–204.

Valletutti, P., & Mopsick, S. I. (1973). A conceptual model for correctional education programs: A special education perspective. In A. R. Roberts (Ed.), *Readings in prison education* (pp. 115–127). Springfield, IL: Charles C. Thomas.

Weinrott, M. R., Jones, R. R., & Howard, J. R. (1982). Cost effectiveness of teaching family programs for delinquents: Results of a national evaluation. *Evaluation Review, 6,* 173–201.

Name Index

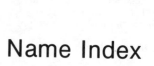

Subject Index

Abt Associates, 67
Academic treatment model, 127–128
Achievement Place Model. *See* Teaching Family Model
Acquittal, 33
Adaptive behavior, 168
Adjudicated
  handicapped youth, 251, 253
  juvenile delinquents, 230
Adjudication, 33
Adjustment to work, 194–195
Administration on Developmental Disabilities, 112
Administrative arrangements, 286
Administrative structures, 63–66
  centralization, 64
  contract/autonomy, 66
  decentralization, 64
  separate educational agency, 64–65
Adult Basic Education (ABE), 55–56, 73–74
Adult correctional education, 73, 75
Adult correctional institutions, 2
  state institutions, 3
Adult Education Act, 73–74
Adult illiteracy statistics, 72
Adult justice system, 24
Adult literacy programs, 74
Adult living skills, 15
  See also Life skills
Adult Performance Level (APL) Project, 58, 72
Adult prison population statistics, 53

Adult reformatory, the first, 20
Advocacy projects for mentally retarded offenders, 114
Aftercare programs, 77
Aggression, 146
  socialized, 143
Aggression-prone adolescents, 228
Aggression-relevant psychological skills, 223–226
  component behavioral steps, 223–226
Aggression replacement training, 234
Aggressive adolescents
  remediation, 234
  skill training, 229
Alabama, 5, 66, 113
Alternative education programs, 215
  for juvenile delinquents, 276–277
Alternative schools, 68
American Association on Mental Deficiency, 107–108, 112
American Bar Association, 105, 118, 120
American Correctional Association, 59, 105, 109, 112
American Prison Association, 21
American Psychiatric Association, 141, 144–145, 157
American Psychological Association
  standards for tests, 174, 185
Antisocial children, 148–149

Anxiety-withdrawal, 143, 146
Appellate review, 33
Arizona, 112
Arizona State University, 281
Arraignment, 33
Arrest
  procedures, 36
  statistics, 36
Arson
  definition, 28
  statistics, 28
Assault
  definition, 27
  statistics, 27
Assessment
  basic skills, 151
  criminal behavior, 33
  decision making, 166–168
  deficits and learning needs, 14
  delinquent behavior, 124–125
  diagnostic, 124, 129–131
  in correctional settings, 165–187
  intelligence, 108, 124, 129, 151
  juvenile offenders, 150–152
  learning disabilities, 124–125
  learning disabilities/juvenile delinquency, 128–130
  model strategies, 267
  nonbiased, 95
  procedures, 264
  program, 166
  reading, 124, 129–131
  remediation programs, 128
  skill areas, 201
  social behavior, 219
  social skills, 57, 204–207
  social skills of youth, 219